Access to Justice in Transnational B2C E-Commerce

Sutatip Yuthayotin

Access to Justice in Transnational B2C E-Commerce

A Multidimensional Analysis of Consumer Protection Mechanisms

Springer

Sutatip Yuthayotin
Central Intellectual Property and International Trade Court
Bangkok
Thailand

ISBN 978-3-319-11130-8 ISBN 978-3-319-11131-5 (eBook)
DOI 10.1007/978-3-319-11131-5
Springer Cham Heidelberg New York Dordrecht London

Library of Congress Control Number: 2014955666

Printed on acid-free paper

Springer is part of Springer Science+Business Media (www.springer.com)

Acknowledgements

First and foremost I would like to thank the Japanese Government, without whose financial support through the Monbukagakusho Scholarship, this Ph.D. research would not be possible. My greatest debts of gratitude go to my principal supervisor, Professor Kono Toshiyuki; without his kindheartedness, professional and valuable criticisms with the foresight of his extensive experience, it would not be possible for me to complete this dissertation.

I was also influenced by my second supervisor, Professor Mark Fenwick, who always kindly listens to my ideas and from whom I received numerous suggestions during the development of this dissertation. The thought of pursuing the doctoral research was first brought to my attention by Professor Caslav Pejovic, who has always believed in me and kindly introduced the Ph.D. research opportunity to me 4 year ago and from whom I always receive gentle support. I have also been particularly fortunate to have benefited from the invaluable guidance of Professor Han Sang Hee, without his advice and suggestions for overcoming all the challenges along the way this thesis would never be completed. I am also grateful to Professor Steven Van Uytsel, who gives me valuable advice and nudges towards writing all it down during the first 2 years of my research. This allows me to finish this project in a respective timeframe. Also I would like to thank Mr. Anand Venkatachalam, SPi Global, India, Professors of Kyushu University, School of Law (i.e. Professor Ago Shin-ichi, Professor Teramoto Shinto, Professor Stefan Wrbka, etc.) for their kind comments on my annual presentation during my three-year research.

Many thanks go to my friends and colleagues; Paulius Jurcys who has contributed to my thoughts and whose advice and support were indispensable in completion of this dissertation. I also wish to deeply thank Sean McGinty for his review and comment on the first draft of this work. Finally and most importantly, I must thank my family, without their encouragement, moral support and love, I would not be able to undertake and complete this project.

Abbreviations and Constructed Terms

BBB	Better Business Bureau
CIArb	UK Chartered Institution of Arbitrators
CRD	Directive 2011/83/EU of the European Parliament and of the Council of 25 October 2011 on consumer rights
DPD	Directive 95/46/EC of the European Parliament and of the Council of 24 October 1995 on the protection of individuals with regard to the processing of personal data and on the free movement of such data
ECD	Directive 2000/31/EC of the European Parliament and of the Council of 8 June 2000 on certain legal aspects of information society services, in particular electronic commerce, in the Internal Market
ECJ	European Court of Justice
ESCP	Regulation (EC) No 861/2007 of the European Parliament and of the Council of 11 July 2007 establishing a European Small Claims Procedure
GNI	Global Network Initiative
GPA	Group Proceedings Act of 2002 of Sweden
ICPEN	International Consumer Protection Enforcement Network
ODR	Online Dispute Resolution
OECD	Organization for Economic Cooperation and Development
OFT	UK Office of Fair Trading
SCP	Small Claim Procedure
UCC	US Uniform Commercial Code
UCITA	US Uniform Computer Information Transactions Act
UTD	Council Directive 93/13/EEC of 5 April 1993 on unfair terms in consumer contracts
Brussels Regulation	Council Regulation (EC) No. 44/2001 on jurisdiction and the recognition and enforcement of judgments in civil and commercial matters

Cooperation Regulation	Regulation (EC) No 2006/2004 of the European Parliament and of the Council of 27 October 2004 on cooperation between national authorities responsible for the enforcement of consumer protection laws
Injunction Directive	Directive 98/27/EC of the European Parliament and of the Council of 19 May 1998 on injunctions for the protection of consumers' interests
Rome I Regulation	Council Regulation (EC) No. 593/2008 on the law applicable to contractual obligation
Second Restatement	US Second Restatement of Conflict of Laws

Contents

List of Figures

List of Tables

Chapter 1
Introduction

1.1 Background

The volume of electronic commerce has grown rapidly along with the advancement in technology and it has been widely adopted in the global market place, including direct sales between business operators and consumers (hereinafter *B2C e-commerce*). It offers consumers access to a vast choice of goods and services without any geographical limitations. The continuously rising number of people with access to the internet, more than 78 % of the 2012 population in North America, 63 % in Europe, 42 % in Latin America and the Caribbean, and approximately 27 % in Asia, has led to an expansion of B2C e-commerce.[1] About one-third of consumers in the European Union shopped online in 2008 and B2C e-commerce has become one of the most common forms of cross border shopping.[2]

However, one characteristic of B2C e-commerce is that it takes place in the virtual world, while the traders and consumers are often located at great distances from each other in the real world, sometimes in different countries. This fact creates greater risks and uncertainties for consumers with regard to breaches of the contracts they enter into than they face in traditional in-person transactions with traders located in the same jurisdiction. Modern communication leads to some key issues that exist in electronic relationships such as the sending of ambiguous communications, the use of personal data, enforcement across long distances and so on, which are difficult to regulate. As many surveys have shown consumers, often lack confidence in B2C e-commerce and are often reluctant to enter into such

[1] *See* Internet World Stats, *Usage and Population Statistics* (February 17, 2013), *available at* internetworldstats.com/stats.htm (visited March 1, 2013).

[2] *See* Eurobarometer, *Consumer Protection in the Internet Market* (October 2008), *available at* ec.europa.eu/public_opinion/archives/ebs/ebs_298_en.pdf (visited March 1, 2013).

S. Yuthayotin, *Access to Justice in Transnational B2C E-Commerce*,
DOI 10.1007/978-3-319-11131-5_1

transactions because of a wide range of questions relating to these crucial matters.[3] Today, the expansion of B2C e-commerce appears to be restricted as a large number of consumers perceive online transactions as risky and remain very conservative when they shop online, especially in transnational sales.[4]

The problems created by new technological tools and distant relationships pose a significant obstacle to the growth of B2C electronic commerce. Given the continuously evolving electronic market, numerous pieces of legislation have been introduced that are designed for the peculiarities of electronic environment and the key issues concerning consumers' need for protection in the online market. Some examples are those electronic commerce laws relating to the formation and validation of electronic contracts, online data protection, and online dispute resolution. These attempts have expanded to the international level where legal harmonization in the context of consumer protection among different countries has been carried out to support the function and growth of the global e-market.

Despite having witnessed the massive growth in legislation dealing with the online market, consumers remain skeptical about shopping online. Some commentators simply claim that the lack of consumer confidence in online transactions is because the existing legal mechanisms fail to provide them with legitimate protection.[5] They believe that regulation of the internet is not necessary since the market itself may correct the failures.[6] Opponents point out that the electronic market poses new challenges, arising mainly out of its technological and transnational nature, which cannot be corrected by market mechanisms.[7] They argue that such

[3] *See e.g.* C. Coteanu, Cyber Consumer Law and Unfair Trading Practices ix (2005) and The Office of Fair Trading (OFT), *Internet Shopping: An OFT Market Study* (June 2007), *available at* oft.gov.uk/shared_oft/reports/consumer_protection/oft921.pdf (visited June 1, 2011), T. Schultz, *Does Online Dispute Resolution Need Governmental Intervention? The Case of Architectures of Control and Trust*, 6 North Carolina Journal of Law and Technology 71, 76 (2004) and L. M. Ponte, *Boosting Consumer Confidence in E-Business: Recommendations for Establishing Fair and Effective Dispute Resolution Programs for B2C Online Transactions*, 12 Albany Law Journal of Science and Technology 441, 442 (2002).

[4] Although the growth of e-commerce is impressive, the average value of each online consumer transaction is very small, and the number of cross border transactions seems to be minimal when compared to the number of business-to-business e-transactions.

[5] *See e.g.* Coteanu, *supra* note 3, at xi and Ponte, *supra* note 3, at 444.

[6] *See* J. P. Barlow, *Selling Wine without Bottles: The Economy of Mind on the Global Net* (1993), *available at* w2.eff.org/Misc/Publications/John_Perry_Barlow/HTML/idea_economy_article.html (visited May 1, 2013), D. Pridgen, *Wyoming Division: Speech: How Will Consumers be Protected on the Information Superhighway*?, 32 University of Wyoming Land and Water Law Review 237, 247 (1997) and T. Hardy, *The Proper Legal Regime for "Cyberspace"*, 55 The University of Pittsburgh Law Review 993–1055 (1994).

[7] It is argued that the e-market condition is inconsistent with generally accepted economic theories because of the occurrence of certain failures of e-market functions that the market cannot self-correct and regulatory interventions are thus needed. Examples include inequality of bargaining power in e-standard terms, inequality of technological information, institutional private litigation failures in cross border e-sales, and behavioral economic failures in e-communication. *See* Coteanu, *supra* note 3, at Chapter 2, R. van den Bergh, *Should Consumer Protection Law be*

challenges should be handled by governmental intervention and regulations specially tailored for the particularities of the electronic market place.[8]

The electronic market initially developed without regulation but, following the boom and burst of the dot-com bubble at the beginning of the 2000 decade, it could no longer be denied that some kind of rules or order appeared to be necessary. In response to such views that regulation was necessary came the argument that the existence of the electronic market gives rise to issues that cannot necessarily be managed by the principles established by the rule of law and that only a private system can ensure that market behavior remains within the boundaries of acceptable social standards.[9] This argument does not totally conflict with the conventional regulation of the e-market but rather considers the value of private ordering and the internet's ability to provide some technical solutions for the wide range of consumer problems in B2C e-commerce that enhance consumer confidence. For instance, consumers may be able to avoid rogue traders by consulting with other consumers through a privately implemented review or rating system before engaging in an online transaction. Therefore, the question becomes whether such mechanisms of consumer protection, which do not rest on the creation of conventional rules of law, are more effective in the context of online transactions and have more advantages than the governmental regulatory approach in the online market. In other words, this research aims to identify mechanisms that enhance consumer confidence in B2C e-commerce.

1.2 Aim and Structure of Research

As one of the main debates concerning today's consumer protection relates to the lack of consumer confidence, the starting point of this study is based on the premise that the lack of consumer confidence in B2C e-commerce needs to be decreased and that, in turn, would lead to the expansion of global commercial exchanges (Chap. 2). Based on such premise, this research therefore identifies mechanisms that have the capacity to promote consumer confidence. There are a wide range of methods that might be used to improve consumer confidence but this study will look at one particular method by arguing that enhancing *access to justice* is potentially an effective means of improving consumer confidence. To put it another

---

Publicly Enforce?, *in* W. van Boom and M. Loos (eds.), Collective Enforcement of Consumer Law 177, 180 (2007).

[8] *See* Coteanu *ibid.*, at xii-xiii, T. Tasker and D. Pakcyk, *Cyber-Surfing on the High Seas of Legalese: Law and Technology of Internet Agreement,* 18 Albany Law Journal of Science and Technology 79, 73 (2008) and S. Zain, *Regulation of E Commerce by Contract: Is It Fair to Consumers*?, 31 The University of West Los Angeles Law Review 163, 165 (2000).

[9] *See* American Bar Association, Jurisdiction in Cyberspace 83 (1999) and G. P. Calliess and P. Zumbansen, Rough Consensus and Running Code, A Theory of Transnational Private Law 153–80 (2010).

way, enhancing access to justice is not the only way to improve consumer confidence in B2C e-commerce but it is a potentially effective method of doing so by generating greater awareness of access to justice from the public.

It seems that many consumers often expect unfavorable future conditions and perceive the likelihood of opportunistic behaviors in online transactions and this leads to the lack of confidence and the avoidance of buying online. Based on this assumption, enhancing access to justice, which ensures that all diverse ingredients of consumer concerns will not be overlooked and the nature of harms suffered by consumers and various aspects of justice necessary to create a fair market environment will be addressed, appears to improve consumer confidence. If an opportunistic behavior does occur, enhancing access to justice means that consumers will be able to obtain restitution and be compensated from the harms they suffered. This would result in the positive change in consumer attitudes that there are more favorable conditions and perception that there is less likelihood of opportunistic behaviors that leads to an increase in *trust* and *willingness* to engage in online purchases. In other words, consumers' trust and willingness to transact, which is a factor that directly link to consumer confidence, can be improved through enhancement of access to justice that contributes to the public perception of a reduced likelihood of opportunistic in B2C e-commerce.

This study starts by examining the existing literature about access to justice (Chap. 3). Much of the existing literature seems to focus on legal representation in litigation. This research then proposes a broader multidimensional approach to access to justice, which includes procedural and substantive dimensions in which both socio-legal and economic considerations are identified as important. The concept of access to justice encompasses not only legal representation or procedural mechanisms, but also the substantive concept of equity. An undeniable goal of the various attempts under the movement to broaden access to justice has been to achieve equal justice by serving various justice interests (such as socio-legal and economic aspects) in people's lives and activities, and public awareness of this broaden concept of access to justice seems to be necessary in enhancing consumer confidence, which is the key issue that this study tries to elaborate. For this research, the words "access to justice" refers to the broader multidimensional approach to access to justice stated above.

The next key issue of this research is to pinpoint the *mechanisms* that are best placed to achieve or facilitate the multidimensional aspects of access to justice. Then, the research constructs a *framework* for conceptualizing access to justice in the context of consumer protection by describing the various reasonable conditions necessary to satisfy consumers in B2C e-commerce (hereinafter the *Framework*) (Chap. 4). The Framework is necessary, as it serves as the benchmark in the evaluation of various consumer protection mechanisms. Concretely, this study is an attempt to lay a foundation for a systematic analysis that can give a complete picture reflecting all aspects of consumers' expectations when they engage in online transactions. There is obviously a need to improve consumer confidence by ensuring that all consumers' interests are well protected and their rights can be practically enforced.

This research then moves on to evaluate different kinds of mechanisms established by legislation using the criterion of the established Framework. It contains a detailed assessment of the roles of *substantive* mechanisms (such as standard terms regulation, information disclosure, cooling off periods and privacy laws) and *procedural* mechanisms (such as small claims procedures, collective actions and regulatory agencies) respectively, which are related to all stages of the online relationship, including the pre-contractual, contractual and post contractual stages (Chaps. 5 and 6).

Subsequently, this study looks at the alternative mechanisms of the private ordering, which do not rest on the creation of rules of law, but rely on technological solution and remedies and their significance for achieving access to justice for consumers in B2C e-commerce (Chap. 7). Nevertheless, before the private ordering are debated and assessed, this study has to turn from the main argument, which largely focuses on the effectiveness of consumer protection mechanisms, to first consider the need for legal harmonization in promoting and facilitating the global e-commerce, one of the important debates on B2C e-commerce that cannot be ignored (Chap. 7, Sect. 7.2). The question that comes to mind is whether the legal harmonization can improve consumer access to justice in B2C e-commerce. By exploring the legal harmonization, which largely relied on a governmental regulatory approach and the private ordering, which based on the private affairs, it helps identify the best institutional arrangement for implementing the mechanisms for enhancing access to justice in the online market. This will shade light on the way forward for improve consumer confidence in B2C e-commerce.

The results from the analysis of legal mechanisms and legal harmonization movements, which largely rest on conventional regulatory interventions, indicate that they have not effectively delivered access to justice to consumers in the online market. Then, this study moves to focus on the mechanisms of private ordering and how they work, identifying their main advantages and pitfalls within the Framework (Chap. 7, Sect. 7.3). This study argues that private ordering appears to be a more satisfactory alternative to address the problems of consumers in B2C e-commerce than the governmental regulatory approach, but there are still difficulties that need to be overcome. In other words, even though the discussion indicates that a model of private ordering can offer greater access to justice, it does not yet fully achieve multidimensional consumer access to justice in accordance with the Framework.

The subsequent key issues that this research tries to elaborate are how the difficulties of private ordering can be limited and how such a system can be designed to effectively deliver access to justice to consumers in the context of B2C e-commerce (Chap. 8). To answer these questions, this study first stresses that although the private institutions, which provide the mechanisms of private ordering are already in place, their problems must be addressed to maximize their effectiveness. The study shows that there is a need for the use of a third party. It puts forward a proposal for using an *intermediary*, a neutral third party playing an integral role in the collaborative task of facilitating various aspects of private ordering as a solution for limiting the risks, justifying the optimal market pressure, and the function of the regime. Such an intermediary would help to ensure that the system meets transparency and accountability standards and, as a result, would attract a higher level of public recognition thereby eliminating the pitfalls of private ordering. To move forward, this study proposes that the state, with its wealth of material resources and incentives, is best equipped as the most suitable institution to act as an intermediary. The state as an intermediary should assume the role of mediator in some suggested areas to ensure that private ordering can better protect multidimensional consumer access to justice and, as a result, help lift consumer confidence in relation to B2C e-commerce. The promising proposal of this study improves the mechanisms of consumer protection in enhancing consumer confidence, and provides a starting point for further discussion on implementable enhancements to the private ordering system in detail.

1.3 Contribution to the Existing Academic Debates

In 1998, the Organization for Economic Cooperation and Development (hereinafter *OECD*) have recognized the new story of borderless e-market place and, as a product of its review, it issued "Guidelines for Consumer Protection in the Context of Electronic Commerce" to assist Member States, traders and consumers in Member States, to create an effective framework for consumer protection in electronic commerce and to facilitate growth in electronic commerce.[10] More than a decade after the OECD released the guidelines, its Member States and non-Member States around the world have modified their existing laws or introduced new laws to keep up with fast changing technology and commercial practices, but consumers' confidence in e-commerce has yet been satisfactorily increased.[11]

If global economic growth is to benefit from the potential of the borderless internet market, a proactive approach is necessary to stimulate favorable market

[10] There are eight core principles under the OECD's guidelines, namely (1) transparent and effective protection, (2) fair business, advertising and marketing practices, (3) information about business, the goods or services and transaction, (4) clear process for the confirmation of sales, (5) secure payment mechanisms, (6) dispute resolution and redress, (7) privacy, and (8) education and awareness. *See* OECD, *Guidelines for Consumer Protection in the Context of Electronic Commerce* (1999), *available at* oecd.org/internet/consumerpolicy/34023811.pdf (visited January 13, 2013).

[11] The following are examples of the adaptation in some principal jurisdictions. The EU has implemented comprehensive legislation and policies for electronic consumer protection which are based on fundamental rules of consumer protection in traditional commercial transactions; such as the Directive on the Protection of Consumers in Respect to Distance Contracts, the Directive on the Protection of Individuals with Regards to Processing of Personal Data, the Directive on the Injunction for the Protection of Consumers' Interests, and so on. The main objective of these legislative measures is to promote consumer confidence in electronic transactions, which is an essential element for electronic commerce to flourish to its full potential. In the US, a series of federal statutes and regulations have been enacted to control and regulate business operators, who are engaging in certain enumerated electronic activities, to prevent fraudulent activities from being committed via electronic networks. The federal agency, called the Federal

conditions that will support the development of the global e-market. One main question pertaining consumer protection policy is how to improve consumer confidence in B2C e-commerce. The fast development of technology and the emergence of multi-jurisdictional concerns make the policy and law makers somewhat reluctant to solely rely on the traditional consumer policy of safeguarding consumers within a national boundary. This may be mainly because it is not clear what constitutes an effective consumer protection approach that can improve their confidence in the e-market.

This study develops an effective model that helps to ensure effective consumer protection and improve consumer confidence, thereby contributing to the existing debates on the appropriate approach to the online market. By synthesizing the theoretical rationales and perspectives on consumer protection and recent thoughts on the lack of consumer confidence, this study proposed that one key factor to enhance consumer confidence is to increase public awareness in relation to enhancing access to justice in the multidimensional sense. This proposed approach to access to justice is broader than most consumer protection literatures that seem to specifically focus on either the redresses and remedies, economic interests or other narrow senses of protection. The discussion presented in this study is made under a broader assumption that the primary goal of consumer protection is to deliver a just environment in the market, which includes socio-legal justice and economic interests for consumers in all aspects encompassing all stages of online activities. Such assumption seems to serve a wide range of interests and preferences of consumers, which have potential influence toward consumers' attitude and willingness to engage in online transactions. This study provides the *framework* for conceptualizing access to justice in the context of consumer protection in multidimensional senses by describing the various reasonable conditions necessary to satisfy consumers in B2C e-commerce—the goal and benchmark for consumer protection. This is a normative guideline on how a consumer protection model needs to be adapted to accomplish the challenges brought about by the transnational B2C e-market and how these adaptations can be implemented.

The latter part of this research argues in favor of private ordering as a meaningful consumer protection mechanism because it has the potential of enhancing the multidimensional approach to access to justice for consumers in B2C e-commerce. Indeed, this research further introduces the need to address the deficits that lead to the resurgence of private ordering mechanisms to sustain the growing volume of e-sale transactions. The proposal going forward is to consider the *state as the intermediary*, a neutral third party playing a role in facilitating various aspects

Trade Commission (FTC) was granted the power to take legal action against the registered website operator, in the event that an illegal act is committed. Apart from that, the protection of electronic consumers is also represented by the Uniform Computer Information Transactions Act (UCITA), which grants electronic consumer some basic rights including the right to return. *See* J. Graubert and J. Coleman, *The Impact of Technological Change in the Canada/U.S. Context: Consumer Protection and Antitrust Enforcement at the Speed of Light: The FTC Meets the Internet*, 25 - Canada-United States Law Journal 275–6, 284–5 (1999).

of private ordering as a solution for limiting the risks under the function of the private ordering regime. This would help shaping the private ordering approach to become a more effective mechanism in delivering access to justice, resulting in the enhancement of consumer confidence.

1.4 Methodology

This study relies on a combination of different academic sources and several theoretical and normative elements, which largely apply to the same consumer protection issues. The analysis of various perspectives will result in a solution to the consumer protection in e-commerce question that uses all of the insights derived therefrom. This study commences by exploring the access to justice concept, which is the goal for consumer protection. It is then followed by the establishment of a *framework* for conceptualizing access to justice in the context of consumer protection in B2C e-commerce that will provide the criterion for the analysis of different types of mechanism throughout this study. The outcomes of these assessments will help draw the main argument of this study in identifying the mechanisms that enhance consumer confidence and the need to adjust the existing mechanisms to provide a more effective consumer protection that is necessary for the future.

Instead of presenting a comprehensive comparative study of various legal systems, this study seeks to explore the *ius commune* or the common core of consumer protection by reviewing the legal debates and looking at some crucial issues and particular problems found in certain legal systems. The common core presented in this study appears to be universal and can be used in future research to assess and provide guidelines to enhance specific legal systems and consumer protection mechanisms. This is not necessarily limited to the online market, but may also be applied to offline consumer activities where one party lacks comparable power in terms of bargaining, information, knowledge, or skill.

1.5 Scope of Research

To map out consumer problems, this study takes a broad approach in the sense that it considers not only the legal aspects, but also general economic theories, which have an influence on consumer protection laws and policies.

In addition, issues related to competition law generally fall outside the scope of this study. However, as the competition law works as a compliment to consumer protection by addressing monopoly problems that helps to create a fair atmosphere and promotes competition in the market,[12] this study sometimes has to broadly refer

[12] *See* Bergh, *supra* note 7.

to it where relevant. Furthermore, there are three types of business relationships in e-commerce activities, namely business-to-business transactions (hereinafter *B2B*),[13] business-to-consumer transactions (hereinafter *B2C*),[14] and consumer-to-consumer transactions (hereinafter *C2C*).[15] This study only focuses on B2C activities where businesses sell their products and services to the public or to general consumers. The other forms of e-commerce fall outside the scope of this study.[16]

The outcomes of this study can be applied not only to cross border transactions but also those domestic transactions arising out of the online marketplace, where parties do not have physical contact. Also, it is sometimes difficult to clearly separate traditional transactions from online sales because consumer issues emerging in the e-market are more or less similar to those in off line consumer activities, and some online problems are sometimes solved by relying on mechanisms used in the traditional environment.

The assessment of this dissertation covers both substantive regulations and enforcement tools because, to efficiently improve consumer protection, substantive and procedural mechanisms are interdependent and needed to develop in parallel.[17] To do so, some specific legal systems must be evaluated to learn lessons on how to create more effective consumer protection systems and mechanisms. This study thus looks at the laws of the United States (hereinafter *US*), the European Union (hereinafter *EU*) and some of its Member States. These jurisdictions have been selected because their debates on B2C e-commerce appear to be the most developed.[18] However, where relevant, this dissertation also expands its analytical

[13] Business-to-Business (B2B) includes all commercial transactions between trading parties, which are assumed to have equal bargaining powers and positions.

[14] Business to Consumer (B2C), which is the focus of this study, occurs at the business to consumer level when the consumer, one party to the contract, is an end user and the business, the other party to the contract, acts based on business purposes.

[15] Consumer-to-Consumer (C2C) refers to electronic auctions and second hand products electronically offered for sale by an individual acting outside his or her trade or profession to general consumers. eBay, for example, is the most successful website of C2C relationships with a large number of goods being put on auction at any given time.

[16] In B2B transactions, parties to the contract are not considered consumers because both parties act in the course of his or her business or profession. In C2C activities, both parties to the contract do not act in the course of his or her business or profession. However, both are deemed to have equal position and bargaining powers for entering into a C2C contract. Thus, protective provisions are not necessary, as there is an assumption no weaker party exists in such case.

[17] *See* K. J. Cseres, *Enforcement of Collective Consumer Interests: A Competition Law Perspective, in* W. van Boom and M. Loos (eds.), Collective Enforcement of Consumer Law 123, 125–6, 132 (2007).

[18] The United States, the leading e-commerce economy with the highest volume of e-consumer transactions, presents a worthy example for our study. The European Union consumer law relating to e-sales is one of the most recently developed and it has benefited from the accumulated experience and good practices of all of its 27 member states, the majority of which are economically advanced jurisdictions. In addition, domestic laws of certain EU Member States that have interesting features relevant to the issues being discussed will be referred to for providing the key issues to develop the best mechanisms to ensure consumers' access to justice.

approach, referring to the laws of other jurisdictions to demonstrate shared or common aspects. It should also be noted that some consumer protection mechanisms used in the e-market such as those relating to product safety, misleading online advertisements and online fraud are not discussed or evaluated. Due to the limited space and time allowed to develop this study, the analysis within the confines of this research uses a number of mechanisms as examples that are best suitable to illustrate the relevant consumer protection insights. The law and mechanisms explored in this research are those effective as of 28 June 2013.

It must be admitted that to evaluate them accurately, more information on the effects of each mechanism is needed. It is difficult to assess some consumer protection mechanisms when the relevant data and empirical research are lacking, especially the recently implemented laws and mechanisms which have not yet been subjected to statistical analysis.[19] This study does not cover some statistic survey, but it provides measurements mainly based on a theoretical, conceptual, and normative approach rather than conducting empirical research on consumer protection mechanisms.

Moreover, the discussions of the proposed strategy in the final chapter (Chap. 9) intend to contribute to an enhancement of current consumer protection approaches in achieving access to justice. The detailed and elaborated functions and their costs and side effects should be explored in-depth before their practical implementation. This is to ensure that it, as promised, would effectively enhance consumer protection and improve consumer confidence in the online market. This study as a result hopes to provide a meaningful starting point for further discussion on the possible implementation and development of the private ordering, which is consumer protection mechanisms in B2C e-commerce.

---

[19] For instance, the EU Consumer Right Directive and the Swedish Small Claims Procedure were introduced within recent years. Consequently, there are not any empirical studies with regard to their practical performance and efficiency.

Chapter 2
Consumer Protection in B2C E-Commerce: Enhancing Consumer Confidence

2.1 Introduction

The electronic market (hereinafter *e-market*) is special in its potential influence and cross-border expansion because of its advanced technological features. Through internet technology and electronic means of communication, traders enjoy great benefits including speed, convenience, lower investment cost, and boundary-free market access. Consumers also benefit from more choices offered, greater information, and the convenience of purchasing products and services from sellers located at a great distance and at any time. Taking a closer look, the e-market has a great potential role to play in this new global economy through its transformative effects that allow goods and services to be flown to markets that up to now have largely been ignored because of geographic barriers. The e-market also has a definite role to play in enhancing competition and communication and affords market access to businesses and consumers on a global scale. However, many empirical studies show that the majority of consumers lack confidence to utilize the e-market, especially with respect to cross border purchases.[1] Given the significant benefit of the e-market to the economy, consumer protection measures are necessary to improve consumer confidence, promote the expansion of global commercial exchanges, and allow e-commerce to grow to its full potential.

This chapter revisits some of the preliminary concepts and issues of B2C E-Commerce. It starts with a brief history and describes the distinctive features of

---

[1] *See e.g.* Commission of the European Communities, *Proposal for a Directive of the European Parliament and of the Council Concerning Unfair Business-To-Consumer Commercial Practices in the Internet Market and Amending Directives 84/450/EEC, 97/7/EC and 98/27/EC Explanatory Memorandum 18.6.2003 COM (2003) 356 final 2003/0134 (COD)*, Eurobarometer, *European Opinion Research Group N. 57.2 (April-June 2002)* (2002), *available at* issda.ucd.ie/documentation/eb/s3640cod.pdf (visited January 15, 2012) and C. Poncibo, *Some Thoughts on the Methodological Approach to EC Consumer Law Reform*, 21 Loyola Consumer Law Review 353–71 (2009).

S. Yuthayotin, *Access to Justice in Transnational B2C E-Commerce*,
DOI 10.1007/978-3-319-11131-5_2

B2C "e-transactions" and their growth in the global and emerging market economies. It then discusses why consumers in B2C e-sales need legal protection. This includes an examination of competing rationales for consumer protection by looking at the four main traditional rationales, namely (I) the lack of knowledge and information asymmetries, (II) the lack of bargaining power and standard contract terms, (III) the behavioral economic problems and (IV) the failures of traditional forms of litigation, and by discussing the new emergence of consumer confidence in global debates on *B2C* e-sales respectively. Conclusions drawn from this chapter will shed light on the rationales behind the need for effective mechanisms of consumer protection in B2C e-sales that help to improve consumer confidence which form the main argument of this chapter.

2.2 Transnational B2C E-Commerce, Economic Growth, and Emerging Markets

2.2.1 A Brief History of B2C E-Commerce

In the 1980s, internet technology, an electronic means of communication, was first introduced to the general public and has since become widely used around the world because of its ability to deliver significant amounts of information in seconds, and because of its ease of use.[2] As the field enlarged, all players made use of the technology to fulfill their objectives. Businesses and commercial entities, for examples, expanded their economic capability into websites that gave them access to the borderless internet environment. Today, e-commerce, a type of business transactions where purchasing and selling of good or services are carried on through internet or other forms of electronic communications or computer networks has commonly conducted.

To distinguish the B2C e-commerce which is the focus of this study from other forms of e-commercial activities (B2B and C2C transactions), the nature of B2C transactions, which are often called "consumer sales" or "consumer transactions", will be briefly explained.

The legislation providing special provisions for consumer transactions—in contrast to those rules governing commercial transactions and other transactions in general—are inspired by policies attempting to protect consumers because of the perceived inequality in economic and bargaining power between consumers and

[2] Internet research was initiated by the U.S. military in 1969. It was later introduced to the public as a consumer friendly medium in 1989. *See* T. T. Reith, *Consumer Confidence: The Key to Successful E-Commerce in the Global Marketplace*, 24 Suffolk Transnational Law Review 467, 469–73 (2001) and R. T. Griffiths, *History of the Internet, Internet for Historians* (October, 2002), *available at* let.leidenuniv.nl/history/ivh/chap2.htm#back%20to%20top (visited January 1, 2011).

businesses.[3] According to most consumer protection legislation,[4] they apply only to transactions by reference to the characteristics of the parties to a contract and to the purpose of the contract.[5] Based on very general criteria, one party to the contract must be a "consumer", acting outside the scope of his course of this trade or profession.[6] Secondly, the other party to the contract, who can be a natural person or legal entity, must be acting in the course of their business.[7] Lastly, consumer sales should be restricted to contracts for the supply of goods for personal family

---

[3] Consumers are entitled to be protected because *"[t]he economic position being one of weakness in comparison with the sellers by reason of the fact that they are private final consumers and are not engaged, when buying the product acquired on installment credit terms, in trade or professional activities." See* Case 150/77 *Bernard v Ott*, [1978] ECR 1431, para 21. The recognition of consumers' weakness has been clearly documented since 1978, when the ECJ decision in *Bertrand v Ott* introduced the definition of consumers who are often economically weaker than businesses. For the idea of unequal bargaining power in consumer transactions, *see* I. Ramsay, Consumer law and Policy, Text and Materials on Regulating Consumer Markets Chapter 2 (2007).

[4] There are no internationally or universally adopted definitions of consumer sales or B2C transactions. In European laws, for example, there are no precise definitions on who is considered a consumer. It largely depends on the definition defined under the particular piecemeal national legislations governing such activities. In German credit law, the term "consumer" is defined as any natural person if the agreement did not stipulate that a credit contract is intended for the pursuance of an existent professional activity. In the English credit law, a consumer who is also a debtor is an individual who has been granted credit under a credit agreement. *See* J. Hill, Cross-Border Consumer Contracts 2 (2008).

[5] These references of the purpose of the contract and the characteristic of the parties to the contract seem to be an *"objective characteristic"*, regardless of whether or not there is an actual imbalance of bargaining power between the parties. According to one argument, such a legal test is based on objective characteristics that are too broad. Not all sales contracts between consumers and business operators that meet such elements should be regarded as a consumer sale. These are, for example, sale contracts for high value goods and services. Consumers will usually seek expert advice from lawyers or financial advisers and the weakness and inequality of the consumers can be eradicated by the professional advice. In this situation, special rules to overcome the inequality that general consumers often confront, is not necessary. This leads to the question of to what extent the regulations designed to protect consumers should be applied to the sale of high value goods and services. To be consistent with the objective of consumer law of protecting consumers as a weak party, the law should rather attempt to identify consumer sales based on the "*subjective characteristic*" of the inequality of bargaining power of the contracting parties. The protective provisions should cover all kinds of sale transactions, if there is an imbalance of bargaining power between parties in such circumstances, the focus should be on the unequal element between the parties. *See ibid.*, at 263.

[6] One important element of a consumer sale is that one party of the contract should act "outside one's trade or profession" for he or she to be considered a "consumer". This leads to the question of what does the term 'outside his or her trade, business, or profession' mean. For detailed discussion on the diverse interpretation of this element, *see ibid.*, at 4–5 and Z. S. Tang, Electronic consumer contracts in the conflict of laws 21–8 (2009).

[7] The component is that the other party to the contract should be acting in the course of their business. However, some legislation only specifies the characteristics of the consumer but omits to address the status requirement of the opposite party, for examples, the Rome Convention Article 5 (1) and the Brussels I Regulation Article 15. The silence of these legislations should not be interpreted to mean that the other party can be anyone.

and household use.[8] If these three conditions are satisfied, the sales transaction, in relation to which there is often deemed an inequality of bargaining power between the seller and the purchaser, is considered a consumer sale or a B2C transaction.

Clearly, the e-market offers traders and consumers in B2C transactions great benefits over traditional forms of commerce. These benefits include greater speed and convenience, and lower transaction costs. Consumers have been handed powerful instruments for exploring information, products, and services online. They can virtually communicate and agree with traders on everything through the internet or other forms of computer networks without any human negotiation or interaction. The formation of a contract is simply concluded through electronic communication such as e-mail exchanges or by clicking the button through active websites, with payment carried by electronic medium or other similar arrangements. Consumers simply click though an operating website and the sales contract is legally concluded. The most prevalent B2C e-sales are the purchases of goods and services including a wide range of books, CDs, clothing, software, airline tickets, and hotel bookings. Payment from the consumers is made online, but the seller's delivery of goods or services takes place later in the real world. For the purpose of this research, the words "e-commerce", "online" or "internet" sales refer to the same characteristics as B2C e-transactions where consumers virtually order goods or services via active websites or other forms of computer networks according to which the characteristic obligations of contractual performance, namely, the payment and delivery, will take place.

2.2.2 *Distinctive Features of B2C "E-Transactions"*

When compared to traditional sale transactions, obvious dissimilarities of B2C e-sales appear in the ways the goods and services are offered for sale, and the means used by consumers to purchased them, which are largely based on technological communications.

2.2.2.1 Absence of Face-to-Face Communication

A B2C e-sale is mediated by technology processes and lacks face-to-face communication. This feature is undeniably different from the traditional form of com-

[8] There have been several legal attempts to define this term and it has been diversely interpreted as personal, family, or household use, private end user, or a person that satisfies personal needs in relation to private consumption. For a different direction of interpretation on this term, *see Bertrand* case, *supra* note 3, at para 21 and Case C-269/95 *Benincasa v Dentalkit* [1997] ECR I-3767, para 17.

merce.[9] In an offline sale, consumers will travel to physical stores or places of service to obtain the desired goods and services. Such physical establishments give consumers a certain degree of assurance that a trader's business is in operation and will remain there even for a temporary period.[10] Moreover, in offline sales, consumers who enter stores are allowed to see and touch products, samples or try them if they want. Consumers can also consult with sale staff if there are questions. Even though technology improves the time and convenience of entering into sale transactions, the said actions that are associated with traditional sales are not possible in the online market. Thus, consumers may feel skeptical about purchasing products or services online for fear that e-traders may not be truly established and the products and services may not have the desired quality.[11] All these physical relationships seem to create some degree of certainty and assurance between parties and the targeted transaction, which may be one of the necessary elements before entering into a legal relationship.[12] However, there is no such tangible feature or physical element that can help assure consumers in B2C e-sales. As the key element that is essential for trust does not exist, consumers in B2C e-sales may not have the same degree of trust and confidence in traders as they would in traditional sales.

2.2.2.2 Moveable, Dynamic, and Voluminous Information

While information on traditional sales at brick and mortar stores are usually based on documents that are static, the internet allows information to be amended at any time and provides unlimited possibilities and dynamics regarding the information displaying formats for the voluminous electronically stored information.[13] The contents and elements of a web page can be instantly changed simply upon website providers saving the revisions on their web pages.[14] Notices on traders' websites can be given to consumers through various formats of electronic presentation, for instance scroll bars, pop-up windows and the bottoms of web pages. Some online terms are not even immediately shown when navigating a web site, but only later when visiting another web page or further using particular designed functions of a web page, such as filling in a form or applying for a membership. This is the

[9] *See* T. Tasker and D. Pakcyk, *Cyber- Surfing on the High Seas of Legalese: Law and Technology of Internet Agreement*, 18 Albany Law Journal of Science and Technology 79, 105–6 (2008).

[10] *See* Z. Saami, *Regulation of E-Commerce by Contract: Is It Fair to Consumers?*, 31 University of West Los Angeles Law Review 163, 167 (2000).

[11] *See also ibid.*

[12] In virtual online transactions, it is clear that the physical face-to-face communication envisioned in traditional contract law does not exist. E-consumers may be at a greater risk of not having the same level of certainty and assurance as when they make offline purchases. Greater protection for consumers in B2C e-sales is necessary. *See ibid.*

[13] *See* Tasker and Pakcyk, *supra* note 9, at 105.

[14] *See* L. Lemay, Sams Teach Yourself Web Publishing with HTML and XHTML in 21 days 14–5 (2001).

so-called delayed notice.[15] In addition, a webpage can be overloaded with various information and designed interactive features such as animations, movies, and sounds, which are likely to divert or distract consumers' attention. Also, the use of trick-or-click computer button uniquely affects consumers' experiences in making contracts. A simple action to indicate an acceptance in the online purchase is, though convenient, often open to errors or miscommunications.

2.2.2.3 Cross Border/Transnational Nature

The borderless or transnational characteristic is an obvious and distinct part of B2C e-sales. The power of the e-market to offer products and services to unlimited geographic targets from a single website at very low operating cost is a great benefit for e-commerce. Although telephone, telemarketing, and mail order sale transactions have long been utilized, the rise of B2C e-sales has significantly and exponentially widened the transnational sales volume because it is simpler, cheaper, faster, and more convenient form of transacting.[16] However, its cross border nature also creates challenges for traders and consumers as well as governments.[17] Many consumers, on one hand, may be concerned that if something goes wrong in an e- transaction with a foreign trader, there is a risk that they will be unable to benefit from the protection he or she can expect when buying something in a more traditional way within their countries.[18] The businesses, on the other hand, are opposed to the recommendation that they should comply with "a patchwork of regulatory schemes and varying requirements of all the jurisdictions in which their various clients or potential clients may be located."[19] Form states' perspective, they have been challenged by the transnational nature of e-commerce, particularly with respect to the areas of choice of law, forum and enforcement of judicial decisions.[20] One of the key issues that has been the focus of both scholars and legislators is the creation of well-designed online consumer protection mechanisms that are neatly responsive to the global nature of internet transactions. Without these, consumers' confidence will be impaired and the growth of online businesses will be limited.

[15] *See* Tasker and Pakcyk, *supra* note 9, at 103–4 (2008).

[16] *See* R. Tasse, M. Faille and G. L. Henderson, *Online Consumer Protection: A Study on Regulatory Jurisdiction in Canada, The Paper Prepared for the Office of Consumer Affairs, Industry Canada* (July 2001), *available at* ulcc.ca/en/civil-section/102-civil-section-commercial-law-strategy/electronic-commerce/370-online-consumer-protectionstudy-on-regulatory-jurisdiction-in-canada (visited January 30, 2012).

[17] *See ibid.*

[18] *See ibid.*

[19] *See ibid.*

[20] *See ibid.*, at 2.

2.2.3 B2C E-Commerce and Global Economic Growth

E-commerce brings the opportunity for the evolution of a single global market. Jay Tannenbaum has stated that "there is great potential for this new commercial tool to change the economy landscape, allowing goods and services to be delivered to a market that largely ignores political and geographic barriers-improving productivities and communication and providing global market access to businesses and consumers worldwide."[21] The benefits of the e-market include greater choices of products and services, more information,[22] increased competition,[23] lower prices,[24] and the convenience of purchasing from businesses based anywhere at any time.

---

[21] *See* OECD, *Gateways to the Global Market Consumers and Electronic Commerce* 21 (1998).

[22] The electronic network allows business and consumers to transact business without the restraint of geographical boundaries. Without the cost of physical offices established in various locations, businesses can easily offer goods or services online, expanding worldwide access. This even encourages small businesses to bring their trade into the international level. In a virtual world, consumers can enjoy a greater range of information of products and services and simply conduct an electronic purchase at home, around the clock, even with the company located thousands of miles away. *See* K. Alboukrek, *Adapting to a New World of E-Commerce: The Need for Uniform Consumer Protection in the International Electronic Marketplace*, 35 George Washington International Law Review 425, 429 (2003).

[23] In general, consumers will look for information and compare it before selecting the best deal based on the information given. Those businesses who offer low quality of goods or services or non-competitive consumer goods or services, will not be selected by consumers. In online markets where consumers have greater opportunities to look for information and a wider range of offers without any geographical restrictions, businesses may have to be very competitive to survive in such a market environment. As a result, it would positively enhance the quality of goods and services offered to consumers. It is likely for online businesses to be free from numerous burdensome operating costs (e.g. physical infrastructure, labor, advertisements) so that they can enhance the quality of their products and services, including before and after sale support with the remaining budget. *See ibid.*, at 429–30.

[24] The e-market also brings greater profits and lower prices. In traditional consumer sales, manufacturers rely on traditional supply chains for the distribution of the massive volume of products. Consumers residing in different corners of the world cannot purchase certain kinds of goods or services unless they are provided with convenient access. Long chains of wholesalers and retailers have become important intermediaries in such transactions; especially in case those consumers are located in remote regions or other countries. This is no longer the case in the internet market where manufacturers can short cut the conventional intermediaries or even contract directly with end consumers via electronic means. In this circumstance, products can be sent to consumers directly from the manufacturers or take out long conventional lines of intermediaries, creating greater profits to the manufacturer. For the consumers, they will enjoy lower prices offered because the manufactures or businesses can reduce the cost of the transaction by cutting the long supply chain, thereby reducing the operating costs. In addition, internet sales require minimal human intervention. The internet shop can manage their operation of their website by computer software. This of course saves labor cost. At the same time, consumers will experience lower prices as electronic commerce affords potential cost saving to businesses that are likely to pass these benefits to consumers in terms of lower prices. *See* OECD, *supra* note 21, at 30–1.

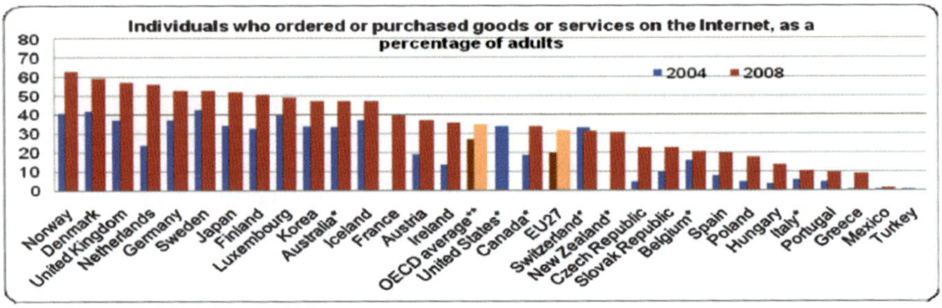

Fig. 2.1 Percentages of adults who ordered and bought goods and services on the internet by countries for the period from 2004 to 2008 (*See* OECD, *OECD Conference on Empowering E-Consumers, Strengthening Consumer Protection in the Internet Economy, Background Report, Washington D.C., 8–10 December 2009* (2009), *available at* oecd.org/ict/econsumerconference/44047583.pdf (visited January 12, 2013)). *Note*: * The available information on the exact period is unavailable. The shown percentages were based on the available information of the nearby periods (Australia's data for 2007 instead of 2008, Belgium's data for 2005 instead of 2004, Canada's data for 2003 instead of 2004 and 2007 instead of 2008, Italy's data for 2005 instead of 2004, New Zealand's data for 2006 instead of 2008, Switzerland's data for 2005 instead of 2008, United States' data for 2003 instead of 2004. *See ibid.*).** Average percentage of the available data

Given the benefits of the e-market to the global economy and to consumers, many policies have tended to encourage the potential growth of e-commerce. As a result, the volume of B2C e-transactions has shown a continuous raise. The statistics of the Organization for Economic Cooperation and Development (hereinafter *OECD*)[25] confirms this continuous rise in e-trades.[26] According to Fig. 2.1, the amount of B2C e-sales in the OECD members increased from 2004 to 2009. During that period, the numbers of individuals who bought goods and services online rose from 26.9 to 35 %. More than half of the adults in Japan, the United Kingdom, as well as a number of European countries entered into the B2C e-sales in the year 2008.

Moreover, some prominent leaders in commercial activities have also displayed the same trend. A survey conducted in the United Kingdom, for example, indicated the continued expansion of the online market. The data published by the UK Office for National Statistics demonstrated a 30 % growth in B2C e-sales within one year, to £163 billion in 2007 as compared to 2006.[27] In the US, the situation is similar. In

[25] The OECD is an international organization comprising thirty three democratic nations, including most countries in the European Union, the United States, Japan, and South Korea, with the aim to support sustainable economic growth.

[26] Some may argue that the percentage of consumer sales in the OECD area does not draw a full picture as in other part of the world, considerable variations may exist. The statistics of electronic trading is unfortunately not obtainable in many countries and this may affect the global picture of e-commerce utilization.

[27] *See* UK Office of National Statics, *News Release, Internet Sales Rose by 30 % in 2007* (November 21, 2008), *available at* statistics.gov.uk/pdfdir/ecomnr1108.pdf (visited March 26, 2013).

2007, 66 % of American consumers ordered and purchased goods and services online, a noticeable increase from 2001 when the figure was only 46 %.[28] Many studies predicted that e-consumer sales would continue to grow steadily even though the possible economic crisis may affect its potential.[29] Today, it may be true that traditional forms of sales have now transformed into e-sales[30] and international trade, once solely the preserve for business, now has expand to consumers through the B2C e-activities.[31]

2.2.4 *B2C E-Commerce and Economic Growth in Emerging Markets*

Emerging markets comprise countries where commercial transactions and social activities are in the evolutionary process of rapid expansion and industrialization.[32]

---

[28] *See* OECD, *OECD Conference on Empowering E-Consumers, Strengthening Consumer Protection in the Internet Economy, Background Report, Washington D.C., 8–10 December 2009* (2009), *available at* oecd.org/ict/econsumerconference/44047583.pdf (visited January 12, 2013).

[29] One of other supporting pieces of evidence for the growth in B2C e-sales is the tremendous success of eBay. eBay operates an online auction and shopping website where businesses and consumers buy and sell a wide range of goods and services. Today, it is a multi-billion dollar business with operations in more than thirty countries worldwide. Based on eBay' annual report in 2008, there were one million visitors to its website per day with 86.9 million active users around the world and a total income of US$1.78 billion in that year alone. Additionally, the success of Amazon, the online retailer which begun business as an online bookshop, but later developed to sell a broad range of products such as CDs, computer software and instruments, video games, electronics, apparel, clothes, furniture, food, toys and so on, are also another confirmation. Today, Amazon has many separate websites in various countries around the world. Canada, the United Kingdom, Germany, France, Italy, Austria, Japan, and China are examples. International delivery or shipping to some specified countries is also related service of Amazon. *See* C. Riefa and J. Hörnle, *The Changing Face of Electronic Consumer Contracts in the Twenty-First Century: Fit for Purpose?, in* L. Edwards and C. Waelde (eds.), Law and the Internet 89, 90 (2009).

[30] *See* I. Colon-Fung, *Protecting the New Face of Entrepreneurship: Online Appropriate Dispute Resolution and International Consumer-To-Consumer Online*, 12 Fordham Journal of Corporate and Financial Law 233, 233 (2007).

[31] *See* Tasse, Faille and Henderson, *supra* note 16, at 1–2.

[32] It is very difficult to give a precise definition to emerging economies. Although many studies have researched the topic of emerging markets, the indication of how a market is considered to be at an emerging stage is not so clear. For example, the 2008 Emerging Economy Report prepared by the Center for Knowledge Societies describes the emerging markets as those nations which "experiencing rapid informationalization under conditions for limited or partial industrialization". *See* The Center for Knowledge Societies, *Emerging Economic Report* (2008), *available at* emergingeconomyreport.com/ (visited February 1, 2011). Differently, Marois Thomas argues that in identifying emerging economies, the financial imperative is a much more important factor to consider. *See* M. Thomas, States, Banks and Crisis: Emerging Finance Capitalism in Mexico and Turkey (2012).

Countries with low-to medium per capital income are usually classified as emerging economies.[33] Even though many groups and organizations have tried to label different list of countries as emerging economies, their analysis shares the common opinion that emerging markets largely include nations in Asia (e.g. China, India, Indonesia, Malaysia, The Philippines, Thailand), South America (e.g. Brazil, Mexico), Eastern Europe (e.g. Russia), the Middle East (e.g. Egypt, Turkey) and African countries (e.g. South Africa).[34]

In 2008, the Internet World Statistic Report revealed that 54 % or approximately 712 million from the total of 1.32 billion worldwide internet users live in the emerging markets and the number of internet users in these markets continued to experience dramatic growth.[35] For instance, China and India,[36] the two most populous nations in the world, have experienced steep growth in internet use of 833 and 1,100 % from 2000 to 2007, with 210 and 60 million internet users respectively.[37]

There has always been a focus on the rapid growth of e-commerce in the countries of emerging markets.[38] The rank of the middle class in these countries is growing at a far greater pace than in the more advanced countries and the rapid increase of their upper class numbers is also evident.[39] For instance, in the Asia Pacific region, the size of the high net worth population is as large as in Europe.[40] Thus, venture capitalists have heavily injected capital in the emerging markets. Many new traders have emerged and the Asia Pacific B2C e-market has been rapidly developed.

---

[33] *See* K. Rouibah, O. E. M. Khalil and A. E. Hassanien (eds.), Emerging Markets and E-Commerce in Developing Economies (2008).

[34] There are many lists labeling countries as emerging economies such as the International Monetary Fund list, Columbia University EMGP List, FTSE list, S&P list, and the Dow Jones list. Although those lists are not exactly the same, one common understanding of the emerging economies that they share is that they are countries undergoing rapid development and reforms. These countries have approximately more than 80 % of the world population and represent 20 % of the global economy. *See ibid.*

[35] *See ibid.*

[36] China and India are very attractive for companies looking to make B2C e-commerce investments because of their fast growing economies. *See* J. Harris, *Consumer Discretionary* (December 12, 2012), *available at* fidelity.com/viewpoints/consumer-discretionary-sector-2012 (visited December 12, 2012), L2 Block Digital Digest, *China Leads Emerging Markets for "Retail E-Commerce Potential"* (June 26, 2012), *available at* l2thinktank.com/china-leads-emerging-markets-for-retail-e-commerce-potential/2012/ (visited December 12, 2012) and Z. D. Wigder, M. Bahl, K. Willis and L. Varon, *Trends in India's eCommerce Market* (August 23, 2012), *available at* assocham.org/arb/general/Forrester_Trends_In_Indias_eCommerc.pdf (visited January 12, 2013).

[37] *See* Rouibah, Khalil and Hassanien, *supra* note 33.

[38] *See* Harris, *supra* note 36, at 3.

[39] *See ibid.*, at 4.

[40] *See* Merrill Lynch Wealth Management, World Wealth Report 2010 (2010).

Along with it, infrastructure, logistics, methods of payments, and communication have been improved.[41] The fast technological development and the sustained revenue growth in emerging markets are likely to be critical to the future expansion of e-commerce in the global market.[42] For instance, China, with the second largest online market with a total transaction value of $23 billion in the year 2011,[43] is predicted to grow around 29 % per year for the next 5 years.[44] The evolution of Chinese infrastructure and its consumers' purchasing behavior will soon drive China to the top of the table of countries with the most B2C e-transactions and support its strong potential growth.[45] The website Taobao appears to dominate the B2C online market in China, having 50 million visitors per day and representing about 50 % market share of Chinese B2C online transactions.[46] Globally, Taobao also has a powerful position, being the 12th most visited website in the world.[47] India is another example where the e-commerce market is growing at a very rapid pace as more and more online population spend and purchase online. Revenue from B2C e-transactions (including C2C) is forecasted to increase up to five times by 2016, from $16 billion in 2012 to reach $88 billion in 2016.[48]

China and India, two examples of emerging economies that are often looked upon by their neighbors as having stable economies and being influential financial forces in their geographic regions, have been experiencing very fast expansion of online B2C sales in recent years. China, with its huge online market and the dominance of Taobao, cannot be underestimated. Although India may have a smaller market the data indicates that it is growing rapidly, with increasing opportunities as people start spending more and more online. Both emerging markets and B2C e-transactions thus are important to global economic growth because not only they have a strong potential upside, but also because they can anchor B2C e-activities in the global economy, linking emerging markets in Asia, South America, Eastern Europe, the Middle East, and Africa. This will of course promote the single global market through e-commerce.

---

[41] *See e.g.* Wigder, Bahl, Willis and Varon, *supra* note 36, L2 Block Digital Digest, *supra* note 36 *and* A. T. Kearney's Global Consumer Institute, *E-Commerce Is the Next Frontier in the Global Expansion* (2012), *available at* atkearney.com/documents/10192/348450/2012-E-Commerce-Index.pdf/83c81d46-fa4f-4421-850a-ef501d92afbd (visited December 12, 2012).

[42] *See also* Harris, *supra* note 36, at 3.

[43] It is second only the United States. *See* L2 Block Digital Digest, *supra* note 36, at 2.

[44] *See ibid.*

[45] *See ibid.*

[46] *See* M. Brown, *Evaluating Emerging eCommerce Markets-China and* Brazil (January 31, 2012), *available at* pfsweb.com/blog/evaluating-emerging-ecommerce-china-and-brazil/ (visited January 12, 2013).

[47] *See ibid.*

[48] *See* Wigder, Bahl, Willis and Varon, *supra* note 36, at 4.

2.2.5 B2C E-Commerce and Consumer Confidence

Although the rise of B2C e-transactions both globally and in specific emerging markets is obvious as discussed earlier, it is still in its relative infancy and has a long way to progress. The number of B2C e-transactions remain much less than B2B ones. The United Kingdom is a good example of this. Retail sales or B2C was only 21 % of the total e-commerce transactions in 2005, whereas B2B was at 79 %.[49] Also, there was a great imbalance between the figures of online and offline purchases. The same survey revealed that internet shopping was about 3 % of the total retail sales in the United Kingdom in 2005.[50] In addition, even though there is a wide range of products available for online purchase such as electronics, CDs, airline tickets, books, clothes and so on, the vast majority of electronic consumer sales were low value transactions. Research conducted in 2005 indicated that an average value of each online sale is only around £ 55.[51] One cannot overlook the substantial imbalance between the volume of B2B e-activities and consumer e-transactions as well as online and offline sales, and the limited value of the products and services that consumers usually purchase.

Even though the benefits of B2C e-sales have often been recognized and many states have attempt to boost their growth by simply modernizing laws and regulations originally designed for brick-and-mortar stores to deal with this new electronic based type of transaction. To date the expansion of B2C e-sales appears to be somewhat contained as discussed above. This may be because of the fact revealed by empirical research that a large number of consumers do not trust the internet and lack the confidence necessary to engage in e-transactions.[52] Consumers remain very old fashioned when they shop online, particularly when making cross border purchases. Research conducted in 2006, for example, indicated that more than 40 % of consumers in the UK engaged in cyber purchases with local suppliers in 2005, whereas only 7 % bought goods and services from vendors in other jurisdictions, in the same period.[53]

A recent EU survey on consumer confidence revealed that the confidence level of e-consumers is extremely low.[54] Approximately 56 % of the surveyed

---

[49] *See* UK Office of Fair Trading (OFT), *Internet Shopping: An OFT Market Study* (June 2007), *available at* oft.gov.uk/shared_oft/reports/consumer_protection/oft921.pdf (visited January 12, 2012).

[50] *See ibid.*, at 18.

[51] *See ibid.*, at 19.

[52] *See ibid. See also* T. Schultz, *Does Online Dispute Resolution Need Governmental Intervention? The Case of Architectures of Control and Trust,* 6 North Carolina Journal of Law and Technology 71, 76 (2004) and L. M. Ponte, *Boosting Consumer Confidence in E-Business: Recommendations for Establishing Fair and Effective Dispute Resolution Programs for B2C Online Transactions*, 12 Albany Law Journal of Science and Technology 441, 442 (2002).

[53] *See* Eurobarometer, *Consumer Protection in the Internal Market* (September 2006), *available at* ec.europa.eu/consumers/topics/eurobarometer_09-2006_en.pdf (visited January 12, 2012).

[54] *See* Eurobarometer, *supra* note 1.

e-consumers gave the reason that foreign businesses are less likely to comply with consumer protection law.[55] Around 71 % of the consumers surveyed cited the extreme difficulty in resolving disputes, e.g., those that may arise from the return of goods, price settlement, warranties, etc., as the reason for such lack of confidence.[56] About 65 % of the surveyed consumers believe it would be problematic if they change their mind and return the products that they purchased online from a merchant locating abroad.[57]

The situation is similar in the emerging markets that one important impediment to the growth of B2C e-activities is obviously the lack of confidence on online shopping. Most consumers are often paranoid that they may be conducting business with fraudulent websites and their order might consequently be cheated.[58] They often perceive online transactions as a risk because of possible fraud, anonymity of traders, unsecured e-payment, personal information theft, and unreliable mode of delivery.[59] A study revealed, for example, that 23 % of Indian consumers quit before completing the online registration process required by websites because of online fraud concerns.[60]

Looking at the above data, it can be said that consumers around the world have no great confidence in e-commerce and this constitutes an important barrier that prevents consumers from participating in online sales. This, as a result, undermines the potential growth of B2C e-transactions.[61] In a global debate on consumer protection in the online market, a lack of consumer trust in the existing consumer protection standard is the main problem that needs to be addressed.[62] The confi-

---

[55] *See ibid.*

[56] *See ibid.*

[57] *See ibid.*

[58] *See e. g* P. R. Chowdhury, *Raising Consumer Confidence to Boost E-Commerce Growth* (November 15, 2011), *available at* bizxchange.in/u47/S-16P-16A-20111115201111151423515756f54b764T-16N-/IT-Zone-Feature-Article.html (visited January 30, 2013) and S. Lu, *On Consumer Confidence in the Online Store* (2009), *available at* bizxchange.in/u47/S-16P-16A-20111115201111151423515756f54b764T-16N-/IT-Zone-Feature-Article.html (visited January 30, 2013).

[59] Lack of confidence is prevalent among consumers in both China and India. *See* Lu, *ibid.* and S. Jain and B. Kapoor, *Ecommerce in India-Boom and the Real Challenges* (2012), *available at* vsrdjournals.com/MBA/Issue/2012_02_Feb/Web/3_Sharad_Jain_597_Research_Communication_Feb_2012.html (visited January 2012, 30).

[60] *See* Jain and Kapoor, *ibid.*

[61] *See* Commission of the European Communities, *supra* note 1.

[62] An obvious confirmation is in the preamble of the EU laws, namely the directive 2005/29/EC of the European Parliament and of the Council concerning unfair business-to-consumer commercial practice in the internal market and directive 2011/83/EU of the European Parliament and of the Council of 25 October 2011 on consumer rights. They similarly confirm that one of the main policies of the EU Commission is to raise consumer confidence in e-sales within the EU.

dence issue has become the central focus for designing consumer protection mechanisms in most countries.[63]

To effectively create confident cross border consumers, who can contribute to the strengthening of the global market, it is necessary at first to establish an understanding of the concept of *consumer confidence*. This concept initially arose from economic and psychological studies concerning consumer's assessment of current economic conditions and his or her future economic expectations.[64] To indicate consumer confidence, Gourge Katona first developed an argument that an evaluation as to what extent psychological variables influence consumers could lead to a true understanding of the behavior of economic agents.[65] He further suggests that the two important factors that dominate the consumer decision-making process about purchasing are (i) an objective factor called *ability or capacity to buy* and (ii) a subjective factor called *willingness to buy*.[66]

Relying on these indicators, the *willingness to buy* appears to be the main essence of what the consumer laws and policies of today are trying to capture. For example, if a consumer has sufficient economic status (ability or capacity to buy), but when he or she has an expectation of negative future outcomes, he or she will postpone discretionary purchases. This tends to be the case in wealthy countries where their economies have already been fostered by a high income level and the majority of the population has significant discretionary income.[67] However, consumers in matured economies still feel that it is very difficult to accept the potential high risks in the e-market as they perceive the potential for negative future consequences when it comes to making purchasing online.

Many studies attempt to explain why consumers have no confidence in e-sales.[68] It has been found that most consumers feel that there is a high possibility for

[63] The EU law is an example. Consumer confidence has been always referred to as a fundamental argument to justify a reasonable standard and safety for consumers in e-sales. At the same time, the harmonization of consumer laws within the EU has been focused on improving consumers' confidence in e-sales. *See* T. Wilhelmsson, *The Abuse of the "Confident Consumer" as a Justification for EC Consumer Law*, 27 Journal of Consumer Policy 317–37 (2004). The issue of consumers' confidence has been a subject of discussion in the US and Canada as well. *See e.g.* Tasse, Faille and Henderson, *supra* note 16 and C. Coteanu, Cyber Consumer Law and Unfair Trading Practices 19 (2005).

[64] *See* Poncibo, *supra* note 1, at 361.

[65] *See* G. Katona, Psychological Economics (1975). *See also* C. P. Haugtvedt, P. M. Herr and F. R. Karders (eds.), Handbook of Consumer Psychology (2008).

[66] *See ibid.*

[67] *See also* Poncibo, *supra* note 1, at 362.

[68] Many studies reveal that consumer perception toward B2C e-sales is that there are greater risks and uncertainties lurking in cyberspace. The situations are alike in both advanced and emerging economies. *See e.g.* Wilhelmsson, *supra* note 63, Tasse, Faille and Henderson, *supra* note 16, Chowdhury, *supra* note 58 and Lu, *supra* note 58.

opportunistic behavior in online transactions. The advanced technology of the cyber world provides a suitable environment for the practice of giving misleading or false information and for outright fraud, especially concerning payment and privacy in online transactions.[69] In addition, websites or online shops can simply be set up without any great cost and without clear regulatory control, especially in the cross border market. Traders who commit wrongful acts can turn up and disappear quickly. The risk of misrepresentations about goods and services being made and the failure of goods to be delivered after purchase payment has been made exist because of the lack of physical contact and the great distance that separates sellers and buyers. When that happens, consumers will face a more difficult and complex situation compared to the case of traditional sales. It is hard for consumers to track down traders that are not physically close to them in the electronic network. Where and how consumers can obtain redress from business operators, whose locations are difficult to identify, can also be very burdensome and costly. The above factors arising from the distinctive features of the e-market are instances that lead to the lack of consumers' confidence. Today, the thinking of many consumers that there is a high likelihood of opportunistic behavior in online transactions which causes a lack of consumer confidence appears to be one factor that has been undermining the potential growth of B2C e-transactions. Therefore, changing this attitude of consumers is necessary to make them more willing to make online purchases. This has been a subject of interest in modern countries as it tends to boost consumer confidence in B2C e-transactions.

In emerging markets, the situation appears to be more complex, as another confidence indicator—"the ability or capacity to buy"—come into play. Such economies are in the process of raising the level of individual income and increasing consumers' discretionary purchase money. Thus, consumers' capacity to buy still plays a very important role in influencing their consumption and their economic behavior. For example, consumer will not purchase things other than necessities or postpone discretionary buying if he or she perceives his or her personal economic status to be unfavorable. Moreover, apart from economic and income factors, the prevalent lack of consumer knowledge and awareness may constitute another factor that discourages consumers in emerging markets from shopping online, thus limiting their capacity to buy online. In the emerging economies, the majority of people still have a lower level income as compared to those in the advanced economies. It has been argued that those lower income consumers are less rational in their purchasing behavior and they are unlikely to be able to digest market information.[70] According to this argument, many consumers in emerging economies may not pay attention to their legal rights, even though consumer protection laws and mechanisms are available to protect them. This is confirmed

[69] *See* Saami, *supra* note 10, at 167.

[70] *See* A. Best and A. Andreasen, *Consumer Response to Unsatisfactory Purchases: A Survey of Perceiving Defects, Voicing Complaints, and Obtaining Redress*, 11 Law and Society Review 701–42 (1977).

by actual experiences in many developing countries where their consumers do not recognize their rights, and even ignore or pay no attention to the information provided such as products' descriptions.[71] Such situation may be because the relevant governments do not actively provide or cultivate consumers with basic knowledge and an understanding of their rights in e-transactions.[72]

As consumers are not aware of their rights, unreasonable expectation regarding online transactions may occur, resulting in a lack of the confidence necessary to enter into transactions. For example, even if the current economic conditions are favorable or the consumer has the economic capacity to make a purchase, because of lack of knowledge or awareness, he or she may still be unable to appraise whether their future economic condition will be positive or negative. Thus, the consumer is likely to postpone discretionary purchases. To complete these puzzles of consumer confidence with a particular reference to the emerging economies, such confidence is not only driven by their economic status but, more importantly, by their understanding, knowledge and awareness.

Based on the above understanding of the notion of consumer confidence, it is the product of complex construction resulting from a wide range of factors influencing the decision making process of consumers and their consumption behaviors. In this framework, there is an assumption that consumers avoid buying online because they expect unfavorable future conditions and perceive the likelihood of opportunistic behaviors in online transactions. More specifically, concerning consumers in the emerging markets, their capacity to buy and their knowledge to appraise future conditions must also somehow be regulated to effectively address the lack of confidence in their particular economic environment. There are a wide range of methods that can be employed to improve consumer confidence. Nevertheless, this study will only focus on the consumer protection mechanisms that are able improve consumers' willingness to participate in e-transactions, in other word of enhancing consumer confidence via enhancing their trust in online transactions.

2.3 Competing Rationales for Consumer Protection

The idea of inequality of status and bargaining power between consumers and businesses has long been underlined as the primary rationale for consumer law, aiming to protect vulnerable consumers.[73] More recent paradigms for consumer

[71] *See e.g.* S. Supanitaya, Private Organization for Consumer Protection (2001) and J. Nethin, *A Comparative Study of Problems in Consumer Protection Laws for Electronic Commerce (E-Commerce) in Thailand and the United States*, 13 Thailand Journal of Law and Policy (2010), *available at* thailawforum.com/articles/comparative-study-of-problem-5.html (visited January 12, 2013).

[72] *See* Supanitaya, *ibid.*

[73] For example, many governmental and academic reports were published between the 1960s and 1970s with an emphasis on the idea of inequality between consumers and merchants.

protection rely on the economic rationale of market failures that focus on the economic interests of consumers with an emphasis on adequate information and behavioral economics.[74] In connection with B2C e-sales, consumer confidence has been emphasized as another important rationale for consumer law. The following Sections discuss major rationales for consumer protection laws and mechanisms in the online market.

2.3.1 Traditional Rationale I: Lack of Knowledge and Information Asymmetries

The concept of "appropriate information", referring to both sufficient and accurate information, is a fundamental principle of fairness and an essential element of consumer protection.[75] It can be regarded as a *pre contractual obligation*[76] of business operators as consumers have the basic right to receive relevant knowledge and information from business operators prior to entering into contracts. Information such as the price, quality, and terms and conditions of the purchase are critical to the consumer's purchase decision-making process.[77] Such information will help consumers assess whether the goods or services being considered meet their needs and whether they are affordable. The availability of sufficient information to consumers will also allow them to send demand signals to the suppliers of goods and services. This will enable the market to flexibly adjust to consumer preferences.[78]

It is an unfortunate truth that consumers are often not adequately informed about products and services. This situation is often referred to as the *asymmetry of information*. This occurs when the business has more information about the product and service than the consumer does.[79] Some businesses often omit necessary information regarding goods or services to minimize the risk that the consumer

---

[74] *See* Ramsay, *supra* note 3, at Chapter 2.

[75] *See* Saami, *supra* note 10, at 167.

[76] The pre contractual obligation is classified as a matter relating to a contract. It is justified by policy reasons as it is better for sound administration. *See* Tang, *supra* note 6, at 33.

[77] *See* Coteanu, *supra* note 63, at 127.

[78] Under market competition, suppliers will be pressured to improve and modify their products, to satisfy the changing consumer demands. The market conditions will then be adjusted to best reflect consumer requirements. *See* Ramsay, *supra* note 3 at 119–20.

[79] The asymmetry of information is based on the economic models created by George Akerlof, Michael Spence and Joseph E. Stiglitz in 1970. In 2001, they received the Nobel Prize for their work on identifying that the market will suffer the problem of deterioration of product quality if vendors possess more information than consumers, and vendors may gain unfair profits in such situations. *See* Coteanu, *supra* note 63, at 127, H. Luth, Behavioural Economics in Consumer Policy, The Economic Analysis of Standard Terms in Consumer Contracts Revisited 28 (2011).

may be displeased with such information and turn to other vendors.[80] This results in the problem of *adverse selection*, where consumers are unable to accurately assess the quality of products because of inadequate information.[81] If consumers cannot do so, they are likely to opt for lower price products as a safe haven.[82] What is left in the market is the competition based on price offered, while product quality plays no role in market selection, resulting in the market being filled with inferior quality products.[83]

False, misleading, or inaccurate information is another problem usually driven by the pressure on the vendor to generate quick revenue and profit.[84] If a lot of incomplete or "false information in relation to a product or service is fed into the market, market performance is adversely affected. Distortion of the marketplace harms both consumers and honest competitors. Consumers are precluded form

[80] Vendors do not inform consumers of negative effects from the consumption of the products. Examples include tobacco companies not stating that smoking is harmful to health and vendors not notifying consumers of ancillary costs associated with the products, including after sale maintenance costs and transportation costs that are higher than those charged by other vendors. *See* Coteanu, *ibid.* and Ramsay, *supra* note 3, at 69.

[81] For detailed discussion of *adverse selection*, *see* Luth, *supra* note 79, at 57 and Ramsay, *ibid.*, at 67.

[82] Generally, consumers may be willing to pay higher prices for products of higher quality or for those that more precisely meet their demands. Under the circumstances where they are unable to distinguish products based on quality because of lack of information, consumers may avoid purchasing high price products that they are unsure of the quality of and opt to purchase lower price products, with the aim of limiting the possible economic damage from wrong selection. By doing so, consumers believe they will at least be able to avoid the risk of paying high price for low quality products. This situation is known as a *race to the bottom*. For more details of the *race to the bottom*, *see* Luth, *supra* note 79, at 22–3. In some cases where there is inadequate information, consumers may not choose to buy the cheapest products available, but prefer to buy more expensive products from better known vendors. By doing so, they believe it would help mitigate the risk of buying low quality products because better known vendors are generally perceived, validly or not, by consumers to carry superior quality products. Such perception can be misguided because a vendor's reputation does not necessarily translate to the quality of the products they carry. On the other hand, well-known vendors may lack the drive to improve the quality of their products because consumers cannot distinguish the products they carry on based on quality. Instead, such vendors would focus on building their reputations by means other than product quality, such as effective advertisement or after sale services. They may also take advantage of their reputations by offering products at prices that are excessive relative to product quality. This also similarly leads to the situation of a race to the bottom.

[83] Adverse selection will be widespread in the market and it may result in gradual deterioration of the quality of products. Vendors are no longer motivated to continuously improve the quality of their products as the quality is no longer a criterion in customer decisions. The reputation of vendors may also be another factor that consumers consider in case they cannot distinguish the products on their quality. *See ibid.*

[84] Examples of these are the "fly by night" and "tourist trap" situations, when vendors are not interested in maintaining long term relationships with customers, but only interested in making a quick profit, before moving on to a new market location. Some vendors even think that such "slash and burn" practices will generate a better profit yield. *See* Ramsay, *supra* note 3, at 67.

marking informed purchasing decisions and firms are denied the ability to compete on a level playing field."[85]

Due to this, the disclosure of true and sufficient information is a critical component of the continuous improvement of product quality. Without true and sufficient information, consumers will not be able to make purchase selections that match their exact requirements, resulting in an unfair situation for consumers. Therefore, information remedies have long been one of the main traditional policies of consumer protection.

2.3.2 Traditional Rationale II: Lack of Bargaining Power and Standard Terms

In the process of general commercial contracts, the contractual parties enter into negotiations and the resultant agreement is then mutually approved. Things seem to be straightforward as the parties to the contract are assumed to have equal bargaining power.[86] However, in the area of consumer transactions, the consumer is generally considered to be an economically weaker party with a lower level of experience and knowledge concerning transaction.[87] In respect of consumer sales, one party, the seller, often has significant influence over the other party, the purchaser. The seller usually controls most, if not all of, the contract terms, via standardized consumer contracts. There is often little to no room for negotiation in

[85] *See* Coteanu, *supra* note 63, at 127. The author cited the statement of Rachel Larabie-Lesieur, Deputy Director of Investigation and Research Competition Bureau, Industry Canada, in Misleading Advertising on the Internet: Competition Law Enforcement in the Electronic Marketplace, Remarks to the Canadian Corporate Shareholder Services Association on September 19, 1996.

[86] *Emptio venditio* or the principle of sales has become one of the most remarkable achievements of the Roman law. It has great influence over today's legislators as it provides us the basic instruments for shaping the way of thinking and formulating sales. Under Roman law, private autonomy or *"Lus Vigilantibus Scriptum"* has been the core principle of sale contract that has promoted an archetype of *"cold-blooded"* boundary and hard structure. The sale contract was solely consensual, where the coincident obligations are to deliver or to transfer the object of sale and to pay the purchase price that was agreed upon between purchaser and seller. There was little attempt in the classic Roman law to limit the freedom of sale contract. It only provides the framework where the purchaser and the seller may freely act without any interference with the main feature of economic liberalism. Its fundamental axiom is that the contract doctrine should be extensively incorporated within the parties' intention, with a clear promise of enforceability, focused on efficiency. From a Roman law standpoint, legal intervention would be an inappropriate infringement of freedom of contract, which is a reflection of the well-recognized liberalistic spirit of the Roman law of sale. Nevertheless, at the time of Roman law, the picture of sale contract does not explicitly refer to consumer sales and its protective functions. For a detailed explanation of Roman law of sale, *see* R. Zimmermann, The Law of Obligations Roman Foundations of the Civilian Tradition 231, 250, 258 (1992). *See also* M. A. Chirelstein, Concepts and Case Analysis in the Law of Contracts 8 (2001).

[87] *See* Ramsay, *supra* note 3, at 4.

consumer sales. The seller, being in a stronger economic position, is often able to impose oppressive terms over the more vulnerable consumer through standard terms of consumer contracts or the *contracts of adhesion*. As a result, such a contract is not created by the parties' bargaining as in the conventional contract theory, but instead are one-sided pre-drafted terms. Such contracts are often not negotiable and there is no freedom for consumers to choose the terms as their only option is to either *take it or leave it*.

However, it is well acknowledged today that standard terms of contract in consumer sales are legally enforceable, given their significant role in facilitating business efficiency by reducing transaction costs and standardizing transactions.[88] The pre-drafted terms offer advantages to the market by providing stability to mass business transactions, reducing the risk of unpredictable contract terms and saving the cost of transactions.[89] In addition, in high volume mass consumer transactions, businesses cannot afford to accommodate individualized negotiations as this would mean unacceptably high costs and time consumption by repeating the same procedure for every transaction. Standard terms reduce the cost of production that is reflected in the lower prices of goods and services in the market.[90]

Therefore, the issue of whether the standard terms of contract are legally acceptable is no longer the point. Rather, the characteristics of consumer sale with standardized contracts leads to another question, whether the purchasers in consumer sales can escape from "unfair or unwanted terms" attached to the standard contracts. This is because the use of standard terms may not always include only fair and efficient terms. Under the high pressure of price competition, the sellers may transfer possible risks to consumers through even more unequal standard terms of contract.[91]

The standard term characteristic of consumer sales has long been recognized and this has led to many attempts to distinguish consumer sales from other commercial activities to provide safeguard provisions.[92] In other words, governmental intervention should help consumers, who are generally considered the weaker party, to avoid undesirable terms that are attached to the standard consumer sale contracts. As a result, some laws have been introduced to combat any possible unjust

---

[88] From economic perspectives, the use of standard terms is beneficial to both seller and purchaser because, in a perfectly functioning market, the standardized contracts will include only fair and efficient terms that give the advantage to the class of purchasers. *See* M. Zhang, *Contractual Choice of Law in Contracts of Adhesion and Party Autonomy*, 41 Akron Law Review 123, 124 (2008).

[89] *See* N. S. Kim, *Evolving Business and Social Norms and Interpretation Rules: The Need for a Dynamic Approach to Contract Disputes*, 84 Nebraska Law Review 506, 547 (2005).

[90] *See* S. E. Friedman, *Giving Unconscionability More Muscle: Attorney's as A Remedy for Contractual Overreaching*, 44 Georgia Law Review 317, 320 (2010).

[91] *See* A. Robertson, *The Limits of Voluntariness in Contract*, 29 Melbourne University Law Review 179, 194 (2005).

[92] *See* C. Edwards, *Freedom of Contract and Fundamental Fairness for Individual Parties: The Tug of War Continues*, 77 University of Missouri at Kansas City Law Review 647, 669 (2009).

exploitation, render aid to the weaker party, and alleviate the rigidity of the standard term contract.[93]

2.3.3 Traditional Rationale III: Behavioral Economic Problems

Economists conventionally rely on *rational choice models* to predict consumers' behavior in markets.[94] It is assumed that, with adequate information provided, consumers are able to make rational decisions in their own best interests after weighing all relevant factors.[95] Nevertheless, such an assumption is not always valid.[96] Consumer decisions are often influenced by several biases, such as hyperbolic discounting,[97] over-optimism,[98] time-related bias,[99] context and framing effect,[100] and anchoring and adjustment.[101] The effects of these biases seem to result in harm and damage to consumers themselves.

Many case studies have similarly concluded that businesses often take advantage of a consumer's behavioral biases.[102] A frequently cited example is auction sales, where vendors are likely to obtain better prices for their products than ordinary sales. Consumers in an auction are driven in part by their egos and in part by a desire to win. They are likely to place their bids in excess of the amount that they would normally be willing to spend on such products in non-competitive settings.[103] Another example is when vendors apply the *discount heuristic strategy*,

[93] For examples, the Australia Consumer Law, the national, states and territorial regulations, includes unfair terms regulations. The UK Unfair Terms in Consumer Contracts Regulations 1999 protects consumers from unfair standard terms in contracts drafted by traders.

[94] *See* Ramsay, *supra* note 3, at Chapter 3.

[95] *See ibid.*

[96] The attempt to understand the impact of such influences on consumer decision-making processes, and their departure from the said conventional economic assumptions, gave rise to a discipline called "behavioral economics".

[97] *See* Ramsay, *supra* note 3, at 72.

[98] *See ibid.*, at 51.

[99] *See* Luth, *supra* note 79, at 52.

[100] *See* Ramsay, *supra* note 3, at 53.

[101] *See* Ramsay, *ibid*, at 74.

[102] *See e.g.* J. Hanson and D. Kysar, *Taking Behavioralism Seriously: Some Evidence of Market Manipulation*, 112 Harvard Law Review 1420, 1424–5 (1999).

[103] This is proven by a famous experiment where a group of people was given a mug and questioned how much they would want to pay to keep the mug. Another group was not given the mug but was asked to answer a similar question of the price they would pay to receive the mug. It was found that the first group would pay a higher price than the latter. *See* D. Kahneman, J. L. Knetsch and R. H. Thaler., *Experimental Tests of the Endowment Effect and the Coase Theorem*, 98 Journal of Political Economy 1325–48 (1990). In addition, Amos Tversky, a Nobel laureate in

by posting "discount" or "sale" signs on their products, although the prices on these signs are normal prices. These signs will attract consumer attention and mislead them into believing that these products are bargains.

Today, many policy makers have noticed the problems of consumers' biases and their potentially unfair impact on consumers, especially when unscrupulous merchants take advantage of them. Apart from lengthy education programs, policy makers are attempting to eliminate or at least mitigate unfair behavioral economic practices toward consumers by enacting certain consumer protection laws and policies.[104] This emphasizes the idea that any business practices that adversely distort economic behavior of consumers are not acceptable and confirms that protecting consumers' ability to make informed decisions is one of the most important concerns and that such ability must not be impaired by any means, whether directly or indirectly.[105]

---

economics, concluded from his study that behavioral economic is indeed widely practiced by merchants, especially in used car business advertisements. *See* Ramsay, *supra* note 3, at 77.

[104] Although the problems of consumers' behavioral biases may be resolved with substantive measures by passing laws barring vendors' actions that can unfairly influence consumers' decisions as mentioned above, substantive measures alone may not be fully sufficient as it is difficult to comprehensively identify all forms of vendors' actions that may have potential unfair effects on consumers' choices. Other measure such as "nudging" consumers to make the optimal choices in their best interests, through the use "heuristic devices" that help minimizing consumers' making decisions based on their biases, are also essential. For the detailed discussion on this issue, *see* Luth, *supra* note 79, at Chapter 3.

[105] The European Union directive 2005/29/EC of the European Parliament and of the Council concerning unfair business-to-consumer commercial practice in the internal market (Unfair Commercial Practices Directive) is an example of a legislative response to this problem. Article 5 of the Directive provides that:

> Prohibition of unfair commercial practices
> 1. Unfair commercial practices shall be prohibited.
> 2. A commercial practice shall be unfair if:. . .
> (b) it materially distorts or is likely to materially distort consumer's economic behavior with regard to the product of the average consumer whom it reaches or to whom it is addressed, or of the average member of the group when a commercial practice is directed to a particular group of consumers" 3. Commercial practices which are likely to materially distort the economic behavior of consumers who are particularly vulnerable to the practice or the underlying product because of their mental or physical infirmity, age or credulity in a way which the trader could reasonably be expected to foresee, shall be assessed from the perspective of the average member of that group. This is without prejudice to the common and legitimate advertising practice of making exaggerated statements or statements which are not meant to be taken literally.

2.3.4 *Traditional Rationale IV: Failures of Traditional Forms of Litigation*

After a consumer sales contract has been executed, if there is a dispute arising from a breach of contract terms by the business, from the quality or characteristics of the product differing from those agreed to in the contract, or from the product being defective or hazardous or some similar ground, consumers should be entitled to an effective and just recourse. The system of private law has long been the traditional means of enforcing such rights of consumers. However, it has been widely criticized for its ineffectiveness in coping with consumer-related litigation, which usually involves small value claims.[106] There are a number of commonly known obstacles to consumers' access to justice via traditional litigation, including the lengthy duration of the process and its high cost relative to the amount of dispute. This may be because the traditional rules of civil procedure were not originally been designed to deal with diffuse or small value claims.[107] Also, the vast majority of consumers are ordinary individuals who often lack sufficient understanding of the law and legal process, especially when they have to take actions against businesses who are usually more economically powerful and well-organized. This often results in a "psychological barrier" that makes consumers ambivalent about bringing their disputes to court.[108]

Today, there is a consensus among scholars that, because of consumers' perception that the law and legal process is complicated, they often choose not to enforce or seek redress for the violation of their rights and simply blame their misfortunes on bad luck.[109] Various forms of informal dispute settlements (direct negotiation, conciliation, mediation, or arbitration) and special procedures for consumer cases are also promoted to help reduce costs, simplify the process, and shorten the time of traditional private procedures.[110] In addition, the bundling of consumer claims in a procedure known today as class actions, collective actions or group actions, depending on the jurisdiction, has been extensively discussed as an alternative form of consumer redress.[111]

---

[106] *See* K. J. Cseres, *Enforcement of Collective Consumer Interests: A Competition Law Perspective, in* W. van Boom and M. Loos (eds.), Collective Enforcement of Consumer Law 123, 129 (2007).

[107] *See ibid.*

[108] *See ibid.*

[109] As Kati Cseres, the author mentioned: "Consumer concerns are complex, diverse and diffuse both over consumer groups and over time. The adverse effects of consumer might realize later in time. They are moreover unpublicized and therefore difficult to detect and address." *See ibid.*, at 161.

[110] *See* M. Cappelletti and B. Garth (eds.), Access To Justice VOL I: A World Survey (1978).

[111] The settlement of mass consumer disputes has been given attention by group litigants for compensation. Group litigation, which may be defined differently from country to county, can be similarly defined as a court' s litigation initiated by a plaintiff acting on behalf of a specific group and for the benefits of that specified group. In-group litigation, the court decision is binding on all

As discussed above, various attempts have evolved over time. This development is driven by the important need to provide consumers with effective weapons in addressing the violations of their rights. This is incorporated in international principle in the United Nations Guideline Consumer Protection, which states that:

> Government should establish or maintain legal and/or administrative measures that are expeditious, fair, inexpensive and accessible. Such procedures should take particular account of needs of low income consumers. Governments should also encourage enterprises to resolve consumer disputes in a fair, expeditious and informal manner and information on redress should be available to consumer.[112]

2.3.5 *The Emergence of "Consumer Confidence" in Global Debates on B2C E-Commerce*

As discussed in previous Sections, many states have been promoting e-commerce, including B2C transactions, based on the idea that the expansion of such commercial activities will promote competition among merchants in various countries, which will in turn foster the evolution of a single global market.[113] In most debates on consumer protection in B2C e-transactions, it is well accepted that the level of consumer confidence is surprisingly low. Under conditions where consumers hesitate to enter into e-market, the role of the internet will be undermined and the efficiency and full competitiveness of the market will not be achieved. As Erin Ann O'Hara argues, "[i]f consumers are unwilling to experiment with unknown vendors, then the Internet fails to create competitive pressures that serve to erode online price

members of that group. Such a claim bundling concept has received substantial favor in the last decade as a better option for consumers' access to justice over traditional civil procedures In the United States, for example, class action litigation has become greatly popular for consumer mass disputes. However, the United States Government cannot overlook the pitfall of the great expense incurred in the class action procedure. To address this shortcoming, the United States passed the Class Action Fairness Act in 2005 to curb the costs of this type of litigation, which were spiraling out of control, by imposing a limit on attorney's fees. In any event, the settlement of mass consumer disputes continues to depend on traditional civil procedures, which are time-consuming and often more costly than the cost of an individual case in normal civil procedure because of the large number of plaintiffs. In today's market society where most products are mass-produced, it is usual for a large number of consumers to share common problems or suffer similar damages; coupled with the problem that traditional civil procedures do not fit well in dealing with consumer disputes, this has given rise to the collective action. For a detailed discussion on group actions or collective actions, *see* W. van Boom and M. Loos (eds.), Collective Enforcement of Consumer Law (2007).

[112] *See* United Nations, *Resolution Adopted by the General Assembly, 39th Session, 16th April 1985 on the Report of the Second Committee (A/39/789/Add2)* (1985).

[113] *See* K. Alboukrek, *Adapting to a New World of E-Commerce: The Need for Uniform Consumer Protection in the International Electronic Marketplace*, 35 George Washington International Law Review 425, 429–30 (2003).

dispersions between vendors. When competitive pressures are relaxed, consumers pay more for their products, and consumer welfare is thus not maximized."[114]

Based on this standpoint, the lack of consumer confidence has become the central focus in designing consumer protection mechanisms for the e-market.[115] This absence of confidence may be caused by the lack of trustworthy references that consumers usually use to assess the reliability of offline activities. This often results in consumers thinking that there is a high likelihood of opportunistic behaviors in online activities. As Thomas Schultz explained in his work, "[w]hen we consider engaging in a relationship, be it personal or commercial, we use points of reference or indicators of trust to assess the risks related to the relationship. For instance, when we intend to make a commercial transaction, we assess the risks of this transaction by examining the other party, the community in which the transaction is to take place, and what can be done if a problem occurs."[116]

In traditional sales, local stores have an established physical presence, giving consumers an assurance that the business is truly in operation and, in all likelihood, will trade in accordance with the relevant laws and regulations of its location. If things go wrong, the consumer can turn to the store or to the relevant government authorities in their jurisdiction, such as an ombudsman or the courts. However, for an internet business, the points of reference appear to be ambiguous. The cost of setting and running a website is much cheaper than a shop. Frauds through websites are easy because of their low costs of establishment and maintenance and the fact that they can withdraw from the market in seconds.[117] This may be one of important factors resulting in a lack of consumer confidence.

For consumers in the emerging markets, confidence issues seem to be more crucial. In addition to the absence of reliable references as mentioned above, many consumers in emerging economies may have yet to attain a mature economic status and their lack of knowledge and awareness regarding their basic rights (including benefits and the online market system) limit their ability to buy and holds them back from engaging in e-transactions. All of these of course undermine their confidence in the online market. To strengthen consumers' confidence, the above-discussed points are essential. To establish them, it is important to analyze which elements

---

[114] *See* E. A. O'Hara, *Choice of Law for Internet Transactions. The Uneasy Case for Online Consumer Protection*, 153 University of Pennsylvania Law Review 1833, 1897 (2005).

[115] The EU law is an example. Consumer confidence has always been referred to as the fundamental argument to justify a reasonable standard and safety for consumers in e-sales. At the same time, the harmonization of consumer laws within the EU has been aiming on improving consumers' confidence in e-sales. *See* Wilhelmsson, *supra* note 63, at 317.

[116] *See Schultz*, *supra* note 52, at 75–69. The author indicates that the absence of traditional points of reference with which consumers can assess the trustworthiness of conventional sale is a major cause of the lack of confidence in e-sales. In addition, Thomas Wilhelmsson also identifies the abuse of the concept of consumer's confidence in great detail. *See* Wilhelmsson, *ibid.*, at 317–37.

[117] *See* R. Starek and L. Rozell, *A Cyberspace Perspective: The Federal Trade Commission's Commitment to On-Line Consumer Protection*, 15 The John Marshall Journal Computer & Information Law 679, 681 (1997).

usually impair confidence so that we can answer exactly what is needed to restore confidence.

2.4 Interim Conclusion

At present, there has been a prevalent consensus that the internet market provides greater opportunities to businesses and corresponding advantages to ordinary consumers. The benefits have included global access, greater information and choices, lower prices, improved completion and convenience. It also has a great potential to create a transnational landscape that allows goods and services to flow freely without geographic barriers, and provides borderless market access to traders and consumers around the globe. Given such significant advantages to the global economy, for businesses and consumers alike, it is important for all stakeholders to ensure that these benefits are fully recognized.

Clearly, the online market has somehow achieved enormous transactional volume, with the fastest growth occurring in both mature economies and emerging economies. Notwithstanding this, one should keep in mind that, in e-commerce, the role of B2C e-transactions is relatively limited, although its volume is undoubtedly growing. The fact that many consumers lack confidence in B2C online sales can provide an explanation for this limitation. This chapter has shown that the fear of opportunistic behaviors because of the distinctive features of B2C e-transactions (e.g. the absence of physical contract, the dynamic and voluminous amount of information and its cross border nature) and the absence of basic knowledge and awareness concerning e-commerce, especially among those consumers living in emerging economies, appear to be the main factor that ruins consumer confidence. Therefore, it is the challenge for governments and stakeholders to find a way to assure consumer confidence in B2C e-commerce. There may a wide range of methods that might be used to improve consumer confidence but this study will look at one particular method. This study argues that enhancing "access to justice" is an important key factor for enhancing consumer confidence. Chapters 5–7 will discuss the abilities of various consumer protection mechanisms to ensure consumer access to justice that in turn would improve consumers' willingness and confidence to make online purchases and create an opportunity for the expansion of global commercial exchanges. However, before the potential mechanisms of consumer protection are debated and weighted up, it is expedient to explore the concept of *access to justice*, a major principle in the development of consumer protection in B2C e-commerce in the first place, to provide more understanding that will be used when the mechanisms are assessed in the following chapters. Exploration of the concept of access to justice will be made in the next chapter.

Chapter 3
Access to Justice: A Goal for Consumer Protection

3.1 Introduction

In consumer contracts the consumer, the party to the contract who is acting outside the course of his or her trade or profession, is generally considered to be the weaker party with less economic power and a lack of experience and knowledge.[1] They often are at a greater risk of not getting the spirit of bargain because of the use of standard contract. Due to this concern, some protective provisions must be afforded to them. This protective idea appears to be largely influenced by the concept of *Access to Justice*. Under its development, diffuse or fragmented interests of individual consumers and the injury or damage suffered by individual consumer is not economically and financially justify any redress. Consumers are initially recognized as a group that initiates various efforts to find measures to promote justice and equality for themselves.[2] Such attempts are later explained as means to create a bridge for consumers to reach not only social and legal justice but also economic equality—the so called the multidimensional aspects of justice, through fair transactions in the market, being a core principle justification for consumer protection laws.[3]

This chapter discusses, on a theoretical level, the concept of access to justice that underlies the idea of consumer protection law and policies. It starts with the historical development of access to justice with particular reference to its currently debated implications for consumer protection. It then follows with a discussion about contemporary views on the roles of consumer's access to justice and how these have been influenced by past development. This will especially focus on the

[1] *See* Chap. 2, Sect. 2.3. *See also* I. Ramsay, Consumer law and Policy, Text and Materials on Regulating Consumer Markets 4 (2007).

[2] *See* M. Cappelletti and B. Garth (eds.), Access to Justice Vol I: A World Survey (1978). *See also*, I. Ramsay, *Consumer Redress and Access to Justice, in* C. E. F. Rickett and T. G. W. Telfer (eds.), International Perspectives on Consumers' Access to Justice 17, 18–9 (2006).

[3] *See* Ramsay, *ibid.*, at 19.

S. Yuthayotin, *Access to Justice in Transnational B2C E-Commerce*,
DOI 10.1007/978-3-319-11131-5_3

multidimensional concept of access to justice, which does not includes only procedural aspect of remedy or redress but also substantive dimension where both socio-legal and economic considerations are identified as important, will be the subject of an in-depth examination. This chapter will lay a foundation for a true understanding of the access to justice concept, which is the core principle underlying the evolution of consumer protection laws, including those which govern in the online environment. The conclusions drawn from this chapter will reveal the origin, spirit and genuine objective that gave birth to consumers' protection and will in so doing establish an appropriate framework to be used as a benchmark in the evaluation of laws and measures for the protection of consumers in electronic sales in subsequent chapters.

3.2 Historical Debate on Access to Justice

The notion of access to justice is recognized in the constitutional laws of many countries in the forms of legal aid, the right of access to a judicial process, and the right to have appropriate legal remedies.[4] However, if one investigates deeper into the history of its theoretical development, access to justice is a broader and more complicated concept than those specified in these constitutional laws.

3.2.1 Review of Main Points from the Nineteenth Century

In the past it is clearly evident that, whether or not they were officially sanctioned by the state, caste systems have been prevalent in one form or another in virtually all societies throughout human history.[5] In traditional societies, each individual understands and accepts their rights and duties which are determined by society based on their birth. In pre-*Meiji* Japan for example the caste system was comprised

[4] *See* E. Sotrskrubb and J. Ziller, *Access to Justice in European Comparative Law, in* F. Francioni (ed.), Access to Justice as a Human Right 177, 178 (2007).

[5] In the past, social issues, one of the most important fundamentals that gave rise to inequality, were not considered or measured. Thus there had been no attempts to mitigate the suffering of the poor and less privileged that came with social injustice. Lawrence Friedman criticized the development of access to justice in the 19th century: "I do not mean to deny the importance of 19th century efforts- the invention of legal aid, the right to free counsel, and the reforms of legal procedure. But in essence, these reforms only tinkered with the system. This was not the fault of the earnest and dedicated people who struggled to make justice real. The topic simply did not sit very high on social agendas; and, from the modern standpoint, even the most passionate spokesmen did not grasp the problem very well." *See* L. M. Friedman, *Claims, Disputes, Conflicts and the Modern Welfare State, in* M. Cappelletti (ed.), Access To Justice and the Welfare State 249, 252 (1981).

of *samurai*, the ruling class, the farmer, the artisan and the merchant.[6] Another example of these systems which is still deeply rooted in society and which has survived to the present day is the caste system of India.[7] Under that system, members of society are divided into four distinct classes, namely the *Brahmin, Kshatriyas*, *Vaishyas* and *Shudras* in order of their place in society, modes of materials, natures and their professions.[8]

When a society industrializes and law in its modern sense becomes widely accepted, the traditional concept of society assigning different rights and duties to members of society on the basis of their birth is viewed as inherently unjust. There emerges the *Rule of Law* or *Rechtsstaat* under which it is though that the law should be born of rationale thought and can be universally and equally applied to every member of society.[9] From this standpoint, a thought on *modern law* which gives substantial focus and importance to various kinds of rights, has been developed.[10] Every person irrespective of their birth, gender, age, race, nationality, occupation, income, sexual orientation, social status or station in life, must be afforded the same rights and protection under the law. These are commonly known as *equal rights* which were the driving force behind the birth of the access to justice concept in the early nineteenth century.[11] As a result, there were a large number of legal reforms in many countries aimed at improving laws to make them easier to understand and apply and at providing a universally applicable judicial process that could be accessed by all citizens.

However, the outcomes of these early legal reforms have not been so satisfactory. At that time, it seemed only the middle class of the society benefitted from the improved access to equal justice while the lower classes of society received little benefit from these new legal modifications.[12] For instance, statistics show that those who exercised their legal rights through judicial processes in both civil and criminal cases mostly came from the members of the middle class such as tradesmen or technicians.[13] This is because these were the only groups whose members could

[6] *See* K. Szczepanski, *The Four-Tiered Class System of Feudal Japan, available at* asianhistory.about.com/od/japan/p/ShogJapanClass.htm (visited November 1, 2011).

[7] *See* J. Heitzman and R. L. Worden (eds.), *India: A Country Study* (1995), *available at* countrystudies.us/india/89.htm (visited November 1, 2011).

[8] The caste system of India still wields substantial influence in the law, culture, administration and government of that country. For detail of the four different India castes, *see ibid.*

[9] *See* L. M. Friedman, *On Legal Development,* 24 Rutgers Law Review 11–53 (1969–1970) and Sotrskrubb and Ziller, *supra* note 4, at 178–9.

[10] Admittedly, the problem access to justice for the poor is a very old issue but there were a few systematic attempts to deal with it. *See* Friedman, *supra* note 5, at 253–5.

[11] *See ibid.*

[12] The attempts to make the law "fair and equal" to everyone was not really free from the class *system.* The law moved to the notion of liberal economics which unexpectedly served the interests of manufacturers, business operators and businessmen. *See* L. M. Friedman, *Access to Justice: Social and Historical Context, in* M. Cappelletti and J. Weisner (eds.), Access to Justice Vol. II: Promising Institutions 10, 10–11 (1978).

[13] *See ibid.*, at 11.

afford the cost of the judicial process. Thus, the initial attempts to establish a rational structure of law and equal justice still contained the remnants of traditional social stratifications, maintaining an invisible barrier between certain groups of the population (the poor and working class) and the judicial process.

3.2.2 Initial Focus on Legal Representation

The notion of access to justice became a strong influence on legal reform in the early 1960s.[14] It began with the idea of providing assistance to the poor to enable them to participate in the judicial process.[15] Such assistance took the form of state funded legal aid agencies providing free legal representation and advice to the poor.[16] The view of the time was that the poor had no financial means of litigating and lacked adequate legal knowledge to protect their legal rights.[17] Due to this, they were often at a disadvantage when they were involved in the judicial process. To comply with the modern idea of law where every individual is treated as having the same legal rights and protections, states came to be viewed as having an obligation to provide necessary assistance to those members of the population who could not afford due legal representation in the judicial process.[18] Such a state duty was

[14] The discussion on the history of access to justice in this paper is largely based on the study of Mauro Cappelletti and his colleagues, who published a detailed analysis on the drive and direction of the development of modern access to justice in the 1970s and 1980s. Their comparative analysis of the experience of various countries sought to better identify the components, structure and essence of access to justice. In their studies, they concluded that the evolution of access to justice came in three different waves, namely, the legal representation wave, the diffuse interest wave and the broader concept of access to justice wave. These three waves were distilled from historical movements on the laws and measures in real world practice and they clearly reflect the spirit of access to justice that are still influenced and accepted by today's jurists. *See* Sotrskrubb and Ziller, *supra* note 4, at 178.

[15] The first important movement on "access to justice" occurred in the 1960s among Anglo-American scholars, who invented and gave great emphasis to the creation of institutions concerning legal aid. *See* Cappelletti and Garth, *supra* note 2, at 22.

[16] Having the state bear the cost of legal representation for the poor was a pioneering initiative to promote universal equality in participation in the judicial process. *See ibid.*, at 23.

[17] *See ibid.*

[18] Legal aid has been given much attention and has developed quickly and continuously, evidencing its success. However, underneath the surface, there are a number of limitations. One barrier is that it requires a substantial amount of public funding. With limitations on state budgets, legal aid in England, for example, has faced difficulties and fewer people can benefit from its inadequate services. For more detail on these difficulties, *see* Lord Chancellor's Advisory Committee on Legal Aid, *The 26th Legal Aid Annual Reports* (1975–1976). Another problem is the lack of volunteer lawyers. Legal aid seems to attract only young and inexperienced lawyers because of its low compensation paid from state funding. This results in inadequate legal representation for the poor both in quality and quantity. Free legal aid is unqualified and itself becoming a major obstruction on the road to justice. France is an example that demonstrated this predicament in

largely influenced by the concept of the welfare state where the government should provide social services for its citizens.[19]

Throughout the 1960s, many other public activities and state measures were duplicated around the world to implement the notion of access to justice. For instance, Germany and England were the first countries that provided free legal representation to the poor in 1919 and 1949 respectively.[20] In the United States in 1965 the Legal Aid Service program was introduced.[21] Sweden follows by issuing its "public legal aid law" in 1972.[22] In addition, Germany, Austria and the Netherlands also responded to the access to justice trend by amending their laws to make it the state's responsibility to give appropriate compensation to public defenders to encourage voluntarism from the legal community to provide legal services to the poor in the spirit of the legal aid program.[23]

3.2.3 Movement Toward a New Kind of Rights: The "Diffuse and Fragmented Rights"

Since 1965, the concept of access to justice has evolved further and expanded its scope to include other "forgotten" members of society including consumers, employees, lessees and others.[24] The members of these groups usually have diffuse or fragmented interests as the injury or damage they individually suffer may not economically or financially justify recourse to litigation.[25] Lawrence Friedman

---

1974. Although the compensation for lawyers in the legal aid program has increased by up to one third, the number of lawyers serving in the legal aid program is still insufficient. *See ibid.*

[19] *See* Ramsay, *supra* note 1, at 14 and Sotrskrubb and Ziller, *supra* note 4, at 179.

[20] Between 1919 and 1923, Germany started the legal aid that called for the system of state compensation for private lawyers to provide for the protection of the rights of all people. In England, major legal aid reform began in 1949 with the establishment of the legal aid and advice programme through the operations of the Law Society and the National Association of Solicitors according to the Legal Aid and Advice Act of 1949. This Act was later called the Legal Aid Act of 1974.

[21] The United States' legal aid program was operated by the Office of Economic Opportunity in accordance with Title I of the Economic Opportunity Act of 1964 which authorized state funds for community programs.

[22] *See* The Public legal Aid Law of Sweden (May 26, 1972).

[23] *See* Cappelletti and Garth, *supra* note 2, at 24.

[24] In fact, the recognition of various kinds of new rights according to the modern law concept initially appeared in 1948 when the Universal Declaration of Human Rights was adopted and implemented by the General Assembly of the United Nations. It recognizes and protects many new rights that are too numerous to describe in a few pages. These newly recognized rights led to a number of issues that had never been discussed before such as the diffuse rights of unrecognized groups of people such as consumers. Nevertheless, the development of consumer protection just became obvious from 1965 onwards.

[25] *See* Cappelletti and Garth, *supra* note 2, at 34–5.

points out that among these groups of people, the "ways in which justice is denied are various – justice costs too much, or is, for whatever reason, too difficult, too alien, or too slow for the group or type shut out."[26]

However, in aggregate, their injury or damage may be substantial and have a wide impact on the population.[27] Therefore, it is in the public interest for the state to find means for these types of groups to litigate their claims.[28] Many measures to allow for collective litigation, including class action, representative action, and so on have subsequently been introduced. This type of litigation can be called "*public interest litigation*".[29] As a result of this, the access to justice concept is no longer limited to the provision of financial assistance to the poor; it now also gives groups, including consumers, who are diffuse or fragmented, rights that can be more effectively enforced.

As a result of this trend, agency representative organizations and public councils have been established for administering diffuse, fragmented and collective rights.[30] For instance, in 1974 the United States led the way by giving fragmented interests assistance in the form of a new public interest institution called a "*public advocate*"[31] that administers and oversees public interest work, including litigation relating to the public interest.[32] The goal of this agency is to act in the interest of the general public on matters that are overlooked by the Government, including various types of diffuse interests such as consumer protection, labor protection and environmental protection.

Across the Atlantic, the Consumer Ombudsman of Sweden, which is influential as an example to many countries even today, was established in 1970 as the representative for consumers on matters relating to collective fragmented interests. Its activities include the initiation of litigation against business operators engaging in unfair practices, such as the making of misrepresentations, on behalf of consumers.[33] It also serves as consumers' representative in negotiations with business operators, a recognition of the fact that a consumer acting alone would not carry any bargaining power into a negotiation with a business operator.[34]

However, a governmental agency requires a substantial amount of public funding to effectively manage rights that are diffuse, fragmented and collective.

---

[26] *See* Friedman, *supra* note 12, at 5.

[27] *See* Cappelletti and Garth, *supra* note 2, at 35.

[28] *See ibid.*

[29] *See* A. Chayes, *The Role of the Judge in Public Law Litigation*, 89 Harvard Law Review 1041, 1048 (1976).

[30] *See* Cappelletti and Garth, *supra* note 2, at 35–6.

[31] *See* US Council for Public Interest Law, Balancing the Scales of Justice: Financing Public Interests Law in America (1976). During the growth of public interest law firms in the United States, it has been said that "The public interest lawyers believe that the poor are not the only people excluded from the decision making process on issues of vital important to them. All people concerned with environmental degradation, with product safety, with consumer protection, whatever their class, are effectively excluded from the key decision affecting their interests." *See* C. L. Halpern, *Public Interest Law: Its Past and Future*, 58 JUDICATURE 119, 120 (1974).

[32] *See* Cappelletti and Garth, *supra* note 2, at 38.

[33] *See* Ramsay, *supra* note 2, at 20. *See also* R. James, Private Ombudsmen and Public Law (1997).

[34] *See ibid.*

A lack of such funding could cause the relevant mechanisms or the competent organization to be unsuccessful.[35] Support provided to the private sector to look after diffuse interests has been recognized as an alternative approach that minimizes national budget constraints.[36] For example, consumer cases can also be pursued through the private formation of interest groups that collectively procure lawyers to initiate legal actions to set legal precedents or "*test cases*" for others who may suffer the same problem in the future. A good example of a private group defending a public interest relating to consumer transactions can be seen in Germany where, in 1977, the Standard Terms of Contract Law was enacted to allow a consumer association to bring a consumer case to court.[37] This new law encourages private groups to litigate petty cases in the interest of their individual members. This is especially true in common law countries such as England and Australia which also encourage litigation by such private groups.[38]

In addition the group action has been developed as another important measure designed to reduce the burden of excessive costs borne by either the state or private actors in the defense of diffuse interests. It is also known as the class action, the collective action or the public interest action depending on the jurisdiction.[39] A group action is carried out by a person acting as a representative of a large group of people in certain cases where there are injured parties suffering the same form of harm. The first and foremost purpose of this type of action is to reduce the cost and repetition of similar litigation by collecting similar cases with petty value into a single action to optimize their economic efficiency. Such actions will also improve the bargaining power of individuals with diffuse interests when their rights are violated because if the defendant loses it may be subject to substantial liability because of the large number of class action plaintiffs.[40]

---

[35] Its reliance on public funds means it may have to bow to political pressures that may result in it not being able to fully defend public interests that are contrary to the interests of politically influential entities. Examples of these are consumer, labor and environmental interests. The work of a public advocate organization that relies on governmental funds may be undermined by the political pressures from politicians or politically influential entities such as big businesses which normally are major political contributors.

[36] The role of private groups as supplemental or alternative for the role of government agencies still has its shortcomings. The transparency, credibility and effectiveness of these private groups remain in question as they usually comprise a large number of people and are difficult to organize and manage. Also, they may need to have a large number of members to adequately contribute to their costs and have personnel with appropriate expertise who can dedicate sufficient time for the work of the group. Without any of the above, the private group may not be influential or be able to effectively serve its role in providing access to justice.

[37] *See* The Standard Terms of Contract Law of Germany (December 9, 1976).

[38] *See* Cappelletti and Garth, *supra* note 2, at 42.

[39] *See* A. Stadler, *Cross-Border Mass Litigation: A Particular Challenge for European Law*, in J. Steele and W.H. van Boom (eds.), Mass Justice: Challenges of Representation and Distribution 73 (2011).

[40] It should be noted that in group action, a lawyer who is capable and experienced in the relevant specialty is critical to collect evidence and conduct the case to satisfy various demands from different people in a single case. If the lawyer is inexperienced, incapable or unorganized, the risk of losing the case would be greater than in the normal case. The lawyer must also possess great

3.2.4 "Universal Thoughts" on Access to Justice

As the above indicates, the historical development of access to justice has put an emphasis on promoting legal representation for the poor and for those holding diffuse rights. In its subsequent development, the concept has expanded beyond provision of assistance in litigation, dispute resolution and redress, to encompass "*preventive measures*".[41] This movement was brought about by the desire to truly provide equal justice to every member of society, expanding justice to cover all relevant institutions, organizations, persons, measures and other procedures and providing dispute avoidance measures.[42] Some scholars have called this "broader conception" an "access to justice approach".[43]

As a result, there has been a significant proliferation of regulations and laws assisting the relatively weak members of society, resulting in a defining notion of state welfare.[44] State welfare has come to mean more than an increase in the power of public officials over citizens or the delivery of new law. It is meant to involve the entire society through legislation, education, other material components and institution initiatives, which are intended to protect citizen's rights and achieve social and economic justice.[45] Thus, access to justice incorporated the idea of the welfare state. They have evolved into various dimensions, not only providing assistance in the judicial process or legal representation, but also modifying substantive law to avoid possible problems. This has resulted in the creation of many new protection mechanisms and special laws for certain members of society whose individual rights are normally overlooked, such as consumers and labor.[46]

Additionally, under this broader approach, a wide variety of procedural reforms relating to dispute settlement processes have continued to evolve. Alternative means of dispute resolution such as arbitration, conciliation, and other similar procedures that are characterized as having simple steps and being fast, convenient and less

---

skills in negotiation and dispute resolution, which are required to minimize the risk of losing the case which would have a great financial and emotional impact on the group. Solutions for effective protection of diffuse interests will need to be further studied and developed. Although it might not be consistent with the direction taken by the movement under the third wave, it does not mean that the problems discussed in the second wave needs not be given attention. *See* M. Cappelletti (ed.), Access to Justice and the Welfare State (1981).

[41] This approach also blended the thinking from the first two movements that were considered to be important elements in paving the road to universal equal justice. It is not possible to develop, protect and strengthen individual legal rights and diffuse interests by giving legal representation alone. It is difficult to ensure the effectiveness and influence of diffuse interests through a relatively new legal right given to specific groups in society such as consumers, employees, lessees and other similar members of society who lack bargaining power. *See ibid.*, at 14–23.

[42] *See ibid.*

[43] *See* Cappelletti and Garth, *supra* note 2, at 49.

[44] *See* Cappelletti, *supra* note 40, at 21.

[45] *See ibid.*

[46] *See* Cappelletti and Garth, *supra* note 2, at 49.

costly, are the fruits of the reform under this new line of thought.[47] For example, since 1971, disputing parties in France have the options of bringing their disputes into an informal dispute resolution process whereby judges will play the role of arbitrator in an informal setting.[48] In 1976, the State of California also introduced the concept of compulsory arbitration at the petition of the plaintiff,[49] which has become widely accepted by disputing parties. In Japan, the concept of conciliation conducted by a third party has also been widely adopted. Under the Japanese system of conciliation, the panel consists of three members, at least one of whom must be a judge by profession, who will hear the dispute and make recommendations impartially.[50]

The establishment of a specialized state agency or a specialized court is another focus of reforms arising from the universal access to justice idea.[51] These have come about because traditional judicial system is not usually economically practical for certain type of claims, especially those having low value.[52] Phrased differently, the characteristics of the regular court system, including its highly complicated process and high cost, are not suitable for enforcing consumer rights at the individual level. Establishment of a specialized court or special procedure can be a solution, allowing small value cases to be handled under simpler, faster, lower cost processes than those offered by the general system of litigation.[53] For example, small claims tribunals in Australia and the English Small Claims Court have been established with the objective of improving the effectiveness of judgment debt collection.[54] It is well recognized that a special procedure for small claims can be adjudicated in less time as they are distributed to a better equipped specialized court.[55]

3.3 Contemporary Debates on Access to Justice

3.3.1 New Movements of Access to Justice

Throughout its evolution, many intellectuals have attempted to establish the perimeters of access to justice. For instance, André Tunc in his article "*The Quest for*

---

[47] *See ibid.*

[48] *See ibid.*, at 60.

[49] *See ibid.*

[50] Despite its great popularity and success, study shown that conciliation practices in Japan is on the decline since 1974. *See ibid*, at 61.

[51] In reality, specialized courts have a long history and were not newly introduced in the third wave movement. They have long been used as a tool for administering rapid changes in substantive law. The advantage of specialized courts has once again been promoted during the third wave where there have been rapid changes in substantive law.

[52] *See ibid*, at 67.

[53] *See ibid.*

[54] *See ibid.*, at 72–3.

[55] *See ibid.*, at 69–73.

Justice" agrees that access to justice is a very broad subject and it can be broadly divided into three components.[56] The first is *access to legal justice* which relates to the enforcement of legal rights and removing barriers from obtaining remedies and redresses under traditional legal mechanisms.[57] The second component is *access to the machinery of justice of the welfare state* which places emphasis on the protection of new legal rights that have not been recognized under the traditional fields of law such as rights of employees, rights of consumers and rights to environmental protection.[58] The last component is access to "Justice", with a capital "J", meaning that access to justice is not only limited to access to a judicial process, but also awareness and action to achieve social justice and equality.[59] This last component with the capital "J" appears to correspond to what Cappelletti and Garth pointed out, which is that in the development of access to justice socio economic aspects are also important.[60]

In the definition of access to justice recently given by Stefan Wrbka, who offered its ideological framework, access to justice is "[t]he term of access to justice consists of two parts: *access* and *justice*. In its literal meaning, *access* stands for the chance to reach or accomplish something, whereas *justice* refers to fairness and reasonableness and embodies the concepts that everybody's rights are safeguarded."[61]

Although many academic and legal experts have offered myriad explanations on access to justice, it may be difficult to give a single all-inclusive definition because of its multidisciplinary nature, complexity, and the difficulty inherent in discerning the justice concept.[62] John Rawls notes that "[a]ll social values – liberty and opportunity, income and wealth, and the bases of self-respect – are to be equally distributed unless an unequal distribution of any, or all of these values are to everyone' advantage."[63] Ronald Dworkin chose to say that "individuals have a right to equal concern and respect"[64]

---

[56] *See* A. Tunc, *The Quest for Justice, in* M. Cappelletti (ed.), Access to Justice and the Welfare State 315, 315–17 (1981).

[57] *See ibid.*

[58] The objective of this component is to achieve a modern welfare state which will bring about equality and a social and economic environment that is suitable to all members of society. *See ibid.*

[59] The latter "J" has the meaning, in the German language, of not only *Justiz* but also includes *Gerechtigkeit. See* Sotrskrubb and Ziller, *supra* note 4, at 188.

[60] *See e.g.* Cappelletti, *supra* note 40, at 20–3. In the following period the notion of access to justice incorporated the idea of the welfare state and had an impact on the structure of the judicial process, through the creation of specialized courts and the integration of consumer and social issues into judicial thinking. The concept of the welfare state also brought about the belief that the state has the responsibility of creating, supporting and perpetuating the welfare state, through such means as offering financial assistance to the unfortunate poor who become a party in litigation and other assistance aiming to establish social fairness surrounding their citizens.

[61] *See* S. Wrbka, *European Consumer Protection Law: Quo Vadis? Thoughts on the Compensatory Collective redress Debate, in* S. Wrbka, S. van Uytsel and M. Siems (eds.), Collective Actions: Enhancing Access to Justice and Reconciling Multilayer Interest? 23, 27 (2012).

[62] *See also* Cappelletti and Garth, *supra* note 2, at 54.

[63] *See* J. Rawls, A Theory of Justice 62 (1971).

[64] *See* R. Dworkin, Taking Rights Seriously Chapter 6 (1977).

Despite many explanations and debates on access to justice, most of today's scholars share the common goal of attaining universal justice, which includes the goal of social justice and equity for all members of society.[65] In other words, the aim of the concept encompasses not only legal discipline, but also sociology and the concept of equity. The remaining question is in what direction the path of access to justice will move forward to.

3.3.2 Enhancing Access to Justice

Due to its expansive scope, the access to justice concept may be perceived as meaning different things to different people. Nevertheless, one undeniable goal of the various attempts under the recent movement to broaden access to justice has been to achieve equal justice by serving various dimensional aspects of justice interests (e.g. socio and legal aspects) in people's lives and activities. From its historical development, it is obvious that the current trend of access to justice does not ignore the ideas from the earlier movements. Rather, it has absorbed each footstep along its path rather than continually replacing the old ideas with new ones. This may be because each step of its development has been a critical component and none may be ignored.[66] Without the components gained from any phase of its past development, the structure of access to justice may not be as strong. As Mauro Cappelletti summarized, the past waves of access to justice could each be viewed as sound waves continuing to radiate out into further reform.[67]

Presently, legal aid, the fruit of the first wave of development, still plays a substantial role and flourishes in the constitutional laws of many nations.[68] Also, the focus on the recognition and protection of "diffuse interest" of underrepresented people in society which arose from the second wave of access to justice

[65] Mauro Cappelletti and Bryant Garth state that, although the access to justice development varies from one country to the next, for example, Germany, a country that focuses on the government's obligation to provide legal aid, has laid out a foundation that imposes a strict duty on the court in providing fair and equal justice, while giving less emphasis to viewing the problem from the "public law interest" perspective. On the other hand, the US links its implementation of access to justice with public policy, and administers active lobbying and class actions. Nonetheless, in implementing access to justice, both countries share a clear common goal of attaining universal social justice for all members of their societies. *See* Cappelletti and Garth, *supra* note 2, at 2, 5 and 54.

[66] *See* Cappelletti, *supra* note 40, at 20–3.

[67] *See ibid.*

[68] *See* Sotrskrubb and Ziller, *supra* note 4, at 184. For example, legal aid has been recently given a place in the law of the European Union. Article II – 46 of The Charter of Fundamental Rights of European Union and Article II–107 of The Treaty Establishing a Constitution for Europe provide that "legal aid shall be made available to those who lack sufficient resources in so far as such aid is necessary to ensure effective to justice." The Constitution of the Netherlands of 1883 is another example of the law that recognizes personal rights (the rights to natural judge) one of which is the right to legal aid. In Article 17, "No one may be prevented against his will form being heard by the courts to which he is entitled to apply under the law."

development is also playing a crucial role. Many enactments of laws for the protection of newly recognized rights are continuously being developed in fields such as consumer law, labor law and environmental law.[69] Also, there have been many dispute resolution reforms that promote special procedures, including informal and non-confrontational means of dispute resolution. Some examples of these are the small claims procedure, group or collective actions and alternative dispute resolution processes.[70] This well received new concept makes it more convenient and economical for the disputing parties by saving them both time and money.[71]

It can be concluded here that all past waves of access to justice have embodied a coherent effort to improve and promote todays' notion of justice. The access to justice concept produced an immense number of implications and it now appears to be a grand subject that may require a comprehensive reform of the entire legal system.[72] A clear difference that can be noticed when it is compared to the past notions of access to justice is that the current trend appears to take various dimensions of justice into account (e.g. social and legal aspects), while in the earlier stages of development it only focused on the one dimension of the legal representation (Fig. 3.1).

3.4 Important Underlying Consumers' Access to Justice

Based on the previous discussion, the idea of access to justice clearly gave rise to the rationales underlying consumer protection. In the consumer context, it started to emphasize the protection of diffuse interests and the establishment of the welfare state wherein the State is mainly obliged to provide public interest services to the underprivileged.[73] The practical outcome has been the tipping of the formal balance of power between individual consumers on the one side and entities that are deemed to be more powerful, such as corporations, industries, manufacturers, governments and the like, on the other.

[69] An important example is the issuing by the European Commission of many laws for the protection of diffuse interests of consumers including Directive 84/450/EEC concerning Misleading Advertising, Directive 2005/29/EC on Unfair Commercial Practices and Directive 93/13/EEC on Unfair Contract Terms. For instance, in 2007, Norway passed the Act on Civil Procedures *(Tristeloven)* prescribing special civil procedures for small claims apart from the procedures for normal litigation. Lithuania and Czech Republic also have specially dedicated civil procedures for small claims. Group actions have been adopted by Sweden and Norway, among many other countries.

[70] *See* Cappelletti and Garth, *supra* note 2.

[71] *See ibid. See also* J. Hörnle, Cross–broader Internet Dispute Resolution (2009).

[72] *See* Cappelletti and Garth, *supra* note 2, at 54.

[73] *See* H. Street, *Access to the Legal System and the Modern Welfare State: A European Report from the Standpoint of an Administrative Lawyer, in* M. Cappelletti (ed.), Access to Justice and the Welfare State 295, 301 (1981).

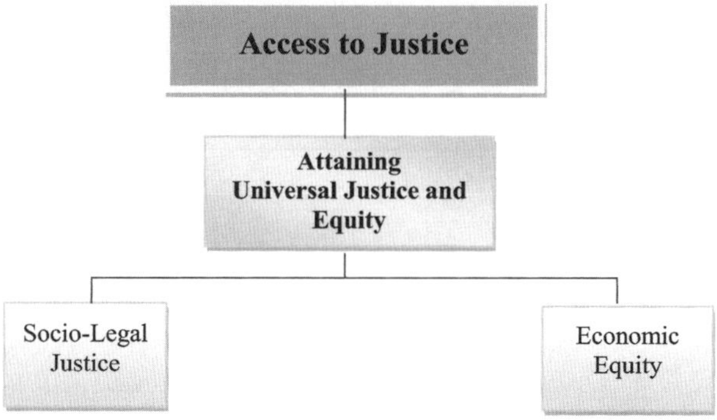

Fig. 3.1 The components of justice in relation to the contemporary concept of access to justice

3.4.1 Consumers' Access to Justice I: Socio-Legal Perspective

The debates on consumers' access to justice indicate that the attempts at reform have largely involved arguments concerning "cost and delay" and "justice for individuals" with an emphasis on providing affordable justice to every member of society by eliminating the economic unaffordability and delays that exist in the traditional judicial process. This development was sometime called the *power approach* which gives tools to individuals to make them well equipped to handle any dispute or litigation they may face in society.[74] This is because consumers are considered to be one of the groups holding diffuse interests that have often encountered difficulty in protecting their rights because of their often being in a lower position than their opponents (the businesses) in various ways including their economic status, knowledge and bargaining power.[75] Based on this, various attempts have been made to devise new measures to mitigate the imbalance of powers between consumers and businesses.[76]

Nevertheless, in the beginning such efforts appeared to be unsuccessful. Violations of consumers' rights by manufacturers or merchants continued to increase without any redress for consumers, especially during the industrial revolution.[77] This may have been because consumers were ordinary citizens who almost never had any influence on the legislative process and thus the designed laws and mechanisms at that time did not fully take into account their rights. This is especially true when we look at the difficulties of traditional litigation processes that consumers are faced with. In litigation, consumers have to prove that manufacturers or merchants have committed the offences and this is not an easy task.[78] For example, in the cases where defective goods or substandard services involve

[74] *See* Friedman, *supra* note 12, at 7.
[75] *See* Street, *supra* note 73, at 301.
[76] *See ibid.*
[77] *See ibid.*
[78] *See ibid.*

complex machinery or professional services, such as medical services, an ordinary consumer cannot be expected to have the thorough understanding of the features of such goods or services.[79] To do so, it would also be costly and highly burdensome for a consumer, resulting in burdens that can far exceed the amount one could hope to recover in litigation.

As a consequence, many alternative measures have been invented to remedy the shortcomings of traditional litigation. Among these are conciliation and mediation which do not subject the consumer to the burden of proof as is done in court proceedings.[80] Another is the establishment of a specialized court or department to handle consumer protection cases with a special or simplified procedure to avoid imposing excessive burdens on consumers.[81] For example, the court could call an expert witness at the court's own cost to assess the cause of the defect or determine whether the service was substandard and the amount of damage the consumer should receive.[82] Another form of assistance for consumers in traditional procedures that is often used in many jurisdictions is to shift the burden of proof to the manufacturers or merchants to prove that the damages were not caused by their own fault.[83]

Additionally group or collective actions, which were first developed in the United States and are based on private litigation, are considered to be an effective means of helping individual consumers achieve access to justice.[84] Such group actions improve the bargaining power of consumers by bundling their diffuse or fragmented interests together. If the defendant loses it may be subject to substantial liability because of the large number of consumer plaintiffs.[85] However, some scholars prefer the use of the ombudsman employed in Nordic countries as a more effective alternative for consumer protection because its function is based on the mandatory power of the state.[86] Even today differing views on various strategies to facilitate consumers' access to justice have brought about continuous discussion.

---

[79] *See* Ramsay, *supra* note 1, at 4. *See also* K. J. Cseres, *Enforcement of Collective Consumer Interests: a Competition Law Perspective, in* W. van Boom and M. Loos (eds.), Collective Enforcement of Consumer Law 123, 146–50 (2007).

[80] *See* Street, *supra* note 73, at 302.

[81] *See ibid.*

[82] The Australia tribunal-based system is a good example. It is not bound by the traditional rule of evidence and procedure. *See* A. J. Duggan, *Consumer Access to Justice in Common Law Countries: A Survey of the Issues from a Law and Economics Perspective, in* C. E. F. Rickett and T. G. W. Telfer (eds.), International Perspectives on Consumers' Access to Justice 46, 58 (2003). Similar designed procedure can also be found in the consumer case procedure of Thailand. *See* Section 33 para 2 and 36 para 1 of Thailand's Consumer Case Procedure Act (B.E. 2551).

[83] *See ibid* and Section 29 of Thailand's Consumer Case Procedure Act (B.E. 2551).

[84] Class action has for example proved to be a successful bridgehead in Brazil. *See* J. R. de Lima Lopes, *Social Rights and the Courts, in* T. Wilhelmsson and S. Hurri (eds.), From Dissonance to Sense: Welfare State Expectations, Privatisation and Private Law 567–92 (1999).

[85] *See* Cappelletti, *supra* note 40.

[86] For general analysis of Ombudsman, *see* R. James and P. Morris, *The New Financial Ombudsman Service in the United Kingdom: Has the Second Generation Got It Right?*, *in* C. E. F. Rickett and T. G. W. Telfer (eds.), International Perspectives on Consumers' Access to Justice 167–95 (2003).

3.4.2 *Consumers' Access to Justice II: Economic Perspective*

In today's market-driven society the growth of consumer markets along with the general expansion of the global economy have led to an increasing number of consumers and a high volume of consumer transactions. While the conventional problems plaguing consumer protection still remain, the fields where they operate have expanded into another dimension. The matter of consumer's access to justice is thus no longer restricted to the traditional socio-legal disciplines (equal justice). The economic element has also started to play a role. As André Tunc has observed "[e]conomic regulation is a poor substitute for social ethics; social security, a poor substitute for spontaneous community solidarity, but both are unavoidable for the protection of man, in our present societies"[87] and suggested that there should be concentration placed on both "economic and social regulation on what appears to be of significant importance..."[88]

At present, access to justice for consumers has arrived at a crossroads where these two academic disciplines have converged. In other words, consumer protection laws and measures, invented in the 1960s with an initial emphasis on equalizing the imbalanced powers of bargaining,[89] is now being challenged by the arrival of modern market economies and the evolution of economic theories.[90] This is confirmed by Michael Trebilo's argument that consumer protection in the twenty-first century is substantially more difficult and complex than it was 30–40 years ago.[91]

In traditional economic theory, it is generally believed that free market competition will result in the optimal and effective allocation of resources, as each resource will be acquired by the consumer who values it the most through the process where prices and quality are matched with the demands of the consumer.[92] In such a competitive environment, manufacturers and merchants will be driven to offer goods and services at the most appropriate price and quality to ensure that they are selected by consumers, resulting in a perfect market where there is a large spectrum of goods and services for consumers' to choose from.[93] Such a highly competitive sphere also helps to maximize the individual welfare of consumers by creating a situation where the optimal selection of goods and services at appropriate prices are efficiently distributed to all consumers, serving their preferences and

---

[87] *See* Tunc, *supra* note 56, at 358.

[88] *See ibid*, at 356.

[89] *See* Ramsay, *supra* note 1, at 53.

[90] One of the major contributions to such difficulty and complexity is the rapid progress in technological development, which brought about the globalized market and evolution of economic theories around such market structures. *See* M. J. Trebilcock, *Rethinking Consumer Protection Policy, in* C. E. F. Rickett and T. G. W. Telfer (eds.), International Perspectives on Consumers' Access to Justice 68, 68 (2003).

[91] *See ibid.*

[92] This assumption is based on the laissez-faire theory which argues that an effective competitive system leads to a perfect market, rejecting any need for governmental intervention. *See* C. Coteanu, Cyber Consumer Law and Unfair Trading Practices 18 (2005).

[93] *See ibid.*

desires.[94] With the countless number of choices available in a competitive market, the preferences and desires of individual consumers are likely to be fulfilled, giving them a greater deal of autonomy in making decisions.[95] This brings justice to individual consumers because they have the same complete freedom in managing their affairs in the market that is available to other members of society. However, such a scenario also relies on the assumption of neo-classical economic theory that consumers are capable of making optimal decision with sufficient information.[96]

Based on this, the economic rationale for state intervention is grounded on the *invisible hand* notion where state action is not viewed as necessary in the consumer market except to serve certain public interests.[97] Instead, the government's role should be to provide an environment where the consumers can make optimal market decisions, such as by ensuring that manufacturers and merchants disclose adequate and relevant information on their products to the market.[98]

Nevertheless, in reality, the market does not work as perfectly as the said economic theory suggests it should. The perfect optimal market does not exist in the real world because various failures that often work to undermine it.[99] Gillain Hadfield, Robert Howse and Michael Trebilcock have listed some characteristics of the market that fails to achieve such optimality and seem to generate unfairness to consumers as follows:

1. Repeat transactions are rare, and consequently the performance incentives created by the possibility of repeat business from satisfied customers are blunted.
2. Entry and exist costs in the industry are low, leading to the possibility of a large number of fly by night operators with few sunk costs and only modest investments in reputational capital.
3. Many sellers or producers are extra jurisdictional, marking redress through private law more difficult for consumers.
4. Sellers characteristically have few assets against which a judgment may be enforced.
5. The costs to consumers of a "bad" transaction are delayed or potentially catastrophic, making ex post relief an inadequate or unsatisfactory solution.
6. The small size of a typical transaction creates a significant disincentive to seeking ex post relief through the courts.[100]

---

[94] This is based on the economic concept of individual welfare which is "the extent to which the preference of individuals can be fulfilled with the means and goods that are available to them." *See* H. Luth, Behavioural Economics in Consumer Policy, The Economic Analysis of Standard Terms in Consumer Contracts Revisited 15 (2010).

[95] *See ibid.*

[96] *See ibid.*, at 41. Under such theory, laws and regulations that will manipulate or interfere with the market mechanisms are not necessary as consumers are assumed to be very capable of making the best possible market decisions.

[97] *See* Coteanu, *supra* note 92. *See also* Ramsay, *supra* note 1, at 55.

[98] *See* Ramsay, *ibid.*, at 61. This idea is also supported by the *consumer sovereignty* notion, an important economic perspective pursuant to which each consumer is afforded autonomy as they are capable of making decisions and taking actions in their own best interests. "Consumer sovereignty is seen in traditional economic viewpoints as a crucial instrument to allow welfare maximizing decisions to be taken by consumers, as consumers have an incentive to promote their own welfare." *See* Luth, *supra* note 94, at 26.

[99] *See* Ramsay, *ibid.*, at 57.

[100] *See* G. Hadfield, R. Howse and M. Trebilcock, *Information Based Principles for Rethinking Consumer Protection Policy*, 21 Journal of Consumer Policy 131–69 (1998).

Inequality of bargaining power in standard terms, information asymmetry, economic behavior and the incapacity of redress institutions appears to be the main causes of the situations where optimally competitive market fails to occur.[101] In such circumstances, problems of unfairness (as listed above) arise. Given these critical problems, government intervention in the market is necessary to deal with them.[102] To effectively do so, the economic approach can assist in forecasting or estimating the impacts from the implementation of any law and identifying market reactions that may be anticipated.[103] This will enable the legislature to more precisely design laws and measures to achieve the *perfect market* without suffering from unexpected side effects.[104]

At present, many agree that economics is influential and plays a role in contemporary paradigms on consumer protection law and policy.[105] In his view, Van den Bergh argues on this point that in a market where there is perfect competition, market equilibrium and appropriate market structures in accordance with the economic theories, the consumers will be afforded proper and fair protection.[106]

It can be said that the economic approach is also essential in helping consumers achieve access to justice. The governments have to take economic aspects into consideration when determining their level of intervention in the interest of promoting consumer access to justice.[107] The question has been raised as to what extent the state should impose mandatory rule to replace consumers' individual preferences while avoiding destroying the decision making mechanisms of consumers that forms the corner stone of the free market.[108] The imposition of state selection may be because the circumstances in the market where consumers are unable or choose not to assess the available information and make optimal choices on product purchases.[109] In other words, states should be step in when consumers act irrationally. As the scope of this paper does not include a deep economic analyses this issue will not be further examined here. Instead, the economic aspects in this paper are only used to establish a basic understanding of how economic principles influence the consumer protection laws and measures of today.

---

[101] *See* Chap. 2, Sect. 2.3.

[102] *See* Ramsay, *supra* note 1, at 55 and Luth, *supra* note 94, at 25.

[103] *See* Ramsay, *ibid.*, at 55–71 and Luth, *ibid.*, at 19–24.

[104] *See ibid.*

[105] *See* Ramsay, *ibid.*, at 55.

[106] *See* R. J. van den Bergh, *Competition Law and Consumer Protection Legislation, in* A. N. Hatzis (ed.), Economic Analysis of Law: A European Perspective 2222–23 (2003).

[107] *See* Ramsay, *supra* note 1, at 69.

[108] Many papers have drawn attention to the concept of "paternalism", wherein an individual's free choice is replaced or substituted by selections made by the state because of the collapse of effective market competition caused by market failures. For a discussion of paternalism concept, *see* Ramsey, *ibid.*, at 100–1, 163–4 and Luth, *supra* note 94, at 72–3.

[109] *See ibid*, Ramsay, at 163.

3.4.3 Contemporary Debates

From the above discussion it can be seen that the concept of consumers' access to justice is not limited to the socio-legal aspects of procedural justice but has other aspects, including preventive measures to ensure various dimensions of justice for consumers and issues of economic equity.

3.4.3.1 Ex Ante Mechanisms Versus Ex Post Mechanisms

In discussing the various dimensions of justice for consumers, Lawrence Friedman pointed out the significant conflict that arose from past reforms-the two different models of justice delivery, namely *routinization* and *individualization*.[110] Routinization provides justice by creating rights for individuals using bright line rules and minimizing the involvement of discretionary decisions of agencies or officials, thereby facilitating a simple, urgent and effectively administered form of justice, with ascertainable outcomes.[111] Such bright line rules can be seen in various forms of substantive laws that offer and protect consumer rights and underline the importance of consumer protection law.[112]

Individualization on the other hand involves tailoring rules according to a given circumstance or individual through the exercise of discretion, fulfilling different needs of different individuals.[113] This way is believed to provide a custom made form of justice as it takes into account the human uniqueness of individual consumers.[114] Based on this idea, many procedural reforms, whether formal or informal (e.g. small claim procedures and informal dispute settlements), have been implemented.

Obviously, these two models have had material impacts on the current development of consumers' access to justice.[115] Consumer protection mechanisms can be classified into two types of tools based on the time of intervention, distinguishing substantive rule mechanisms (routinization) from procedural or enforcement

---

[110] *See* Friedman, *supra* note 12, at 16.

[111] *See ibid. See also* Ramsay, *supra* note 2, at 39.

[112] For the path breaking argument on this issue in Arthur Leff's work, *see* A. Leff, *Unconscionability and the Crowd: Consumer and the Common Law Tradition,* 31 University of Pittsburgh Law Review 349–58 (1970). This argument has continued to be a focus, *see* J. Braucher, *the Repo Code: A Study of Adjustment to Uncertainty in Commercial Law*, 75 Washington University Law Quarterly 549–625 (1997).

[113] *See* Friedman, *supra* note 12, at 22.

[114] *See ibid.*

[115] Although these two types of justice delivery were first discussed in 1978, they still influence the thinking of today's consumer law scholars. For example, Iain Ramsay argued in support of routinization that it plays an important role in consumer protection as evidenced by the wide spread application of laws in the licensing regimes of today, *see* Ramsay, *supra* note 2, at 40. For similar position, *see* Braucher, *supra* note 112.

mechanisms (individualization).[116] The first are *ex ante* mechanisms, which are largely based on substantive regulations[117] that seek to control unacceptable or unwanted acts prior to the commission of such acts.[118] Many current studies have focused on these *ex ante* measures for dispute avoidance, examples of which include information disclosure, license control product warranties, standard terms of contract and cooling off period regimes.[119] This may be because the difficulties and time-consuming nature of procedural processes of individual actions help redirect focus and attentions to these *ex ante* mechanisms as the means to protect and afford justice to consumers at earlier stages.[120]

The second type is *ex post* mechanisms, which deal with harms that have already occurred because of the infringement of *ex ante* rights or substantive rules.[121] They have monitoring functions that heavily rely on enforcement through measures such as small claims procedures and collective actions.[122] These mechanisms are largely based on the view that justice will be better served according to a specific individual's needs and requirement for redress, although this model may be more time-consuming and complicated to administer than one based on *ex ante* measures.

Although *ex ante* tools are impressive as they perform at the very early stage, preventing possible problems and conflicts, it has been recognized that *ex ante* strategies that merely control specific behaviors may not be sufficient to discipline the consumer market.[123] For example, they cannot assist injured parties in complex cases such as those involving a latent product defect where the seller has already complied with all the rules and regulations applicable to the manufacturing of the product.[124] In such cases, *ex post* mechanisms that offer quick, economical and effective dispute resolution may be more useful.[125] The question then is how to

---

[116] There is no clearly defined line that separates interventions of *ex ante* control and *ex post* monitoring, and an often referred to classification between these two interventions is that they are solely rules on the one hand and third party intervention from judiciary on the other, which are always difficult to distinguish. *See* Luth, *supra* note 94, at 150. Sometime scholars often refer to these different mechanisms as substantive law and procedural law when discussing the topic of consumer protection. Kati Cseres points out that "[T]he focus of discussion in both European and international market regulation have been shifted from substantive issues to enforcement and institutional matters", *see* Cseres, *supra* note 78, at 120.

[117] *See* Luth, *supra* note 94, at 150.

[118] *See* R. van den Bergh, *Should Consumer Protection Law be Publicly Enforced?, in* W. van Boom and M. Loos (eds.), Collective Enforcement of Consumer Law 184, 200–1 (2007).

[119] *See e.g.* Ramsay, *supra* note 1, at 216 and W. van Boom and M. Loos (eds.), Collective Enforcement of Consumer Law 3 (2007).

[120] *See ibid.*

[121] *See* Bergh, *supra* note 118, at 200–1.

[122] *See* Luth, *supra* note 94, at 150.

[123] *See* Cseres, *supra* note 79, at 123–76.

[124] *See* E. G. Thornburg, *Privatisation and Power: Dispute Resolution for the Internet, in* C. E. F. Rickett and T. G. W. Telfer (eds.), International Perspectives on Consumers' Access to Justice 300, 300–1 (2003).

[125] Consequently, the choice of *ex post* tools or enforcement means needs to be taken into consideration to improve and make future regulatory choices for consumer protection. *See* Cseres, *supra* note 79, at 125.

achieve the optimal balance between *ex ante* and *ex post* mechanisms in the field of consumer transactions in a way that best serves justice.[126]

3.4.3.2 Individual Interests Versus Public Interests

The past emphasis on providing justice to individual consumers by eliminating the high costs and delays inherent in the traditional judicial process allows the system of judicial adjudication to support not only private interests through the provision of individual remedies but also public interests by setting social standards of acceptable behavior on a wide social scale.[127] In other words, the dispute resolution process that, in the past, emphasized providing individual redress to consumers has now extended its role to include the facilitation of social justice, especially in cases involving a large number of interested parties.

Past efforts to provide assistance in the form of legal representation to individuals in pursuing claims alone may not be adequate to serve both private and public interests in the consumer market. Even though legal aid is available, many consumers appear to still prefer not to bring their disputes to court for judicial adjudication because their individual interests may still be too small to justify the complicated process of litigation.[128] Well known barriers to litigation include the excessive time and effort required and the psychological barriers it presents.[129] Even though various ways to assist traditional litigation such as test cases,[130] small

---

[126] Kati Cseres has stated that "If consumers are granted substantive rights without providing mechanisms to ensure their effective exercise, these rights have no practical value." Therefore, the effectiveness of consumer protection relies on the functioning of both *ex ante* regulatory mechanisms as well as *ex post* procedural mechanisms. For the synergy effect of consumer protection, *ex ante* commands and *ex post* tools have to develop inter-linkages and work in parallel, as the interplay between them obviously exists. *See* Cseres, *supra* note 79 at 126. Lawrence Friedman also emphasizes the importance of both substantive and procedural aspects of access to justice: "It hard to draw the line between failure of justice in procedural sense and failure of justice in the substantive sense…sometimes the two are bound closely together, as when divorce law is simplified and reformed to make it easier both in rule and in process." *See* Friedman, *supra* note 12, at 6.

[127] As previously discussed, the judicial adjudication has an important role to play in public policy and regulation because it affects social standards and behaviors on a wide scale. It is commonly recognized that the judicial settlement process can promote both public and individual interests. *See* W. van Boom and M. Loos, *supra* note 119.

[128] *See* Cappelletti and Garth, *supra* note 2, at 27.

[129] *See ibid.*, at 28.

[130] Test cases are cases brought to a competent court to set a precedent which subsequent cases of a similar nature will follow. *See* K. Viitanen, *Enforcement of Consumers' Collective Interests by Regulatory Agencies in the Nordic Countries, in* W. van Boom and M. Loos (eds.), Collective Enforcement of Consumer Law 81, 92 (2007).

claims procedures[131] and group representation[132] have been promoted these processes are still largely based on private litigation. With the highly complicated process remaining largely unchanged, these techniques often have offered little benefit to consumers as research has revealed that stimulating such lawsuits will conventionally advantage middle class interests rather than consumers living below the poverty line.[133] Even though the group action seems to provide a solution to the individual incentive problem, as it consolidates widely fragmented small value claims, the cost of litigation and the difficulties of forming processes remain obstacles to consumers accessing the courts.[134] Looking at the Swedish group action as an example, only six cases have been brought since its establishment in 2003.[135] This puts a limit on the public value as the judicial process cannot play their important role in regulating and guiding social standards via their decisions on cases.

Therefore, public enforcement or administrative power by special purpose governmental organizations or agencies may also be necessary. For instance, the Nordic ombudsmen, which are state agencies, have the authority to investigate and fine business operators who violate consumer protection law and recover damages for consumers, serving both public and private interests at the same time.[136] Nevertheless, such administrative agencies often demand large budgets from the state and, as a result, they may not be fully independent or may not fully serve to protect the public interest and the interest of individuals.[137] The experiences of the Nordic Ombudsmen have shown that the limit of public resources appears to be one reason for the unwillingness and inactiveness of the competent authorities to initiate consumer cases.[138]

At present, the question of whether public enforcement (e.g. ombudsmen) or private enforcement (e.g. small claim procedures, group actions) are more effective in promoting both individual interests and public interests has been subject of huge debates.[139] More specific to consumer protection is the question of which of

[131] This is the process designed to divert cases away from general judicial litigation and to encourage dispute resolution in more economically efficient ways. Measures include lower court fees and faster and simpler processes. For a detailed historical note on the development of the small claims courts and procedures, *see* Cappelletti and Garth, *supra* note 2, at 64–84.

[132] For a deep analysis and detailed debates on the consumer group actions, *see* J. Steele and W. H. van Boom (eds.), Mass Justice: Challenges of Representation and Distribution (2011).

[133] This is especially true in the test case and the small claims procedure. *See e.g.* H. Kötz, *Public Interest Litigation: A Comparative Survey, in* M. Cappelletti (ed.), Access to Justice and the Welfare State 82, 89 (1981) and Cappelletti and Garth, *supra* note 2, at 64–84.

[134] *See* Viitanen, *supra* note 130, at 96.

[135] *See* Viitanen, *ibid.*

[136] *See ibid.*, at 81–103.

[137] *See* F. Caffaggi and H. W. Micklitz, New Frontiers of Consumer Protection, The interplay Between Private and Public Enforcement 2, 5 (2009).

[138] *See* Viitanen, *supra* note 130.

[139] For detailed debate on public and private enforcements in consumer transaction, *see* Boom and Loos, *supra* note 119.

(i) administrative enforcements by special purpose governmental agencies on behalf of consumers; or (ii) private enforcements by individual or private representatives such as class actions, group actions or collective actions, can better serve to protect consumer and market interests. While prevention is the foremost objective of public enforcement, it is the secondary objective of private enforcement for which "redress and compensation for damages" is the foremost concern. The question that many countries, particularly in Europe, are pondering is how to prioritize these objectives, in other words how to balance private and public enforcement.

3.4.3.3 State Regulations Versus Self-Regulations

Under the access to justice concept, social justice has come to the fore in addition to legal justice. The "welfare state" concept wherein the state provides social services to promote social justice and equality has been the subject of attention throughout the history of access to justice.[140] It later evolved into the border concept of "social positive welfare"[141] which recognizes that the welfare improvement must address all aspects of problems, going beyond income transfers and giving rise to many issues of justifiability including social planning and economic strategies.[142] It not only imposes a duty of supporting justice in society on the state but also encourages the private sector to do so.[143] The standards of professions or codes of conduct established by private actors, which regulate duties and roles to meet standards expected by society, for example, have become important measures that may have large implications for access to justice.[144] This includes the duties of legal professionals to clients, physicians to patients and the duties of banks and other financial institutions to customers.[145] Such standards or codes of conduct may also help instill confidence in society as a whole as they assist in creating positive welfare by listening to what consumers and society want. If the standards were set according to social expectations, they may help minimize the occurrence of possible disputes which is another way of serving justice to the members of society and, at the same time, creating social norms that recognize the importance of fair dealing in each industry.

The UK, for example, is a country that always encourages private entities to participate in providing justice in the market through self-regulation regimes.[146]

---

[140] *See* Street, *supra* note 73, at 295–6.

[141] *See* A. Giddens, Beyond Left and Right: The Future of Radical Politics (1994).

[142] *See ibid.*

[143] *See ibid.*

[144] *See* Sotrskrubb and Ziller, *supra* note 4, at 179 and Ramsay, *supra* note 1, at 14.

[145] *See* Ramsay, *ibid.*

[146] *See* OECD, *OECD Reviews of Regulatory Reform: United Kingdom: Challenges at the Cutting Edge* (2002), *available at* keepeek.com/Digital-Asset-Management/oecd/governance/oecd-

This is obvious in the area of consumer protection as each industry is allowed to establish their own appropriate and acceptable standards for dealing with consumers.[147] These self-regulatory regimes have been well received and further spread to dispute resolution processes. For example, in 2004, the International Standards Organization issued an international standard to provide guidance for forms and conducts concerning commercial and non-commercial complaints, as well as e-transactions. These guidelines offer frameworks, formats and procedures for fair and informal dispute resolutions, which will be continuously improved in the future and become an important roadmap for private sector self-regulation. A prominent characteristic of this new approach is to cause the codes of practice or fair dealing guidelines to transform certain standards or practices into new social norms in the hope that such norms will help move society towards universal justice and equality.[148]

It can be said that today we have discovered the "alternative to conventional regulations". While the classic regime gave the principal regulatory role to the state, the alternative took away some parts and gave them to the private sector to "self-regulate" in the hope that it would further advance social goals. One certainty is that this new approach helps the state save costs while promoting the private sector's participation in creating positive welfare in society. On the other hand, some are skeptical that the trend of self-regulation may be harmful as the private sector may not be sincere in conducting best practices in the public interest or promoting positive welfare and social justice.[149] When the role of the state is more restricted, injustice and violation of rights of individuals may surface, undermining the progress of access to justice. Due to this, the benefits and pitfalls of the "classic regulatory approach" and "new self-government" will need to continue to be further studied and given a closer look when they are going to be applied in any particular market.

---

reviews-of-regulatory-reform-united-kingdom-2002_9789264199255-en (visited January 12, 2012).

[147] To view this issue more clearly, the Office of Fair Trading (OFT), a Government agency responsible for the protection of consumers' rights in the United Kingdom for the past 40 years, usually issues rules and regulations in an unofficial manner that provides for voluntary compliance. In the 1980s, the OFT issued codes of practices as guidelines for various types of business to follow in maintaining good standards for dealing with consumers. As a European Union report mentioned: "[t]he United Kingdom has a distinctive preference for self-regulation". *See* I. Ramsay, *Globalization, the Third Way and Consumer Law: The Case of the U.K., in* J. K. Winn (ed.), Consumer Protection in the Age of the Information Economy 59, 64–5 (2006).

[148] Rather, they may collude to tighten their grasp of the supply side of the market in their own self-interest because individuals consumers, the other parties, often have less bargaining power in relation to self-regulating business operators. *See* Ramsay, *supra* note 1, at 115.

[149] One danger of self-regulation is that its characteristics are likely to support the development of a cartel because the market is largely regulated by trade associations or private industries. *See ibid*, at 116.

3.4.3.4 Consumers Protection Versus Global Economic Interests

New technologies brought forward in todays' borderless and global market provide consumers with an ever greater selection of goods to choose from and competitive prices. This new form of market largely ignores political and geographic boundaries, which distinguishes it from conventional markets that are generally divided at the national level. Many nations today are pushing for full and free competition in trade and investment to benefit from globalization. It is also in their interest to protect consumers from unfair trading practices that may arise in transnational activities. As the presence of such practices is no longer limited to any particular jurisdiction, the issue of how to protect consumers has become more complicated and difficult. The borderless nature of today's market has brought about the issue of conflicts of law, for example, where a consumer in one jurisdiction makes a purchase from a manufacturer or merchant in another. If the purchased goods are defective, which jurisdiction's laws and procedures should be used? Moreover, the attractiveness of diffuse interest proceedings, that are usually already time-consuming and costly, may be greatly reduced because there may be uncertainty about whether a judgment can really be enforced in a foreign jurisdiction. This scenario, which is a reality of the global market, may further impede consumers from access to justice.

With its different characteristics from conventional markets, some scholars have the view that, in the frontier-less landscape of the global market, "self-help" by consumers may be the most appropriate solution.[150] Various laws and measures may not be necessary because in such a highly competitive global market place the market will be driven to its optimal point.[151] In addition, the benefits provided by the global market, including its great convenience, low cost and wide selection, will have to be balanced with the disadvantages it brings which includes the requirement that the consumers must adapt to the concept of "self-help" in looking after themselves and beware of the risks for which there is no recourse or only a form of recourse that would not be worth pursuing.[152]

On the contrary, David Levi-Faur argues that it is necessary to develop a new form of global regulation to ensure fairness to consumers in this period of globalization. He suggests this should consist of: "greater regulation within government to prevent the classic problem of regulatory "capture" and to maintain public trust; the rise of new instruments of regulation that involve increased internal monitoring by corporations; increased international regulation through technical standard; and the diffusion of regulatory ideals worldwide through regulatory networks"[153]

[150] *See* Coteanu, *supra* note 92, at x.

[151] *See ibid*, at 18–9.

[152] *See ibid* and J. Hill, Cross-Border Consumer Contracts 20–1 (2008).

[153] *See* D. Levi-Faur, *The Global Diffusion of Regulatory Capitalism*, 598 The Annals of the American Academy of Political and Social Science 12–32 (2005).

Between these two differing standpoints an obvious dichotomy between economic rationale and justice in the market appears. To illustrate this clear contradiction, the e-market with its transnational nature may serve as an illustrative example. Without any clear regulation, e-merchants may easily use their technological expertise to take advantage of consumers through such means as unclear notices on their websites, the collection of data without obtaining consent from, or even giving notice to, consumers and so on. These create environments that are unfair to consumers in the e-market. Additionally, traders may also set a "forum clause" in their pre-drafted standard contract which provides that any dispute relating to such contract must be brought to the jurisdiction where their head offices are located. Such clauses may impose a great burden on consumers who are usually located at great distances, or even in a different country, from the merchant. Nevertheless, regulations in the global e-market should not be too draconian as they may become an obstacle for the evolution of the global consumer market. State rule-based regimes are often difficult to sustain in the transnational e-environment where jurisdiction is not so clear and enforcement is extremely difficult.[154] For example, if a business offers their goods or service online in many countries, that business may have to comply with all the mandatory rules of all the relevant countries to ensure its legal compliance. Therefore, businesses may limit the geographical scope of their sales to avoid being forced to comply with the laws of various countries which would impose some costs on them.[155] This erodes market competition and consumer's choices, two of the main benefits of the transnational online market. How to find this optimal equilibrium to balance of the values of the economic interests of the global market and fairness to consumers in the today market is not an easy task.

3.4.4 Enhancing Consumers' Access to Justice

From a historical perspective, the notion of access to justice started from the recognition of equality under the rule of law. Consumers are members of society who often have limited access to justice when compared to other groups in society. From this recognition the focus then turned to enhancing consumers' rights, reducing the gap between consumers and the more powerful merchants and making access to justice more available to consumers. This led to various attempts at legal reforms to both the substantive law (*ex ante* mechanisms) and procedural processes (*ex post* mechanisms), with the parallel objectives of serving both public and private interests.

"Socio legal justice" is one important dimension of consumers' access to justice that focuses on delivering comprehensive justice to consumers, irrespective of

[154] *See* P. Cortés, Online Dispute Resolution for consumer in the European Union 34 (2011).

[155] *See* Hill, *supra* note 152, at 357.

whether such justice is provided by the state or the private sector.[156] This is based on the desire to provide equal justice to every member of society and thereby achieve universal justice. Within this objective, the most traditional and well-known development is the procedural reform in respects of the enforcement of consumers' rights and the provision of remedies and redresses under legal mechanisms (e.g. collective or group actions, special courts or alternative dispute resolution mechanisms).

The arrival of the modern market economy has led to the evolution and integration of economic theories into consumer law and policies. Since then, "economic interest" has become another dimension of consumers' access to justice. Today, it is universally recognized that "market efficiency" based on free competition will bring the optimal selection of goods and services at the optimal price and quality, creating a just environment to all players, particularly consumers in the market, being one of the main avenues for consumer to access to justice. Such market efficiency comes about when the optimal selection of goods and services at appropriate prices are efficiently distributed to all consumers. This serves the preferences and desires of consumers[157] and allows for their "individual welfare development", which promotes their autonomy by enhancing their freedom of choice. This brings another aspect of justice relating to economic context to individual consumers (Table 3.1).

3.5 Interim Conclusion

From its historical development the main goal of access to justice can be summarized as the provision of justice to certain members of society who have less access to justice than other groups of people in society. Consumers with their diffuse interests are one of the disadvantaged segments of the population who often suffer from a lack of access to justice. They are often at a disadvantage both financially and in terms of their access to information, especially when they have to face strong institutions or large organizations. The notion of access to justice clearly gave birth of consumer protection law and policy.

Various approaches have been driven by protective ideas, which were initiated by past social inequality, including the provision of legal aid and alternative dispute resolution mechanisms to reduce the existing gap between the more powerful parties (traders) and consumers in their relationship. Later, the concept took a broader approach, which included problem or dispute avoidance through substantive mechanisms which certify and grant substantive rights to consumers. Under the current universal access to justice idea, it is quite clear that consumers' access to justice includes multidimensional aspects. Its scope covers not only socio-legal

[156] *See* Sotrskrubb and Ziller, *supra* note 4, at 178.

[157] *See* Luth, *supra* note 90, at 15.

Table 3.1 Historical development of the concept of access to justice and its relationship with the movement for consumers' access to justice

The development of access to justice	Historical periods (prior to nineteenth century)	Legal aid (early nineteenth century)	Diffuse and fragmented interests (mid 1960s)	Universal justice (1970s)	Contemporary development (present)
How access to justice is defined?	Equal rights	Assistance for the poor in judicial processes	Protection of unrecognized groups of people	Broader concept (including "preventive measures")	Concept includes not only socio-legal justice, but also economic justice (that embodies everybody's rights)
Consumer access to justice	N/A	N/A	Consumers as one of the unrecognized groups who need protection (e.g., public bodies provide assistance to consumers, etc.)	Preventive measures for consumers' problems (e.g., special laws for consumer protection and consumer courts, etc.)	Economic perspectives have been integrated into the concept of consumer protection (e.g., promote market efficiency, enhance consumers' bargaining powers, etc.)
Outcomes	Legal reforms in relation to various new rights (e.g., human rights, woman rights, etc.)	Free legal representation and legal advices from states	Public interest institutions, public interest litigation and group or class actions for particular groups of people (e.g., laborers, consumers, etc.)	Proliferation of special laws (substantive laws to prevent injustice), ADR, special courts and welfare state	Recognition on interrelationship between *ex ante* and *ex post* mechanisms and between public and private enforcement and the emerging of self-regulations

justice (e.g. individual redress and a fair market environment) but also recognizes economic interests (e.g. market efficiency and individual welfare development) with the ultimate objective of creating justice in both the private and the public spheres. In other words, consumers' access to justice has been expanded to all aspects of justice embodying consumers' activities and is aimed at establishing minimum standards in the market place, facilitating equal access to consumption opportunities and enforcing consumer rights.[158] By exploring and understanding the concept of access to justice, which is the core fundamental rational of consumer protection in this chapter, the next chapter will draws an appropriate framework or a measurement tool to be used as a benchmark in the evaluation of consumer protection measures in e-sales in Chaps. 5–7.

[158] *See also* Ramsay, *supra* note 1, at 88.

Chapter 4
Towards a Multidimensional Approach to Access to Justice: Setting a Framework for Consumer Protection in B2C E-Commerce

4.1 Introduction

The previous chapter described the historical development of the concept of access to justice with particular reference to its application in debates on consumer protection. The main argument of the chapter was to suggest that—historically, at least—the concept of access to justice in its early stages of development referred to the use of *procedural* legal mechanisms (or legal representatives) to provide justice to certain groups within society to whom justice had been less accessible in comparison to other members of society. Consumers have been regarded as one such *disadvantaged group* who have often had limited access to justice because justice is often too costly, too difficult, or comes too late. The focus of consumers' access to justice turned to enhancing consumers' rights, thus reducing the gap between consumers and more powerful merchants or traders and making access to justice better available to them. The chapter went on to suggest that in recent developments there has been a shift in the focus of the debate from the role of *procedural* law towards a greater focus being placed on the role of *substantive* law with an emphasis on consumers' rights in achieving access to justice.[1]

---

[1] Today, many consumer law scholars often refer to substantive law and procedures when discussing the topic of consumer protection and access to justice. For example, Iain Ramsay argued in support of substantive aspects that they play an important role in consumer protection as evidenced by the widespread application of laws on the licensing regimes of today. *See* I. Ramsay, Consumer law and Policy, Text and Materials on Regulating Consumer Markets 40 (2007). For similar position, *see* J. Braucher, *The Repo Code: A Study of Adjustment to Uncertainty in Commercial Law*, 75 Washington University Law Quarterly 548–625 (1997). For discussion of the similar situation in the EU, Kati Cseres points out that "[t]he focus of discussion in both European and international market regulation have been shifted from substantive issues to enforcement and institutional matters", *see* K. J. Cseres, *Enforcement of Collective Consumer Interests: A Competition Law Perspective*, *in* W. van Boom and M. Loos (eds.), Collective Enforcement of Consumer Law 123, 125 (2007). Some authors often refer to the two models for the legal intervention of consumer contracts. The first is *ex ante* regulation or substantive issues.

S. Yuthayotin, *Access to Justice in Transnational B2C E-Commerce*,
DOI 10.1007/978-3-319-11131-5_4

Rapid technological changes and globalization have expanded the consumer market and made available a wide range of goods and services to consumers in all corners of the world. This has made consumer interests increasingly complicated and introduced various new forms of trading practices which today's consumers are faced with. On one hand, the complexity of the expanded range of products and trading practices that consumers face today has driven the growth of the global economy with various side effect to market function. On the other hand, consideration must be given to the question of what consumer interests have to be protected and what are the best ways of doing so. As consumer interests have become more complex, diverse and diffuse over the time, consumers have not only suffered from a lack of social justice and remedies against unfair trading practices, but they have also been deprived of economic welfare as provided for by market efficiency, the freedom of meaningful individual choice and so on. These have become material concerns.

Therefore, a discussion about effective means of consumer protection cannot disregard the multidimensional aspects of today's diverse and complicated consumer interests. Prospective protection mechanisms, currently consisting of substantive rules that influence market behavior, depend on institutional procedures to provide the effective enforcement of consumer rights and easy access to justice. In shaping these, the diversity and complexity of consumer interests must be considered.[2]

This chapter will build on existing discussions—particularly the recent emphasis on multidimensional aspects within the consumers' access to justice debates–and propose a *multidimensional framework* for conceptualizing access to justice which include procedural and substantive focuses in the context of consumer protection which give equal importance to both socio-legal and economic considerations (hereinafter the *Framework*). As consumer transactions are associated with a long tradition in the law of contracts, commercial activities, consumer protection and their relevant theoretical concepts are thus used as the fundamental underpinnings of the proposed framework. It is worth noting that from the historical development of the concept of access to justice, its evolution heavily depends on how society receives the meaning and scope of justice. The established Framework represents the thoughts on consumers' access to justice today, while this concept will continue to evolve along with human society long into the future. Also, the Framework is not an exhaustive list and does not offer priority elements of the concept of access to justice. This because the discussion on how to prioritize or balance different aspects of justice appears to be a political question which has to be discussed in the context of the legal system and conception of access to justice in a specific country.

Table 4.1 illustrates the multidimensional framework comprising the conditions necessary to satisfy the multidimensional aspects of access to justice in B2C

The second is *ex post* mechanisms in court. *See e.g.* H. Luth, Behavioural Economics in Consumer Policy, The Economic Analysis of Standard Terms in Consumer Contracts Revisited (2011).

[2] *See* Cseres, *ibid.*, at 161.

Table 4.1 The conditions necessary to satisfy the multidimensional aspects of access to justice in B2C e-transaction

A Multidimensional Framework for Access to Justice
4.2 Accurate and Sufficient Information and Ability to Digest Information
4.3 Variety of Goods and Services at Appropriate Prices
4.4 Ability to Make Rational Decisions and Freedom of Choice
4.5 Fair Terms and Conditions
4.6 Right of Withdrawal
4.7 Performance of Obligations
4.8 Consumers' Privacy
4.9 Consumers' Safety
4.10 Reasonable Cost of Transaction
4.11 Right to Conduct Dispute Resolution in a Convenient Location
4.12 Access to Effective Dispute Resolution
4.13 Enforcement of Remedies or Redress
4.14 Fair Trading Practices
4.15 Recognition of Consumer Rights and their Roles in the Market

e-transactions, which will be the subject of detailed discussion in this chapter. The framework will then be used as the benchmark for the evaluation of various consumer protection laws and mechanisms implemented in the e-market discussed in Chaps. 5–7 respectively.

It is necessary to point out that, in this chapter, the proposed multidimensional framework will bring two advantages in the development of consumer protection mechanisms in e-sales.

First, the multidimensional approach to access to justice ensures that all relevant interests of consumers are considered. In the previous chapter, it was suggested that the emphasis on legal representatives or procedural mechanisms in earlier debates on access to justice undoubtedly promoted the enforcement opportunities for a particular class of individuals—e.g. consumers—thus promoting social justice. However, this type of approach resulted in the neglect of certain other interests. Interests that were not incorporated into this approach include the private interest in maximizing autonomous individual choice, as well as the public interest in market efficiency and other aspects of social justice. The multidimensional framework being advocated here serves the broader objectives of protecting all aspects of justice embodying consumers' activities with the aim of establishing minimum standards in the market place, facilitating equal access not only to socio-legal justice, but also to economic justice and serving both the public and private interests.

Second, another advantage of this multidimensional framework is that it points out the essential development of various elements that provide the conditions for consumers' access to justice as a scale and it highlights the centrality of "trade-offs" within any debate on whether any particular legal mechanism is more desirable than others. Different legal mechanisms may have benefits in one dimension and costs in another and this will be made clear in Chaps. 5–7.

Therefore, this chapter presents various conditions necessary to satisfy the multidimensional aspects of access to justice in the consumer context through the Framework. These are being suggested as the essential or minimum reasonable conditions necessary for achieving consumers' access to justice. At the end of the discussion on each condition, specific issues relevant to B2C e-sales will be introduced which have advanced technological aspects that give them a transnational nature.

4.2 Sufficient and Accurate Information and the Ability to Digest Information

Taking into account the needs and interests of consumers, it is widely recognized that consumers should be provided with sufficient and accurate information prior to entering into a contract to allow them to make informed decisions about their transactions.[3] Information about the identity of the seller, the goods or services offered (e.g. price, quality, etc.), the characteristics of the transaction (e.g. the terms and conditions of the purchase, method of payment, etc.) and so on enable consumers to assess whether the transactions being considered meet their needs and are affordable to them.[4]

If consumers are not sufficiently informed, the information asymmetry that arises can decrease the efficiency of contractual exchanges and harm the proper functioning of the market. Nobel Prize Laureate George Akerlof has argued that asymmetries in information appear to destroy particular markets for consumers' products.[5] Uncertainty of quality because of lack of information erodes consumers' decision-making process, causing adverse selection and quality deterioration.[6] For example, if consumer cannot distinguish between good and bad quality products beforehand because of the unavailability or inadequacy of information, they may buy goods at purchase prices that are too high relative to the quality and utility that they can receive from those goods. The contractual exchanges will not be *Pareto Optimal*—the situation where both parties must be better off.[7] Eventually, goods of

---

[3] *See e.g.* E. Rubin, *The Internet, Consumer Protection and Practical Knowledge*, *in* J. K. Winn (ed.), Consumer Protection in the Age of the Information Economy 35–55 (2006) and United Nations, *United Nations Guidelines for Consumer Protection (as expanded in 1999)* (2003), *available at* unctad.org/en/docs/poditcclpm21.en.pdf (visited March 12, 2013).

[4] *See* C. Coteanu, Cyber Consumer Law and Unfair Trading Practices 127 (2005).

[5] *See* G. Akerlof, *The Market for Lemons: Qualitative Uncertainty and the Market Mechanism*, 84 Quarterly Journal of Economic 488–500 (1970).

[6] *See ibid.* For detailed discussion of adverse selection, *see* Luth, *supra* note 1, at 22–3 and Ramsay, *supra* note 1, at 67.

[7] *See* Rubin, *supra* note 3, at 37.

decent quality will be driven out of the market by goods of bad quality because those selling the former will find that the market prices at which the majority of consumers are willing to pay are lower than the true value of their products.

In such a situation, the traders of good quality products may decide to cease their offers and leave the market. Once a sufficient number of such traders decide to leave the market, there will be a decline in the average product quality, a drop in product prices and only low quality products will be offered for sale.[8] This situation is also known as *a race to the bottom*.[9] This process of adverse selection as described by Akerlof seems to be more serious in the market for consumers' products that are not regularly purchased (e.g. second-hand cars, products or services purchased at tourist traps) and those with qualities that are difficult to assess (e.g. standard terms of services provided by physicians and other professional services). One often cited reason why information asymmetries occur is that the trader omits necessary information regarding goods or services to minimize the risk that the consumer might not be pleased with such information and turn to other traders.[10]

To some extent, the market itself may correct the information problem. For instance, reputation may be an indicator or signal of quality and serve as a disciplinary guideline for repeat purchasers.[11] When consumers are not fully informed, some consumers may choose not to buy the cheaper products and instead choose to buy products that are more expensive from well-known traders because those traders are generally perceived, correctly or not, by consumers to carry superior quality products. However, such perceptions can be misguided as reputation may not necessarily translate into quality products.[12] Well-known traders may build their reputations through means other than improving product quality, such as effective advertisements or after sale services. They may also take advantage of their reputations by offering products at prices that are excessive relative to product quality.[13] This may also lead to a race to the bottom.

---

[8] *See* R. van den Bergh, *Should Consumer Protection Law be Publicly Enforced?*, *in* W. van Boom and M. Loos (eds.), Collective Enforcement of Consumer Law 177, 188–9 (2007).

[9] *See* Luth, *supra* note 1, at 22–3.

[10] Traders do not inform consumers of negative effects from the consumption of their products such as, for example, that smoking is harmful to health. Vendors also do not notify consumers of ancillary costs of the products, including after sale maintenance costs, transportation costs, etc., that are higher than those charged by other vendors. *See* Coteanu, *supra* note 4, at 127 and Ramsay, *supra* note 1, at 69.

[11] *See* P. Nelson, *Advertising as Information*, 82 Journal of Political Economy 729–54 (1974).

[12] *See* Bergh, *supra* note 8, at 189.

[13] One possible way that traders with dominant market position can seek to maximise their profit is to reduce the warranty protection that they provide. This is likely true when consumers cannot distinguish the products they carry based on quality. *See also* R. A. Epstein, *Contract, Not Regulation: UCITA and High-Tech Consumers Meet Their Consumer Protection Critics*, *in* W. van Boom and M. Loos (eds.), Collective Enforcement of Consumer Law 205, 228 (2007).

The second difficulty relating to information problems is that the disclosed information may be false, misleading, or inaccurate. If "incomplete or false information in relation to a product or service is fed into the market, market performance is adversely affected. Distortion of marketplace harms both consumers and honest competitors. Consumers are precluded form making informed purchasing decisions and firms are denied the ability to compete on a level playing field."[14] Such false or misleading information will also bring about adverse selection because consumers will misinterpret the information and falsely perceive that the goods or services are of better quality than they actually are. As a result, consumers will make incorrect selections on that basis. Practices of false or misleading information are often driven by the traders who wish to generate quick revenue and profit, such as the "fly by night" or "tourist trap" situations. These traders are not interested in maintaining long term relationships with customers, but are only interested in making a quick profit, before moving to a new market location.[15]

Considering the possible deterioration of product quality and the capture of unfair profits that may occur if consumers lack or receive false information there is a strong case to be made for compelling disclosure, which has been the dominant response to the above stated problems.[16] It is logical enough that regulation require information be sufficiently and accurately disclosed to consumers.[17] However, experiences with compelled disclosure may not yet be satisfactory. The problem is that asymmetry of information can bring about failures of the market that are more intractable than the supporters of information disclosure have assumed.

To start with, the mere disclosure of information will not turn out to be so effective if the disclosures are too difficult to understand or digest. If difficult or ambiguous language is used in disclosing the information, or the disclosure is made in a format that is difficult to look at, such disclosure may be as useless to consumers as if there had been no disclosure at all. For instance, there is substantial evidence indicating that the disclosure of legal terms and conditions of consumer

---

[14] *See* Coteanu, *supra* note 4, at 127. The author cited the statement of Rachel Larabie-Lesieur, Deputy Director of Investigation and Research Competition Bureau, Industry Canada, in *Misleading Advertising on the Internet: Competition Law Enforcement in the Electronic Marketplace, Remarks to the Canadian Corporate Shareholder Services Association on September 19, 1996.*

[15] Some traders even think that such "slash and burn" practices will generate a better yield of profit. *See* Ramsay, *supra* note 1, at 67.

[16] *See* Bergh, *supra* note 8, at 189 and Z. Saami, *Regulation of E-Commerce by Contract: Is It Fair to Consumers?*, 31 The University of West Los Angeles UWLA Law Review 163, 167 (2000).

[17] Information disclosure can be regarded as a "*pre contractual obligation*" of traders, which is classified as a required matter relating to a consumer sale contract. It is justified on policy grounds as it is better for sound administration. *See* Z. S. Tang, Electronic Consumer Contracts in the Conflict of Law 33 (2009) and Saami, *ibid*., at 163,167. Please note that one often cited benefit of information disclosure is that it allows consumers to express their demand for goods and services through their selection processes. Under market competition, suppliers will be pressured to improve and modify their products, to satisfy the changing consumer demands and the market conditions will then be adjusted to best reflect consumer requirements and preferences. *See* Ramsay, *supra* note 1, at 119–20.

contracts are not particularly helpful because a large number of consumers cannot understand these.[18] Another example is when the information is presented in fine print footnotes and the question of whether that constitutes effective communication to consumers.[19] Such practices may not be fair to consumers if some key information that is necessary for consumers to decide whether to enter into the sales contract is presented in fine print footnotes. Information presented in that way can easily be overlooked by consumers before entering into contracts because of such inappropriate forms of presentation.[20] These practices tend to produce the same effect as a lack of disclosure. Christina Coleanu emphasizes the importance of the content, format, and presentation of information: "[t]he positive impact of disclosures depends on the fact that disclosures are made in a clear language that is understood by consumers. To avoid the risk of information asymmetries, traders and advertisers should use clear language and syntax and avoid legal or technical jargon. Also, incorporating extraneous material into the disclosure also may diminish the message that must be conveyed to consumers."[21]

Moreover, efforts to comply with the disclosure requirements may create *information overload* problems that undermine consumer ability to digest and comprehend necessary information. Some scholars indicate that excessive information will reduce the ability of a person to digest it and to make proper decisions based on such information.[22] With excessive information provided consumers often selectively read only parts of the information, which may lead them to overlook things that may be truly essential for making proper decisions, such as product properties.[23] This premise is supported by a specific study in the instant food industry, where it was discovered that the majority of consumers ignore excessive information on product packages because of its volume.[24]

In the case of B2C e-sales where consumers and traders are often located far apart, consumers may need even more assurances from the additional key information regarding the vendor and the transaction. These include such things as the address of the vendor, the method of contacting the vendor in case there are

---

[18] *See* Rubin, *supra* note 3, at 35–5.

[19] The information presented in this form is printed in much smaller letters than other information. It may not be conspicuously placed in the middle, but may be placed at the end, at the margin or in the back of the advertising medium. As a result, it will not be as easily seen by consumers as other part of the advertisement.

[20] *See* Coteanu, *supra* note 4, at 126.

[21] *See ibid.*, at 127.

[22] *See* Ramsay, *supra* note 1, at 75.

[23] Robert Matthews identifies some of the potential negative effects of information overload: "(1) consumers make poorer decisions; (2) consumers faced with too many choices may be more likely to respond to price promotions that provide a simple method of justifying their choice; and (3) consumer may avoid making decisions where they have a wealth of alternatives and show grater satisfaction when purchasing from a small choice set." *See* R. Matthews, *The Agonies of Too Much Choice*, Financial Time, January 6, 2006, at 7.

[24] *See ibid.*

problems with the product and so on. Such additional key information should also include means and processes for recovering compensation in the event that the vendor breaches the contract. All these are because of the fact that consumers in e-sales do not have the opportunity to meet and familiarize themselves with the traders and their places of business, an important opportunity that is available to consumers in the traditional market setting but not in e-sales. Unfortunately, according to a study on Web Sweep Analysis conducted by the Office of Fair Trading (hereinafter *OFT*) of the UK 14 % of the websites in the survey did not provide the physical addresses of the e-traders and 34 % did not provide their e-mail addresses. This resulted in injustice to consumers in e-sales.[25]

Furthermore, it is recognized that the information contained in electronic means can be quickly transmitted and can be easily changed at any time.[26] Such special characteristics enable e-traders to easily present false or misleading information that will be difficult to investigate and prosecute because such unfair practices can easily be subsequently removed from the e-market.[27] For example, a trader can place an advertisement selling the product at a low price on the internet, but when the consumer wants to actually make a purchase, the price charged by the vendor might be higher than the internet advertised price. If the consumer wishes to bring a case against the trader over the provision of such false or misleading information, he or she may face the difficulty of providing proof as traders would likely and quickly have changed such e-information. Additionally, the consumer would have a greater burden in obtaining proof in such scenario than he would in a traditional sale where the consumer and trader are both physically present at the sales point and information is conveyed through paper. Again, the study of the OFT of the UK revealed that 44 % of the surveyed websites contained misleading information on prices and ancillary costs of the products by subsequently including various additional charges at the checkout stage, thus creating an unfair environment for e-consumers.[28]

In addition, an e-sale is normally associated with a device's inherent technical constraints such as limited memory and storage capacity or the various capabilities with regard to the display format.[29] Such qualifications can undermine consumers' ability to digest electronic information easily compared to a traditional sale where communications are usually carried out via normal human sensory perception without reliance on technology. Problems arising from e-communication include

---

[25] *See* OFT, *Web Sweep Analysis* (March 2008), *available at* oft.gov.uk/713560/publications/reports/consumer-protection/oft982 (visited March 12, 2013).

[26] *See* T. Tasker and D. Pakcyk, *Cyber- Surfing on the High Seas of Legalese: Law and Technology of Internet Agreement,* 18 Albany Law Journal of Science & Technology 79, 87 (2008).

[27] *See* Coteanu, *supra* note 4, at 23.

[28] *See* OFT, *supra* note 25, at 4.

[29] *See* Tasker and Pakcyk, *supra* note 26, at 87.

information overload,[30] information being frequently provided in fine print at the bottom of a web page or otherwise being hidden from plain view—the so-called *browser wrap*[31] where the graphics, sound, creative letter types and dynamic visual presentation obscures it or negatively affects consumers' ability to digest it.[32] Additionally, delay in notice has been the subject of recent discussion in connection with the timing of compelled disclosure in e-transactions.[33] For instance, the practice of delaying the disclosure of the aggregate price that consumers have to pay for a product or service and only disclosing the existence of additional costs at the checkout stage after the online sale contracts have been entered into, thereby causing great hassle for online consumers to cancel the purchases if they do not agree to these additional costs.[34] This delayed release of material information seems to be disfavored by commercial law and consumer law as their underpinning points tend to prefer effective advanced disclosure of material information and terms.[35] Some e-vendors even take advantage of e-sales by not revealing some key information that may not be appealing to consumers until after the sales contract has been entered into and the payment has been made.[36]

All these examples represent the manipulation of technology and the way of presenting information to undermine consumers' ability to digest such information,

---

[30] As practically unlimited quantity of information can be stored or contained by e-means, in most cases, e-consumers cannot digest all the information dumped onto them by vendors. *See ibid.*, at 83.

[31] Consumers are required to scroll down the page or click a hyperlink to view them. *See* G. E. Maggs, *American Law in a Time of Global Interdependence: U.S. National Reports to the XVITH International Congress of Comparative Law: Section VI Regulating Electronic Commerce*, 50 American Journal of Comparative Law 655, 660 (2002).

[32] *See* Coteanu, *supra* note 4, at 126.

[33] *See e.g.* J. K. Winn (ed.), Consumer Protection in the Age of the Information Economy (2006).

[34] *See* OFT, *supra* note 25, at 18–20. The likely outcome of the survey has been confirmed by the study of the European Commission, which revealed that airline websites often practice deceptive pricing by dividing costs into many items without providing the total price until after the consumers have made the purchase. The total prices are usually greater than the prices the consumers perceived them to be before entering into the sale contracts. *See* P. Masons, *One in Three Airline Sites Break Consumer Laws*, Out-law.com, May 13, 2008, *available at* out-law.com/page-9113 (visited December 30, 2011).

[35] *See* J. Braucher, *New Basics: Twelve Principles for Fair Commerce in Mass-Market Software and Other Digital Products, in* J. K. Winn (ed.), Consumer Protection in the Age of the Information Economy 177, 193 (2006). *See also* R. A. Hillman, *Online Consumer Standard Form Contracting Practices: A Survey and Discussion of Legal Implications, in* J. K. Winn (ed.), Consumer Protection in the Age of the Information Economy 283, 298 (2006).

[36] This is often the case in software licensing contracts where the consumers are often required to enter into contracts and make payment before downloading the products. Only after the download will the consumers be able to see the full contract terms or, if there is a disc, the sealed envelope containing the product must be torn to access the paper containing the full contract terms. This type of products cannot be returned once downloaded or the sealed envelope containing the product is tampered with even if they are not satisfied with the full contract terms after reviewing them. *See* J. Braucher, *Delayed Disclosure in Consumer E-Commerce as an Unfair Deceptive Practice*, 46 Wayne Law Review 1805–67 (2000).

resulting in injustices. The consumer may in fact not thoroughly notice all information that is innumerably presented in those technological means.

While technology provides today's consumers with greater access to a wider range of information and fast and convenient means of communicating with sellers than ever before, the question has arisen as to whether such information and communication is being properly and effectively conveyed to consumers. This issue has been acknowledged by many scholars and policy makers as evidenced by its inclusion as one of the twelve principles in the book called "Stop before You Click" published by the Americans for Fair Electronic Commerce Transactions (hereinafter *AFFECT*) as follows: "Customers are entitled to readily find, review, and understand proposed terms when they shop..."[37]

4.3 Availability of Variety of Goods and Services at Appropriate Prices

Considering the economic interests and needs of consumers, it have been recognized that consumers should have the right to access the best possible choice of quality, the reasonable prices and adequate supplies of goods and services that are necessary for them.[38] These appear to be a common goal of competition and consumer protection law and policy, which aim to make markets work to better ensure the efficient allocation of resources in the economy and to maximize consumer welfare by protecting consumers' economic interests.[39]

---

[37] *See* Braucher, *supra* note 35, at 183.

[38] This principle is affirmed by the United Nations Guidelines for Consumer Protection of 1985, as amended in 1999. One of the main objectives of the Guidelines is set out as: "(g) To encourage the development of market conditions which provide consumers with greater choices at lower prices". *See* United Nations, *United Nations Guidelines for Consumer Protection (as expanded in 1999)* (2003), *available at* unctad.org/en/docs/poditcclpm21.en.pdf (visited March 12, 2013).

[39] The objectives of consumer protection policy and competition policy are a convergence, similarly aiming at increasing consumer welfare. Once the two policies are applied, they have a complimentary effect in the market, reinforcing each other. Although they deploy different approaches, on one hand competition law focuses on an establishment of a well-functioning market, on the other hand, consumers laws seek to protect consumer interest from unfair practice, the end of both objectives are essentially the same, ensuring a fair market and increasing consumers' welfare. *See* M. Kisyombe, *Competition and Consumer Protection Policy: A Tanzanian Perspective, Paper for Presentation and UNCTAD Ad-hoc Expert Group Meeting on the Interface between Competition Policy and Consumer Welfare, Thursday 12 and Friday 13 July 2012* (July 13, 2012), *available at* unctad.org/meetings/en/Presentation/ciclp2012_EMCP_S3_Kisyombe_en.pdf (visited March 12, 2013) and CUTS International, *Competition Policy and Consumer Policy* (2005), *available at* google.com/url?sa=t&rct=j&q=&esrc=s&frm=1&source=web&cd=1&ved=0CDMQFjAA&url=http%3A%2F%2Fwww.cuts-international.org%2Fdocuments%2FCompetition%2520and%2520consumers%2520view.doc&ei=zp9XUaLhCoeCkwXxwoHQDA&usg=AFQjCNG8NJ3Z5rwA6lnWPVdTOtdS6bAurw&sig2=V7e67Z1MhcIsai3DotfRFA (visited March 12, 2013).

Based on the above-stated objective, the point is that ensuring effective markets appears to be the main strategy to facilitate the efficient distribution of resources in response to the needs and desires of consumers and to increase consumer welfare by providing access to a wide range of goods and services.[40] A competitive environment consequently must be promoted to achieve such an optimal market environment where there are a sufficient number of traders offering a variety of products in the market. An adequate number of traders will lead to competitive market conditions where traders must continuously adjust their prices, and the quality of their goods and services, to best meet consumer expectations and demands to be chosen by consumers. Through this process, the market will attain a state of equilibrium between demand and supply. Consumers will have a wide, reasonably priced selection of goods and services that meet their demands, from which they can freely and fairly choose from, thus promoting their welfare by allowing them to make individual choices according to their wishes and needs.

On the contrary, in a market that lacks competition, a single or a few vendors will be able to manipulate and control the price and quality of goods and services, increasing the likelihood of inappropriate or unfair price increases.[41] To put it differently, it brings about a market failure effect that causes the market to lose the state of competition that will eventually lead to the rise of monopolies or oligopolies. Consumers in such a situation would have less alternative sources of supply for the products that truly serve their demands. Such a market state is clearly detrimental to the economic interests of consumers. As Iain Ramsay has stated in a market where there is an absence of competition, or where there is an obstruction to market entry by new traders, market failures may occur that require government intervention to protect the interest of consumers.[42]

Another important concern is not about the availability of choices but rather access to goods and services. In other words, this concern relates to the unequal distribution of goods and services. It has always been the case that the underprivileged have less access to goods and services, be it in terms of variety or quality, than the privileged.[43] For instance, in the rural areas of most of the emerging markets or less developing world, professionals such as physicians and attorneys are very limited in number.[44] To access such services, regular people located in

---

[40] Consumer welfare may mean different things depending on the needs of different groups of people. In the developed world where people are relatively rich with adequate economic resources to afford all that they need, people seem to be concerned about the variety of goods and services offered. Differently, for those having weaker economic status, particularly those in the developing countries, their main concerns relate to accessibility rather than number of choices. *See* CUTS International, *ibid*.

[41] *See* Ramsay, *supra* note 1, at 56.

[42] *See ibid*., at 55–6.

[43] *See* F. William (ed.), Why The Poor Pay More 1–4 (1997).

[44] Thailand, one of the emerging market countries, is for example. The popular medical tourists in Bangkok have caused a shortage of doctors in public hospitals, especially in rural areas. A Thai patient named Malai said that "she has come in from a district in southern province of Phetchaburi

those rural areas, have to make long and difficult journeys, at a cost that they often cannot afford. Once they reach the service providers, the quality of services offered to them are frequently of lesser quality because of their limited financial means.[45] Such a situation is another form of injustice to consumers.

In a study titled *Paying More: Getting Less*, the situation where only certain groups of consumers enjoy a variety of reasonably priced goods and services is called *cherry picking*. The study explained that "[c]ompetition can help prices down, but providers *cherry-pick* the most profitable consumers using increasingly sophisticated marketing techniques. Inadequate market intervention has meant that some socio-economic groups benefit less from price competition than others, consumers who are costly to supply are charged in excess of their ability to pay or denied service altogether. The increasing reduction of socially motivated consumer cross subsidies has compounded this problem".[46]

Despite the existence of market competition with a wide selection of products available, the benefits often only go to certain groups in society. The reason may be that the availability and variety of goods and services is usually limited to areas where the consumers have greater purchasing power and thus greater profits are there to be made.[47] Areas populated with underprivileged consumers are often ignored and these consumers are not able to access certain products. This constitutes one form of market unfairness toward the underprivileged consumers.

In the B2C e-transaction context, although the availability of products offered in the global online markets undoubtedly leads to a greater selection of goods and services (and probably at lower prices) because of the use of speedy, cost-saving and borderless means of communication, it also brings about the same *cherry picking* problem. This is because only certain groups of consumers are able to enjoy the benefits offered by the internet. These consumers are usually of good economic standing and are often residing in developed countries or urban areas. For those less privileged consumers, particularly those in remote areas of the developing world who usually lack electronic means of communication or related technological skills and knowledge, the enjoyment of the same variety of products and services at the same prices provided by the global e-market is out of their reach. They seem to somehow be excluded from the technological market.

because she felt sick and her leg hurt. She also has hepatitis. She left her home at 3 a.m. to travel three hours to the hospital. She will probably have to wait several hours to get two or three minutes with a doctor. Then she will wait some more for test results or a prescription. Malai said she will not get home until 9 p.m. A recorded message asks for patience. It is a constant reminder that Siriraj hospital does not has nearly enough doctors." *See* J. Hamilton, *Medical Tourist Creates Thai Doctor Shortage* (November 29, 2007), *available at* npr.org/templates/story/story.php?storyId=16735157 (visited March 15, 2012). *See also ibid.*

[45] *See* Ramsay, *supra* note 1, at 89.

[46] *See* Child Poverty Action Group, *Paying More and Getting Less: Exclusion from Utilities*, *available at* cpag.org.uk/info/Povertyarticles/Poverty120/utilities.htm (visited December 2, 2011).

[47] *See* William, *supra* note 43, at 1–4.

To promote the adequate supply of goods and services at reasonable prices in both online and offline markets in the long run, greater competitiveness leading to a greater range of product choice and development and the resulting greater accessibility of goods and services are both necessary. Competitiveness, which is more closely related to the concerns of competition law, seems to be more important in developing countries. Development (e.g. of education, knowledge and infrastructure), which is the main concern of consumer protection, is much more focused on the less developed world. Both factors are central to the promotion of the economic interests of consumers as they are complimentary to each other in achieving the common goal of equal access to a variety of goods and services at reasonable prices.

4.4 Freedom of Choice and Ability to Make Rational Decision

The concept of consumers' rights places importance on the notion of individual autonomy in making choices. In other words, the idea is that consumers should have complete freedom in managing their personal affairs and have the same right to make personal choices as other groups in society.[48] Hugh Collins's view is that consumer protection is designed to protect individual dignity and personal autonomy and that it should not ruin individual self-respect.[49]

Based on this, the use of duress or undue influence, or any action that seeks to coerce consumers into entering into a contract or otherwise restrict or undermine their freedom of choice, are unacceptable.[50] This is because consumer transactions rely on contracts as a legal instrument that sets out the rights and obligations, which consumers and traders have consented to. Where there is a meaningful exchange between the parties, the validity of the contract can be ensured in a fair and reasonable manner.[51] An example of an *act of economic duress* would be a situation where a contracting party threatens to terminate the contract if the other party does not agree to additional terms that are more favorable to the terminating party.[52] To illustrate this, consider a case where a customer brings his car for repair to a garage. The mechanic then takes the car apart as part of the repair and suggests to the customer more parts be replaced than are actually necessary. If the customer disagrees, the garage could refuse to carry out the repairs or even to reassemble

---

[48] *See* S. Deutch, *Are Consumer Rights, Human Rights?*, 32 Osgoode Hall Law Journal 537, 551–3, 576 (1994).

[49] *See* Ramsay, *supra* note 1, at 97.

[50] *See ibid.*, at 322–3.

[51] *See* M. Zhang, *Contractual Choice of Law in Contracts of Adhesion and Party Autonomy*, 41 Akron Law Review 123, 125–6 (2008).

[52] *See ibid.*

the car.[53] This type of unfair situation may occur because traders often have more knowledge about goods or services that they specialize in, particularly those concerning complicated processes or technical fields. This tends to limit the ability of consumers to freely choose products or services.

Ready-made or standardized consumer contracts with the features of a *contract of adhesion* are another example of a way where the freedom of consumers to make their own choices can be eroded.[54] Standard consumer contracts pose a challenge because of the pressure they put on the underlying concept of mutual assent.[55] The enforcement of standard form contracts pushes the assumption of mutual assent to such a point that it may not require the true volition or equal bargaining power of the parties or even some basic level of voluntary consensus, understanding or meaningful informed choice.[56]

Unfortunately, a trader in a consumer transaction can communicate to the consumer that it wishes to sell its product under standard terms of contract by implying a *take it or leave it* nature of the transaction where the specific needs of the individual consumer may be ignored. Consumers' consent to standard terms may not always represent their true intent. Sometimes they are pressured into consenting by the fact that even if they do not agree there are no other products available to them because of the common use of similarly phrased contracts by all traders in the same industry.[57] In such cases, the rejection of a trader's standard terms is not an attractive option for consumers and, as a result, they are indirectly coerced into agreeing to terms that may not accurately reflect their true will and intention. As Margaret Jane Radin argues free "[c]onsent requires a knowing understanding of what one is doing in context in which it is actually possible for one to do otherwise, and an affirmative action in doing something, rather than a merely passive acquiescence in accepting something".[58]

Software products that offer only one authorized dealer or servicer provide a real life example of a transaction that involves a lack of true consumer consent. If the consumer finds the terms of the standard contract unsatisfactory or unfair, they would have no choice but to agree to them as there would be no other traders who could offer the consumer better terms.[59] This lack of alternatives for consumers has raised awareness regarding the fairness of standard term contracts because they can sometimes impose a coercive contracting process which restricts consumers from freely exercising their ability to choose or to agree to contract terms.[60]

---

[53] *See ibid.*

[54] *See ibid.*, at 98.

[55] *See* S. E. Friedman, *Giving Unconscionability More Muscle: Attorney's Fees as a Remedy for Contractual Overreaching*, 44 Georgia Law Review 317, 320 (2010).

[56] *See ibid.*, at 321.

[57] *See* Hillman, *supra* note 35, at 283–309.

[58] *See* M. J. Radin, *Human, Computers, and Binding Commitment*, 75 Indiana Law Journal 1125–62 (1999). The author has an opinion that there is a lack of free consent in the case of end user license agreements (EULAs).

[59] *See* Braucher, *supra* note 35, at 184–5.

[60] *See ibid.*

In addition, in some situations where there is complete freedom of choice, consumers may themselves make irrational choices or mistakes.[61] Behavioral research indicates that many basic assumptions in standard economic models relating to cognitive processes are inconsistent with how people actually make decisions and the rational choice model has been challenged in light of several behavioral biases.[62] For instance, experiments have revealed that many consumers are over-optimistic.[63] They often enter into suboptimal contracts such as fitness center membership contracts because they overestimate the number of times they will use the service in the future.[64] Also, consumers seem to rely on a variety of heuristics in their purchasing decisions. It has been suggested that many individuals believe that the unit price of products packed in large quantity is cheaper than those in smaller packages and that bigger malls offers better prices than smaller ones.[65] Traders often draw on these individual cognitive biases when designing their marketing and selling strategies. Thus, the insights of behavioral biases that are frequently commented on in the behavioral economic literature have consequently become influential issues in designing consumer protection law and policy.[66] Today, it is widely recognized that the importance of biases can have a negative influence and distort consumers' decision-making processes, leading to suboptimal decisions and potential unfairness for consumers, especially when practiced by rogue traders. Therefore, protecting the consumers' ability to make rational decisions and avoiding behavioral biases have become important concerns in the area of consumer welfare and justice.[67]

---

[61] *See e.g.* J. Hanson and D. Kysar, *Taking Behavioralism Seriously: Some Evidence of Market Manipulation*, 112 Harvard Law Review 1420, 1424–5 (1999).

[62] *See* Luth, *supra* note 1, at 47 and Ramsay, *supra* note 1, at 71.

[63] *See* Luth, *ibid.*, at 51 and Ramsay, *ibid*, at 73.

[64] *See* Ramsay, *ibid.*, at 75.

[65] *See ibid.*

[66] *See* Luth, *supra* note 1, at 47 and Ramsay, *supra* note 1, at 71–2.

[67] The European Union Unfair Commercial Practices Directive is an example of a legislative designed to response to the behavioural economic problem. Article 5 of the Directive provides that:

> Prohibition of unfair commercial practices
> 1. Unfair commercial practices shall be prohibited
> 2. A commercial practice shall be unfair if:
> ...(b) it materially distorts or is likely to materially distort the economic behaviour with regard to the product of the average consumer whom it reaches or to whom it is addressed, or of the average member of the group when a commercial practice is directed to a particular group of consumers. 3. Commercial practice which are likely to materially distort the economic behaviour only of a clearly identifiable group of consumers who are particularly vulnerable to the practice or the underlying product because of their mental or physical infirmity, age or credulity in a way which the trader could reasonably be expected to foresee, shall be assessed from the perspective of the average member of that group. This is without prejudice to the common and legitimate advertising practice of making exaggerated statements or statements which are not meant to be taken literally. *See* Directive 2005/29/EC on Unfair Commercial Practices.

In e-sales, technology seems to have increased the likelihood of diminishing or destroying consumers' freedom of choice and their ability to make rational decisions. This is because

e-communication creates an environment where it is easier to express intentions by simply clicking the computer's mouse and, as such, the consumer's true intentions may not be as accurately expressed as they would be through traditional forms of communication with human interaction. Electronic communication utilizes computer programs to transmit human's instructions without the actual human's verification or review.[68] This, coupled with the fact that the information is transmitted in seconds, makes it easier for contracts to be formed through computer programs that do not accurately reflect the intention of one of the parties.[69]

The *click it or leave it* characteristic of e-commerce may result in consumers accepting the terms of an e-transaction by mistakenly clicking the "accept" button without actually intending to accept all of the terms of the contract. Phrased differently, there are great risks of the *input error* in online activities because of the use of a mode of communication that fails to give an opportunity for a consumer to confirm his or her e-input.[70] Consequently, consumers may subject themselves to enforceable obligations under the terms of the contract and information on the website without actually assenting to them. In such cases, if the price of the product is not a high price, the consumers will simply ignore this shortcoming and proceed with the transaction rather than cancelling or correcting the transmission to avoid the hassle and the time required to make the cancellation or correction because of the distance between consumers and trader. As a result, the consumers will remain subject to contractual obligations that are not consistent with their true intentions.

Although the problems of consumers' behavioral biases may be resolved with substantive measures by passing laws barring vendors' actions that can unfairly influence consumers' decisions as the above EU law, substantive measures alone may not be fully sufficient as it is difficult to comprehensively identify all forms of vendors' actions that may have potential unfair effects on consumers' choices. Other measures such as "nudging" consumers to make the optimal choices in their best interests, through the use "heuristic devices" that help minimizing consumers' making decisions based on their biases, are also essential. Unlike substantive laws which set out rights and obligations in a mandatory nature, these "heuristic devices" work by having third parties persuade or facilitate consumers to make the best decisions for themselves, thereby resulting in justice for consumers. Nonetheless, consumers are free not to follow such persuasions. As a result, it can be seen that making consumers choose in their best interests may not be accomplished by substantive mechanisms alone. It must also be supported by procedural conditions with the third parties' help or intervention. *See* Luth, *ibid.*, Chapter 3.

[68] For the discussion of electronic agent, *see* Coteanu, *supra* note 4, Chapter 6.

[69] *See ibid.*, at 74.

[70] *See also* the Organization for Economic Cooperation and Development (OECD), *OECD Policy Guidance for Address Emerging Consumers Protection and Employment Issues in Mobile Commerce* (2008), *available at* oecd.org/sti/consumer/40879177.pdf (visited March 12, 2012).

This leads to the erosion of their freedom in selecting goods or services and the terms of contracts in e-sales.

Also, the advancement of technology allows traders to easily store the personal information of consumers almost without limit and they may later use such information for future commercial and marketing strategies to maximize their business profits. A study by Gllenn Ellison and Sara Fisher Ellison suggests that e-traders collect consumer information to analyze consumers' behavior to categorize consumers into groups and help formulate effective marketing strategies by offering prepared terms and conditions that are likely to convince the targeted consumers to purchase their products or services.[71] Sometimes, traders will apply such information to identify and formulate measures to create behavioral biases for each group or individual consumers in the interest of selling their products and maximizing their profits without regard to whether such practice is unfair to consumers.[72] The fact that the technology enables e-traders to procure the personal information of consumers more easily than in the traditional sales setting and from such information, they can easily develop sales tactics and strategies that take advantage of the economic behavior of consumers to maximize the vendors' own gain, contributes to the unfairness of consumers.

4.5 Fair Terms and Conditions

One of the characteristics of a ready-made or standardized consumer contract is that the trader is usually the only party who drafts the contract. This feature of a *contract of adhesion* may create an unfair environment for consumers. Many studies have similarly confirmed that traders as sole contractual drafters often draft contracts in their best interests, without considering the adverse effects of contract terms on consumers.[73] However, even though the standard term of a contract may be unfair to consumers, it brings the irresistible economic benefits to the market by reducing the transaction costs of mass consumer transactions.[74] Contemporary discussions on this subject matter are no longer focused on the refusal of standardized contracts per se, but are directed at the appropriate contents of the ready-made terms to be offered to consumers as mentioned earlier.[75] The reason is that standardized

[71] *See* G. Ellison and S. F. Ellison, *Search, Obfuscation, and Price Elasticities on the Internet*, 77 Econometrica 427–52 (2009), *available at* econ2.jhu.edu/People/Harrington/2611/ee_09.pdf (visited March 12, 2012). *See also* Ramsay, *supra* note 1, at 139.

[72] *See ibid.*

[73] An example is James Maxeiner's study. There is an interview of a legal consultant to the 500 American enterprises. He confessed that the priority objective in drafting contracts is to protect and maximise the interests of his clients (the enterprises), not to provide fairness to consumers. *See* J. R. Maxeiner, *Standard-Terms Contracting in the Global Electronic Age: European Alternatives*, 28 Yale Journal of International Law 109, 109–82 (2003).

[74] *See* Chap. 2.

[75] *See ibid.*

consumer contracts may lead to injustice to consumers because they are usually prepared by one contractual party and thus were made without any process of negotiation between the parties. Thus, monitoring unfair terms in standardized consumer contracts is another important component as, in the interest of justice, consumers should not be bound by terms of contracts that are unfair to them as they have did not have the opportunity to negotiate such unfair terms. Thus, there is a need for more policing on the possible unfairness of non-negotiated transactions. The theory of assent to standard contracts—the so-called *blanket assent* introduced by Karl Llewellyn—seems to be the most influential principle of assent to standard forms.[76] This states that when it comes to standard terms, specific assent is not required except for terms that are unlikely to have been accepted if there had been a negotiated process.[77] In other words, this principle states that there is blanket assent to all reasonable terms in standard contract in mass market transaction, but not to terms that are unfair or unreasonable.

Presently, there are two important measures to prevent consumers from being victims of unfair standard terms. The first is the prevention at the procedural stage, and the second is the prevention in dealing with substantive or content issues. Prevention at the procedural stage can be enacted by shaping the processes that lead to the formation or conclusion of contracts.[78] This may involve the manipulation of the supply of appropriate information thereby allowing consumers to protect themselves by avoiding entering into those consumer contracts that contain onerous terms.[79] The second is the creation of mandatory substantive rules that protect consumers by not allowing the contents of unfair terms to be enforceable in consumer contracts. This can take the form of the banning of specific onerous terms by legal provisions.[80] Another form of substantive rule relies on court interpretation and discretion in determining cases relating to unfair contract terms. Virtually all systems of law have developed legal doctrines that can be used by courts to test unfair contract terms. Despite different names for these tests, such as the *fairness test*, *reasonable test* and *unconscionable test*, they are

---

[76] *See* Braucher, *supra* note 35, at 191.

[77] *See* K. Llewellyn, The Common Law Tradition: Deciding Appeals 370 (1960).

[78] There is an argument that the compulsory term mechanism in consumer contracts – the so-called "paternalism" – which provides necessary information and states designed terms may direct a decision that is in the best interest of consumers and protects them from unfair standard term contracts. *See* D. Kennedy, *Distributive and Paternalist Motives in Contract and Tort Law, with Special Reference to Compulsory Terms and Unequal Bargaining Power*, 41 Maryland Review 563, 631 (1982).

[79] *See ibid.*

[80] In many legal systems, there are the black and grey listed provisions. The black list will legally identify onerous terms as unfair terms which will not be enforceable. The grey list will identify onerous contract provisions that are assumed unfair. The Netherlands' law of Unfair Contract Terms, for example, includes grey and black lists. Also, the EU Unfair Contract Terms Directive specifies a grey list. However, the US legal system does not implement this kind of coloured list, but it relies on a court discretion approach based on the legal substantive test.

substantially similar.[81] All these attempts at banning unfair contract terms indicate that consumers should not be bound by them, thereby ensuring basic justice for them.

The problem of unfair terms is also one of the foremost problems in B2C e-sales. Due to its cross-broader dimension, in practice business operators usually prescribe in their standard forms of contract that their contracts are governed by the law and are under the jurisdiction of the country of their place of business in the event of disputes. They may also prescribe methods of dispute resolution other than formal judicial proceedings to circumvent the application of foreign laws, or submission to the foreign jurisdiction of the consumer's country.[82] These kinds of terms may constitute difficult situations for consumers as they impose unfair burdens on consumers seeking to take legal actions and redress in the unfamiliar judicial system of the business operator's country. It may even force the consumers to agree to waive their rights to litigate against the business operators but provide for dispute resolution methods that may be more costly and disadvantageous to consumers. The question of whether or not the choice of law and forum clause and the alternative dispute resolution clause in standard commercial contract term in e-sales are unfair to consumers remains the topic of continuous discussions and is subject to differing views.[83]

[81] The *fairness test* appears in the EU Unfair Contract Terms Directive. According to Article 3, the contractual term "shall be regarded as unfair if, contrary to the requirement of good faith, it causes a significant imbalance in the parties' rights and obligations arising under the contract, to the detriment of the consumer." In Article 4, reads that "the unfairness of a contractual term shall be assessed, taking into account the nature of the goods or services for which the contract was concluded and by referring, at the time of conclusion of the contract, to all the circumstances attending the conclusion of the contract and to all the other terms of the contract or of another contract on which it is dependent." European Commission, *Unfair Contract Terms* (July 4, 2007), *available at* europa.eu/consumers/cons_int/safe_shop/unf_cont_terms/index_en.htm (visited June 28, 2012). Differently, the US employs a concept called *the unconscionability test* whereas the Unfair Contract Terms Act 1997 of US clearly contains "the reasonable test". This unfair term test doctrines may be differently implemented in details in different jurisdictions, but their share the fundamental principles and objectives. For a discussion on the fairness test in European civil law and the unconscionability concept of the US, *see* R. A. Hillman and J. J. Rachlinski, *Standard-Form Contracting in the Electronic Age*, 77 New York University Law Review 429, 456–8 (2002).

[82] *See* A. J. Schmitz, *Embracing Unconscionability's Safety Net Function*, 58 Alabama Law Review 73, 83 (2006).

[83] According to the EU legislation, the choices of law and forum clause and the alternative dispute resolution clause must be executed as an available option to consumers after the dispute arises rather than in adhesive contracts. On the other hand, in the United States, the choice of law and forum clause and the alternative dispute resolution clause are often considered subject to the parties' freedom to contract any way they like. The consideration of whether they constitute unenforceable unfair contract terms must be made on a case by case basis at the discretion of the court. *See* S. McGill, *Consumer Arbitration Clause Enforcement: A Balanced Legislative Response*, 47 American Business Law Journal 361, 365 (2010). For detailed discussion on this the choice of forum, *see infra* Chap. 7.

4.6 Right of Withdrawal

Even after the entry into a contract or after a trader has partially performed their contractual obligations, in some circumstances consumers should have the opportunity to review their decisions and, if they wish, change their minds within a brief specific period. Door to door sales where sale persons will visit the homes of consumers in an attempt to complete a sale, is one example of a situation where this would be appropriate. Under the pressure of the uninvited home visit that is central to the door-to-door sales strategy, consumers will make unnecessary purchases of products that they do not really want, often at a price higher than they would have paid at a store.[84] Therefore, this kind of sales transaction appears to put unfair pressure on consumers. In such circumstances the right of withdrawal, which is a consumer's right to reconsider the decision during a relatively short "cooling off", should be available.

It has been said that the "right of withdrawal", often known as the "cooling off period", is a new field in private law.[85] This may be because one important pillar of traditional contract law is the principle of *pacta sunt servanda* which provides that once a contract has been entered into, the contracting parties must be bound by all the terms and perform the obligations to which they have agreed.[86] The right of withdrawal seems to deviate from that traditional principle of contract law by allowing them to escape from contractual terms that have already been agreed to. However, upon looking deeper, one finds that the principle of *pacta sunt*

[84] *See also* Ramsay, *supra* note 1, at 10, 70, 331. The UK, the first country to introduce "the cooling off period" has been addressing the problem of unfair pressure in door to door sales. As of today, the consumer's right of withdrawal have been accepted and incorporated in the laws of many countries including the US's cooling off period rule issued by the Federal Fair Trade Commission. Under the Federal Trade Commission's (FTC)'s Cooling-Off Rule, consumer also have a three day period to cancel purchases of $25 or more if you buy an item in your home or at a location that is not the seller's permanent place of business. For detailed discussion on the US's cooling off period rule, *see* FreeAdvice®, *Cooling-off Rule* (May, 1996), *available at* law.freeadvice.com/resources/gov_material/ftc_cooling_off_rule_5_96.htm (visited December 4, 2011). For Japanese consumers, they have the opportunity to *cool down* and delay contracting for 8 days from the day contract documents are received in door-to-door sales under Article 9 of the Specific Commercial Transaction Law. *See* International Policy Division General Affair Department FUKUI Prefectural Government, *Cooling-off System* (2004), *available at* info.pref.fukui.jp/kokusai/tagengo/html_e/konnatoki/9horitu/g_cool/1.html (visited December 4, 2011). Similarly, the laws at the supranational level of the EU contain the provisions about the right of withdrawal. Some examples are the Doorstep Selling Directive, Council Directive 85/577/EEC of December 20, 1985 to protect the consumer in respect of contracts negotiated away from business premises, which aims to protect consumer regarding contracts concluded away from trading's expects and the Distance Selling Directive, Directive 97/7/EC of the European Parliament and of the Council of May 20, 1997 on the protection of consumers in respect of distance contracts, which aims to protect consumer in respect of distance sales.

[85] *See* M. Loos, *Rights of Withdrawal*, *in* G. Howells and R. Schulze (eds.), Modernizing and Harmonizing Consumer Contract Law 237, 239 (2009).

[86] *See ibid.*, at 241.

servanda is based on the premise that the contracting parties entered into the contract voluntarily, with complete free will. In consumer markets, such a premise does not always hold true because the consumer often enters into a contract under pressure or misunderstanding, with false, incomplete information, or under duress. Such consumer contracts are made in the absence of the consumer's true consent. Therefore, the consumers' right of withdrawal in fact does not contradict to the principle of *pacta sunt servanda*. Rather, it is something that should help consumers escape the burden of unfair conditions.

At this point, it may be said that, at least in some circumstances, the consumer should be entitled to the right of withdrawal as a means of redressing certain injustices they may suffer. Such a right is not in conflict with any law or legal principle. As Claus Welhelm Canaris has offered as an argument in support: "[t]he right of withdrawal may be seen as just another example of the fact that the formal and material notions of freedom of contract need not always coincide, as already follows form more familiar instruments as fundamental mistake, deceit and fraud."[87]

In the e-market, one main difficulty for consumers in exercising their right of withdrawal is the expense of doing so.[88] As the financial cost of cancelling the purchase and returning the products usually falls on the consumer, this has become an obvious obstacle for them in exercising such rights. This is because the relevant processes can be extremely burdensome which leads to the expenses that can be quite high, especially when the products are to be returned to a trader in a different country, which may not be worth doing in light of the value of the products.[89]

Another problem is when consumers try to exercise their rights of withdrawal in B2C e-sales and find that the traders do not allow them to do so or do not give a full refund for the returned products. The Web Sweep Analysis conducted by the OFT of the UK indicates that 15 % of the surveyed websites do not allow purchase cancellation (not giving consumers information on their right to cancel) and 31 % do not offer a full refund.[90] In another online shopping survey, in more than 30 % of the surveyed cases traders failed to provide refund and of the 70 % of those traders who provided a refund, about half of them failed to refund the delivery charge.[91] This may be because the traders not wishing to bear the risk of consumers located far away cancelling the purchase and returning the products, without first being able to inspect the products' condition before deciding whether to accept the return of

[87] *See ibid.*

[88] *See* C. Scott, *Regulatory Innovation and the Online Consumer*, 26 Law and Policy 476, 470–80 (2004). *See also* Hillman, *supra* note 35, at 299.

[89] *See* Scott, *ibid.*

[90] *See* OFT, *supra* note 25, at 5.

[91] The European Consumer Centre Network (ECC-Net), *Realities of the European Online Marketplace, A Cross-Border E-Commerce Project* 2003 (2003), *available at* ec.europa.eu/consumers/ecc/docs/european_online_marketplace2003_en.pdf (visited March 12, 2012).

the products.[92] Therefore, they are not willing to allow the return of the products as commonly practiced in traditional sales that are conducted physically between vendors and consumers. As a result, it can be stated that the "right of withdrawal" or "cooling off period" in e-sales is subject to obstacles that prevent it from becoming as fully effective as it is in traditional sales transactions.

4.7 Performance of Obligations

As a contractual party of sales transactions, consumers have to perform their obligations as buyers by paying the prices of products or services. On the supply side, sellers who received such payment have a duty to deliver the products or services in accordance with the quality and characteristics described, whether by advertisements or through the word of sales people.[93] If, after the purchase, the quality and characteristics of the goods or services meet the consumer's fair expectation as they had been informed, the traders will be deemed to have performed their obligations to consumers as contractually agreed. If that is not the case (for example, in the case of non-delivery or the delivery of goods or services that are different from their descriptions), the consumer's fair expectation regarding the goods or services is not met. Consumers then suffer unfair economic and financial harm as they have already performed their contractual obligations as a buyer by paying the prices for the products or services.[94]

A defective product is one example of a trader's failure to meet their obligations. In a case study titled *Buying Problems: Consumers, Unsatisfactory Goods and the Law* by the National Consumer Council of the UK,[95] it was discovered that over 25 % of the consumers in the study experienced problems in their first purchases, of whom 20 % complained that their products did not work. In this regard, a product warranty that legally imposes the obligation on trader to repair or replace defective products for consumers at no charge, was designed to be a measure to ensure the full performance of traders' obligations, particularly with respect to the quality and characteristics of the products.[96] This kind of mechanism apparently emphasizes

[92] *See also* J. Hill, Cross-Border Consumer Contracts 221–2 (2008).

[93] The supply of information concerning the quality and characteristics of goods and services by traders through advertisements or sales people is an important factor in assisting consumers in making purchasing decisions.

[94] *See* Ramsay, *supra* note 1, at 604.

[95] *See* UK National Consumer Council, *Buying Problem: Consumers, Unsatisfactory and the Law* 18–20, 22, 25 (1984).

[96] Today, product warranties are widely used in consumer markets. Such warranties will help to reduce the expenses from disagreements between consumers and traders, avoiding the possibility of having a dispute. Many jurisdictions have placed product warranties as legal obligations, for instance, Directive 99/44 of the European Parliament and of the Council of 25 May 1999 on certain aspect of the sale of consumer goods and associated guarantees, the Australian Consumer Law of

and demonstrates the importance of the full performance of traders' obligations to meet consumers' fair expectations in providing a fair market environment for consumers.[97]

In e-sales, consumers do not have an opportunity to see and inspect the products because traders are often located far away. Sometimes the properties and qualities of the products received by the consumers are not consistent with those reasonably to be expected based on the traders' electronic description or advertisements.[98] Despite potential solutions provided by product warranties and the possible return of the products (the right of withdrawal), consumers still have to suffer the hassle and expense of claiming the warranties or returning the products if the e-trader is living in a different country.[99] This is often the case in cross border B2C e-transactions. Therefore, the warranty measures and the cooling off period may not be so effective in protecting consumers in the online market.

In the worst situation, consumers in B2C e-transactions may not receive the delivery of the products or services that they ordered at all. In a survey conducted by the European Consumer Center's Network, 30 % of the consumers who electronically ordered products did not receive the products that they ordered.[100] Consumers who did not receive the products may decide not to take any action against the vendors as the values of the products may not be worth the hassle and cost of taking action against traders located overseas. All of these contribute to the risk of not receiving the repayment of obligations, creating unfairness to e-sale consumers who must face the greater possibility of unfairness in exchange for the convenience and selection of products in the transnational e-market.

2011 and the Consumer Guarantee Act 1993 of New Zealand. *See* The EU Sale of Goods and Associated Guarantees Directive, *available at* eur-lex.europa.eu/LexUriServ/LexUriServ.do?uri=CELEX:31999L0044:EN:NOT (visited March 12, 2012), the Australian Consumer Law of 2011, *available at* mst.com.au/library_news.php?New-consumer-guarantees-under-the-Australian-Consumer-Law-346 (visited March 12, 2012) and the Consumer Guarantee Act 1993 of New Zealand, *available at* legislation.govt.nz/act/public/1993/0091/latest/DLM311053.html (visited March 12, 2012).

[97] An express legal prescription of product quality standards is another measure to ensure that consumers' fair expectations on product quality are fulfilled. For example, Articles 14 and 15 of the Sale of Goods Act 1979 of the UK prescribe criteria for "satisfactory quality" by requiring that a product must meet the standards that can be expected by a reasonable person. *See* The Sale of Goods Act 1979 of the UK, *available at* http://www.legislation.gov.uk/ukpga/1979/54 (visited December 2, 2011). For discussion of legal consequence of the Sale of Goods Act 1979 of the UK, *see* Ramsay, *supra* note 1, at 620–1.

[98] *See* Scott, *supra* note 88.

[99] *See ibid.*

[100] *See* ECC-Net, *The European Online Marketplace: Consumer Complaints 2004* (2004), *available at* ec.europa.eu/consumers/ecc/docs/european_online_marketplace2004_en.pdf (visited March 12, 2013).

4.8 Consumers' Privacy

In various commercial transactions, traders may collect the information of consumers for reference in future transactions with the same consumers. Such information may include consumers' identities, activities, personal interests, telephone numbers and e-mail addresses, as well as payment related data such as credit card numbers, identification card numbers, etc. If consumers are recognized and their consent is given, such collected personal information would normally be for use by a specific trader and not shared with others. Unfortunately, in many cases consumers are not aware or have not consented to such data collection. They are not always informed of the way their personal information is kept and cannot be sure that it will not be passed on to other traders.[101] Many consumers are now coping with unsolicited sales calls and e-mails as their personal information has been passed to numerous traders. Without notice and consent, consumers would have no means of preventing or stopping such violation of their privacy, putting them in an unfair situation.[102]

---

[101] The US Feral Trade Commission found that in 1997, 85 per cent of internet business operators collected consumers' information. Only a small number of them informed those consumers in respect of their information protection practices. *See* J. Graubert and J. Coleman, *The Impact of Technological Change in the Canada/US Context: Consumer Protection and Antitrust Enforcement at the Speed of Light: The FTC Meets the Internet*, 12 Canada-United States Law Journal 275, 286–7 (1999).

[102] The US and the EU are the two examples of jurisdictions that have awaken to the issue of consumers' privacy protection. They have obviously adopted the Organization for Economic Cooperation and Development's (OECD) Recommendations Governing the Protection of Privacy and Transborder Flows of Personal Data. The EU has announced the use of the Directive on Data Protection focusing on the protection of individual's right to privacy in his or her personal information. It aims to protect consumers' privacy right and promote the free flow of information among Member States by harmonizing privacy laws. *See* Directive on Data Protection, which became effective on October 25, 1998. Differently, the US has put emphasis on vendors' self-regulation in the area of consumers' personal data protection. The US Federal Government has largely encouraged the private sector to bear the development of a private policy. At the same time, it has also enacted a number of pieces of legislation to protect consumers' personal data. The first federal privacy law is the Fair Credit Reporting Act (the first federal privacy law) which was followed by a wide variety of laws that enable consumers to access their personal information kept by vendors. With a wide range of laws concerning consumers' privacy, the US Federal Trade Commission, as the consumer protection agency, may have jurisdiction over industries not already regulated by laws, such as: Fair Credit Reporting Act, Bank Secrecy Act, Children's Online Privacy Act, Freedom Of Information Act and Patriot Act. Apart from these two jurisdictions, Canada has established guidelines to encourage the protection of consumers' rights and fair practices. These guidelines incorporate recommendations on privacy and security of payment and personal information, among which are limiting the collection, the use, disclosure and retention, individual access, and so on. Such activities of many countries highlighted above indicate the importance and necessity of the protection of consumers' privacy, recognized as one form of justice that consumers should be entitled to in today's market. For detailed discussion of the laws of US and Canada, *see* T. T. Reith III, *Consumer Confidence: The Key to Successful E-Commerce in the Global Marketplace*, 24 Suffolk Transnational Law Review 467–86 (2001)

In e-sale transactions, consumers are often required to provide personal information to the traders through e-means before completing a transaction. With the advancement in the technology of the online market, a massive volume of information can be stored and easily transmitted to others via e-networks. This makes it even more difficult for e-consumers to control their personal information that has been electronically put into the e-market because it is a fact that the majority of individual consumers do not have sufficient technical knowledge to do so. In many cases, e-traders often store such information for their business uses and may sell it to other traders that are not their competitors. This leads to the problem of widespread unsolicited e-mail advertisements that violate the privacy of many e-mail users in today's e- market.[103]

In addition, traders can also utilize consumers' personal information to analyze consumer behavior, interests and personal preferences. From such analysis, traders may selectively target consumers who are willing to pay higher price for certain products than others. This is one way for traders to gain greater profits from consumers' private information. Such practices can cause consumers to suffer by taking unfair advantage of their personal information without their awareness. Due to the complexity of the technology involved, ordinary consumers have no means of controlling or preventing nonconsensual collection and transmission of their private information. Therefore, the natures of e-transactions are contributing to the easy violation of consumers' personal rights and privacy.

4.9 Consumers' Safety

After the consumers have agreed to make a purchase, the purchased product must, in addition to meeting the consumers' fair expectation as discussed earlier, not cause harm to the consumers' health and well-being.[104] The complex manufacturing process of today's products bars consumers from knowing and selecting hazard-free products. For instance, pharmaceutical products, electrical products and vehicles often possess certain dangers that are not completely known to consumers. Consumers should not solely bear the risk of harms from hazardous products that do not arise from the consumer's own fault.[105] Supply of adequate product information

---

and Working Group on Electronic Commerce and Consumers, *Principles of Consumer Protection for Electronic Commerce, A Canadian Framework* (1999).

[103] Spam or unsolicited e-mails are a great annoyance and violations of the privacy of all e-mail users. OECD has issued guidelines to remedy the problem of unsolicited e-mails or spam including legal prohibition and sanctions against transmitters of spam e-mails, raising awareness of the problem among vendors and education. *See* OECD, *OECD Recommendation on Cross Border Cooperation in the Enforcement of Laws against Spam* (2006). *See also* Ramsay, *supra* note 1, at 149.

[104] *See* Ramsay, *ibid.*, at 691–2.

[105] *See ibid.*, at 691.

and warning to consumers is a basic economic solution to mitigate the problem of product safety.[106]

However, there is an argument that information remedies alone may not be an adequate solution for consumers' safety problems because of two important reasons. Firstly, one study indicates that the understanding of product hazards is largely based on consumer's personal experience.[107] Therefore, the assessment of product hazards cannot be made solely through the study of product information.[108] Secondly, product errors can cause large-scale damages that are too critical to depend only on the disclosure of information and provision of warning, an approach that is driven largely by an economic cost and benefit analysis.[109] The Chinese milk scandal in 2008 is an example.[110] This involved infant formula mixed with another ingredient with melamine and affected an estimated three hundred thousand victims.[111] Such events create tremendous pressure on the relevant governments to take immediate remedial action, such as suspension of the sale of the hazardous product, the imposition of strict controls and harsh penalties such as punitive fines on manufacturers and traders, rather than relying on soft measures such as providing information to consumers which are less costly but require a longer time to accomplish.[112] As Iain Ramsay has stated "[t]here is the further objection to the use of cost-benefit analysis in making decisions about consumer safety that certain values ought not to be subject to such an analysis. This objection reflects the ethical argument that there is a special value to life-that there is a 'right' to safety which can only be reconciled with other values through moral judgment."[113]

Based on the above argument, measures relating to product safety need to go beyond those suggested by an economic assessment of relative costs and benefits. Rules that are mandatory in nature or impose an additional financial burden on manufacturers or traders may be necessary. Such measures can include controls on the manufacturing process of the product[114] or imposing the burden on manufacturers or traders to achieve a "safe product" that meets society's standards. This will help to ensure consumers' safety that is one aspect of the justice that they should be entitled to.[115]

---

[106] *See ibid.*

[107] *See ibid.*

[108] *See ibid.*, at 691.

[109] *See ibid.*, at 698.

[110] In China, there was a food safety incident in 2008 involving nutritional contamination in milk. *See* BBC New Asia-Pacific, *China Diary Product Found Tainted with Melamine*, BBC New, July 9, 2010, *available at* bbc.co.uk/news/10565838 (visited June 12, 2012).

[111] *See ibid.*

[112] *See* L. Chiu, *Summary of China's Tainted Milk Scandal* (2008), *available at* chineseculture.about.com/od/2008milkscandal/a/Milksummary.htm (visited March 12, 2013).

[113] *See* Ramsay, *supra* note 1, at 698.

[114] *See ibid.*, at 703–4.

[115] *See ibid.*, at 698. The EU passed Directive 2001/95/EU of the European Parliament and of the Council on General Product is an example. It provides that: "Section 2...(b) "safe product" shall

The new globalization of the e-market renders it more difficult to regulate and ensure consumer safety because of the variation in product safety standards, regulations, and controls in different countries.[116] Products purchased through transnational e-sales will be delivered to consumers in many countries making it virtually impossible for the government of a consumer's country to regulate the safety of the products that may not meet the required safety standards. To ensure an appropriate level of product safety for e-sale consumers, it has been claimed that internationally accepted product safety standards may need to be established and enforced.[117] As a result, the governments, manufacturers, and traders will realize and give priority to product safety issues to ensure product safety to consumers in e-sales.

4.10 Reasonable Cost of Transaction

Average consumers not only bear the costs of the products they purchase, they also bear "transaction costs" that may not merely be in the form of monetary expenses but also include various other forms of consumer efforts and time spent in the completion of transactions. Broadly, typical transaction costs consist of information and search costs, negotiation costs, contracting costs, and monitoring and enforcement costs.[118] Excessive transaction costs will lead to injustice for consumers, as these bring about an inefficient allocation of consumer resources.[119]

---

mean any product which, under normal or reasonably foreseeable conditions of use including duration and, where applicable, putting into service, installation and maintenance requirements, does not present any risk or only the minimum risks compatible with the product's use, considered to be acceptable and consistent with a high level of protection for the safety and health of persons, taking into account the following points in particular: (i) the characteristics of the product, including its composition, packaging, instructions for assembly and, where applicable, for installation and maintenance; (ii) the effect on other products, where it is reasonably foreseeable that it will be used with other products; (iii) the presentation of the product, the labeling, any warnings and instructions for its use and disposal and any other indication or information regarding the product;(iv) the categories of consumers at risk when using the product, in particular children and the elderly. The feasibility of obtaining higher levels of safety or the availability of other products presenting a lesser degree of risk shall not constitute grounds for considering a product to be "dangerous". This law clearly acknowledged and confirmed consumers' right to hazardous free products in the market. *See* Directive 2001/95/EC of the European Parliament and of the Council of 3 December 2001 on General Product Safety, *available at* eur-lex.europa.eu/LexUriServ/LexUriServ.do?uri=CELEX:32001L0095:EN:NOT (visited March, 12 2012).

[116] *See also* A. F. Perez, *Consumer Protection in the America: A Second Wave of America Revolutions?*, 5 University of St. Thomas Law Journal 698, 711–3 (2008).

[117] *See* Consumers International, *Decision Marketing in the Global Market: Trader, Standards and the Consumer* 5, 45–8 (2005).

[118] There are three important costs in operating market transactions (transaction costs). They roughly include: 1. Information search costs 2. Bargaining and decision costs and 3. Monitoring and enforcement costs. *See* I. Ramsay, Rationales for Intervention in the Consumer Marketplace 15–24 (1984). *See also* Luth, *supra* note 1, at 19, 27- 8.

[119] *See also* Luth, *supra* note 1, at 27–8.

It is a fact that not all consumers can enjoy a variety of goods or services offered, as some of them may not be able to afford the additional transaction costs involved in procuring them. For instance, low-income consumers may lack sufficient spending power to pay for the costs of travelling in search of good quality products at lower prices. These consumers, who are unable to afford transaction costs, frequently have to settle for products of lower quality, at higher prices, offered near their homes.[120]

Controlling excessive transaction costs are an important issue in consumer policy making, which helps consumers to broaden their access to goods and services, thus achieving justice in the market. With reasonable transaction costs, the affordability of products will not be inflated by excessive transaction costs, allowing consumers to choose from a wider variety of good quality products at lower prices. One of the most commonly used forms of market intervention, in many jurisdictions, is the use of legislatively stipulated default rules in consumer contracts.[121] This helps to minimize the expense of the contractual drafting process and avoids the necessity of spending time negotiation with each individual consumer.[122] Using default rules allows traders to avoid drafting large numbers of consumer contracts and allows consumers to avoid the costs of reviewing them. Consumers would normally need to accept these costs of reviewing contracts to make a decision as to whether to enter into a transaction with a particular trader.[123] Under government imposed default rules, consumers may already be assured that the contracts used in the market will at least comply with the default rules, thus affording them some level of fairness.

However, transaction costs are not only limited to the expenses that occur before and during the contracting process (e.g. information searching costs, bargaining and decision making costs, the costs for completing contractual procedures, etc.). Additionally, there are transaction costs relating to the enforcement of the rights of individual consumers. The time required to be spent by consumers, the difficulty in dealing with complex procedures and the uncertain outcome of cases can result in additional transaction costs that put an excessive burden on consumers.[124] Therefore, procedural mechanisms are used to regulate transaction costs at the enforcement stage. For example, the establishment of a small claims court, the creation of group, collective or class action litigation processes, or the allowing of consumers' representatives (be they private actors or state agencies) to enforce consumers rights on behalf of consumers.

In e-sales, e-communication can clearly help consumers to save on transaction costs by allowing them to conveniently search for information and locate products

[120] *See* William, *supra* note 43, at 2.

[121] The standard terms also help to reduce transaction costs, decreasing the cost of negotiation and drafting. *See* Luth, *supra* note 1, at 134, 140.

[122] *See* Chap. 2.

[123] *See* Luth, *supra* note 1, at 140.

[124] *See* Ramsay, *supra* note 1, at 56, 124.

without having to make trips to find them. It cannot be denied that products and services may often be sold at lower prices in the online market than the physical market because of traders' lower operating costs and consumers' cheaper information searching costs.[125] However, in terms of economic benefit, e-traders never stop searching for a way to maximize their profits. One way of doing so in e-sales is to offer lower prices as a means of attracting consumers and then later add extra charges or other related transaction costs to maximize their profits.[126] The practice of charging overpriced delivery costs is an example.[127] This strategy adds a new form of transaction costs that e-sale consumers must unnecessarily bear, resulting in unfairness to them.

4.11 Right to Conduct Dispute Resolution in a Convenient Location

Generally, the jurisdiction principles governing private transactions were influenced by *actor sequitur forum rei*, the famous legal rule which states that the "individual should be sued in the court of the place where they are domiciled".[128] In other words, the basic jurisdiction principle or the rule of forum that relates to the competent court having legal power to hear and determine a case provides for jurisdiction at the location of the domicile of the defendant, unless the disputing parties agreed otherwise. When it comes to commercial transactions, including consumer transactions, "the place of performance of obligation in question" or "where the transaction is or should have been completed" would be another alternative for the asserted forum.[129] However, because a consumer is theoretically considered the weaker contracting party because of his possession of less information, bargaining power, and litigation experience, the jurisdiction rules that apply to consumer contracts should be different. If these general rules are applied to consumer claims, a consumer who is a plaintiff may have to file a claim against a trader defendant in the jurisdiction of such trader's residence or domicile. The consumer will be put in a disadvantageous position and they may not succeed in

[125] *See* Chap. 2.

[126] *See* OFT, *supra* note 25, at 18–9.

[127] *See* Ramsay, *supra* note 1, at 138.

[128] For Detailed discussion on the *actor sequitur forum rei* rule, *see* A. T. V. Mehren, Theory and Practice of Adjudicatory Authority in Private International Law: A Comparative Study of the Doctrine, Policies and Practices of Common-and Civil-Law Systems 179 (2002).

[129] *See e.g.* The Council Regulation (EC) 44/2001 on Jurisdiction and the Recognition and Enforcement of Judgments in Civil and Commercial Matters (The Brussels Regulation). *See also* The EC Brussels Convention on Jurisdiction and the Enforcement of Judgements in Civil and Commercial Matters, Article 5(1).

securing remedies. Such a situation is particularly true with traders living in jurisdictions where the expensive costs of long-distance litigation far exceeds the small amount involved in the dispute. Thus, consumers should be granted an option to initiate an action against trader in a forum that is to their convenience or in the location of their domicile as this would widen their ability to access justice and remedies.[130]

In the reverse situation where the consumer is the defendant, many traders are able to preserve their advantage of choice of forum through the standardized terms that they drafted. Unfortunately, evidence suggests that in many standard consumer contracts a forum of dispute clause is inserted which usually uses the place of residence or domicile of the trader as the selected forum.[131] Thus, the trader's advantageous position of not having to conduct legal proceedings in a remote venue is protected under the standardized terms. Consumers bound under such terms seem to be in an even worse position if he or she becomes a defendant because they have to conduct the case against the trader in a distant venue (i.e., the jurisdiction of the trader's residence or domicile).[132] Litigation in such a remote and unfamiliar forum puts the consumer at a great disadvantage because of their limited financial means.

As some choice of forum clauses creates an unfair situation for consumers, many efforts have been made to render such clauses unenforceable. For example, the EU jurisdiction law clearly sets forth legislative provisions emphasizing the consumers' convenient location by specifying that unless the forum selection clause is favorable to consumers it will be deemed unenforceable.[133] Another example is the US. Even though the US courts would normally strictly adhere to the principle of freedom of contract, they are unwilling to enforce a contract term that is unfairly oppressive, unconscionable or which generates outcomes beyond the reasonable expectation of the consumer.[134] It can be said from the above stated examples that there is a clear legal trend that the requirement that a consumer conduct legal proceedings in the trader's home jurisdiction may be considered unfair unreasonable to the consumer.

When it comes to the global e-commerce market, in many cases, the trader's home jurisdiction is often very far away in a country unfamiliar to the consumer. Therefore, the part of an e-consumer contract concerning the dispute forum should be subject to especially careful scrutiny to equalize the playing field between the consumer and the long-distance trader. E-consumers should be afforded the convenience of conducting legal proceedings in the jurisdiction of their residence or

---

[130] *See e.g.* Hill, *supra* note 92, at 187–8.

[131] *See ibid*, at 194–6.

[132] *See* Brauche, *supra* note 35, at 188.

[133] *See* Article 17 of the Brussels Regulation.

[134] For discussion of the related US's cases law relating to the issues of jurisdiction, *see* P. Cortés, Online Dispute Resolution for consumer in the European Union 31 (2011).

domicile as this would constitute a means of providing them with better access to justice.[135] One example to support such a position is set out in one of the AFFECT's twelve principles: "consumers are entitled to have their disputes settled in a local convenient venue."[136]

4.12 Access to Effective Dispute Resolution Process

Civil proceedings in private law have long been the traditional means of enforcing personal rights and it usually involves disputes between private parties where one party is attempting to defend their own rights.[137] If a consumer dispute arises because of a breach of contract, or because of a defective or hazardous product, consumers should be entitled to effective and just redress through the private law system, which is also a main channel for consumers to defend their rights.[138]

The defense of individual rights through traditional private law only represents one side of the coin when it comes to consumer related disputes. The other side of the coin is the protection of the public interest in consumer markets.[139] Consumers' success in their good faith claims against rogue traders will show the general public that the wrongdoer will not go unpunished if they violate consumers' rights. In the

---

[135] On the contrary, it has been suggested that the uncertainty of jurisdiction imposes a big burden on e-traders because of the unpredictability of their legal duties and obligations. This may result in limitations of the growth of e-commerce. *See* Hill, *supra* note 92, at 152.

[136] *See* Braucher, *supra* note 35, at 183. This is consistent with Article 16 of the Brussels Regulation. It provides the forum selection of the European Union Member States which reads as following:

> 1. A consumer may bring proceedings against the other party to a contract either in the courts of the Member State in which that party is domiciled or in the courts for the place where the consumer is domiciled. 2. Proceedings may be brought against a consumer by the other party to the contract only in the courts of the Member State in which the consumer is domiciled. 3. This Article shall not affect the right to bring a counter.

See The Brussels Regulation, *available at* europa.eu/legislation_summaries/justice_freedom_security/judicial_cooperation_in_civil_matters/l33054_en.htm (visited December 2, 2011).

[137] Even though in consumer cases, consumer advocate groups or government agencies may conduct the proceedings on behalf of consumers, the procedures are usually based on the traditional private law mechanism. For consumer disputes, "the basis for claims can be twofolds: To use the language of the two Rome Regulations, claims can either be based on 'contractual obligations' or 'non-contractual obligations'. Both have their roots in private law concepts: private autonomy in the first and 'tort/delict', unjust enrichment, *negotiorum gestio* or *culpa in contrahendo* in the second case." *See* S. Wrbka, *European Consumer Protection Law: Quo Vadis? Thoughts on the Compensatory Collective Redress Debate, in* S. Wrbka, S. van Uytsel and M. Siems (eds.), Collective Actions: Enhancing Access to Justice and Reconciling Multilayer Interest? 23, 37 (2012).

[138] *See ibid.*

[139] *See* H. Kötz, *Public Interest Litigation, in* M. Capperlletti (ed.), Access to Justice and the Welfare State 83, 86 (1981).

opinion of Kati Cseres, consumer redress not only creates direct or concrete solutions for individual consumers, but is also beneficial to a broad class of consumers who are similarly situated, in that "[c]onsumer redress is aimed at deterring firms form transgressing the law and modifying their behavior in a way that they will comply with the law and thus operate in a pro-consumer manner. Beside actual solutions, optimal deterrence, and behavior modification consumer redress also seeks meaningful compensation for consumer harms".[140]

Unfortunately, the private law system has long been criticized for its ineffectiveness in coping with consumer related disputes.[141] The time and money that have to be spent in relation to the small amount at stake in a dispute coupled with a lack of knowledge and understanding of the dispute resolution process are among the various commonly known obstacles to consumers' access to justice via traditional private litigation. So long as consumers make their decisions based on a personal cost and benefit analysis and conclude that disputes are not worth pursuing, their lawful rights will go undefended.[142] In the circumstances where consumers decided to forego any attempt for recourse, their rights will likely be ignored, resulting in injustice to them.[143]

Due to this, many laws and measures have been suggested and implemented to help consumers defend their rights and provide them with effective dispute resolution. Effective dispute resolution relates not only to the question of access (e.g. fast, easy, and economical), due process is also important to ensure that parties to a dispute settlement process are fairly and equally treated and the resolution is rational, reasonable and accurate within a just process.[144] Various means of dispute resolution have been established with the main aim of eradicating the long duration and high cost of disputes through a fair and standardized procedure. For instance, there is an important on-going discussion on having a government agency represent consumers in the enforcement of their rights in a dispute resolution process, thereby shifting the barriers in conducting consumers' disputes to the state.[145] Alternatively, the existence of large numbers of consumers sharing common problems or suffering similar damages (coupled with the fact that traditional procedures do not fit well in dealing with small value of consumer disputes) led to the idea of bundling consumer claims into what are known today as class actions, collective actions or

[140] *See* Cseres, *supra* note 1, at 130.

[141] *See ibid*, at 129.

[142] *See ibid*, at 129–30.

[143] *See* Kötz, *supra* note 139, at 86. Kati Cseres made a similar argument that: "Consumer concerns are complex, diverse and diffuse both over consumer groups and over time. The adverse effects of consumer might realize later in time. They are moreover unpublicized and therefore difficult to detect and address." *See* Cseres, *supra* note 1, at 161.

[144] *See* J. Hörnle, Cross-Border Internet Dispute Resolution 18 (2009).

[145] So-called "public enforcement" may be an effective alternative in compensating individual consumers and at the same time elevating standard practices of vendors to meet the needs of consumers, the public, and society.

group actions, depending on the jurisdiction.[146] Other options that helps reduce costs, simplify the process, or shorten the time of traditional private procedures are also promoted. These include informal dispute settlements (direct negotiation, conciliation, mediation, or arbitration) and special procedures for consumer cases.[147]

These significant developments are driven by the important need to provide consumers with effective weapons in addressing the violation of their individual rights. In addition, the exercise of consumers' rights also plays an important role in promoting the broader public interest by putting pressure through sanctions on traders to recognize and respect consumers' rights, thereby elevating market and social standards for the public as a whole. As a result, various dispute settlement mechanisms have evolved overtime to build the most effective means of consumer dispute resolution, one of the rubrics of consumers' access to justice.

In case there is a dispute concerning an e-sale, the traditional problems in consumer litigation such as costs, delays, and psychological barriers seem to worsen in cross border litigation. Consumers must identify processes to initiate claims and enforce their rights against overseas vendors that they may not be familiar with and may require extensive expert advice in the area of private

---

[146] The settlement of consumer mass disputes has made use of group litigation for compensation. In-group actions, the plaintiff can be classified into three different types; "Firstly, we may identify a proper *class action*, where the plaintiff is a member of the group and seeks, e.g. redress also for his own damages which he has suffered. A second possibility is that the plaintiff is not a member of the group, but a public authority responsible for the supervision of collective rights of a certain group. Thirdly, there are actions where the plaintiff is a private group, e.g. a consumer organization, which has received legal standing. These actions have been call *action by organization*". This claim bundling concept has received substantial favor in the last decade as a solution for consumers' access to justice over traditional civil procedures. In any event, the settlement of mass consumer disputes continues to depend on traditional civil procedures, which are time-consuming and often more costly than the cost of an individual case in normal civil procedure because of the large number of plaintiffs. In the United States, for example, class action litigation has become greatly popular for consumer mass disputes. However, the United States Government cannot overlook the great expense occurred in class action procedures. To address this shortcoming, the United States passed the Class Action Fairness Act in 2005 to curb the costs of this type of litigation, which were spiraling out of control, by imposing limit on attorney's fees. *See* K. Viitanen, *Enforcement of Consumers' Collective Interests by Regulatory Agencies in the Nordic Countries, in* W. van Boom and M. Loos (eds.), Collective Enforcement of Consumer Law 81, 91, 96 (2007).

[147] In the opinions of many scholars, among various option schemes, alternative dispute resolution outside the court may be the most appropriate option for consumer cases, as such processes are quick, simple, and inexpensive. *See* Hörnle, *supra* note 144 and Cortés, *supra* note 134. On the other side of idea, such processes may carry less prestige and credibility than traditional civil procedures in the eyes of many. Such perception of the alternative dispute resolution is derived from various factors, including the lack of vendor's cooperation or good faith participation in the process; the opinion of the dispute resolution body not having the legal enforceability of a court judgment; or the absence of transparency or credibility in the process because of the partiality of the dispute resolution body, which may not be as independent as a court of justice. *See* Cseres, *supra* note 1, at 167.

international law, especially on the complex issues and rules concerning jurisdiction and applicable laws. The costs and complexity of cross border claims are likely to make it not worthwhile for consumers to take action for low value purchases.

These obstacles to consumers' access to justice seem to be more prominent in the e-market. In this regard, the establishment of the appropriate rules on jurisdiction and applicable laws in the area of private international laws have been claimed to be necessary to give clarity to consumers when making cross border claims, coupled with the application of effective dispute resolution procedures, will enable consumers to have a proper access to justice in e-market to the same degree as they would be in the traditional market.[148]

4.13 Enforcement of Remedies or Redress

The true success of a consumer dispute resolution also lies in the consumer's ability to enforce their rights in accordance with the dispute resolution outcome, whether it is in accordance with a court judgment, arbitral award, or an informally agreed settlement. In traditional legal proceedings, enforcement is usually carried out through the competent officers of the court and such processes are often inconvenient, time-consuming, and costly. Unsurprisingly, such processes are not popular in relation to low-value consumer disputes. Many consumers would no longer be willing to bear the expense of enforcing the dispute resolution outcome. Some of them may decide to stop at the point where there is the recognition of their rights under a court judgment, arbitral award, or agreed settlement, without proceeding further to actually enforcing the remedies or redresses under such judgment, award, or settlement.

In consideration of these related difficulties, some forms of enforcement on behalf of consumers have been developed to provide an effective enforcement. For example, some countries in the EU have not only permitted enforcement on behalf of consumers in the form of collective redress by representatives through group or collective actions[149] but have also extended this to enforcement by consumer organizations that have the authority to conduct and enforce consumer

---

[148] Online Alternative Dispute Resolution is an example of a mechanism designed to avoid the difficulties of the private international laws. It has recently been promoted as the new alternative dispute resolution for e-commerce and has become a subject of contemporary debates. For detailed discussion on the global harmonisation of the private international laws, *see infra* Chap. 7.

[149] Class action enforcement was created to compensate for the shortcoming of state support in the enforcement of the diffuse interests of consumers. *See also* Viitanen, *supra* note 146, 81–103 and G. Howells, *Cy-près for Consumers: Ensuring Class Action Reforms Deal with Scattered Damages*, *in* J. Steele and W. H. van Boom, Mass Justice, Challenges of Representation and Distribution 58–72 (2011).

cases on behalf of consumers.[150] Some countries allow consumer organizations that are operated by state agencies or private entities to act on behalf of consumers under different restrictions and manners prescribed by the laws.[151] Well-known examples include the Nordic Ombudsmen, the governmental consumer agencies that have been established as representatives of consumers in seeking redresses and remedies for consumers.[152]

Today's debates concerning the most efficient legal enforcement of consumer claims continue to be hotly contested, especially between the proponents of private group enforcement such as class actions or actions by consumer organizations, and the proponents of public intervention or enforcement by state agencies.[153] Creating mechanisms that truly provide consumers with the remedies they are legally entitled to receive is an essential element in providing justice in society. As Kati Cseres argues that, if consumers possess substantive rights but lack appropriate tools to ensure those rights can truly be exercised, such rights will not be of much value.[154] Therefore, consumers cannot attain access to real justice if they cannot enforce the remedies or redress to which they are legitimately entitled.

Enforcement of consumer remedies is more complex in case of transnational e-sales. Even though a consumer may be successful in a dispute resolution process, if the trader who becomes a judgment debtor does not comply with the judgment or dispute resolution award, the consumer will have go through the proceedings at the execution stage to enforce such judgment or dispute resolution award.[155] There can be problems if the trader does not have any assets in the country of the consumer because the consumer will need to enforce the judgment or award in the foreign jurisdiction where the vendor's assets are located. The feasibility of enforcing such a judgment or award will depend on whether such foreign jurisdiction recognizes and accepts a judgment or award issued by another jurisdiction, which usually depends on the existence of a bilateral or multilateral enforcement treaty between the country of the consumer and the country of the trader.

Even with the existence of the necessary treaty, the relevant procedures for enforcement and execution of a foreign judgment are still very complex and

---

[150] Various EU Directives, namely the Misleading Advertising Directive 97/55/EC, Unfair Contract Terms Directive 93/12/EEC 97/7EC, Distance Selling Directives 97/7/EC and Consumer Right Directive 2011/83/EU, allow Member States to grant the right to take legal actions in respect of consumer protection law to consumer organizations. Consequently, most Member States have given this kind of right to certain consumer organizations.

[151] *See also* Howells, *supra* note 149, at 67.

[152] For a discussion on the duties and functions of the Nordic ombudsmen, *see infra* Chap. 6. Another example of these agencies is the Office of Fair Trading of the United Kingdom. These agencies also serve as public law regulators with the duty to monitor and suppress violations of consumer protection laws.

[153] *See* W. van Boom and M. Loos (eds.), Collective Enforcement of Consumer Law 6 (2007) and Wrbka, *supra* note 137.

[154] *See* Boom and Loos, *ibid*, at 6.

[155] *See* Hill, *supra* note 92, at 60, 127, 130.

costly.[156] Unfortunately, many forms of efficient legal enforcement on behalf of consumers, either the private group enforcement or public enforcement by state agencies, have been developed over the years but they have not yet reached the level where these consumer representative agencies can help enforcing and executing consumers' rights in multi or foreign jurisdictions. Due to this, e-sale consumers' full access to remedies or redresses continues to be elusive.

4.14 Fair Trading Practices

Honesty and fairness by merchants in conducting their business will help reduce the risk of disputes between consumers and traders and consequently promote consumers' confidence. This is one of the basic principles of socio-legal and economic notions in consumer markets.[157] Richard Stewart and Cass Sunstein refer to this notion as one of the "community values in consumer protection".[158] They believe that the values of honesty, fair dealing, and risk sharing in business practices will maximize economic growth and the protection of individual rights and interests in the market.[159] It is easier said than done to ask traders to compromise or sacrifice their business interests to advance these values, but it is something that many scholars are hoping for to promote consumers' access to justice, resulting in an increase of their confidence in the market.

In the environment where consumers have confidence and trust in traders, they will be able to make the best market decisions and be more likely to gain satisfaction from such transactions. With a high level of confidence and trust, the number of consumer transactions will increase thereby contributing to greater economic growth. As Kenneth Arrow argues that:

> ...[f]rom the point of view of efficiency as well as from the point of view of distributive justice, something more than the market is called for. The government may indeed perform somewhat better than the private sector in realizing social feeling, trust, and emphathy, but within limits....[160]

Due to this, the concept of consumers' access to justice must include honesty and fair dealing by traders as an element. The EU is an obvious example of a group of nations that places emphasis on developing social norms with the aim of achieving trust and confidence in the market. The policy making process of the EU relating to consumer protection does not consist only of calculating the economic advantages

---

[156] *See* J. Hörnle, *The Jurisdictional Challenge of the Internet, in* L. Edwards and C. Waelde (eds.), Law and the Internet 121, 152–3 (209).

[157] *See* Ramsay, *supra* note 1, at 99.

[158] *See* R. B. Stewart and C. R. Sunstein, *Public Programs and Private Rights*, 95 Harvard Law Review 1193, 1238 (1982).

[159] *See ibid.*

[160] *See* K. J. Arrow, The Limits of Organization 23 (1974).

and disadvantages of the policy, but also includes the advancement of social notice towards the appropriate degree of honesty and fair dealing of traders in the market. The norm of consumers in society towards standards of commercial practices is often considered essential as what the majority of consumers is thinking should be applied as the benchmark in determining whether a trader's conduct constitutes an unfair commercial practice.[161] A trader is expected to be aware of and maintain the standard commercial practice that the majority of consumers have come to expect. This will promote consumers' confidence and fair practices in the market, thereby enhancing consumers' access to justice.

In B2C e-transaction, fair trading practices and consumers' confidence are also critical problems. In a borderless market, different countries have different standards of trading practices and related domestic laws. In such circumstances there is an uncertainty as to the applicable law and this has been claimed to be one of the factors undermining consumers' confidence.[162] Consumers may not be so sure when entering into e-sales with foreign traders whether they will be protected by the familiar law of their residential countries, or whether their rights and obligations will be in accordance with the laws of the traders' country, particularly where the country of the consumers have higher standards of fair trading practices and consumer protection law.[163] Due to this, consumers may not want to risk buying products from vendors in other countries, thereby preventing e-commerce from being developed to its full potential.[164]

With today's global market, the harmonization of consumer protection laws and mechanisms and the establishment of internationally accepted fair trading standards has become the main subject of discussion.[165] However, it is undeniable that universal consensus will be difficult to attain as different countries will have different views based on their cultural background as to what constitutes acceptable fair trading practices.[166] Despite the difficulty because of different cultures and ideas in different countries, various attempts continue because there is a belief that a common standard of trading practices is one of the key solutions for the problem in consumer protection in the global environment that should be implemented.[167]

---

[161] *See* The concept of "standard of average consumer" under Article 5 and 5(3) of the EU Unfair Commercial Practice Directive, *available at* eur-lex.europa.eu/LexUriServ/LexUriServ.do?uri=CELEX:32005L0029:en:NOT (visited December 2, 2011).

[162] *See* Hill, *supra* note 92, at 12.

[163] *See ibid.*, at 46.

[164] *See ibid.*, at 12.

[165] *See* Coteanu, *supra* note 4, at Chapter 8.

[166] This controversial issue is indeed an obvious example in the attempt to harmonize the consumer protection laws among the different legal cultures of the Member States of the European Union. *See* Coteanu, *ibid* and Perez, *supra* note 116, at 711–3.

[167] Many scholars claim that the establishment of a common standard of fair trading practices is essential and necessary to ensure consumers' confidence, providing a reasonable fairness that every individual consumer is entitled to. For a detailed discussion on the harmonization of consumer protection law, *see infra* Chap. 7.

4.15 Recognition of Consumers' Rights and Their Role in the Market

Manufacturers and traders are typically large, professionally managed business organizations with abundant expertise in their business. It can be said that they are "highly well organized". They appear to play a major role in generating revenue and growth for their countries and are extremely influential in shaping the legal, social, and economic policies of their nations.[168] In contrast to this, typical consumers are ordinary individuals who make decisions about the products they want based on the information fed to them and their decisions are sometimes not necessarily optimal or appropriate.[169] As an individual who usually spends a small amount of money in the market, a consumer's interests are often overlooked because of his or her limited economic and political influence.

The imbalance power between consumers and traders are even clearer when looking at standard terms and the "take it or leave it" nature of consumer contracts, which are solely drafted by traders. This shed light on concerns over and unfair influence on the market. Karl Llewellyn and Friedrich Kessler were the earliest scholars to raise this concern.[170] They point out that the lack of negotiation and uneven bargaining powers between the strong trader and the consumer, a weaker party, under standard contracts are likely to bring about the complete control of the contractual terms and the dictation over market direction by traders, the more powerful party.[171] Under such conditions, unfair contractual practices can easily surface. It is unfortunately true that the terms of standard contracts in use today are, within given industries, virtually identical or at the very least very similar to each other.[172] Given such consistent industry practices, consumers do not have many alternatives as the contractual terms offered by one trader do not substantially differ from those offered by another.

One way of empowering consumers concerning the instant standard terms that is currently being debated is the use of "the negotiated model forms of standard consumer contracts".[173] The application of this model will lead to negotiation

---

[168] *See* The UK Broad of Trade, *Final Report of the Committee on Consumer Protection (Monopoly Committee), Cmnd 1781* (1962).

[169] *See ibid.*

[170] *See* K. Llewellyn, *Book Review on the Standardization of Commercial Contracts in English and Continental Law, by O. Prausnitz*, 52 Harvard Law Review 700–5 (1939) and F. Kessler, *Contracts of Adhesion-Some Thoughts About Freedom of Contract*, 43 Columbia Law Review 629–42 (1943).

[171] As part of their observation, they further point out that the preservation and promotion of consumers' freedom to choose is critical as it will enable consumers to only enter into contracts with the terms that are fair and true to their intents.

[172] *See ibid.*

[173] Today, this model of negotiation practice, which is usually conducted between the business operators, consumer representatives and state authorities, is becoming more prevalent as a new government approach in regulations and is currently implemented in various countries among the

between consumers' representatives and business operators in the process of drafting standard contractual terms. In this way, consumers' voices are likely to be heard and they are given a chance to be involved in the process of determining standard terms, which will lead to the improvement of the quality of standard terms and the exclusion of unfair ones. As Hanneke Luth argues, if consumers' interests represented by consumer organizations or representative, it would constitute a way that allows the voice of the consumer to be heard in the drafting process of standard contract forms.[174] Such a proposal may offer a solution by affording consumers the opportunity to help frame the terms of standard contracts, thereby mitigating the one-sided nature of the contract in favor of the vendors.

The example above is one of the important ways of promoting the development of an appropriate role and power of consumers in the market through allowing consumer representatives to participate in the process of drafting standard contracts along with traders, with relevant government agencies assisting and mediating the process. In the Final Report of the Committee on Consumer Protection, the Board of Trade of the UK stated that: "... [t]hrough many of the submission reaching us there ran the theme that piecemeal improvement would not ensure that a proper balance between buyer and seller would be wholly restored and permanently maintained... The idea of a 'consumers' sovereignty' was fallacious. In truth, it was said, the producer easily prevailed over the welfare of the consumer; and would continue to do so until the consumer was provided with an organization of equal weight of protect and represent him..."[175]

Additionally, the establishment of strong consumer interest or representative organizations is another means of enhancing the role of consumers in the market. A strong consumer interest or representative organization with substantial membership will give loud voice to individual consumers that cannot be easily ignored by the government or large vendors, thereby increasing consumers' power. If consumers are allowed to play their appropriate role and are granted status and bargaining power in the market, greater access to justice will be available to them.

Member States of the EU, the Nordic countries (Norway, Sweden, Finland and Denmark), the Netherlands, Belgium, and so on. The consumer ombudsman in the Nordic countries, for example, often acts as a consumer interests' representative in the negotiation on the contents of standard terms with traders. This negotiated model form will help improve the quality of contract terms by excluding unfair standard terms presented to consumers in the market. Through their participation in this process, consumers could freely exercise their autonomy and freedom to choose various appropriate terms available before them as they need or desire. The situations where there is no choice because all traders offer similar unfair terms will be eradicated, creating a greater way for consumers to access justice. *See* Luth, *supra* note 1, at 269–81.

[174] *See ibid.*, at 277.

[175] *See* The UK Broad of Trade, *supra* note 168.

In online market, technology creates new form of communication that is non-physical and relies on the processing by computer program without human verification. With traders' superior technological knowledge, it somehow allows them to design and control information and presentation format that can manipulate consumers in some ways.[176] As a result, consumers often discover that there are no alternatives. Standard contract in e-market are for example usually similarly drafted because traders usually strictly control contract to minimize the risks that may arise from borderless e-transactions.[177] Within this new face of online market, technology seems to increase the disparity and advantage in e-transactions in favor of traders, lowering consumers' power and their important roles in the market. As Cristina Coteanu confirms that "... whilst information technology should continue its role in creating solutions that are effective for consumers, the growing disparity between consumer knowledge and the characteristics of technological environment creates new rationales for consumer protection"[178]

Based on the above argument, it appears that there is a wide gap between traders and consumers because of their unequal levels of technological knowledge. To put it differently, the bargaining power of consumers in the e-market tends to be even lower than it is in the traditional sales market because of the superior technological knowledge of traders. Therefore, the establishment of an appropriate role, status, and increase of bargaining power of consumers in the e-market is necessary to protect their rights and interest from powerful traders who possess greater technological knowledge that they use to unfairly and unilaterally control that market.

4.16 Interim Conclusion

History reveals that to adhere to the concept of consumer access to justice and the effective enforcement of consumer rights, designers of consumer protection mechanisms have to be very well aware that procedural and substantive issues are essentially interdependent. The focus has been shifted from the initial debates on procedural roles (e.g. legal aids, legal representations, etc.) to substantive issues promoting consumer rights in achieving justice.

Technological development and the emergence of globalization have expanded the consumer market into a mass product market with a wide range of goods and services being offered. This leads to the increasingly complicated and magnified concerns of consumers which include not only the social justice of the market (e.g. fair trading practices, remedies, etc.), but also consumer economic interests and welfare (e.g. market efficiency, individual meaning choices, etc.). Therefore, a discussion on effective consumer protection mechanisms cannot ignore these

[176] *See* Sects. 4.2 and 4.4.

[177] *See* Coteanu, *supra* note 4, at 206.

[178] *See ibid.*

multidimensional aspects of access to justice, which include procedural and substantive issues and the diverse concerns of consumers where the justice aspect of both socio-legal and economic considerations are identified as essential elements.

In designing the most efficient and effective consumer protection mechanisms for the B2C market, the designers cannot disregard the diverse ingredients of consumer concerns that have to be protected, the nature of harms suffered by consumers and the multidimensional aspects of justice necessary to satisfy a fair market environment. Therefore, the proposed multidimensional framework in this chapter serves broader objectives of protecting all aspects of justice embodying consumers' activities, both substantive and procedural. These are considered crucial issues when aiming to establish minimum standards in the market place. It not only facilitates equal access to serve the social aspect, but also offers economic justice. Its main aim is to satisfy the diversity and complexity of the relevant interests of consumers and ensure that all relevant consumer concerns are considered when designing consumer protection measures. The Framework proposed in this chapter can be meaningfully applied as criteria when considering how consumer protection mechanisms can be designed to protect consumers and ultimately assist in achieving optimal social justice and economic efficiency for the B2C e-market. The next step in the progress of this study is to analyze different kinds of consumer protection mechanisms using the criteria of the established Framework. It starts with a detailed assessment of the substantive mechanisms that will be dealt with in the next chapter.

Chapter 5
Substantive Mechanisms for Achieving Access to Justice

5.1 Introduction

Many consumer transactions are often characterized by unfairness for reasons including the use of misleading advertising, the provision of goods of poor or defective quality and the unauthorized use of personal data.[1] Many laws and regulations have been introduced on the grounds of protecting consumers against these types of deceptive and unfair practices, requiring traders to treat all consumers fairly.[2] As is the case with traditional transactions, consumers in the online market are also often faced with these unfair practices. However, there are other unfair practices in B2C e-transactions that are even more difficult for many consumers to deal with because of the associated advanced technology that created the transnational environment for such e-transactions.[3] With its unique characteristics including the absence of national boundaries and the speed of communication, the emergence of today's e-market has transformed the procedures and manners of conducting business and allowed unfair commercial practices to occur more easily as traders manipulate technology to their advantage.[4] A question arises as to how

[1] *See* I. Ramsay, Consumer law and Policy, Text and Materials on Regulating Consumer Markets 268 (2007).

[2] This is true of various countries' statutes. These laws require that sellers treat all competing consumers on the same fair basis. This fair trading requirement affects not only consumers but also eradicates the risk of unfair competition between different competing businesses. For a detailed explanation of the regulation of deceptive and unfair commercial practices, *see ibid.*, at 267–77.

[3] *See* C. Coteanu, Cyber Consumer Law and Unfair Trading Practices 159 (2005).

[4] Among various unfair practices, an often found example in online transaction is the unauthorized use of identity and account information. With the advent of the online market, traders can easily collect personal data about the behavior of consumers without notice or consent and then use such collected data to maximize future sales and profits, thus bringing an unfair commercial practice into the online market. Price discrimination strategy is an example of the unauthorized use of personal data that constitutes an unfair commercial practice. This happens when a trader is

S. Yuthayotin, *Access to Justice in Transnational B2C E-Commerce*,
DOI 10.1007/978-3-319-11131-5_5

well the existing consumer protection mechanisms can cope with advanced information technology and the fast changing environment of the online market. A lack of effective tools for dealing with these problems would lead a large number of consumers to refrain from participating in e-transactions, resulting in B2C e-commerce not achieving its full potential.

Therefore, this chapter assesses the effectiveness of the consumer protection mechanisms prevalently used in the online market by exploring selected examples of good consumer protection practices[5]—namely the mechanisms of the EU and the US. This is not to say that the e-consumer protection regimes in the US and the EU are the best in the world. The fact is that these are the two leading jurisdictions with the highest volumes of B2C e-transactions that have had long head starts in developing regulations concerning e-sale activities ahead of other jurisdictions.[6] In doing so, the proposed multidimensional framework set out in Chap. 4, which highlights various conditions that are necessary for achieving consumers' access to justice, will be used as benchmarks in assessing the merit of each existing mechanism and shedding light on future directions and improvements of consumer protection mechanisms, particularly for dealing with the advanced technological and transnational nature of the online market. This latter point will be discussed in Chap. 8.

---

charging different prices for the same goods or services to different groups of consumers based on the analysis of their personal data. Relating to this problem, Robert Weiss and Ajay Mehrotra have stated that, in traditional consumer markets, traders often segmented their consumers to charge them different prices. Customers of amazon.com who discovered that they bought identical DVDs at different prices are a clear example. *See* R. Weiss and A. Mehrotra, *Online Dynamic Pricing: Efficiency, Equity and the Future of E-Commerce,* 6 Virginia Journal of Law and Technology (2001), *available at* vjolt.net/vol6/issue2/v6i2-a11-Weiss.html (visited August 21, 2012).

[5] It is impossible to analyze all consumer protection mechanisms existing in the online market. Within the limited scope of this study, mechanisms that are recently developed and have been the subject of extensive discussions and studies are selected as case studies to reveal the difficulties that the existing consumer protection mechanisms are encountering because of the special characteristics of the online market.

[6] The US and the EU have long been considered the most advanced economies, with the highest level of consumer consumption. The emerging economies have recently exerted their influences because of their rapidly increasing rates of consumer spending in the global economy. However, e-consumption is still largely based in North America and Western Europe. In effect, the US and the EU have become the pioneers in introducing and developing consumer protection laws, including those related to online transactions. The laws of the US and the EU are always subjected to many international studies. Therefore, the study of the laws of these jurisdictions is indispensible to help analyze and compare the effectiveness of different consumer protection mechanisms in e-sales. *See* C. G. Christopher, Jr. and E. Johnson, *Emerging Consumer Markets: The New Drivers of Global Economic Growth,* 4 CSCMP' Supply Chain Quarterly 2011 (March 18, 2013), *available at* supplychainquarterly.com/columns/201104monetarymatters/ (visited March 23, 2013).

The content of this chapter begins with the standard term mechanisms that are the principle measure for protecting consumers from unfair contract formation processes[7] and unfair substantive terms contained in standard term contracts. It then follows with an analysis of the information disclosure mechanism, a tool designed to fight information asymmetries in the e-market. Next, there will be a discussion on the withdrawal mechanism. This mechanism is designed to mitigate the problems that may occur because of the distance between consumers and traders and the absence of the opportunity to inspect the products in e-transactions. The final section will appraise the privacy rule, a critical issue in the context of the internet, where the technology affords traders the ability to easily store and transfer consumers' personal information. The question that this chapter attempts to answer is whether these currently available mechanisms can safeguard and protect consumers in e-transactions given the special characteristics of the e-market because of the ease and convenient use of complex communication that this environment provides.

5.2 Standard Term Mechanism

This section discusses the standard term mechanism created to help consumers avoid being subjected to unfair standard contracts as the vast majority of consumer contracts, including e-contracts, are *standard form* contracts or *adhesion* contracts, where the consumer is not likely to have the opportunity or bargaining power to negotiate changes to the standard drafted language used.[8] As part of the discussion of the standard term mechanism, this section will describe and evaluate the standard term validation principle, which protect consumers from an unfair process of contractual formation, and unfair contract terms rules. In this regards, relevant legal principles, including court precedents established by the judiciary, as well as the substantive laws of the US and the EU, will be the main subject of discussion.

[7] For instance, in browser wrap agreements, which are often found in e-sales, the terms and conditions of an e-sale are frequently provided in fine print at the bottom of the page, or hidden from plain view, so the consumers are required to scroll down the page or click a hyperlink to view them. It does not require consumers to click any button or type any words to indicate their assent to those terms and conditions. The offer and acceptance rules under the contract law require interpretation and analysis to determine whether (1) adequate consent has already been given and was made and (2) how to interpret the scope and extent of such assent in the e-commerce setting.

[8] *See* D. Horton, *Flipping the Script: Contra Proferentem and Standard Form Contracts,* 80 University of Colorado Law Review 431, 444–6 (2009). For a detailed review of the court roles in standard contract, *see* C. Edwards, *Freedom of Contract and Fundamental Fairness for Individual Parties: The Tug of War Continues*, 77 University of Missouri-Kansas City Law Review 647, 655–7 (2009).

5.2.1 *Overview of Standard Term Validation Principles*

For e-sale transactions, signatures are not the indicator of the contracting parties' acceptance of the terms and conditions of e-contracts as they are in traditional commercial contracts. Instead, online e-contracts may utilize various kinds of *wraps*, as indicators of acceptance and incorporation of terms into e-contracts. In this regard, court judgments (especially in US courts) play a substantial role and have a material influence on the path of development of e-contract formation and validation mechanisms by setting relevant legal principles which have evolved in parallel with the technology in e-sales.[9]

5.2.1.1 Click Wrap

In a click wrap agreement, the terms and conditions of a contract are presented to the consumer via their computer monitor, where the consumer may show his or her assent by clicking on an icon or by typing "yes" into a text box.[10] The legal validity of the click wrap method of acceptance appears to be recognized by law at the same level as the legally bound terms by human signatures.[11] In

---

[9] In the EU, this issue of recognition and validation of e-contracts clearly appears in the substantive law. Article 9 (1) of the European Directive 2000/31/EC on E-Commerce (ECD) confirms the validity of contracts concluded by electronic means by providing that the legal requirements applicable to contractual processes shall neither create obstacles for the use of e-contracts nor result in such contracts being deprived of legal effectiveness and validity on account of their having been made by electronic means. Various forms of contracts made exclusively by the exchange of e-mails or equivalent individual communications, or concluded through websites, are also legally certified by the ECD according to Articles 10 and 11. Due to the general recognition and validation of e-consumer contracts under this law, various forms of contracts made exclusively by the exchange of electronic means such as e-mail, e-chat, the world wide web and so on, are legally certified under the EU law. This helps assure merchants and consumers alike that electronically executed contracts are as legally binding and enforceable as traditional paper written contracts, supporting confidence among contracting parties that promissory exchanges through e-communication can be enforced. For a discussion of the typology of internet services to consumers, *see* Coteanu, *supra* note 3, at 53.

[10] *See ibid.*

[11] For instance, in the US case, *Groff v. America Online, Inc.*, the plaintiff claimed that he "never saw, read, negotiate for or knowingly agreed to be bound by the choice of law..." present in a click wrap method. The court rejected the claim and explained that, by clicking an "I agree" button located next to a "read me" button or an "I disagree" button at the end of the online merchandise ordering process, the plaintiff as the subscriber is deemed to have agreed to have been bound by the contract terms and conditions displayed on the website including the forum selection clause. The court further concluded that by placing an online order, the plaintiff could not claim that he is not aware of the contract terms that are presented on the website in the form of click wrap agreement and therefore a binding contract should not have been formed under contract law. *See Groff v. America Online, Inc.* 1998 WL 307001, R.I. Sup Ct., May 27, 1998. In another case of privacy litigation, the court's ruling confirmed that a click wrap agreement is binding on an online user, including the arbitration clause contained in the final paragraph of the click wrap agreement under

other words, the use of an "I agree" button can and does create legal binding obligations.[12]

5.2.1.2 Browse Wrap

The browse wrap agreement refers to the contents of the agreement that may be accessed or read by clicking a hyperlink from the website home page.[13] Such an agreement is unassociated with any required manifestation of acceptance by an action, such as clicking an icon or typing "yes" in a space as used in click wrap agreements. However, the use of a browse wrap agreement can be as legally binding and enforceable as a traditional paper contract with the signatures of the contracting parties just like with a click wrap agreement.[14] Without a manifested acceptance, the contract terms and conditions in a browse wrap must be displayed in

---

a "miscellaneous" heading which also contained the choice of law and forum clauses. Also, the US court is of the view that the arbitration clause was in the same font and size as other contents of the contract. The online user had full access to read, inspect and review the click wrap agreement without any time restriction. *See Real Networks, Inc., Privacy Litigation*, 2000 WL 631341, N.D. III May 8, 2000, *available at* internetlibrary.com/pdf/In-re-RealNetworks-N.D.-Ill.-May-8-2000.pdf (visited April 12, 2013). *See also Moore v. Microsoft Corporation,* NY Sup Ct App Div 2nd Dept, April 15, 2002. The ruling states that the use of an "I agree" button could be legally binding and creates enforceable legal obligations.

[12] Today, the US is not the only country that recognizes click wrap agreements (as evidenced by the above court judgments). The laws of many other countries have also adopted the click wrap method of contract formation to keep up with the advancing electronic communication technology. The UK is an example. Although there is no case law confirming the validity of click wraps in the UK, the click wrap method for the ordering of goods and services via website is well accepted and is regarded as equivalent to the contract terms made under the parties' signatures. *See* C. Riefa and J. Hörnle, *The Changing Face of Electronic Consumer Contracts in the Twenty-First Century: Fit for Purpose?, in* L. Edwards and C. Waelde (eds.), Law and the Internet 89, 110 (2009).

[13] *See* Coteanu, *supra* note 3, at 53.

[14] Depending on the circumstances, the US courts have reached divergent opinions regarding the enforcements of the browse wrap agreements in form of hypertext links. *See* T. Tasker and D. Pakcyk, *Cyber-Surfing on the High Seas of Legalese: Law and Technology of Internet Agreement,* 18 Albany Law Journal of Science & Technology 79, 83–4 (2008). One example is that a court confirmed that a browse wrap agreement can be valid and enforceable if the terms of the agreement can be viewed on the homepage or a different web page that is linked to the homepage. *See ProCD Inc. v. Zeidenberg* 86 F. 3d 1447 (7th cir.1996). Another example is *Ticketmaster Corp. v. Tickets.com, Inc.:* the US District Court clearly established a guideline that for the terms and conditions in a browse wrap to be legally binding and enforceable as a contract, they must also display a prominent notice on the homepage stating that if the user wishes to continue to use the website, he or she must agree to be bound by such terms and conditions of use as set out in the browse wrap. *See Ticketmaster Corp. v. Tickets.com, Inc.,* C. D. C. a., March 7, 2003, *available at* internetlibrary.com/cases/lib_case25.cfm (visited January 12, 2013). By contrast, in the EU, there is very little judicial guidance concerning the browse wrap method. The focus is placed on different strategies, including an explicit registration of e-merchants and monitoring of unfair terms. *See* Riefa and Hörnle, *supra* note 12, at 111.

a manner that the consumer could be considered to know, or to ought to have known, or where it can be said that a reasonable notice has been given to the consumer.

5.2.1.3 Shrink Wrap

A shrink wrap agreement is often used in a software sale where the software's container or package contains a notice which states that use of the software will subject the user to the contract terms and conditions listed on that software's container or package.[15] It is commonly found that the majority of shrink wrap agreements specify that if the purchaser does not wish to enter into the agreement and be bound by the terms and conditions on the product's container or package, the purchaser has to return the product and receive a refund within a given period.[16] Similar to a click and a browse wrap agreement, a shrink wrap agreement used in the e-market can be legally binding if such wrap agreement is executed in a manner that satisfies particular criteria, namely that there be a clear and conspicuous notice of the shrink wrap agreement's existence, a requirement for some form of affirmative act of acceptance at the beginning of the use and an option for return.[17] These three conditions constitute the guidelines for e-merchants to ensure the validity of their shrink wrap contract terms.[18]

---

[15] *See* Coteanu, *supra* note 3 at 49. For a detailed analysis of shrink wrap agreements in mass market software, *see* J. K. Winn (ed.), Consumer Protection in the Age of the Information Economy (2006).

[16] *See e.g. Specht v. Netscape Communications Corporation,* 150 F. Supp. 2d 585, S.D.N.Y. July 5, 2001, *Hill v Gateway 2000, Inc*., 105 F. 3d 1147 (7th Cir.), cert. denied, 522 U.S. 808 (1997) and *Brower v. Gateway 2000, Inc*., 246 A.D. 2d 246, 676 N.Y.S. 2d 569 (N.Y. App. Div. 1st Dep't 1998).

[17] In *ProCD Inc. v. Zeidenberg*, the U.S. Court of Appeals opined that the terms of the shrink wrap agreement are enforceable if such agreement is formed based on certain criterion set out in the judgment. The judge gave his view, which was focused on how and when the contract was made, that in forming a contract the merchant may specify the sales contract is to be formed in the store or thereafter, as in the case of a telephone order where the contract formation can be delayed to the time the customer makes payment, the time the customer has inspected the product or has reviewed the terms of contract. In this case, the merchant invited the customer to indicate acceptance by a specific kind of conduct that can be considered an acceptance. Therefore, the contract was formed when the purchaser accepted or implicitly indicated his acceptance by using the software product after he had the opportunity to learn the terms on the shrink wrap. In other words, the consumer's act of software purchasing was not tantamount to his acceptance but instead his use of the software was. In addition, the facts in this case indicated that the plaintiff, a software company, provided a conspicuous notice that the license terms were in the product package and, at the time of software start-up, the user had to proceed with the "I agree" routine that was splashed out on the monitor. Finally, the user was also provided with an option to return the product within 30 days, thereby providing the opportunity to decline to be bound by the terms of use. *See ProCD Inc. v. Zeidenberg*, *supra* note 14.

[18] However, the question remains as to whether these three prerequisites really protect consumers from possible risks because the consumers could not see or review the terms and conditions of the shrink wrap at the time the products were ordered. For a detailed discussion and recommendations on shrink wrap agreements, *see e.g.* Coteanu, *supra* note 3, at 52–3. *See also* Winn, *supra* note 15.

5.2.2 Evaluation of Standard Term Validation Principles

An often cited argument in favor of acceptance of the various wrap agreements in the e-market is their economic benefits. As shrink wrap contracts can be legally completed easily and conveniently, they appear to support and facilitate the growth of internet transactions. If consumers and traders are able to enter in to a transaction within a second regardless of their location this would benefit the competitive market, increasing number of goods and services available and facilitating convenient shopping from unlimited traders located everywhere at any time.[19] This corresponds to Sect. 3.2 of the Framework on availability of variety of goods and services at appropriate prices. Also, despite the distance between contractual parties, wrap agreements can be instantly executed via computer network. There is no requirement for travel or physical interaction in the process of forming wrap agreements, reducing the burden of transaction costs on consumers. This corresponds to Sect. 4.10 of the Framework on the reasonable cost of transaction. In addition, a wrap agreement can also serve as an evidence to ensure consumers regarding traders' performance of their contractual obligations under wrap terms. If a trader fails to comply with their legally binding e-contract, a consumer may enforce such obligations on the trader and/or subject the traders to a contractual penalty. This corresponds to Sect. 4.7 of the Framework on the performance of obligations.

Nevertheless, the ever changing and more complex technology may sometimes render contracting through the online wrap method unfair to consumers. This may occur, for instance, when a consumer visits a trader's websites and information is downloaded onto their computers, resulting in automatic, unauthorized changes to the configuration of their computer.[20] Even if those consumers would later review the click wrap agreement and decide not to enter into it, their computer's operating systems would have already been changed. This case appears to be unfair to consumers because they did not really give any assent to the terms and conditions provided through such advanced technological processes. Unfair practices may also occur with browse, web or shrink wraps where consumers can easily be taken advantage of because of the requirement for affirmative action. Consumers may easily be bound by the substantive content of an agreement without even being aware of their existence.[21]

---

[19] *See* OECD, *OECD Conference on Empowering E-Consumers, Strengthening Consumer Protection in the Internet Economy, Background Report' Washington D.C., 8–10 December 2009* (2009), *available at* browse.oecdbookshop.org/oecd/pdfs/free/2498011e.pdf (visited June 21, 2011).

[20] The users were no longer able to use the internet services of non-AOL service providers or to run non-AOL programs. They could not access their e-mails and various personal files provided by non-AOL providers. The court ruled such way of presenting wrap agreements shall not be binding. *See Williams v. America Online, Inc.*, 2001 WL 1356825 (Mass. Supr., February 8, 2001).

[21] This affirmative action of clicking the relevant button in a click wrap agreement is usually deemed to be an express declaration stating that the user has assented to the terms and conditions

Consequently, the judicial institution has to enforce wrap contracts with care and transform its direction to ensure that the technological formation process of wrap agreements does not cause any unfairness toward consumers.[22] To deal with these possible unjust practices, the courts appear to rely heavily upon traditional legal principles as legal guidelines were drawn up through analogies with cases with no internet context.[23] The courts are likely to enforce e-terms in wrap agreements (especially browse or shrink wrap agreements) only if they are displayed in a manner that satisfies the requirement for reasonable notice (e.g. clear and conspicuous form).[24] This is clearly in accordance with the doctrine of reasonable notice, which has been well developed in the law governing traditional transactions.[25]

In most litigation related to the wrap agreements, the question of whether the consumers actually noticed or could have reasonably noticed the e-terms has been considered to be a prerequisite for admitting such terms.[26] However, in analyzing

---

of the agreement. Unlike the click wrap agreement, the browse warp, web wrap and shrink wrap do not require any active action to indicate assent, bringing about a crucial issue on consumer assent. In one case, the US court stated that the browse wrap agreement was not incorporated and thus unenforceable, because the terms were displayed on the website without any clear indication of intent to be bound by the browse terms. *See Specht v. Netscape Communications Corporation*, 150 F. Supp. 2d 585 (S.D.N.Y. July 5, 2001). A similar direction was also found in a shrink wrap agreement case. A shrink wrap agreement offered by a software vendor was not enforceable because there was no required action that was equivalent to expressly assenting to the terms contained in the shrink wrap standardized contract from the user. *See Step-Saver Systems, Inc. v. Wyse Technology* 939 F. 2d 91 (3rd Cir. 1991). *See also Arizona Retail Systems, Inc. v. Software Link, Inc.*, 831 F. Supp. 759 (1993).

[22] For instance, in *America Online, Inc. v. Superior Court*, the California Court of Appeals also refused to enforce a click wrap contract on the grounds of public policy concerns and promoting social justice. In that case, the court established that the forum selection clause in a click wrap contract that was executed or displayed to the user during the installation process on a CD-ROM constituted an unfair contract making process on the user for the following four reasons. First, there were no negotiations. Second, the terms and conditions of the contract were prepared in a standardized form. Third, the clause was in small text and located at the very end of the contract, rendering it difficult for the user to read. Finally, the contract was contrary to California public policy that encourages and promotes appropriate and fair legal remedies for its citizens. Any restrictions on consumers' legal rights are not viewed favorably under California public policy. *See America Online, Inc. v. Superior Court,* 90 Cal. App. 4th 1 (2001).

[23] *See* M. E. Budnitz, *Consumers Surfing for Sales in Cyberspace: What Constitutes Acceptance and What Legal Terms and Conditions Bind the Consumers?*, 16 Georgia State University Law Review 741–87 (2000).

[24] Technological display of the terms during computer use without any required action of consumers or delayed terms can demonstrate a lack of reasonable notice to establish any clear or implied manifestation of assent. *See i.e. Hill v. Gateway 2000, Inc.*, 105 F. 3d 1147 (7th Cir. 1997), *ProCD, Inc. v. Zeidenberg*, 86 F.3d 1447, 1452 (7th Cir. 1997) and *Brower v. Gateway* 2000, Inc. 246 A.D. 2d 246, 251 (NY App. Div. 1998).

[25] According to the reasonable notice rule, consumers must be given reasonable notice of contract terms for unsigned contracts (e.g. tickets or other commercial materials) to constitute or indicate their assent. The rationale for this rule is that consumers might negotiate the contract terms or decide to walk away from the unfavorable terms of contracts. *See* Ramsay, *supra* note 1, at 167.

[26] *See* Tasker and Pakcyk, *supra* note 14, at 91.

the question of sufficient notice there are divergent views, depending on the individual judges' opinion. In the US jurisdictions, some judges require consumers to have actual notice and conduct actions by clicking on phrases that expressly state their assent, while some jurisdictions focus on placement and the existence of a reasonable opportunity to acknowledge the electronic terms and conditions.[27] Another may recognize mere access to a web site as being sufficient to manifest assent to terms and conditions.[28]

It can be inferred that the validation of e-contract mechanism not only recognizes the legal validity of wrap agreements for the purpose of facilitating the growth of e-market without any limitation. Rather, the mechanism also takes into consideration the interests of social justice as cases concerning wrap agreement usually first address the "reasonable notice" question as a means of protecting consumers from an unfair process of forming a wrap agreement. This is to ensure that the terms and conditions of the wrap must be prepared in an appropriate form that gives a reasonable opportunity for consumer to digest them. This corresponds to Sect. 4.2 of the Framework on the sufficient and accurate information and ability to digest information. At the same time, as the reasonable notice principle serves as an indicator to express manifest assent to the terms. With the appropriate opportunity to acknowledge the terms according to the reasonable notice requirement, consumers are enabled to freely make their own selection of terms and conditions that they prefer. This corresponds to Sect. 4.4 of the Framework on the freedom of choice and ability to make rational decision.

However, the flexible way where judges apply the doctrine of reasonable notice to indicate the enforceability of e-contracts is often unclear and unpredictable, lacking any harmonized direction in the judicial decisions as was earlier mentioned.[29] This may result in transactions and market competition not growing as fast as expected because contracting parties are left in doubt as to whether the e-wrap contracts they entered into are actually legally enforceable because the courts are reviewing the enforceability of wrap contracts on a case by case basis. This practice with unclear contractual outcomes somehow may undermine market

---

[27] On one hand, one judge held that the consumer did not agree to clauses that looked like a posted internet advertisement. *See Jones v. Tread Rubber Crop.*, 199 F. Suoo. 2d 539, 544 (S.D. Miss. 2002). Another has involved the placement and the obviousness of a hyperlink where it was "inconspicuously located at the bottom of the internet page", thus providing insufficient notice. *See DeFontes v. Dell Computers Corp.*, No. PC 03-2636, 2004 (R.I. Super. Ct. Jan. 29, 2004). On the other hand, a court found that posted content resembling an advertisement was a sufficient contractual offer that was able to lead to acceptance. *See Lim v. TV Corp. Int'l.*, 121 Cal. Rptr. 2d 333, 336–7 (Cal. Ct. App. 2002). *See also Register.com v. Verio, Inc.*, 126 F. Supp. 2d 238, 248 (S.D.N.Y. 2000).

[28] *See Register.com, Inc. v. Verio, Inc.* 356 F. 3d 393, 403 (2d Cir. 2004). For further refined direction, the repeat consumers to web site are likely to notice the posted terms, being subject to enforcement of browse wrap agreements. *See Druyan v. Jaggar,* 508 F. Supp. 2d 228 (S.D.N.Y Aug. 27, 2007) (holding that where a party repeatedly visited a website for 5 years, the link to the terms that was placed above the link leading to the web page was sufficient notice).

[29] *See* Tasker and Pakcyk, *supra* note 14, at 83.

confidence concerning the performance of contractual obligations. This contradicts Sect. 4.3 of the Framework on the availability of variety of goods and services at appropriate prices.

5.2.3 Overview of Unfair Term Regulations

Council Directive 93/13/EEC of 5 April 1993 on unfair terms in consumer contracts (hereinafter *UTD*) has been adopted and has been in effect since 1993. Its coverage is not limited to contracts that are written on paper, but also applies to e-contracts in consumer sales.[30] Under its provisions, the UTD does not apply to a contract term that is "individually negotiated", but will apply to pre-drafted standard terms according to Article 3 (1) and (2) of the UTD.[31] In general, almost no contracts in B2C transactions are results of the negotiations of the contracting parties. This is especially the case in the online market where e-contracts are typically presented with standardized terms in the form of various wrap agreements. Therefore, almost all e-terms in consumer sales fall under the scope of the UTD and, as a result, any of which that are unfair will not be enforceable on consumers.[32]

To assess which contract provisions constitute unfair terms, it must first be considered whether there exists a significant imbalance in particular rights and obligations under the contract to the detriment of the consumer. Secondly the question of whether such terms are in conflict with good faith, the so called the *fairness test* must be considered.[33] The implementation of this test must take into account "the nature of the goods and services of which the contract was concluded and by referring, at the time of conclusion of the contract, to all the circumstances attending the conclusion of the contract and to all the other terms of the contract or of another contract on which it is dependent"[34] and "the unfair nature of the terms shall relate neither to the definition of the main subject matter of the contract nor to

---

[30] The UTD is one of the Directives of consumer acquis that is currently under review. *See* J. Stuyck, *Unfair Term, in* G. Howells and R. Schulze (eds.), Modernizing and Harmonizing Consumer Contract Law 115, 115 (2009). *See also* European Commission, *Unfair Contract Terms* (July 4, 2007), *available at* ec.europa.eu/consumers/cons_int/safe_shop/unf_cont_terms/index_en.htm (visited 28 June 2012).

[31] *See* Article 3 (1) and (2) of the UTD prescribe general criteria of contracts that are subject to this Directive as: A contractual term that has not been individually negotiated.

[32] According to Article 6 of the UTD, the rules of the UTD always apply to contracts of adhesion that are presented by a "take it or leave it" means, which is in contrast to negotiated contracts. *See* Riefa and Hörnle, *supra* note 12, at 111–2.

[33] *See* Article 3 (1) of the UTD. In Austria, Finland and Luxembourg the fairness test is focused solely on the imbalance of rights and obligations between parties. Differently, in Denmark and Slovakia, this test is limited to moral and honest trading practices. For the further discussion of the fairness test and the scope and meaning of good faith under this Article, *see* Stuyck, *supra* note 30, at 123–4.

[34] *See* Article 4 (1) of the UTD.

the adequacy of the price and remuneration, on the one hand, as against the services or goods supplies in exchange, on the other, in so far as these terms are in plain intelligible language."[35] As examples of the terms that trigger the fairness test, the UTD also provides a list of specific types of contract terms that may be considered unfair in its Annex.[36]

According to the last sentence of Article 5 of the UTD, where the merchant prepares sales contracts in writing, such contracts must be drafted in plain and intelligible language.[37] The requirement under this Article appears not to be restricted only to paper documents, and therefore extends to e-records of e-contracts that must be presented in plain and intelligible language. In case there is any ambiguity about the meaning of a term, it must be interpreted in the most favorable way to the interest of the consumer. This is the so-called *transparency and interpretation principle* under Article 5 of the UTD.[38]

The provisions of the UTD attempt to set reasonable standards for consumer contracts, including those in the form of e-contracts. It is a fundamental objective of the UTD to afford consumers with sufficient and appropriate protection from the abuse of power by traders where the general and classical contract law alone does not adequately protect them, particularly in the area where the one-sidedly drafted contract terms of merchants unfairly limit or oppress consumers' legal rights.[39]

5.2.4 Evaluation of Unfair Term Regulations

The UTD was apparently designed to help protect consumers from unfair terms by providing that unfair contract terms shall not be legally binding.[40] The UTD may

---

[35] *See* Article 4 (2) of the UTD.

[36] *See* Article 3 (3) and the Annex of the UTD.

[37] *See* Article 5 of the UTD.

[38] *See ibid.*

[39] *See* J. K. Winn and B. H. Bix, *Diverging Perspectives on Electronic Contracting in the US and EU*, 54 Cleveland State Law Review 175, 186 (2006) and Riefa and Hörnle, *supra* note 12, at 111.

[40] *See* Article 6 of the UTD Today, the provisions of the UTD highlighted above have been proven to perform their duty in protecting consumers in e-sales in the EU. A leading example of this occurred in France, when over 30 clauses in a pre-drafted internet access contract of American Online, Inc. (AOL) were found to be unfair and thus unenforceable as they violated the provisions of the UTD. The clauses of AOL's standard contract breached the French domestic law of consumer contract implementing the UTD and AOL was subject to a 30,000 Euro fine and ordered to remove the unfair clauses within one month. In addition, AOL agreed to no longer use the nineteen unfair clauses in its standard contract offered to consumers in Germany. AOL also promised to pay 2,000 Deutsche Marks if it included any unfair terms in its pre-drafted contracts in the future. *See* M. L. Rustad and M. V. Onufrio, *The Exportability of the Principles of Software: Lost in Translations?*, 2 Hastings Science & Technology Law Journal 25, 21 (2010). *See also* Riefa and Hörnle, *ibid.*, at 113 and J. R. Maxeiner, *Standard-Terms Contracting in the Global Electronic Age: European Alternatives*, 28 Yale Journal of International Law 109, 164 (2003).

also have an indirect effect in pressuring merchants, the unilateral drafters of the contracts, to pay careful attention when preparing contracts to avoid terms that may be unfair and thus risk their being found to be unenforceable. This also helps raise the standard of trading practices in this area, thus promoting fair trading practices. This corresponds to Sects. 4.5 and 4.14 of the Framework on the fair terms and conditions, and the fair trading practices and consumers' confidence respectively.

However, when considering standard form contracts in e-sales, which are subjected to the UTD, traders often incorporate certain provisions to minimize the burden and complexity that may arise from the transnational nature of e-sales.[41] In case of a dispute with e-consumers located in other jurisdictions, the traders may be forced to conduct legal proceedings to enforce their legal rights in a foreign jurisdiction at great expenses.[42] Moreover, such proceedings would likely be conducted under the law of a foreign jurisdiction that is unfamiliar to the merchant.[43] To avoid facing this predicament, the merchant often includes an arbitration clause, choice of forum clause or application law clause in their standard form contract. This practice of e-merchants has been confirmed by a survey of 500 large internet retailers. From that survey, it was discovered that 49 % of the examined standard contracts included choice of law and choice of forum clauses.[44] Such mandatory choosing of the forum, applicable law or alternative dispute resolution[45] in standard e-terms could also be considered one-sided terms which may be detrimental to consumers.[46] Therefore, UTD has become a tool that protects consumers from these unfriendly terms.

---

[41] A study on the substantive content of standard terms found that the majority of the explored contracts were more favorable to the drafters or the sellers, particularly the standard terms concerning dispute resolution clauses, as compared to the same issues prescribed in the default rules set by the state. *See* F. M. Wurgler, *Unfair Dispute Resolution Clauses: Much Ado About Nothing?, in* O. B. Shahar (ed.), Boilerplate: Foundations of Market Contracts, 45, 45–64 (2007).

[42] *See also* J. Braucher, *New Basics: Twelve Principles for Fair Commerce in Mass-Market Software and Other Digital Products, in* J. K. Winn (ed.), Consumer Protection in the Age of the Information Economy 177, 188 (2006).

[43] *See ibid.*

[44] *See* R. J. Mann and T. Siebeneicher, *Just One Click: The Reality of Internet Retail Contracting*, 108 Columbia Law Review 984, 999 (2008).

[45] Although arbitration comes with confidentiality, speed and lower cost, the binding arbitration of future disputes in consumer transactions has been criticized and objected to by many scholars. The OECD, for example, has considered cross border consumer dispute resolution in various study documents and mandatory arbitration is not suggested or endorsed by them because it places an unfair burden on consumers. For further arguments regarding arbitration clauses in consumer sales, *see* S. McGill, *Consumer Arbitration Clause Enforcement: A Balanced Legislative Response*, 47 American Business Law Journal 361–413 (2010).

[46] *See* Wurgler, *supra* note 41, at 45–64 (2007).

5.2.4.1 Arbitration Clause

Article 3 (3) of the UTD for example clearly classifies arbitration clauses as unfair provisions. In its Annex, which offers examples of unfair contract terms, terms which have the object or effect of . . .“(q) excluding or hindering the consumer’s right to take legal action or exercise any other legal remedy, particularly by requiring the consumer to take disputes exclusively to arbitration not covered by legal provisions, unduly restricting the evidence available to him or imposing on him a burden of proof which, according to the applicable law, should lie with another party to the contract”[47] are considered unfair terms. This renders a provision in an e-consumer sales contract, where a future dispute is required to be put before an arbitration panel, an unfair term that is thus unenforceable under the UTD.

5.2.4.2 Choice of Forum Clause

In contrast, a choice of forum clause is not clearly listed in the Annex of the UTD as one of the examples of unfair terms as is the case with arbitration clauses. However, when considering the Council Regulation (EC) No. 44/2001 on jurisdiction and the recognition and enforcement of judgments in civil and commercial matters (hereinafter *Brussels Regulation*), which states the rules for determining jurisdiction and the enforcement of judgments that equally applies to cross broader e-consumer sales,[48] Articles 15 to Article 17 guarantees a consumer’s right to file or defend lawsuits in his or her local court.[49] This right may not be contractually waived by the consumer.[50] On this basis, an EU consumer possesses an absolute right to sue and litigate in the court of his or her domicile. This renders the e-trader unable to incorporate a choice of forum clause in its standard form contracts.

Although a choice of forum clause referring to the exclusive jurisdiction of a court located in a city or country is not clearly specified as an unfair term in the Annex of the UTD, such a clause can interfere with the consumer’s right to take legal action, resulting in the violation of Annex (q), which prohibits “excluding or hindering the consumer’s right to take legal action or exercise any other legal

---

[47] *See* Annex (q) of the UTD.

[48] In the European Union, the Brussels Regulation provides the ground rules for jurisdiction of judgments in civil and commercial cases between parties and governs the enforcement of judgments through the Member States.

[49] Article 15 of the Brussels Regulation defines a consumer as someone who is acting “outside his trade or profession” which is the definition used in all of the mandatory rules concerning consumer protection under the European Legislation. Article 17 specifies that consumers cannot waive their rights to initiate or defend litigation in their local or residential courts.

[50] *See ibid.*

remedy" of the UTD as well. In *Oceano Groupo Editorial v. Salvat Editores,*[51] the European Court of Justice (hereinafter *ECJ*) confirmed the position of Annex (q). In that case, the ECJ refused to enforce the seller's choice of forum clause in an e-consumer contract that conferred exclusive jurisdiction on a court in Spain, a country that was not the domicile of the consumer, as such clause was found by the ECJ to be in violation of the provisions of the UTD.[52] The clause required the consumer to defend its claim in a distant jurisdiction, thus constituting an unfair term because it excluded or hindered the right of the consumer to take a legal action.

5.2.4.3 Applicable Law Clause

In analyzing whether an applicable law clause or a choice of law clause, which prescribes the law that would apply in a cross border transaction, constitutes an unfair term under the UTD, one must refer to the Council Regulation (EC) No. 593/2008 on the law applicable to contractual obligation (hereinafter *Rome I Regulation*). It governs the principles courts use in determining which law to apply in EU cross border transactions, including e-sales. It allows B2B contracting parties to choose the law applicable to their contract.[53] On the contrary, in the case of B2C contracts, the Rome I regulation is functionally equivalent to the mandatory rules of the Brussels Regulation, which means that the law applicable to a consumer contract is the governing law of the habitual residence of the consumer.[54] This mandatory governing rule, which also applies to e-transactions, only imposes the condition that the consumer must be an individual person with a "place of residence" in an EU Member State. The Rome I's mandatory rule applies to merchants who have direct activities in jurisdictions of the EU Member States.

In addition, the provision of Article 7 (1) of the UTD requires that "Member States shall ensure that, in the interests of consumers and of competitors, adequate and effective means exist to prevent the continued use of unfair terms in contracts concluded with consumers by sellers or suppliers."[55] This consequently means that choice of law clauses which require a dispute to be litigated under a law foreign to the consumer's place of residence, and thus unfamiliar to the consumer, is not only in violation of the Rome I Regulation, but may also be in breach of the spirit of

[51] *See* Joined cases C-240/98 to C-244/98, *Oceano Grupo Editorial SA v. Rocio Muciano Quinterno* and *Salvat Editores SA v. Jose M. Sanchez Alcon Prades, Jose Luis Copano Bacillo, Mohammed Berroane and Emilio Vinas Feliu*, 2000 E.C.R I-4941.

[52] The ECJ ruled that the forum clause violated the UTD because consumers were compelled to settle their dispute far away from their home. Also the court additionally reasoned that where the cases involve a small monetary amount, the consumers seem to have no redress because the cost of litigation will highly exceed the possible recovery. Therefore, such choice of forum clauses are considered to have the effect of excluding or hindering the rights of consumer to pursue legal action.

[53] *See* Article 4 of the Rome I Regulation.

[54] *See* Article 4 of the Rome I Regulation.

[55] *See* Article 7 (1) of the Rome I Regulation.

Article 7 (1) of UTD where the Member States have to act as necessary to fight those unfair terms that appear to limit the potential interest of consumers in filing or defending their disputes.

From the discussion of the UTD so far, it can be said that the UTD is a potent substantive mechanism that can be applied against standardized terms that have the potential to be unfair to consumers and renders them unenforceable. This includes those used in e-sale transactions, where e-merchants usually place contract terms such as arbitration clauses, choice of forum clauses or applicable law clauses that are favorable to themselves to avoid the hassles of cross border transactions as mentioned above.[56]

However, at the same time, such features of the UTD may be too one-sided, as it does not take into consideration the negative effects it may have on traders.[57] Under the UTD, the burdens, hassles, and costs of cross border dispute resolutions in e-sales are imposed solely on e-traders as they have to comply with the cost and complexity of law and enforcement in foreign jurisdictions at consumers' locations.[58] A study shows that 47 % of e-retailers from the survey group decided to limit their business to within their jurisdiction because the need for compliance with unfamiliar foreign regulations is a big obstacle to cross broader e-sales.[59] Due to possible burdens arising from a cross border dispute in e-sales, a certain number of merchants may choose to confine their business activities to their domestic markets, leaving the transnational e-market completely. This contradicts Sect. 4.3 of the Framework on the availability of variety of goods and services at appropriate prices. Also, to survive in the cross border market, an e-trader might pass on these risks to consumers in the form of higher prices for goods and services or higher transaction costs when possible.[60] Moreover, this contradicts Sect. 4.10 of

---

[56] In the original proposal for a Directive of Consumer Rights which was the result of the Review of the Consumer *Acquis* launched in 2004 by the Commission with the aim of improving and modernizing the existing consumer directives, it includes a blacklist of terms that are unfair in all circumstances and a gray list of terms that are presumed to be unfair, replacing the UTD. The blacklist may be an effective tool for consumers in struggling against compelled arbitration clauses, unfair choice of law and forum clauses that are commonly found in wrap agreements.

[57] The intervention in the market to protect or benefit consumers can have a distributive effect toward others. The merchant will suffer from certain costs to comply with the set regulations. *See* H. Luth, Behavioural Economics in Consumer Policy, The Economic Analysis of Standard Terms in Consumer Contracts Revisited 113 (2011).

[58] The requirements for businesses to comply with foreign laws and litigate in foreign jurisdictions add cost to those who do business across borders. *See also* European Commission, *Proposal for a Directive of the European Parliament and of Council Concerning Unfair Business-to-Consumer Commercial Practices in the Internal Market and Amending Directives 84/450/EEC, 97/7/EC and 98/27/EC Explanatory Memorandum, 18.6.2003 COM* (2003) 356 final 2003/0134 (COD) (June 18, 2003), *available at* eur-lex.europa.eu/LexUriServ/LexUriServ.do?uri=CELEX:52003PC0356:EN:NOT (visited March 1, 2013).

[59] *See* European Commission, *Unfair Contract Terms* July 4 2007), *available at* ec.europa.eu/consumers/cons_int/safe_shop/unf_cont_terms/index_en.htm (visited 28 June 2012).

[60] Legal obligations will create additional costs to sellers, who will usually pass these on to consumers where possible. This is the so called mandatory allocation or risk. *See* R. J. van Den

the Framework on the reasonable cost of transaction. As the price increases, choices decrease. Not all consumers may prefer this situation. Some might have a preference for lower price and more choice of goods and services and be willing to trade off those preferential conditions with better or fair terms.[61] The provisions of the UTD may put restrictions on consumer choices by mandating certain terms. This would be preferred by consumers who want higher quality terms, but it ignores other consumers who prefer lower quality terms where they lead to lower prices. The intervention of the UTD may somehow undermine the consumers' sovereignty to make their own decision and the freedom to decide what fits their best interests.[62] This contradicts Sect. 4.4 of the Framework on the freedom of choice and ability to make rational decision. Further, the UTD and government interventions may lead to the moral hazard problem. By implementing governmental interventions and removing consumers' individual responsibility, consumers will have no incentive to look after themselves or learn from their experiences and mistakes, relying solely on governmental protection.[63] For example, consumers may no longer be interested in reading essential information and contract terms displayed by the merchant as they believe that the law already gives them sufficient protection from unfair terms.[64] This would bring about bad decision making on the side of consumers, rendering them unable to make rational decisions that will help maximize the value of contractual exchange as reflected in its ability to satisfy their true needs. This contradicts Sect. 4.4 of the Framework on the freedom of choice and ability to make rational decision.

Apart from the previously discussed pitfalls of the UTD,[65] the effectiveness of the UTD in practice remains questionable. Evidence worth mentioning includes a joint survey conducted by the Netherlands' consumer authority, together with

---

Bergh, *Competition Law and Consumer Protection Legislation, in* A. N. Hatzis (ed.), Economic Analysis of Law: A European Prospective 22, 22–3 (2003).

[61] *See* R. J. van Den Bergh, *Subsidiary as an Economic Demarcation Principle and the Emergence of European Private Law,* 5 Maastricht Journal of European and Comparative Law 129, 135 (1998).

[62] "... it would be indeed ironic if greater insight into the complexity of human decision making become the justification of taking the freedom to decide, even if imperfectly, from those very individuals." *See* S. Issacharoff, *Can There be a Behavioral Law and Economic?*, 51 Vanderbilt Law Review 1729, 1745 (1998).

[63] *See Luth*, supra note 57, at 35.

[64] *See* C. P. Gillette, *Rolling Contracts as Agency Problem,* 42 Houston Law Review 679, 716–7 (2004).

[65] Some scholars argue against the UTD that terms of consumer contracts will be automatically efficient in the market as the invisible hand is assumed to drive the information flow, resulting in better and fairer terms. To maximize profit and attract more consumers, sellers will have to draft their standard terms to meet consumers' preferences, in particular those who are reading and shopping for better terms. Other consumers then can free ride on the efforts of the informed consumers who discipline the market unless they can be distinguished and preferentially treated by sellers. For the details of the argument that the competition drives efficient contracts, *see* Luth, *supra* note 57, at 134–5.

institutional partners from Belgium and Luxembourg, on the e-standard terms.[66] From that study, 10 out of 18 large chain retailers with a total of over 3,800 stores were found to insert illegal terms into their standard e-contracts, including imposing additional unfair costs on delivery and repair, establishing unreasonable processes for returning goods.[67] These terms will definitely not pass the fairness test under the provision of the UTD, as they directly infringe the law.

Legal enforcement challenges may well explain the situation. The inherent trans-border nature of the e-market represents a great enforcement challenge to the relevant authorities as their power is often limited within one jurisdiction.[68] The authorities in the UK, for example, stated that they are unable to combat infringement affecting non-English consumers even though the illegal practices are committed in their jurisdiction because of jurisdictional restrictions on their power.[69] Additionally, e-sales represent a great challenge and difficulty for consumer protection authorities in terms of identifying the location of rogue online retailers. Doing so requires a substantial investment of time, money, human resources, and skills training to cope with the fast development of e-technology.

5.2.5 *Overview of Unconscionability Doctrine*

A very well-known test applied by the US courts in determining whether standardized and adhesive terms, including those contained in wrap agreements, are enforceable is the *unconscionability doctrine*.[70] The court will not enforce a standard term if it finds that such term is unconscionable or unfair to consumers. In other words, this doctrine, which deals with the combination of unequal bargaining power and unfair terms,[71] has been applied by the courts in testing the enforceability of e-contracts and in refusing to enforce unfair terms.

The US Courts have developed *the two-pronged test* to examine whether the contract is unconscionable. The test categorizes unconscionability into *procedural* and *substantive* elements.[72] Procedural unconscionability examines the process of

[66] For the translated detailed of this study, namely Consumentenautoriteit's study conducted in 2010, *see ibid.*, at 191.

[67] *See ibid.*

[68] *See* OECD, *supra* note 19, at 30.

[69] *See ibid.*

[70] The substantive rule of unconscionability or unreasonableness has been developed in common law countries, including commonwealth countries. The concept of unconscionability represents a combination of unequal bargaining power and unfair terms. *See* Lord Denning's explanation in *Lloyda Bank Ltd v. Bundy* (1975) QB 326.

[71] *See ibid.*

[72] For the details of first development of the two-pronged test, *see* A. Leff, *Unconscionability and the Code – The Emperor's New Clause*, 115 University of Pennsylvania Law Review 485, 489–546 (1967). *See also Williams v. Walker-Thomas Furniture Co.*, 350 F. 2d 445, 449 (D.C. Cir.

contract formation and whether one of the contracting parties has no other option but to enter into the contract or whether it lacks voluntary consent or knowledge because of uneven bargaining power or being in a weaker position.[73] Similarly, the substantive test scrutinizes contract terms and conditions to see whether their contents or substance are oppressive or unreasonably one-sided.[74]

In general, the courts will investigate whether a contract was unconscionable at the time it was formed. If the contract is found to have both substantive and procedural defects, the unconscionability doctrine will be applied, resulting in its terms and conditions being held to be unenforceable. A procedural defect or substantive defect alone is not enough to trigger application of the doctrine.[75]

When deciding on the application of the unconscionability doctrine, the courts weigh several factors on a case by case basis. Unconscionability cannot be applied merely by looking at the contract. There is also a need for a deeper analysis of commercial practices, objectives, and possible outcomes, including the context where the contract was finally made.[76]

This doctrine is considered a remedy in contract law cases and a legal basis for refusing unfair specific performance, which has evolved from the fairness and equity concerns that underpin the core fundamental idea of contract law.[77] Under

---

1965). The guideline drawn by this court decision mirrors the two-pronged test initially introduced by A. Leff.

[73] *See Parilla v. IAP Worldwide Services VI, Inc.*, 368, F. 3d 269, 276–77 (3d. Cir. 2004). *See also* A. J. Schmitz, *Embracing Unconscionability's Safety Net Function*, 58 Alabama Law. Review 73, 91–2 (2006).

[74] *See Brower v. Gateway 2000*, Inc. 676 N.Y.S. 2d 569, 574 (N.Y.App. Div.1998).

[75] *See* M. Zhang, *Contractual Choice of Law in Contracts of Adhesion and Party Autonomy*, 41 Akron Law Review 123, 153 (2008).

[76] *See Wilson Trading Crop. v. David Ferguson, Ltd.* 23 N.Y. 2d 398, 403 (N.Y. 1968). The court concluded that the question of whether the terms in a contract are unconscionable or not is an issue for the judicial institution to determine based on the background and circumstances surrounding the commercial setting of such contract.

[77] Generally modern contract law has been crafted and advanced by lawmakers and scholars who put emphasis on the freedom of choice and the limitation of state regulation and judicial intervention in promissory exchange. Formalist concepts that promote harsh enforcement of commercial contracts are relatively prevalent. As the society industrialized in the US, the contract rules were then formalized which focused on the idea of modern contract law and transformed into the Restatement (Second) of Contracts and Article 2 of the Uniform Commercial Code (UCC), which governs the sale of goods. However, such formalized contract laws cannot ignore the flexible fairness that lies at the core of contract. The Restatement (Second) of Contracts and Article 2 of the UCC, have appeared to recognize the unconscionability doctrine as a mechanism to flexibly protect fairness and equality. The Restatement (Second) of Contracts states prescribes unenforceable standard terms are that beyond reasonable expectation. The Restatement (Second) of Contracts refers to the unconscionability doctrine that a bargain "is not unconscionable merely because the parties to it are unequal in bargaining position nor even because the inequality results in an allocation of risks to the weaker party". *See e.g.* Braucher, *supra* note 42, at 192, Schmitz, *supra* note 73, at 75, P. S. Atiyah, The Rise and Fall of Freedom of Contract 146–7 (1979) and P. Huber, *Flypaper Contracts and the Genesis of Modern Tort*, 10 Cardozo Law Review 2263, 2268–9 (1989).

the unconscionability doctrine, the court is allowed to scrutinize the conclusion of the contract in the interest of distributive justice, enabling interference by the state concerning contractual activities.[78]

5.2.6 Evaluation of the Unconscionability doctrine

Unsurprisingly, the main objective of this doctrine are similar to those mentioned in the unfair term rules, which is to battle the unfair terms in consumer contracts, functioning as a check that ensures some appropriate degree of contractual fairness. It is a weapon to fight against unfairness in standard contracts, which is based on the view that there is a need for a tool to protect parties that are vulnerable.[79] This corresponds to Sect. 4.5 of the Framework on the fair terms and conditions. Simultaneously, the implementation of this doctrine will also help prevent the abusive use of economic power and unjust business practices.[80] This will ultimately increase confidence and cooperation among market participants, creating fair trading practices.[81] This corresponds to Sect. 4.14 of the Frameworks on the fair trading practices and consumers' confidence.

As for e-contracts, the unconscionability doctrine will be implemented as it is in the case of general contracts. However, in determining whether the doctrine can promote the flexible fairness norm lying at the core of contract, one must consider and analyze past lessons and experiences from the related precedents.

In the procedural unconscionability context, the US courts have taken divergent views as to what constitutes procedural unconscionability in internet transactions. One trial court held that the arbitration clause is procedurally unconscionable as it is

[78] During the 1970s, courts in the U.S. had shown their positions on these debates through their judgments. These judgments confirmed the courts' belief that state actions are necessary for the creation and assurance of basic justice although such state actions may adversely affect the exercise of freedom of contract. In *Jones v. Star Credit Corp.*, for example, the court declared that the doctrine of unconscionability is a state regulation ensuring basic justice while respecting the sanctity of bargain on the basis that contracting parties are free to make decisions to be bound by any contract term that they are truly willing to be bound by. *See Jones v. Star Credit Corp.*, 298 N.Y.S. 2d 264, 265 (N.Y. Sup. Ct. 1969). *See e.g. Rowe v. Great Atlantic & Pacific Tea Co.*, 385 N.E. 2d 566, 569 (N.Y. 1978) and *Ortelere v. Teachers' Retirement Bd. of City of New York*, 250 N.E. 2d 460, 465 (N.Y. 1969).

[79] Policing contractual relationship for unfairness is not a new concept. The unconscionability doctrine is believed to have its roots in the Roman civil law of *laesio enormis* doctrine in the early fourth century. According to this Roman doctrine, the seller could call for revocation if the price of a land sale received was not equivalent or over half the value of the land sold. For further discussion of the historical evolution of unconscionability, *see* S. E. Friedman, *Giving Unconscionability More Muscle: Attorney's Fee as a Remedy for Contractual Overreaching*, 44 Georgia Law Review 317, 334–5 (2010). *See also* Edwards, *supra* note 8, at 672.

[80] *See* Edwards, *ibid.*

[81] *See ibid.*

adhesive to the contract, being drafted by one contracting party having superior bargaining strength, and imposed on the other contracting party who only had the option of either adhering to the contract and all its terms or rejecting it.[82] However, other courts' determinations of procedural unconscionability may not be based on the adhesive nature alone. One has concluded that, by clicking a box on the website which including terms in a hyperlink, the clicking party has indicated lawful assent to those terms and that this did not constitute an unconscionable procedure.[83] In another instance, a lack of negotiation and the existence of unequal bargaining power did not indicate an unconscionable procedure as the consumers were free to shop around on the internet where there are myriad of offerors of goods and services[84] or where a party had a fair opportunity to refuse the electronic standard agreement.[85] Also, some courts have considered that consumers having unlimited time to learn terms and conditions makes forum selection clauses legally enforceable.[86]

On the substantive unconscionability aspect, whether terms are substantive unconscionable usually depends on their particular content and language.[87] One judicial decision, for example, concluded that consumers failed to prove that they would be deprived of any remedy which they were legally entitled to if the arbitration settlement was applied, thus failing to meet the requirements of the test of substantive unconscionability.[88] Another court similarly refused a claim that an agreement was unconscionable based on its content where it included an exclusive forums clause.[89] On the other hand, a different court opined that an arbitration clause is unconscionable because there is a sole determiner of matters concerning disputes, a prohibition against consolidating consumers' claims and the imposition of prohibitive arbitration fees and restrictions on the venue where consumers could conduct proceedings, deeming the contents of the contract to be oppressive.[90]

---

[82] *See Comb v. Paypal, Inc.*, 218 F. Supp. 2d 1165 (N.D. Cal. 2002).

[83] *See DeJohn v. The TV Corp. International*, 245 F. Supp. 2d 913, 915–19 (N.D. Ill. 2003).

[84] This highlighted the difficulty of proving an online contract unconscionable, *see* R. J. Casamiquela, *Contractual Assent and Enforceability in Cyberspace*, 17 Berkeley Technology Law Journal 475, 493–5 (2002).

[85] *See Novak v. Overature Svcs.*, 309 F. Supp. 2d 446, 456 (E.D.N.Y.2004).

[86] *See ibid.*, at 452. *See also Riensche v. Cingular Wireless LLC*, No. C06-1325Z, 2006 U.S. Dist. (December 27, 2006), *available at* aterwynneblog.com/oregon_business_litigatio/files/riensche_order.pdf (visited January 12, 2013).

[87] Contractual content and the content of the language have long been problematic issues in traditional consumer sales and the discussion is still ongoing. This paper has limited discussion in this area as the contractual language is not the main critical issue in the internet context and it does not create any distinctive problems as compared to the related long developed ideas in traditional sales.

[88] *See Hubbert v. Dell Corp.*, 835 N.E. 2d 113, 126 (Ill. App. Ct. 2005).

[89] *See Novak v. Overature Svcs.*, 309 F. Supp. 2d 446, 452 (E.D.N.Y.2004).

[90] *See Comb v. Paypal, Inc.*, 218 F. Supp. 2d 1165 (N.D. Cal. 2002).

In e-transactions, consumers have often argued that a forum selection clause or an arbitration clause is unfair and unconscionable in its content as it appears to limit the use of a class action. There are divergent opinions of courts as to whether the term of a contract that removes recourse to a class action is unenforceable. For example, one court ruled that a seller has no right to constrain the procedural tool of class actions and such contractual limitation (e.g. a forum selection clause or an arbitration clause) has no effect on enforcement.[91] However, another court legally enforced an arbitration clause present in online a wrap agreement as it found there was insufficient evidence of an intention to cheat a large number of consumers.[92]

Also, it is interesting to point out that without the doctrine of procedural unconscionability, the courts have sometimes bypassed considering the issue of substantive unconscionability and whether the contract contains unfair or unreasonable terms. A court once left unanswered the question of whether the content of an applicable law and forum clause which designated the law of a distant, foreign, jurisdiction were inherently oppressive and unfair or not.[93] Instead, the court concluded that because procedural unconscionability was absent, the doctrine of unconscionability would not apply.

The precedents indicate that the courts have different ideas as to what triggers *the two-pronged test* of procedural and substantive elements in e-sales. Sometimes they appear to restrain the implementation of unconscionability doctrine. This is because there is a claim that, "the doctrine attributes conflict with classical *will theory* that supports individuals' freedom to make contract choice and also that courts use the doctrine's flexibility to second-guess contract choices based on subjective determination".[94] In other words, the unconscionability doctrine may distort the liberty of contract at the fundamental core of classical contract law[95] by allowing judges to apply the doctrine as a way of adding their own subjective idea of justice.[96]

---

[91] *See DeFontes v. Dell Computer Corp.*, No. PC 03-2636, 2004(R. I. Sup. Ct.).

[92] *See Provencher v. Dell, Inc.*, 409 F. Supp. 2d 1196, 1201–02 (C.D. Cal. 2006).

[93] *See DeJohn v. The TV Corp. International,* 245 F. Supp. 2d 913, 915–19 (N.D. Ill. 2003).

[94] For the further discussions on this matter, *see* Schmitz, *supra* note 73, at 75.

[95] Contemporary trends in contract law accept the individual's right to pursue their individual interests by contractual means and refuses the imposition of limitations on such rights such as through judicial intervention using the unconscionability doctrine in relation to social justice. *See e.g.* E. A. Posner, *Contract Law in the Welfare State: A Defense of the Unconscionability Doctrine, Usury Laws, and Related Limitation on the Freedom to Contract*, 24 Journal Legal Studies 283, 318–9 (1995) and M. Rosenfeld, *Contract and Justice: The Relation Between Classical Contract Law and Social Contract theory*, 70 Iowa Law Review 796, 776–83 (1985).

[96] At present, there is no current objective criterion for establishing what is an appropriate "just term". *See* R. A. Epstein, *Unconscionability: A Critical Reappraisal, Search Term Begin*, 18 Journal of Law & Economics 293, 306 (1975) and M. Rosenfeld, *ibid*, at 779–840. On the other hand, those who are against the limited application of this doctrine believe that judges are quite qualified to exercise their discretion in relation to social fairness norm as members of society. As members of society judges have a better understanding of such norms than the complex formalized rules or regulations.

Based on the assumptions made by law and economics, an individual can make his best rational contractual choice when he or she has been given all necessary information and the enforcement of the contractual choice made under such conditions will maximize overall economic welfare.[97] Richard Epstein argues that "application of unconscionability in a substantive sense undercuts contractual liberty in a manner that is apt to do more social harm than good".[98] Courts' constrained analysis and application of unconscionability is sometimes necessary to ensure and promote that assumption which will have beneficial effects towards consumers' complete freedom. This corresponds to Sect. 4.4 of the Framework on the freedom of choice and ability to make rational decision.

Another reason for courts to maintain and limit their role in challenging e-contracts based on unconscionability is that the doctrine appears to conflict with the core principle of contracts law focused on promissory enforcement that supports economic growth and market efficiency.[99] A party to a contract may be easily released from obligations they committed to through use of the doctrine regardless of the fact that the party voluntarily entered into the contract and that the terms and conditions as a whole fulfilled the parties' interests at the time the contract was concluded.[100] There is an argument that "economic analysis reveals no grounds other than fraud, incapacity, and duress for allowing a party to repudiate the bargain that he made in entering into contract."[101] For this reason, the strict application of the unconscionability doctrine is necessary as it promotes performance of obligations between parties of the consumer contract. This corresponds to Sect. 4.7 of the Framework on the performance of obligations. Additionally, confidence in the enforcement of contractual performance by market players also fosters market certainty that will promote the parties' long-term benefit and the efficient allocation of resources in society. This corresponds to Sect. 4.3 of the Framework on the availability of variety of goods and services at appropriate prices.

Based on the above reasons, the restrained implementation of the unconscionability doctrine in e-transactions has prevalently been adopted and recognized by many courts' rulings. The U.S. courts now often assume that e-contracts are not procedurally unconscionable because consumers are able to search for information and seek out many options available to them in the internet market and they can freely read them without any time limit.[102] Such assumptions release the courts from being obliged to consider the contents of the contract to determine whether they are substantively unconscionable. As not all unfair e-standard terms will fit the

---

[97] *See* Schmitz, *supra* note 73, at 75.

[98] *See* Epstein, *supra* note 96, at 315.

[99] *See ibid.*, at 293.

[100] *See* A. R. Kamp, *Uptown Act: A History of the Uniform Commercial Code: 1940–1949*, 51 SMU Law Review 257, 335 (1998).

[101] *See* Schmitz, *supra* note 73, at 98. The author explains the economic rationale behind the strict application of the unconscionability doctrine by referring to the statements of many scholars.

[102] *See ibid.*, at 110–1.

demands of *the two-pronged test*, some of them may therefore be legally enforceable.

This is especially true when considering certain provisions that e-merchants like to put in their e-contracts to avoid the costs and hardships associated with cross border transactions such as arbitration clauses, forum selection clauses and applicable law clauses.[103] These e-clauses would often not trigger the unconscionability doctrine and would always be enforceable if the courts strictly applied it. Due to the great alternatives in e-market and the unlimited time consumers have to read the terms, standard e-contracts would not be considered to constitute a form of procedural unconscionability that requires the court to apply the substantive unconscionable test to their content.[104]

In addition, the strict application of unconscionability to disputes using both procedural and substantive tests usually bars courts from releasing consumers form e-click wrap, browse wrap or shrink warp agreements.[105] E-wrap contracts seem to be very adhesive, but often pass *the two-pronged test*.[106] As Amy Schmitz pointed out about the unconscionability doctrine, such "rigid legislative nets also leave gaps that merchants may manipulate by drafting contracts to the edge of permissible practice. They also allow merchants to evade consumer protections through the choice of law clause designing the law of states that strictly enforce form contracts".[107] It is true that some courts may reject or deny the enforcement of choice of law clauses, but many are willing to legally recognize such clauses as a tool to promote and facilitate e-commerce.[108]

With a strictly confined doctrine of unconscionability, the courts may have overlooked its original objective, which focused on justice and equity in contractual

---

[103] These kinds of standard terms do not explicitly conflict with any substantive laws of the US. The Restatement (Second) of Contracts allows parties to freely choose an exclusive forum. Section 114 endorses the forum selection clause which states that the court will broadly enforce the parties' choices of forum clause unless the choice is "unfair or unreasonable". The UCC also entitled the parties' choice of law in standard form unless it was so one sided as to be "unconscionable". Consequently, these terms shall be legally enforceable unless they meet the two prong tests of unconscionability and are found to be unfair or unreasonable terms.

[104] *See* R. J. Casamiquela, *Contractual Assent and Enforceability in Cyberspace*, 17 Berkeley Technology Law Journal 475, 493–5 (2002). *See also Riensche v. Cingular Wireless*, LLC, No. C06-1325Z, 2006 WL 3827477. (W.D. Wash. Dec. 27, 2006).

[105] Due to the fact that the courts respect the inviolability of the freedom of contract theory and value promissory exchange promoting electronic growth and economic developments. *See* Friedman, *supra* note 79, at 342–3.

[106] *See ibid.*

[107] *See* Schmitz, *supra* note 73, at 91–2.

[108] *See* G. A. Michael, *Is There a There There? Toward Greater Certainty for Internet Jurisdiction*, 16 Berkeley Technology Law Journal 1345, 1387–90 (2001). The author noted that the "court generally enforces forum selection clauses and that cases protecting consumers from manufacturers' contractual specifications of applicable law are exception rather than rules."

relationships, and its role in nurturing and promoting distributive justice in the market.[109] This means that the courts should more actively prevent formalist assumptions that some standard terms should be legally enforceable simply because they have been commonly used in practice in the market. Otherwise, "merchant and corporate contract-drafters may successfully transform oppressive form contracts into accepted practice in their industries."[110] Businesses may then finally have monopoly power over contract terms in the consumer context, inserting unfair or unfavorable terms into their standard contract. This contradicts Sects. 4.5 and 4.14 of the Framework on the fair terms and conditions and the fair trading practices and consumers' confidence.

Apparently, the recognition of arbitration clauses, forum selection clauses and applicable law clauses in e-contracts may also lead to unfairness to consumers in the procedural dimension of access to justice as they would bear the burdens and costs of having to conduct dispute resolution according to the unfamiliar law and sometimes in a distance jurisdiction.[111] Also, as the value of the vast majority of e-transactions is relatively modest, consumers may choose not to take any actions to claim or defend their rights under unfamiliar laws in foreign countries.[112] This contradicts Sects. 4.11 and 4.13 of the Framework about the right to conduct dispute resolution in a convenient location and the enforcement of remedies or redresses.

Under such risky circumstances for e consumers, some writers suggest a flexible approach in applying the unconscionability doctrine to maximize the effectiveness of distributing justice and to increase the court's role as protector of justice in e-sales, promoting the initial and historical objectives of the doctrine.[113] With flexible application, the courts should actively resist unreasonable contracting practices that create consumer resentment, moving the focus from the sole economic interests to justice value.

Interestingly, such thinking is also reflected in one case worth mentioning, *Brower v. Gateway 2000, Inc*. where the court applied a flexible unconscionability doctrine, rendering unenforceable an arbitration clause in a shrink wrap agreement by weighing the interests of general justice against the burden of the arbitration clause.[114] The court's view was that an arbitration clause requiring high fees and an

---

[109] *See* Schmitz, *supra* note 73, at 98–102. The author discusses unconscionability's failure to fix contractual wrongs because of bargaining inequalities and unfair terms.

[110] *See ibid.*, at 104. The author further analyzes a numbers of weaknesses concerning strict implementation of unconscionability.

[111] *See* Braucher, *supra* note 42, at 188.

[112] The enforcement of consumer protection law is faced with many challenges. Large numbers of consumers will not go to court because the expected benefits from going to the courts or conducting dispute settlements do not exceed the cost of participating in such processes. In internet sales, the cost of time, effort and money seem to be far greater for e-consumers who lost a small value looking for dispute settlement in a distant place under unknown law. *See* Luth, *supra* note 57, at 151.

[113] *See* Schmitz, *supra* note 73, at 111–2. *See also* Zhang, *supra* note 75, at 152–6.

[114] *See Brower v. Gateway 2000*, Inc., 676 N.Y.S. 2d.

inconvenient forum impeded consumers' legal rights and was thus not enforceable.[115]

Such flexible application of unconscionability as a safety net against unfair terms in e-contracts may give a signal to companies that they should carefully police their pre-drafted terms.[116] As one author has suggested, "this may help curb litigation by transforming companies' healthy fear of unconscionability into more reasonable contracting practices".[117] Businesses may be wise to positively revise their clauses which are likely to be found to be unfair or unreasonable harsh to increase the certainty of the contracts' enforcement.[118] This corresponds to Sect. 4.14 of the Framework on the fair trading practices and consumers' confidence.

It can be said here that an arbitration clause, a choice of forum clause and an applicable law clause in e-standard contracts may sometimes be considered unconscionable, depending on whether the unconscionability doctrine is strictly or flexibly applied.[119] In general, such standardized e-terms are not automatically unconscionable for economic reasons as e-contracts help promote economic growth. In any event, if there is any specific evidence showing that there are excessive burdens being placed on consumers (for example, high costs and long distances to travel to arbitrate under arbitration clauses), the broad and flexible unconscionability doctrine may sometimes be applied by the court and the outcome would be that such onerous terms would not be enforced.

Regrettably, today the U.S. judicial decisions in applying this doctrine and its two-pronged test seem to vary among courts, lacking a bright line rule, resulting in unclear and unpredictable outcomes.[120] As a result, the traders may fear judicial unpredictability in the determination of unconscionability and decide to avoid transactions with parties who may claim unconscionability.[121] This contradicts Sect. 4.3 of the Framework on the availability of variety of goods and services at appropriate prices. Also, there is a caution that the merchant may pass the costs of such unpredictable dispute resolution to consumers in forms of increased price and

[115] *See ibid.*

[116] *See* S. Macaulay, *Elegant Models, Empirical Pictures, and the Complexities of Contract*, 11 Law and Society Review 507, 517–20 (1997).

[117] *See* Schmitz, *supra* note 73, at 114.

[118] *See ibid.*

[119] The difficulty in seeking the optimal balance between protecting consumers from being taken advantage of by business and the promotion of market efficiency pressures the US court to create a special scale of justice for determining the validity of e-consumer contracts. In many cases, the court finds it difficult to balance this special scale and accommodate both of these two equally important interests. *See* S. Burton, Principle of Contract Law 256 (1995).

[120] Contract law principles and the unconscionability doctrine governing standard contracts have long been claimed to be vague, ill equipped and to frequently produce unpredictable outcomes. Some scholar further noted that the lack of clarity of the unconscionability doctrine ruins its value and it should be abandoned and the focus should be directed to other mechanisms. *See also* Schmitz, *supra* note 73, at 95–6, 98.

[121] *See* R. Korobkin, *Bounded Rationality, Standard Form Contracts, and Unconscionability*, 70 University of Chicago Law Review 1230, 1244 (2003).

transactional cost.[122] This contradicts Sect. 4.10 of the Framework on the reasonable cost of transaction.

Similar to the EU unfair term rule the practical effectiveness of the unconscionability doctrine, whether strictly or flexibly applied, is subject to question. Generally, the remedy of unconscionability is nonenforcement or limited enforcement of an unconscionable contract or certain of its terms.[123] Without any harsh sanctions, some merchants may take a risk by putting unfair terms in their standard contracts to maximize their economic advantages because, in the worst case, they will only find their contract or the particular unfair terms to be unenforceable. As Steven Friedman has stated "the doctrine of unconscionability cannot fully meet the challenges posted by standard form contracts without a robust remedy. The lack of an adequate remedy seriously undermines unconscionability's effectiveness."[124] Many scholars propose that stronger sanctions other than nonenforcement may be needed to effectively combat unfair terms in standard forms.[125] Under the current practice the provisions of unconscionability, in the absence of punitive provisions, may not yet be an adequate mechanism for ensuring the fairness of terms and conditions as well as fair trading practice.

5.3 Information Disclosure Mechanism

As e-consumers do not have the opportunity to meet traders to inquire or inspect the goods and a transaction is conducted in a matter of seconds by e-means, such environment may result in disadvantages to e-consumers if appropriate information is not provided in an adequate and timely manner. This section will discuss information disclosure rules that require traders to present certain information to

---

[122] *See* Schmitz, *supra* note 73, at 97.

[123] Under Article 2 of the UCC which applies to sale of good transaction, Section 2-302 states: "1. If the court as a matter of law finds the contract or any clause of the contract to have been unconscionable at the time it was made, the court may refuse to enforce the contract, or it may enforce the remainder of the contract without the unconscionable clause, or it may so limit the application of any unconscionable term as to avoid any unconscionable result." Similarly, the Restatement Section 208 prescribes that: "if a contract or term thereof is unconscionable at the time the contract is made a court may refuse to enforce the contract, or may enforce the remainder of the contract without the unconscionable term, or may so limit the application of any unconscionable term as to avoid any unconscionable result." Therefore, the UCC and the Restatement contain similar statements that have led to the judicial conclusion that the unconscionability does not provide an award of contractual remedy or a cause of any action.

[124] *See* Friedman, *supra* note 79, at 319.

[125] One scholar suggests for example the attorney's fees as a remedy for unconscionable contracts. *See ibid.*, at 334–5. Another propose for the adequately liability toward the drafter, so called *contra proferentem*. *See* Horton, *supra* note 8, at 431.

e-consumers.[126] For the purpose of this section, the EU information disclosure law is the main focus.

5.3.1 Overview of Information Disclosure Rules

5.3.1.1 The Directive on E-Commerce

Directive 2000/31/EC of the European Parliament and of the Council of 8 June 2000. On certain legal aspects of information society services, in particular e-commerce, in the Internal Market (hereinafter *ECD*) is the main directive constituting the back bone of e-contract law in the EU, governing all manners of e-business, whether B2B or B2C transactions. The ECD provides a detailed description that places information disclosure duties on service providers, including e-merchants, particularly during the ordering process, which aims at avoiding possible mistakes and maximizing fairness to consumers.[127]

Under the ECD, a website is not only required to contain the name, address and other necessary information of the merchant,[128] but also a detailed explanation on

---

[126] Traditional commercial law has taken an ambivalent position concerning non-disclosure of some material facts by one contractual party because such disclosure would substantially distort the bargaining value between parties, respecting the doctrine of *caveat emptor*–buyer beware. In consumer sales, the law and economic perspective is calling for information disclosure from sellers which is believed to promote economic efficiency. "…in general it is the case that a requirement of seller disclosure of material facts is more likely to promote efficient information dissemination, without seriously undermining incentives for information generation, than a requirement of buyer disclosure of material fact, which may undermine incentives to invest in information generation relating to privately and socially undervalued assets in the first place". *See* M. J. Trebilcock, *Rethinking Consumer Protection Policy, in* C. E. F. Rickett and T. G. W. Telfer (eds.), International Perspectives on Consumers' Access to Justice 68, 95 (2006). The economic analysis of law further suggests that the government should only intervene in the market's functions to correct market failures, with information failure being the most recognized. Information failure results from information asymmetries, destroying the value of contractual bargaining between parties and undermining market efficiency. Thus, the information disclosure regulations are creatures of well accepted rationale as a tool in the fight against information asymmetries in the market. *See* Ramsay, *supra* note 1, at 53–106 and S. Bainbridge, *Mandatory Disclosure: A Behavioral Analysis*, 68 University of Cincinnati Law Review 1023–60 (2000) and T. Durkin and G. Elliehausen, *Disclosure as A Consumer Protection, in* T. Durkin and M. Staten (eds.), The Impact of Public Policy on consumer Credit 109–48 (2002).

[127] The ECD covers all transactions relating to e-information to ensure that a contract concluded by e-means is based on free and valid consent. The ECD requires the service providers to provide necessary information, appropriate processes for the placing of the order and general obligations to monitor and comply with the relevant codes of conduct. *See* Articles 5 to 15 of the ECD. *See also* Riefa and Hörnle, *supra* note 12, at 113.

[128] *See* Article 5 of the ECD.

how to place an order[129] and the correction of input errors.[130] Article 5 requires the disclosure of the identity and geographical address of the seller, contract details, any professional identification or relevant entries in trade registers and the price including tax and delivery cost.[131] Such information must be rendered clearly, easily, directly and permanently as well as comprehensibly and must be unambiguously accessible to consumers.[132]

Article 10 of the ECD also imposes the responsibility on merchants to present essential information concerning the process of the execution of an e-contract to consumers in a clear, comprehensible and unambiguous manner that allows consumers to understand the process involved the use of technological steps to conclude the e-contract.[133] Every piece of the essential information concerning the online purchase process has to be presented to consumers before the order is being finally placed.[134]

Article 10 (1) (c) read together with Article 11 (2) are designed to help alleviate the problem of input errors in connection with e-commerce sales contract formation because, owing to the rapid speed and the lack of human intervention in e-sales, an error or mistaken input by consumers can easily occur. Service providers who are merchants must select the appropriate technical means for consumers to review and correct input errors at least once before the order is finalized.

5.3.1.2 The Directive on Consumers Rights

Directive 2011/83/EU of the European Parliament and of the Council of 25 October 2011 on consumer rights (hereinafter *CRD*) aims to increase opportunities for

---

[129] *See* Article 10 of the ECD Article 10 (1) of the ECD prescribes that, in case of consumer contract entered into by electronic means, the service provider (i.e. merchant) must provide consumers with the following necessary information before the consumer can place an e-order:

(a) the different technical steps to follow to conclude the contract;

(b) whether or not the concluded contract will be filed by the service provider and whether it will be accessible;

(c) the technical means for identifying and correcting input errors prior to the placing of the order;

(d) the languages offered for the conclusion of the contract.

[130] *See* Article 10 (1) (c) of the ECD requires a service provider, including the merchants, to acknowledge consumers and provide consumers with a technical means for identifying and correcting any input error before the consumers are able to enter the final ordering process. In this regard, Article 11 (2) of the ECD enumerates that the merchant shall provide to the consumer of the service appropriate, effective and accessible technical means allowing him to identify and correct input errors prior to the stage of order placing.

[131] *See* Article 5 (1) (a) to (g) and (2) of the ECD.

[132] *See* Article 5 (1) and 10 (1) of the ECD.

[133] *See* Article 10 (1) of the ECD.

[134] *See* Article 10 (1) of the ECD.

distance sales and to contribute to a high level of consumer protection.[135] In terms of substantive information requirements, e-consumers according to Article 6 must be provided with information concerning the suppliers' identity, the main characteristic of the goods or services, the price, the method of payment, delivery or performance of obligations, the trader's complaint handling policy, the right of withdrawal and the relevant cost of returning, the cost of using remote communication, the duration for which the price offer remains legally valid and the minimum period of the contractual relationship relating to the supply of products or services to be performed permanently or recurrently.[136]

In terms of procedural information requirements, Article 8 (1) requires the means of e-communication to use plain and intelligible language.[137] Also, Article 8 (1) and (2) of the CRD further impose obligations on sellers or traders concerning the confirmation process beyond those required of traditional consumer contracts, which are the terms and conditions of sale presented on the website. These include the requirement that the information, particularly the terms of payment, be presented in a durable medium, directly and conspicuously located near the area where the consumer needs to click to confirm or place the order.[138]

Similar to the ECD, in terms of information transparency requirements the CRD prescribes that the information to be provided should be clear, comprehensive and easily accessible.[139] In effect, according to Article 8, certain information must be presented by means and methods that will give consumers the opportunity to review their decisions prior to concluding the transaction or the contract.[140] Confirmation must be given to consumers in a durable medium, setting out their rights and obligations, within a reasonable time at the latest at the time of delivery.[141]

5.3.2 *Evaluation of Information Disclosure Rules*

As Annette Nordhausen Scholes has said "distance and electronic marketing give rise to their own rationales for information provision, given that the consumer is

---

[135] The CRD prescribes the obligation of trader that trader must disclose necessary information to consumers in distance contracts before entering in to the contract. It contains specific provisions relating to the conclusion of distance consumer contracts by mail order, phone, fax and internet. For the purposes of the ECD, *see* The preliminary Section of the ECD.

[136] *See* Article 6 of the ECD.

[137] *See* Article 8 (1) of the ECD.

[138] *See* Article 8 (1) and (2) of the CRD.

[139] The transparency requirements are to ensure that the information is disclosed in ways that are easy to digest and understand by consumers as well as to maximize the opportunity for consumers to take such information. Articles 5 (1) and 10 (1) of the ECD and Article 6 (1) and 8 (1) of the CRD are considered the transparency requirements.

[140] *See* Article 8 (1) to (4) of the ECD.

[141] *See* Article 8 (7) of the ECD.

dealing with a remote trader, about whom he may know very little: at the very least, he needs to have contract details for the trader and information about the product and services being supplied."[142] Article 5 of the ECD and Article 6 of the CRD appear to be consistent with the above suggestion as they place a duty on traders to provide information regarding themselves and their goods or services, thus correcting information asymmetries regarding transactions and ensuring that consumers are better able to make informed decisions in selecting goods or services based on the information provided.[143]

Moreover, Article 10 of the ECD and Article 8 of the CRD similarly place great emphasis on the form and format of the presentation of e-information, which must be easily understood and presented via durable means that can be restored for future reference. This will help ensure that the consumer not only receives the information, but "the consumer should receive the information at a time and in a form that allows him to make appropriate use of it".[144] In other words, the EU laws provide consumers with the necessary information and facilitate consumers' ability to digest and understand such information. This corresponds to Sect. 4.2 of the Framework on the sufficient and accurate information and ability to digest information.

Further, the mandating of such information disclosure under the ECD and the CRD may put some pressure on traders to carefully police the information that appears on their own websites to ensure that it complies with the specified regulations out of fear that failure to do so may result in legal sanctions against them. This corresponds to Sect. 4.14 of the Framework on the fair trading practices and consumers' confidence. Information disclosure strategies also allow consumers to freely adjust and balance their preferences between price and quality of products and contract terms according to their economic needs by comparing various informative choices provided by many merchants.[145] As Howard Beales, Richard Craswell and Steven Salop confirm "[r]emedies which simply adjust the information available to consumer still leave consumers free to make their own choices, thus introducing less rigidity into the market. Such remedies leave the market free to respond as consumer preferences and production technologies change over time."[146] This corresponds to Sect. 4.4 of the Framework on the freedom of choice and ability to make rational decision.

---

[142] *See* A. N. Scholes, *Information Requirements, in* G. Howells and R. Schulze (eds.), Modernizing and Harmonizing Consumer Contract Law 213, 213–4 (2009).

[143] *See ibid.*, at 217.

[144] *See ibid.*, at 214.

[145] In contrast, the use of direct regulation, which compromise diverse preferences by providing an appropriate pattern, usually imposes a single and similar choice on consumers and may result in a rigid market environment. *See* H. Beales, R. Craswell and S. Salop, *The Efficient Regulation of Consumer Information*, 24 Journal of Law and Economics 491, 513–32 (1981) and Ramsay, *supra* note 1, at 119.

[146] *See* Beales, Craswell and Salop, *ibid.* Phrased differently, information disclosure helps to lead consumers to make appropriate informed decisions to protect themselves according to their

However, it should be noted that with the various benefits stated above, there are several critical points under the ECD and CRD indicate their practical effectiveness in internet market.[147]

5.3.2.1 Information Overload

As technology allows traders to put more information in its communication without any substantial cost, it can easily lead to a large amount of information being presented before consumers, which is likely to be burdensome to digest and understand.[148] This phenomenon referred as *information overload*[149] is a practice where traders present a near unlimited volume of information on their websites that may not turn out to be particularly helpful.[150] An empirical study by George Miller revealed that consumers have the ability to read and understand information in seven aspects.[151] Therefore, the majority of consumers may not be able to assess the more than 20 pieces of information that Article 5 of the ECD and Article 6 of the CRD require e-merchants to disclose to consumers.

Under these circumstances, consumers may choose to focus on a few single items such as price, quantity, and discount, while ignoring other *boiler plate* information presented to them.[152] If only a few pieces of information are assessed in consumers' decision making process, while ignoring other relevant information

different individual interests rather than placing on the state the difficult task of deciding what is the common need for different and diverse consumers' preferences.

[147] The information remedies in e-markets may be complicated and subtle task compared to those in the traditional market because of its technological nature. *See* E. Rubin, *The Internet, Consumer Protection and Practical Knowledge, in* J. K. Winn (ed.), Consumer Protection in the Age of the Information Economy 35, 38–40 (2006).

[148] The problem of information overload seems to be a critical issue in the internet context rather. The opportunity to digest information by internet means is not comparable to the physical inspection of the goods, an inquiry with seller's representative, or reading information printed on paper. In addition, the assessment of an unlimited amount of information may sometimes not be a worthwhile exercise compared to the relatively small value of most e-sales. *See also* O. Ben-Shahar, *The Myth of the 'Opportunity to Read' in Contract Law*, 5 European Review of Contract Law 1, 12–20 (2009).

[149] Many websites insert an overdose of information, confusing consumers rather than helping them. *See* Riefa and Hörnle, *supra* note 12, at 116. *See also* J. Landers and R. Rohner, *A Functional Analysis of Truth in Lending*, 26 UCLA Law Review 711, 722–25 (1979).

[150] *See* Luth, *supra* note 57, 167.

[151] *See* G. Miller, *The Magical Number Severn, Plus or Minus Two: Some Limits on Our Capacity for Information Procession*, 63 Psychological Review 81–97 (1956).

[152] *See* Korobkin, *supra* note 121, at 1230–95. An author further points out that information overload in e-market may render consumers confused and feel paralyzed with cause consumers to refrain from taking any action, including reading them. *See also* T. Brennan, *Consumer Preference Not to Choose: Methodological and Policy Implications* (2005), *available at* papers.ssrn.com/sol3/papers.cfm?abstract_id=854424 (visited July 12, 2012).

that the law wants consumers to know, the problem of information asymmetries will remain uncorrected.

Some scholars have been critical of the effectiveness of the ECD and CRD, which impose a long list of information requirements, but overlook the actual impact they may have on consumers.[153] The contents and details of information required have gradually increased over time during the development of these two EU Directives.[154] Today, many EU traders appear to overload consumers with information to comply with the requirements under the ECD and the CRD provisions but whether such information can be actually and effectively digested by consumers is questionable. The attempts by the ECD and the CRD to cure the problem of asymmetry of information in the online market mainly by providing information may be considered "cheap talk".[155] In fact, it may not really benefit consumers in e-transactions. The increase in "quantity" of information available to consumers without the increase of the "quality" of communication, by virtue of the information disclosure mechanisms, may lead to a flood of useless statements.

5.3.2.2 Delayed Notice

Due to the use of technological means in e-transactions, merchants sometimes do not provide complete and clear information concerning the products or services immediately upon a consumer visiting their website or in an appropriate time period thereafter.[156] There may be a delay in displaying such information by using a feature of the website until after consumers have completed the necessary process for placing an order, but just before consumers having to click confirming the order.[157]

At that stage, consumers usually feel that they are already committed to the e-transaction because they have already spent time and effort in filling in information and following the process, spending a significant amount of time and energy in

[153] *See* G. Howell, *The Potential and Limits of Consumer Empowerment by Information*, 32 Journal of Law and Society 349, 363 (2005), Ramsay, *supra* note 1, at 122 and Riefa and Hörnle, *supra* note 12, at 116–7.

[154] *See* Riefa and Hörnle, *ibid*, at 116.

[155] The term of "cheap talk", according to the economic notion, "consists of statements by a participant in a transaction that do not commit the person to any particular course of action; in other words, for proposes of reaching an enforceable agreement, such talk is useless." Thus, the cheap talk is not beneficial. *See* E. Rubin, *supra* note 147, at 47.

[156] From a technological point of view, information disclosure could be more effective as it is cheaper with fewer limitations in some aspects. However, there is an argument that some businesses are attempting to create a new legal culture in the information economy where it is allowed to hold back some important information until after consumers make payment. *See* Coteanu *supra* note 3, at 129–30.

[157] *See ibid.* and Tasker and Pakcyk, *supra* note 14, at 103.

forming the transaction.[158] Consumers may be hesitant to cancel the order and spend more time looking for a new transaction, even if they are not pleased with the terms and conditions, such as an unexpectedly high total price because of additional, previously unmentioned, costs that have just been displayed to them right before clicking the confirm button, for example.

As Jean Braucher concluded in his study "*New Basics: Twelve Principles for Fair Commerce in Mass Market Software and Other Digital Products*", "[d]elayed terms,. . .can also be seen as a more virulent form bait and switch; the customer in a traditional switch situation can decide not to enter into the transaction, whereas a customer who has already entered into a transaction when the switch occurs has to unwind it before starting on a new search for another deal."[159]

For the delayed notice problem, Article 8 (3) of the CRD is designed to prevent such conduct. It requires that traders must inform consumers of certain information in a clear and legible manner "at the latest at the beginning of the ordering process".[160] However, Article 8 (3) of the CRD requires that the time of disclosure be at the commencement of the ordering process only in relation to the two issues of "any delivery restrictions" and "means of payment are accepted". Apart from the required disclosure at the starting point, Article 8 (2) and (4) of the CRD also similarly deal with the delayed notice issue but at the later stage by requiring certain information to be disclosed "before the consumer place his order"[161] and "prior to the conclusion of such a contract"[162] respectively.

Nevertheless, these two provisions only refer to the information concerning the trader, the product, the price, the contracting period, the termination of the contract,

[158] *See also* K. Engle and P. McCoy, *A Tale of Three Markets: The Law and Economics of Predatory Lending*, 80 Texas Law Review 1255, 1307 (2002) and Rubin, *supra* note 147, at 39.

[159] *See* Braucher, *supra* note 42, at 185. This argument is also confirmed by an observation of consumers' behaviors in lending transactions, which "are typically provided after the contract has been negotiated by the parties, or, to describe the situation more realistically, after the borrowers have been approved for the loan. At this point, researchers have noted, borrowers are already committed to the transaction. . .Consumers are often unwilling to unwind it and incur the cost of seeking another cost". *See* Engle and McCoy, *ibid.*, at 1307, W. Eskridge, *One Hundred Years of Ineptitude: The Need for Mortgage Rules Consonant with the Economic Dynamics of the Home Sale and Loan Transaction*, 70 Virginia Law Review 1083, 1128–29 (1984). *See also* C. Peterson, *Truth, Understanding, and High-Cost Consumer Credit: The Historical Context of the Truth in Lending Act*, 55 Florida Law Review 807, 898 (2003) and Durkin and Elliehausen, *supra* note 126, at 39.

[160] *See* Article 8 (3) of the CRD.

[161] Article 8 (2) of the CRD specifies that "the trader shall make the consumer aware in a clear and prominent manner and directly before the consumer place his order of the information provided for in points (a), (e), (o), and (p) of Article 6 (1)."

[162] Article 8 (4) of the CRD states that ". . .the trader shall provide, on the particular means prior to the conclusion of such contract, at least the pre-contractual information regarding the main characteristics of the goods or services, the identity of the trader, the total price, the right or withdrawal, the duration of the contract and, if the contract is of indeterminate duration, the conditions for terminating the contract, as referred to in points (a), (b), (e), (h) and (o) of Article 6 (1). . . "

the duration of consumer's obligations and the right of withdrawal under Article 6 (1) (a), (b), (e), (h), (o) and (p) of the CRD. The provisions does not touch on other information from its timely disclosure requirement, such information includes the cost of withdrawal, the cost of using distance communication, the cost of returning, the legal guarantee, the after sale services, the available of alternative dispute resolution and so on.[163] As a result, traders may delay the disclosure of the information excluded from Article 8 (2), (3) and (4) of the CRD, even after the consumer has placed his order or the e-contract has been concluded. This may cause unfairness to the consumer as he has already proceeded far too deep into the transaction process without the benefit of some essential information.[164]

5.3.2.3 Technological Variations

To help with mitigating the information problem, both online and offline transactions similarly need a clear and appropriate manner of presenting information to be effective to avoid the risk of consumers being unable to digest or understand it.[165] Unlike information on paper, which is tangible, static and cannot be easily changed, information on web pages is dynamic in nature and depends on the construction and design of web operators.[166]

When looking at disclosure from the perspective of the form of presentation, referring to the placement and proximity of disclosure, there is a significant difference between the traditional and internet markets.[167] Internet based information, including various technological interactive features such as attractive graphics, moving animation and snazzy sounds, may exhaust all of a consumer's

[163] Article 8 (4) states that "... The other information referred to in Article 6 (1) shall be provided by the trader to the consumer in an appropriate way in accordance with paragraph 1 of this Article" and such paragraph 1 (Article 8 (1)) provides that ".. the trader shall give the information provided for in Article 6 (1) or make that information available to the consumer in a way appropriate to the means of distance communication used in plain and intelligible language. In so far as that information is provided on a durable medium, it shall be legible". This means that there is no requirement concerning the time of disclosure for the information excluding from Article 8 (4), unless it otherwise specifies in other particular provisions of timing disclosure requirements such as Article 8 (2) and 8 (3). These are the information required to be disclosed to consumers according to Article 6 (1) (c), (d), (f), (g), (i), (j), (k), (l), (m), (n), (q), (r) and (s).

[164] Also a consumer, at that stage, has already completed almost all of the burdensome steps of the order and may be hesitant to cancel such transaction after such an investment even if the consumer subsequently discovers unfavorable information and they have the right to withdrawal or the right to return.

[165] Generally, the positive outcome of information disclosure does not only require specific content of information that needs to be presented to consumers, it also relies on the fact that such information is presented in clear and understandable language and in a comprehensible manner which allows consumers to digest and understand it.

[166] *See* Tasker and Pakcyk, *supra* note 14, at 105.

[167] *See* Coteanu, *supra* note 3, at 123–6.

senses before they can read the information prescribed by law for their benefit. With these unlimited imaginative features, consumers may have difficulty digesting or reading such critical information. As Ty Tasker and Daryn Pakcyk have said "imagine the difficulty of trying to concentrate on noticing or reading a contract while rapidly moving animation dances before one's eyes, or while a sound effect or a catchy tune are playing"[168]

In addition, a lot of the structures, formats, or designs of communications in the e-market can be displaced or used in divergent ways depending on the design of the providers, presenting information in countless formats through technological and e-means. The clicking of hyperlinks,[169] the scrolling of webpages[170] or the displaying of annoying pop-up windows[171] are some examples of forms of e-presentations that are not easily comparable to turning pages in documents printed on paper.[172] In effect, consumers have often reported that it is difficult to read e-information on their computer screens and this certainly causes a problem to consumers in digesting e-information.[173]

The ECD and the CRD have attempted to prevent and remedy these problems caused by modern forms of communication. Article 10 (1) of the ECD and Article 8 (2) of the CRD similarly require traders to electronically present information in a clear, comprehensive and prominent manner, and directly before the consumer

---

[168] *See* Tasker and Pakcyk, *supra* note 14, at 105.

[169] Texts presented in such means that only appear on the computer screen after the consumer click a relevant button. This form of presentation may easily escape consumers' view or observation, without close direction and guidance from the web operator.

[170] It is an unsettled issue as to whether the use of a scroll bar on a computer monitor to view the information (including terms and conditions) is an obstacle for manifesting consent. The US Courts have divergent views on this matter. However, if the scroll bar connects to a distracting feature which may be able to deter consumers from scrolling further, such form of presentation will be considered an insufficient notice and render the e-contract unenforceable. For a discussion of various trial court decisions concerning the scroll bar method, *see* Tasker and Pakcyk, *supra* note 14, at 97–8.

[171] Pop-up windows have become a standard item in software products. Many consumers click to close the pop-up window without reading information contained therein because of their annoyance. Sometimes, pop-up windows were designed to disappear within a certain period. The pop-up window method may become hidden from view and such means of communication may make information more difficult to be digested by viewers. *See ibid.*, at 98–9.

[172] There is an argument that "the physical effort of scrolling to read terms is analogous to turning pages in paper contracts, and not more onerous". *See Bar-Ayal v. Time Warner Cable Inc.*, No. 03 CV 9905(KMW), 2006 WL 2990032 (S.D.N.Y. Oct. 16, 2006). In contrast, there are arguably enormous differences between information contained on paper and the information conveyed by internet. "Paper is static, while web pages can be dynamic in countless ways, limited only by the imagination and skill of the side developer." *See ibid.*

[173] This e-information may easily escape consumers' view or observation in the absence close direction and guidance from web operator. For a detailed discussion on consumer difficulties with e-shopping and e-communication, *see* S. L. Jarvenpaa and P. A. Todd, *Consumer Reactions to Electronic Shopping on the World Wide Web*, 1 International Journal of Electronic Commerce 59–88 (1996–1997).

places his or her order. This requirement aims at preventing problems that may occur from the countless designs and dynamic nature of electronic means of communication. As a result, some forms of the designed graphic animation and presentation of e-information (e.g. scroll bars, hyperlinks or pop-up windows, the design bypass pages or subpages) may not be considered a sufficiently clear, prominent and direct form of disclosure, being in violation of Article 10 (1) of the ECD and Article 8 (2) of the CRD. However, it should be noted that there is no provisions under the ECD and the CRD that handle the possible insertion of sound in a website that can also be an obstacle for consumers in learning information.

5.3.2.4 Input Error

In the online market where there is an imbalance of technological knowledge, merchants are able to use the technology to dictate the particular acts that constitute assent.[174] For example, traders may design the method of acceptance by just having the consumer press the "enter" button or clicking the computer mouse rather than typing the word "accept" in a designated text box.[175] Another website may apply an inadvertent way where the computer program automatically links from the main entry page to another page, without any required consumers' input, to indicate assent.[176] Additionally, the nature of its ease, speed and the unlimited designs of e-presentation may lead to mistaken inputs as people inadvertently click something without realizing that by doing so they are expressing assent to a contract. All these circumstances can bring about a possibly unintentional act that indicates a consumer's assent.

Unlike in person transactions where the consumer has an opportunity to physically negotiate and to observe any potentially mistaken manifestations of assent, the consumer in a remote e-transaction has no such ability. Therefore, Article 10 (1) (c), when implemented together with Article 11 (2) of the ECD, are designed to help alleviate this problem by requiring the appropriate technical means for consumers to review and correct input errors. Such requirement aims to minimize the technical error of inadvertently clicking to make an order or committing other unintentional acts of assent without actually intending to do so.

In general practice, after a consumer has made an initial response through the website, many websites usually prepare a summary page displaying the details of the order made by the consumer and request that the consumer confirm such details before proceeding to the final steps, such as payment and issuing an e-mail

---

[174] In the internet market, the mere access of a webpage may be a legal manifestation of the assent of consumers to information and terms provided. *See Register.com, Inc. v. Verio, Inc.*, 356 F.3d 393, 403 (2d Cir.2004). *See also* Tasker and Pakcyk, *supra* note 14, at 111.

[175] *See* Tasker and Pakcyk, *ibid.*, at 100.

[176] *See ibid.*, at 95–105. The author discusses various forms of e-presentations (e.g. scroll bars, pop-up windows, design bypassing, etc.) and the designed effects.

confirming the order. Ordering processes designed like that are clearly in accordance with the said provisions of the ECD, as they afford the consumer the opportunity to review and correct any input error before such input is deemed to be part of a valid order. However, it is interesting to point out that consumers must be aware of the existence of an opportunity to revise their orders that is available to them as specified in Articles 10 (1) (c) and 11 (2). If they fail to review the detailed summary of their orders provided and to make any necessary corrections, they will not be able to correct any input errors at a later stage as such summary is usually deemed to be the final terms of the order. As such, consumers will be bound by such terms regardless of whether their inputs were truly or correctly inserted.

This is particularly true in the cases where an e-consumer is in a *click happy* mood wherein they expect to achieve instant enjoyment when browsing e-markets, leading them to be overeager in e-contracting[177] and fail to review their input errors. Such consumers will often click a computer button in an instance without adequate awareness of essential information and the consequences of doing so. In such circumstances, even though the ECD has established requirements to help prevent input error in reality, if many consumers choose to ignore the information and the opportunity to review or correct their orders offered by the laws, the legal provisions appear to be of no value at all.

5.3.2.5 Ineffective Enforcement

Within the online environment, the effectiveness of information disclosure mechanisms such as those contained in the ECD and the CRD is still in question. This is because of the existence of evidence showing that the vast majority of e-merchants do not provide basic information to consumers even though it is required by law. The OFT web sweep's survey, for example, found that 20 % of the surveyed web operators do not post their e-mail addresses on their websites for consumers in violation of Article 5 (1) (c) of the ECD and Article 6 (1) (c).[178] In addition, the survey further revealed that 40 % of e-sellers are not transparent in the process of giving information on the costs of goods and services to consumers,[179] contradicting the transparency requirement regarding the forms of presentation.[180] These merchants often add hidden charges at the checkout stage after the consumer has completed almost all of the steps of the e-transaction for the purchase of the goods or services.[181]

[177] *See* R. A. Hillman and J. J. Rachlinski, *Standard-Form Contracting in the Electronic Age*, 77 New York University Law Review 429, 480 (2002).

[178] *See* OFT, *Web Sweep Analysis* (March 2008), *available at* oft.gov.uk/713560/publications/reports/consumer-protection/oft982 (visited March 12, 2013).

[179] *See ibid.*

[180] The transparent requirements are specified in Article 10 of the ECD and Article 8 of the CRD.

[181] *See* OFT, *supra* note 178, at 178 and Riefa and Hörnle, *supra* note 12, at 115.

The result of the said survey is confirmed by the study conducted by the European Commission on airline websites. It found that insufficient and ambiguous information regarding price is one of the main problems.[182] The ticket prices are often purposely divided into many components and the consumers will only see the final total of the price at the check-out stage of the booking process,[183] when the consumers are unlikely to walk away from the purchase despite being unfavorably affected by the additional hidden cost. Also, an EU-wide investigation on e-sale websites revealed that more than 50 % of e-merchants' websites did not meet the legal requirements, in particular finding that they were misleading about the total cost of products or services and gave incomplete contract details of the sellers.[184] It may have to be conceded here that the nature of mandatory disclosure pursuant to the ECD and the CRD appears to be ineffective in the e-market because of its failure to be enforceable in practice.

The unique and unprecedented characteristics of the internet market itself may well explain the situation. As the costs of entry and exit in the internet market are low, a large number of e-sellers may be unconcerned about their potential long term reputational capital.[185] Fly-by-night traders in the online market, for example, often aim at achieving short term profits and they may not be interested in future sales and may use various aggressive sales techniques, including non-disclosed information tactics, which infringe the provisions of ECD and the CRD.[186] Later, they can simply and quickly walk away from the internet market and any potential legal liability.

In addition, the inherent cross border nature of the online market represents a great challenge to the relevant authorities in relation to enforcement because of jurisdictional restrictions on their power.[187] As previously mentioned, the authority in the UK, for example, has admitted that they lack the capacity to combat infringements affecting non-English consumers even though the illegal practices were committed in the jurisdiction of the UK.[188] Due to its advanced technological and transnational nature, e-sales represent great difficulties for consumer protection

---

[182] *See* Pinsent Masons, Out-law.com, *One in Three Airline Sites Break Consumer Laws* (May 13, 2008), *available at* out-law.com/page-9113 (visited December 30, 2011).

[183] *See* Article 23 (1) of Regulation 1008/2008 on common rules for the operation air services in the communities. It compels airlines to disclose airfares and related costs in a more transparent and clear manner.

[184] *See* OECD, *supra* note 19, at 19.

[185] *See* G. Hadfield, R. Howse and M. Trebilcock, *Information Based Principles for Rethinking Consumer Protection policy*, 21 Journal of Consumer Policy 131, 155–66 (1998). The authors outline the characteristics of the market structures that are similar to internet markets, where there was likely to be a detriment to consumers.

[186] *See* I. D. C. Ramsay, Rationales for Intervention in the Consumer Marketplace 25–35 (1984) and OECD, *supra* note 19, at 30.

[187] *See* OECD, *ibid.* at 30.

[188] *See ibid.*

authorities in identifying the location of rogue traders, arresting them and imposing relevant sanctions on them.

5.4 Withdrawal Mechanism

In the case of an internet purchase, consumer often have a problem in picturing the goods or services purchased because it would be difficult for them to assess the specifications of the goods or services without seeing them to judge whether they meet the consumers' requirement.[189] The introduction of withdrawal mechanisms may actually serve to promote the conclusion of more online contracts by removing a psychological barrier that some e-consumers possess.[190] This section will mainly examine the existing withdrawal mechanisms adopted by the EU Member States.[191]

5.4.1 Overview of the Withdrawal Rules

Many provisions of the CRD provide criteria for the exercise of the right of withdrawal and the associated cooling off periods no matter where the consumer lives or by which means—by telephone, online or in person—the contract was concluded.[192] Article 9 of the CRD gives consumers an unconditional right to withdraw from the contract within 14 days beginning from the day of conclusion of service contracts, or from the day on which the consumer or their representative receives physical possession of the goods according to sale of goods contracts.[193]

---

[189] *See* M. Loos, *Rights of Withdrawal, in* G. Howells and R. Schulze (eds.), Modernizing and Harmonizing Consumer Contract Law 237, 248.

[190] There is an argument put forward for e-sales growth based on the idea that, if more agreements are concluded online, it will ultimately increase the number of cross border transactions. *See ibid.*, at 248.

[191] The right of withdrawal has become an important topic for the revision of the consumer *acquis*, which the European Commission recently adopted. The framework of the CRD is intended to revise the consumer acquis in the EU, including the consumers' rights of withdrawal in sale transactions. The right of withdrawal is sometimes called the cooling off period. It is a new legal concept in private law as it was first mentioned in legislation in the early 1970s. The right of withdrawal initially aims to help consumers out from rash transactional decision. During a short cooling off period, consumers may choose to walk away from a contract that may already be concluded. In the European community, the right of withdrawal was initially introduced by the Doorstep Selling Directive. Since then, this concept has been specified in many EU Directives such as the Directives on Life Assurance, Timeshare, Distance Selling and Consumer Credit. For further detailed description of the history of the right of withdrawal at the EU level, *see ibid.*, at 239.

[192] *See* Article 3 of the CRD.

[193] *See* Article 9 (2) (a) and (b) of the CRD.

Such right will be extended up to 12 months from the end of the initial withdrawal period if the merchant fails to provide the information on the right of withdrawal in writing or in another durable medium.[194] Therefore, the right of withdrawal under the CRD starts tolling from the date on which the merchant informed the consumer of such right.

To exercise the right of withdrawal, the consumer must notify the merchant of his or her wish to exercise such right before the expiration of the withdrawal period. An e-sale consumer may notify the exercise of such right through either an unequivocal statement setting out his withdrawal decision from the contract, through the completion of an e-form provided by the merchant for convenience in terminating the contract, or by sending the model withdrawal form set out in Annex I (B) of the CRD.[195]

The effect of withdrawal is that both the merchant and consumer will return to the *status quo* that existed before the contract and all duties and obligations pursuant to the online contract are extinguished.[196] The trader is legally bound to reimburse the sums paid by the consumer without any charges except for the direct costs of returning the goods.[197] This means that the consumer shall bear the direct cost of returning the good.[198]

The CRD limits the right of withdrawal in some circumstances such as with service contracts after the service has been fully performed, with goods or services for which the price fluctuates according to the market situation, with goods made to order, with perishable goods or goods for which the purchase contract was concluded at a public auction.[199]

Initially, the right of withdrawal, including that specified in the CRD, is usually applied to protect a consumer from making a rash transactional decision under high-pressure by giving him or her a chance during a relatively short cooling off period to go back on his or her decision to enter into the contract.[200] The opposite party to

---

[194] *See* Article 6 and Article 10 of the CRD.

[195] *See* Article 11 (3) and Annex I (B) of the CRD. In the case there is a dispute, the burden of proof of exercising the rights of withdrawal rests on the consumers. *See* Article 14 (1) of the CRD.

[196] *See* Article 12 of the CRD.

[197] *See* Article 13 (1) of the CRD. However, if the consumers use the goods, they will be liable for any diminished value of the goods resulting from the handling of goods other than what is necessary to establish the nature, characteristics and functioning of the goods. The consumer will not be responsible for such diminished value if the merchant fails to provide the notice of the withdrawal right to the consumer. *See* Article 14 (2) of the CRD.

[198] *See* Article 14 (1) of the CRD. It specifies that "[t]he consumer shall only bear the direct cost of returning the goods unless the trader has agreed to bear them or the trader failed to inform the consumer that the consumer has to bear them."

[199] *See* Article 16 of the CRD.

[200] The case of doorstep selling is a clear example. This means of sale had some influence over the establishment of the withdrawal right in legislation. Merchants in door step sales usually make an unsolicited visit to the home of the consumer and induce the consumer to make a decision "he cannot oversee at the moment". Although the introduction of the right of withdrawal is aiming at eradicating the aggressive sale techniques in the market, obviously one may claim that a distance

contract, normally a merchant, is not given any similar opportunity. The rationale for the right of withdrawal is to protect consumers from aggressive sale techniques or other circumstances that a consumer cannot make an informed decision as to whether the goods or services offered to him or her in fact meet his or her demands or needs.[201]

5.4.2 *Evaluation of the Withdrawal Rules*

In the internet sales context,[202] consumers must exercise their imagination to visualize pictures of the products or services from the descriptions or pictures provided on the website and such imaginary picture may often be better than the real products or services delivered. This may result in goods or services purchased in the e-market not truly reflecting the consumer's needs and desires. The right of withdrawal under the CRD then serves to enable consumers to reconsider their earlier decisions. A relatively short 14-day cooling off period according to Article 9 of the CRD in principle allows consumers to reflect on whether their transactional decisions were in accordance with their actual demands, being free from possible misleading, aggressive, or other unfair trading practices.

Based on an economic perspective, the withdrawal mechanism can "prevent the exploitation of irrationality-for example over-optimism at the likelihood of using a timeshare regularly-or exploitation of price ignorance in door to door selling and problems of asymmetric information in distance selling."[203] In other words, it can be used to help those consumers who may suffer from economically irrational behavior. Some behavioral economic scholars positively support this mechanism and label it as *asymmetric paternalism,* which "creates large benefits for those who

---

consumer is also deprived from the chance to assess the quality of product or service offered by the merchant at the time of concluding the consumer contract. In this circumstance, this may create unfairness to consumers and the right of withdrawal should be extended to help them. Macro Loos confirms that "the right of withdrawal serves to enable consumers to rethink their earlier decision, which may not have been made under the influence of the actions of the trader." Today, the right of withdrawal has been adopted in consumer transactions, including those in the e-market. An often seen example is the e-retail trading practice that the purchased goods can be exchanged or returned within a specified time if consumers are not satisfied with them. This may be because the withdrawal right was also founded on the rationale that consumers in e-sales who cannot determine the quality of the products or ascertain the nature of the services before conclusion of contract. For further discussion of the rationales and aims of the withdrawal right, *see* Loos, *supra* note 189, at 245.

[201] The right of withdrawal under the CRD obviously gives the consumers the option to unilaterally go back on their determination to enter into a consumer transaction. The effects of withdrawal mechanisms are far reaching as they protect one party from other party by restricting the binding nature of the contract. *See ibid*, at 241.

[202] It often includes a variety of sales methods such as e-catalogue sales, e-basket shopping, website marketing, unsolicited e-mails and so on.

[203] *See* Ramsay, *supra* note 1, at 330.

make errors, while imposing little or no harm on those who are fully rational. Such regulations are relatively harmless to those who reliably make decisions in their best interest, while at the same time advantageous to those making sub-optimal choices."[204] Without any interference with consumer choices, they seem to be an attractive mechanism to ensure a greater degree of autonomy and freedom to consumers in both online and offline markets by allowing them to freely form contracts.[205] This corresponds to Sect. 4.4 of the Framework on the freedom of choice and ability to make rational decision.

The right of withdrawal also acts to remove barriers to long distance trade, in particular that which occurs via the conclusion of online contracts.[206] With regard to the e-market, consumers have difficulties in evaluating whether or not goods or services meet their demand based solely on merchants' description given online.[207] It is often found that traders' descriptions given in e-sales are inconsistent with the actual nature of goods and services that consumers receive.[208] Due to such concerns, the consumer may choose to purchase goods or services from traders who are operating locally instead of those operating on the internet.[209] Therefore, the function of the right of withdrawal under the CRD also seems to aim at enticing the consumer to purchase in e-transactions by removing some of the potential surprise elements and psychological barriers that go along with online trading.[210] Consumers will tend to be more confident in entering into online transactions that

---

[204] "Cooling off period is very attractive because they do not seem to interfere with consumer choice. Unlike bans or costly licensing procedures they protect individual who wish to cancel without interfering with the other individual choices", *see* Ramsay *supra* note 1, at 346. *See also* C. Camerer, S. Issacharoff, G. Loewenstein, T. O'Donoghue, M. Rabin, *Regulation for Conservatives: Behavioral Economics and The Case for "Asymmetric Paternalism"*, 151 University of Pennsylvania Law Review 1211 (2003), *available at* papers.ssrn.com/sol3/papers.cfm?abstract_id=399501 (visited January 12, 2013).

[205] *See* Ramsay, *supra* note 1, at 346.

[206] *See* Loos, *supra* note 189, at 246–7.

[207] *See ibid.*

[208] *See* Recitals 11, 13 and 14 of the preamble to the Distance Selling Directive.

[209] *See ibid.*

[210] *See* Reticle 5 of the preamble of the CRD. However, there is an argument against the effectiveness of the withdrawal mechanisms. Although it will certainly take away some barriers for trade in distance and cross border transactions, including internet sales, there are many cautions relating to its function and performance. For example, it is difficult to justify the length of the cooling off period. A short cooling off period may be insufficient "where an individual signs up to a long term contract such as a health club. The consumer may not realize until after a month or so that she will not make significant use of facilities". *See* P. Rekaiti and R. van Den Bergh, *Cooling of Periods in the Consumer Laws of the EC Member States, A Comparative Law and Economics Approach*, 23 Journal of Consumer Policy 371, 383 (2000). For the detailed discussion of the limitations of the withdrawal right, *see* Ramsay *supra* note 1, at 345–6 and Loos, *supra* note 189, at 248.

will lead to a greater number of participants in internet markets,[211] resulting in an increase in the variety of goods and services offered online to meet consumers' demands. This corresponds to Sect. 4.3 of the Framework on the availability of variety of goods and services at appropriate prices.

Another objective of the right of withdrawal is to allow a consumer a better opportunity to have access to more information relating to the intended purchase.[212] The European Commission once justified the cooling off period by stating that "[t]he delay allows consumers to shop around after conclusion of the agreement and possibly to find a better offer. This provision is intended to enhance competition".[213] With more opportunity for consumers to search for information concerning their proposed purchases, merchants will be forced to compete to bring goods and services of the quality and price that meet consumers' demands as close as possible into the market. If consumers discover a more attractive offer, they may exercise the right of withdrawal during the cooling off period. The traders will then lose the sale of goods or services. In effect, such a competitive environment in the online market seems beneficial because of the increase of the number of choices offered. This corresponds to Sect. 4.3 of the Framework on the availability of variety of goods and services at appropriate prices.

However, the right of withdrawal may create an unreasonable burden for the business side because of "uncertainty as to the finality of the contract concluded",[214] causing unpredictability in promissory exchange under contractual relationships. By affording consumers the right to change their mind and terminate the contract without any conditions required, one might overlook the hardship placed on merchants because of the uncertainty this imposes on them. As a consequence of this right, the promissory exchange that is the fundamental principle of contract may no longer be sacred. This contradicts Sect. 4.7 of the Framework on the performance of obligations.

Some scholars in their economic analysis argue that the "cooling off period should be limited to situations where the consumer's rationality is likely to be undermined, the seller is likely to have superior knowledge about relevant market prices, and the consumer has difficulty in checking out a purchase before buying."[215] The introduction of the right of withdrawal might substantially and negatively affect businesses. Due to the security of consumers' choices, merchants may have to bear some costs of documentation, loss of sales, and the recovery of

---

[211] It is believed that an introduction of the right of withdrawal is in fact the promotion of concluding online consumer contracts through the internet, which would indirectly and efficiently enhance the rise of the transactional participations in the internet market. *See* Loos, *ibid.*, at 247–8.

[212] *See* Ramsay, *supra* note 1, at 330.

[213] *See ibid.*, at 344.

[214] *See* Loos, *supra* note 189, at 244.

[215] *See* Rekaiti and van Den Bergh, *supra* note 210, at 371–408.

merchandise or services.[216] Robert Hillman, for example, argues that "a cooling off period could make internet contracting prohibitively expensive for e-businesses and for little gain."[217] The interest of the businesses should also be considered and balanced in a way that overly harsh economic burdens are not placed on them by such potential expenses because of the introduction of the consumers' right of withdrawal. Otherwise, merchants may simply pass on the cost of such burdens to consumers in the form of higher prices of the products, greater transaction costs and a reduction in the quality of goods and services provided. This contradicts Sect. 4.10 of the Framework of on the reasonable cost of transaction.

In addition, the possibility of an opportunity to return the products or services may also be problematic because the consumer may not necessarily provide any reason for the withdrawal at the first stage. The abuse of the right of withdrawal may easily be committed because of the likelihood of opportunistic behavior by some consumers who enjoy the product first and then return it,[218] namely moral hazard. With the availability of an avenue for escape from contractual obligations without any valid reasons being required, the consumers may pay less attention in making transactional decisions or even make irrational decisions. This contradicts Sect. 4.4 of the Framework on the freedom of choice and ability to make rational decision.

Nevertheless, once we turn to the detailed function of the withdrawal rights of the CRD in e-sales with the general benefits and pitfalls stated above in mind, the question is to what extent it has been effective in practice in the online market environment.

5.4.2.1 The Start and the End of the Right of Withdrawal

In the case of e-sale transactions, the cooling off period of 14 days starts when the goods are delivered, whereas in the supply of services, it is when the contract is concluded.[219] However, in the case of a failure to notify the consumer of the right of withdrawal, the cooling off period shall never start to run.[220] This is to ensure that the consumers know or should have known of their legal right by encouraging traders to perform their relevant information disclosure obligation.[221] This rule of

---

[216] Based on this economic point of view, some commentators doubt the effectiveness of the withdrawal right in internet contracting. *See e.g. ibid.* and R. Hillman, *Online Consumer Standard Form Contracting Practices: A Survey and Discussion of Legal Implementations, in* J. K. Winn (ed), Consumer Protection in the Age of the Information Economy 283, 299 (2006).

[217] *See ibid.*

[218] For agreements concerning moral hazard problems because of the cooling off period, *see* Rekaiti and van Den Bergh, *supra* note 210, at 371–408.

[219] *See* Article 9 (2) of the CRD.

[220] *See* Article 10 (1) of the CRD.

[221] Unlike the cooling off period rules specified in the various EU directives (such as the 2002 Distance Marketing of Financial Service Directive and the 2008 Consumer Credit Directive) where the extension of cooling off period will be applied if the merchant has not only breached

the CRD follows the court precedent of the ECJ in *Heininger* case that "the cooling off period does not start before the consumer is informed of his right of withdrawal".[222] However, in any event the cooling off period is limited in all circumstances to the period of 12 months from the end of the 14 day period starting from the date of delivery or the conclusion of contract as the case may be.[223] This is because, without any time limitation, an unjust burden would be placed on the merchants, causing them to lose confidence in the promissory exchange in consumer transactions.

However, the intended function of the right of withdrawal under the CRD, with its focus on informing the consumer of the existence of their withdrawal right as a starting point, may not be effective in online sales where high technology in communication tends to obstruct or impair consumers' ability to digest information. Even though the CRD has been attempting to ensure a reasonable notice for consumers by specifying that the cooling off period will begin when the consumer received information relating to the withdrawal right in plain and intelligible language provided on a durable medium,[224] online consumers are faced with burdens and difficulties in learning information because of variations in the technology used to convey information, the large number of presentation formats, the problem of information overloading, and so on. As a result, the right of withdrawal in the CRD may not be able to truly provide protection to consumers in online transactions. If the consumers fail to digest the relevant information at the beginning they will never exercise such right.[225]

---

his disclosure information relating to the consumer right of withdrawal but also other information disclosure obligations, the new CRD explicitly specifies that only the beach of the information to be given on the existence of the right of withdrawal will constitute the extension of cooling off period. For further detailed discussion on this issue, *see* Loos, *supra* note 189, at 250, 257. *In Heininger v. Bayerische Hypo-und Vereinsbank*, the ECJ confirmed that the right of withdrawal shall not be start before the consumer is informed of such right by the merchant. *See Heininger v. Bayerische Hypo-und Vereinsbank*, Case C-481/00, ECR [2001] I-09945, nos. 44–48, AG ECJ 12 December 2001.

[222] Based on the Heininger case, a consumer may be able to withdraw from the transaction as long as one year after the contract was concluded. In this case, the consumer legally exercised his withdrawal right almost 8 years after the conclusion of the contract. *See Hamilton v Volksbank Finlder, ibid.*

[223] *See* Article 10 of the CRD.

[224] *See* Article 8 (1) and Article 6 (1) of the CRD.

[225] Today, there has not been any studied evidence that the right of withdrawal has a positive outcome in EU online sales. It is likely that many online consumers do not notice the right of withdrawal and they rarely use or exercise such right. *See* Ramsay, *supra* note 1, at 143.

5.4.2.2 Difficulties in Exercising of the Right of Withdrawal: Form Requirement

Consumers may choose to express their withdrawal by informing the trader of their decision to cancel the contract in their own statement or a standard withdrawal form to be supplied by the trader, which must meet the requirement prescribed in Annex I of the CRD.[226] In case of a distance sale concluded by an online contract via a website, the consumers may use electronic communication (e.g. fax and e-mail) to deliver their decision to withdraw from the contract.[227]

Obviously, the CRD attempts to introduce a simplified withdrawal process to bring legal certainty in both online and offline sales.[228] However, many remain skeptical of its practical benefits to the majority of consumers in the e-market because of the processes of withdrawal that it requires.[229] This is because the requirement of sending a "notice of withdrawal" under the CRD is likely to protect only more sophisticated consumers in online transactions. Those more vulnerable consumers must overcome the difficulties in handling technological communication when trying to exercise their withdrawal. They are also less likely to be familiar with the documentation necessary to establish their rights.[230] In addition, some commentators also doubt the efficacy of the cooling off period because many online consumers are unlikely to make an effort to exercise their cancellation rights because it requires the investment of time and effort to return the goods or service.[231]

The question to ponder now is what to do if the online consumer fails to meet the form requirement but the merchant is, in fact, fully aware from the communication of the consumer's intention to terminate the contract. For instance, if the online consumer returns the product within the cooling off period but does not explicitly or expressly state that he or she wishes to exercise the withdrawal right. In such circumstances, the CRD's provision of a specific form for notification of withdrawal may work against the consumer because the trader may claim that there is no

---

[226] *See* Article 11 (1) and Annex I of the CRD.

[227] *See* Article 11 (3) and Annex I of the CRD. Such notification can also be given by a letter, a telephone call or by returning the goods with a clear statement of the consumer's decision to withdraw from the contract. *See* Recital 44 of the CRD.

[228] *See ibid.*

[229] Many scholars similarly affirmed the benefits over the cost of the withdrawal right. One example study concluded that "[cooling off period] likely to impose costs on sellers, but the greater costs focus on the sellers who benefit from consumer making hasty, ill-conceived decisions in the heat of the moment." *See e.g.* Camerer, Issacharoff, Loewenstein, O'Donoghue, Rabin, *supra* note 204.

[230] *See* Rekaiti and van Den Bergh, *supra* note 210, at 371.

[231] *See* Hillman, *supra* note 216, at 229. *See also* Rekaiti and van Den Bergh, *supra* note 210, at 371, W. Shanklin and H. King, *Evaluating the FTC Cooling Off Rule*, 11 Journal of Consumer Affairs 101–6 (1977) and Citizen Advise, *Can You Cancel It? CAB/ECC Clients' Experience of Cancellation Rights in Consumer Contracts' CAB Evidence Briefing* (2005), at 4.

valid notice of withdrawal.[232] The result is that the consumer remains bound by the contract and the merchant has no obligation to refund the purchase price.

The objective of the form requirement is basically to serve as evidence and it seeks to provide traders with a certain clear and unequivocal statement of consumer's intention.[233] However, if the consumer's intention to terminate the contract is clearly evident during the cooling off period, even though it does not meet the form requirement, it already serves as a clear and unequivocal notice of intention of withdrawal.[234] In such circumstances, rigorous maintenance of the form requirement may therefore not be necessary. Instead, the flexible implementation of the form requirement would also positively help to protect consumers "who may very well be ignorant of the importance or the meaning of the form requirement".[235] The law of Ontario, Canada, for example, appears to take this argument into account. It permits withdrawal by any means that can prove the date the merchant received the withdrawal notice.[236] Therefore, the form of withdrawal under the CRD may be so overly strict that it leads e-consumers to ignore or choose not to exercise the withdrawal mechanism that the CRD offers.

5.4.2.3 Failure to Comply with the Cooling Off Period's Obligations

The CRD awards consumers the extension of the cooling off period if the merchant has breached his obligation to inform them of their withdrawal right.[237] Without any strong sanction under the CRD other than the cooling off period extension of up to 12 months, there may be no incentive for the trader to perform his or her information obligation on the right of withdrawal. Doing so would raise the consumer's awareness of such right that translates into a greater likelihood that the consumer will exercise it, resulting in the trader losing the benefit of the contract already made with that consumer.

Studies conducted by Terence George Ison and the OFT similarly provide empirical results for the economic hypothesis that "there will be significant

[232] *See* Loos, *supra* note 189, at 263.

[233] "The form requirement is not based on the need for protection of a fundamental interest of the trader as such, but also seeks to safeguard the trader's need for a clear, unequivocal statement by the consumer, whereas that objective has apparently been achieved in the particular case at hand." *See ibid.*

[234] *See ibid.*

[235] *See ibid.*

[236] *See* Ramsay *supra* note 1, at 338.

[237] *See* Article 9 of the CRD. It is interesting to point out that the cooling off period is extended only if the trader has not informed the consumer of his withdrawal right, while the breach of any other information obligation is not sanctioned by the cooling off period extension. Rather, the sanction for the breach of information disclosure requirement is "left to member states to specify in their national laws." For further detailed discussion on this issue, *see* Loos, *supra* note 189, at 250, 257.

incentives for aggressive and fraudulent sale practice in markets where businesses are uninterested in repeated sales or in fostering goodwill"[238] indicating the possibility that a number of them may ignore their obligations under the cooling off period scheme. If compared to the traditional market, such incentives may be much more prevalent in the internet market where there are low barriers to entry into the market and a large number of small size business operators who are more unlikely to be interested in repeated sale volume and customers' goodwill.[239]

According to the studies conducted by the UK's OFT, 15 % of websites were in violation of the withdrawal right disclosure requirement.[240] This problem is even more pressing in the situation where e-traders have not performed or ignored other duties concerning the right of withdrawal. The OFT survey also found that 30 % of online merchants did not refund the full cost of goods returned.[241] This online commercial practice would obviously contradict the provisions of the CRD.[242] As the studies shows that many e-merchants do not comply with the CRD, the withdrawal rules appear to lack practical effectiveness in the e-sale setting. An important reason that leads to increasing legal violations may be the easy and instant communication offered by the e-market. This feature also makes it difficult to regulate the online market as the offending businesses can very well be located outside the jurisdictional authority of the regulator, thus making it very easy for offenders to evade penalty.

5.4.2.4 Non-exercising of Withdrawal Right

Some authors doubt the effectiveness of a cooling off period in internet sales because there are many drawbacks in exercising the cooling off right that may discourage consumers from making use of it.[243] In opting for the internet over brick and mortar shops, the majority of e-consumers demand convenience and speed. However, if they decide to withdraw, they would have to spend time and effort to

---

[238] For the detailed discussion of these studies, *see* Ramsay *supra* note 1, at 338. The author refers to many studies conducted about the cancellation rights. The studies conducted by T.G Ison and OFT are some examples. *See* T. G. Ison, Credit Marketing and Consumer Protection (1979) and OFT, *Doorstep Selling, A Report on the Market Study* (2004), *available at* oft.gov.uk/shared_oft/reports/consumer_protection/oft716.pdf (visited January 12, 2013).

[239] *See* K. Viitanen, *Enforcement of Consumers' Collective Interests by Regulatory Agencies in the Nordic Countries, in* W. van Boom and M. Loos (eds.), Collective Enforcement of Consumer Law 81, 100 (2007).

[240] *See* OFT, *supra* note 178, at 20.

[241] *See ibid.*, at 27–8.

[242] *See* Article 3 of the CRD.

[243] *See* Rekaiti and van Den Bergh, *supra* note 210, at 371 and Hillman *supra* note 216, at 229. In Canada, for example, there is no cooling off period or withdrawal mechanism in e-sales, even though many e-traders offer return policy for their e-consumers. This may be because their policy-makers are skeptic about the benefit of this mechanism. *See also* Ramsay, *supra* note 1, at 134.

return goods or services to the merchants who are usually located at a great distance.[244] Further, some rogue online merchants may restructure the transactions to avoid the cooling off period. For example, merchants may only allow consumers to exchange the goods or they may design an overly complicated procedure for the exercise of cancellation rights. Such business practices may discourage consumers from cancelling their contracts. This claim is confirmed by research showing that individuals experienced problems in attempting to cancel the purchases of goods with the price exceeding £1,000.[245] Another research conducted in the US after the introduction and promotion of the cooling off period for consumers, it found a reduction of consumers' cancellations.[246] At the conclusion of this research, the researcher concluded that "the ability to cancel reduce consumers' doubt about the wisdom of the purchase".[247]

In the event of withdrawal under the CRD, the merchant is obligated to reimburse all payments received from the consumer, including cost of delivery,[248] while the consumer is not responsible for any expenses other than the direct cost of returning the goods.[249] However, the costs of returning the goods at great distance in e-sales are often higher than the costs of returning the goods to brick and mortar commercial establishments.[250] This creates another reason for e-consumers not to exercise their rights to return the goods, particularly in low value purchases. An official report provided by the OFT emphasizes that British consumers, who purchase low price products of less than £35, do not benefit from the cooling off period.[251] This may be because the cost of purchase is small and the cost of

---

[244] Due to these burdens, the right of withdrawal in e-sales may cause internet contracting to be prohibitively expensive for merchants while affording little or no benefit to consumers. *See* Hillman, *ibid.*, at 229.

[245] Some researches show that only a few consumers noticed their withdrawal rights and some found that the exercise of such rights is very complicated. For discussion of these research results, *see* Ramsay, *supra* note 1, at 338.

[246] *See* W. Shanklin and H. King, *Evaluating the FTC Cooling Off Rule*, 11 Journal of Consumer Affairs 101, 105 (1977).

[247] *See ibid.*

[248] *See* Article 13 (1) of the CRD.

[249] *See* Article 14 (1) of the CRD.

[250] During the discussion in the green paper relating to the CRD, there are various opinions on who should carry the burden of returning goods purchased at a distance. Consumer agency alleged that it would be more efficient if the cost of returning the purchased goods would fall on the sellers because the exercising of the right of withdrawal should not cost anything to consumers. In contrast, some merchants claim that in traditional sales when a consumer buys goods or services and he wishes to return them, he has to bear all the costs associated with the return, including transportation costs. In addition, if the cost of returning were to be borne by consumers, it will prevent abuses and excesses. However, both groups similarly argue in favor of having the sellers pay for returning in case of using the withdrawal right by the consumer because the goods and services delivered do not conform to the contract. For detailed explanation on this matter, *see* the review of consumer *acquis* document, at 9–10. *See also* Loos, *supra* note 189, at 267.

[251] *See OFT*, *supra* note 238.

returning the good is far greater than that.[252] In this regard, some academics have alleged that "withdrawing from a contract should not lead to any cost for consumers and that it would be efficient if the cost of returning goods bought at a distance were to be borne by the sellers".[253]

The provision of the CRD, which requires consumers to bear the cost of return in the event of exercise of the withdrawal right may not have taken into consideration the fact that the costs of returning goods at great distance may be exceedingly high. This may cause the majority of e-consumers not to take advantage of the available withdrawal mechanism, resulting in the cooling off period not functioning as effectively as it should. However, it should be noted that "if the withdrawal would not cost the consumer anything, this would ultimately lead to a general increase of prices for all consumers, as the costs are ultimately redistributed over all consumers"[254]

In addition, the lack of awareness of consumers' withdrawal right among a large portion of consumer groups in the e-market may also be another factor that undermines the effectiveness of this mechanism. Many studies, for example, suggest that a significant number of consumers do not read the information on the merchant's website beyond the price and description of the goods or services.[255] With the non-reading behavior that is often found in online transactions, only a few consumers are aware of their rights about the cooling off period. This was true when Citizen Advice filed a complaint to the UK's OFT in 2002 that the majority of British consumers were not fully aware of their legal rights, particularly the withdrawal rights, even though the law required traders to inform consumers of such rights.[256] Therefore, consumers' behavioral tendency to ignore such information in standard consumer contracts may be one of the principal topics for analytical studies to improve consumer law. It may offer a partial explanation as to why the withdrawal rights are not often exercised by consumers.

One thing that can be concluded here is that if the withdrawal right is only used by a minority of marginal e-consumers, the effectiveness of the cooling off

---

[252] *See ibid.*

[253] *See also* Loos, *supra* note 189, at 267. The author explained various opinions and the rationale behind the question of who should bear the returning cost during the drafting process of the CRD.

[254] *See ibid.*

[255] *See* Hillman, *supra* note 216, at 282–300. The author provides the detailed data based on his survey with an explanation of why consumers do not read or only partially read the information and standard terms.

[256] The Citizens Advice is an agency service established in UK, aims to provide the advice people need for the problems they face and to improve the policies and practices that affect people's lives. In 2002, after the Citizen Advice has been informed of various problems relating to consumer transactions from consumers, it made a complaint to the OFT alleging the problems, in particular a lack of knowledge of consumer rights and limitations of cancellation rights provided under the law. In response to such complaints, the OFT conducted a market study identifying detailed problems and making recommendations, *see* OFT, *supra* note 238.

period is obviously limited.[257] Pamaria Rekatti and Roger Van den Bergh have also stated:

> .... Cooling off periods will be ineffective when the cancellation right is exercised only occasionally...The marginal consumer will exercise his right once he realizes that he can conclude a similar contract acquiring products or services of higher quality. In contrast, the infra-marginal consumer will accept what he is given and will not bother the use his withdrawal right, even if he is provided with numerous written notifications and preprinted forms, as most of the regulations analyzed in this paper require. If the number of infra-marginal consumers is higher than the number of the marginal consumers, the trader may not be incited by the mandatory provision of the cooling-off period to provide higher quality. It may be more profitable for him to receive some products back, to repay the marginal purchasers, and to continue to offer low quality to the rest this business, which anyway constitutes the majority of his customers.[258]

5.5 Privacy Mechanism

As the technology in the internet market has become more complicated, privacy concerns emerging from the fear that the information that consumers have faithfully given to online merchants will be violated has increased.[259] Consumers in e-sales have often found that e-merchants are collecting much more personal information than what is necessary to complete purchasing transactions and beyond what consumer are willing to give.[260] In this regard, e-merchants argue that data collection is necessary as a valuable resource that not only allows them to complete transactions, but which also allows them to operate effective marketing and to customize their products and services.[261]

Some studies have explored the relationship between online privacy concerns and online consumer behavior.[262] These have found that, as consumer privacy concerns increased and trust in e-privacy practice consequently declined, consumers have become less likely to enter in to e-transactions as a way of protecting

---

[257] It should be noted that today the role of withdrawal mechanisms specified in the CRD, and its impact on the internet market of the EU, have not yet been thoroughly explored by any study because of its recent implementation.

[258] *See* Rekaiti and van Den Bergh, *supra* note 210, at 383.

[259] *See* A. Rea and K. Chen, *Chapter VIII Privacy Control and Assurance: Does Gender Influence Online Information Exchange?, in* K. Chen and A. Fadlalla (eds.), Online Consumer Protection: Theories of Human Relativism 165, 165–6 (2009).

[260] Generally, if the collected individual information is often used without consumer's consent or for purposes other than what the consumer was informed of, or the data was easily transferred or shared with other parties without the consumer's knowledge, the consumer may be unwilling to disclose personal data to merchants. *See ibid.*

[261] *See ibid.*, at 168.

[262] *See ibid.*, at 177. *See also* A. Gurung and A. Jain, *Chapter VII Antecedents of Online Privacy Protection Behavior: Towards an Integrative Model, in* K. Chen and A. Fadlalla (eds.), Online Consumer Protection: Theories of Human Relativism 151, 159 (2009).

themselves from possible unauthorized access to their personal data.[263] The legislative attempts to eradicate online privacy concerns and build the trust of consumers in online privacy are the central to the focus of this section.[264] The privacy legislation of the EU will be explored to examine to what extent it has been effective in improving consumer's trust concerning privacy issues in e-sales.[265]

5.5.1 Overview of the Privacy Protection Rules

Directive 95/46/EC of the European Parliament and of the Council of 24 October 1995 on the protection of individuals with regard to the processing of personal data and on the free movement of such data (hereinafter *DPD*) was formed with the main objective of facilitating the movement of data throughout the EU and, at the same time, lifting the standards of personal data protection in the EU Member States.[266] For example, merchants face no difficulty in transferring data to their employees from one Member State to another. Simultaneously, the DPD implemented regulations concerning the processing and transferring of data outside the EU to make sure that the issue of data protection is properly handled by individual EU Member States.

---

[263] *See ibid.*, at 159.

[264] This is because "trust in e-privacy practices has been often cited as one cause of the low consumer involvement in business to consumer electronic commerce." *See ibid.*, at 177.

[265] Among EU Member States, Article 8 of the European Convention on Human Rights and Fundamental Freedom (ECHR), Council of Europe Convention for Protection of Individuals with Regard to Automatic Processing of Personal Data 1981 (The Data Protection Convention) and Data Protection Directive 95/46/EC (DPD) have been influential in developing the laws on data protection. However, the most important of these is the DPD, which will be the subject of discussion in this part. These pieces of legislation aimed at protecting personal data in Europe are particularly puzzling because of the distinctive characteristic of the EU law and the quick pace of development. However, it should briefly be noted that Article 8 of the ECHR is the fundamental principle of data protection law created in all EU Member States who are signatories to the ECHR. It specifies that "[e]veryone has the right to respect for his private and family life, his home, and his correspondence." For a general discussion on the implementation of Article 8 of the ECHR by the European Court of Human Rights, *see* A. Mowbray, Cases and Materials on the European Convention on Human Rights (2007). As inspired by Article 8 of the ECHR, the creators of the data protection Convention drawn guidelines for all Member States in prescribing precise principles and norms aimed at preventing the unjust collection and processing of personal data and information. Although the Data Protection Convention is not legally enforceable, it wields substantial influence over the development of data protection laws in the EU. With the influence of the Convention's principles, in 1995 the DPD was introduced. For further detailed development of the EU privacy laws, *see* C. O' Mahony and P. Flaherty, *Chapter XVII The Legal Framework for Data and Consumer Protection in Europe, in* K. Chen and A. Fadlalla (eds.), Online Consumer Protection: Theories of Human Relativism 326, 334 (2009).

[266] In 2002, the DPD was complemented by the Directive 2002/58//EC, which is known as the directive on privacy and electronic communications. However, the main principles were already set in the DPD, which covers computerized files containing personal data, including the data that is not automatically processed if such data forms part of a filing system.

The general provisions of the DRD intended to guarantee that data's owners are informed of their legal rights concerning data protection. It requires that "personal data be processed fairly and lawfully".[267] There are a number of conditions that need to be complied with before personal data can be legally processed, namely, the unambiguously given consent of the data subject, proper controls on the data and protection of the vital interest of the data subject.[268] Processing the data in a manner that reveals the subjects' ethnicity, religious beliefs, political beliefs, membership in a trade union, criminal record, condition of health and sex life are prohibited.[269] Minimum information such as the identity of the controller and of his or her representative, the purposes of the intended data processing, the recipients or types of recipients of the data, whether providing answers to the questions are obligatory or voluntary, as well as the possible outcomes of failure to reply, the existence of the right of access to and the right to rectify his or her data, must be informed to the data subject in cases where the data is collected directly from him or her.[270]

In addition, some information, namely the identity of the controller and of his or her representative, the purposes of the intended data processing, the categories of data concerned, the recipients or categories of recipients, the existence of the right of access to data and the right to rectify the data, must also be informed to the data subject in cases when the data about the subject has been gathered or collected from a third party.[271] In cases of data disclosure to a third party, the data subject must be informed prior to the disclosure.[272] The data subject has the right to object, at any time on compelling legitimate grounds relating to his or her particular situation, to the processing of data relating to him or her or to object, on request and free of charge, to the processing of such data which the controller intends to process for the purposes of direct marketing.[273]

Further, all persons have the right not to be subject to a decision which produces legal effects concerning them or which significantly affect them and which is based solely on the automated processing of data intended to evaluate certain personal aspects relating to them, such as their performance at work, credit worthiness, reliability, conduct and so on.[274]

The DPD also ensures the confidentiality and security of data processing by prescribing important duties for the data controller or the data processor. For example, the controller must implement appropriate technical and organizational

---

[267] *See* Article 6 (1) (a) of the DPD.

[268] *See* Article 7 of the DPD.

[269] *See* Article 8 (1) of the DPD.

[270] *See* Article 10 of the DPD.

[271] *See* Article 11 of the DPD.

[272] *See* Article 14 of the DPD.

[273] *See ibid.*

[274] *See* Article 15 of the DPD.

measures to protect personal data to ensure an adequate level of data security.[275] In addition, the DPD also requires all Member States to adopt suitable measures to ensure the implementation of the DPD and the sanctions to be imposed in cases of infringement of the provision of the DPD.[276] Any transfer of personal data to a third county that is not a Member State may only be carried out in cases where the third country ensures an adequate level of data protection.[277]

5.5.2 Evaluation of the Privacy Protection Rules

Generally, the privacy of consumers[278] is based on the claim that individual data "should generally not be available to other individuals and organization, and that,

[275] *See* Article 17 (1) of the DPD. Also, in the case where the processor carries out the process on behalf of the controller, the processor must procure efficient guarantees in respect of the technical security measures and organizational measures governing the processing.

[276] *See* Article 24 of the DPD. In addition, the DPD further prescribes the establishment of a supervisory authority in each Member State to review the application within its territory of the DPD provisions adopted by the Member State pursuant to the DPD (Article 28 of the DPD). It requires the Member State to make a judicial remedy for any breach of the rights guaranteed by the national law applicable to the processing in question available to any person who has suffered from such infringement (Article 22 of the DPD). The controller will be liable for any compensation to any person who has suffered damage because of unlawful processing operation or any act incompatible with the national provisions adopted pursuant to the DPD (Article 22 of the DPD).

[277] *See* Articles 24 and 25 of the DPD.

[278] In a more specific context, privacy may take many forms. Some scholars view it as moral, legal or consumer rights. Privacy can be defined as "the right of an entity (normally a person), acting in its own behalf, to determine the degree to which it will interact with its environment, including the degree to which the entity is willing to share information about itself with others". Others view it as a "social power effort", "economic theory" or "trust establishment". For various discussions on the meaning and scope of the privacy, *see* J. Campbell and M. Carlson, *Panopticon.com: Online Surveillance and the Commodification of Privacy*, 46 Journal of Broadcasting and Electronic Media 133–145 (2002), T. Hemphill, *Electronic Commerce and Consumer Privacy: Establishing Online Trust in the U.S. Digital Economy,* 107 Business and Society Review 221–239 (2002) and A. Mukherjee and P. Nath, *Role of Electronic Trust in Online Retaining: A Re-Examination of the Commitment-Trust Theory*, 41 European Journal of Marketing 1173–1202 (2007). Many look at it within the context of a need to maintain personal space or an important psychological condition. *See e.g.* G. Gumpert and S. Drucker, *The Demise of Privacy in a Private World: From Front Porches to Chat Room,* 8 Communication theory 408–25 (1998) and R. Clarke, *Internet Privacy Concerns Confirm the Case for Intervention,* 42 Communications of the Association for Computing Machinery 60–67 (1999). For other various different opinions toward the definition and scope of privacy, *see* C. Goodwin, *Privacy: Recognition of a Consumer Right*, 10 Journal of Public Policy and Marketing 149–166 (1991), A. Papazafeiropoulou and A. Pouloudi, *Social Issues in Electronic Commerce; Implications for Policy Makers,* 14 Information Resources Management Journal 24–32 (2001) and P. Han and A. Maclaurin, *Do Consumers Really Care About Online Privacy?*, 11 Marketing Management 35–8 (2002). This study will focus on the consumers' need for privacy or information privacy in B2C e-commerce, which requires the protection of collecting compilation and dissemination of information relating the use of consumers' data.

where data is possessed by another party, the individual must be able to exercise a substantial degree of control over their data and its use".[279] This may be in part based on an ownership concept where the consumers are viewed as the owners of their data or information. Therefore, the consumers should be entitled to "self-determination" in making decisions relating to the data or information they own.[280]

The concern of consumers that their personal information, in terms of data that can be identified with an individual, should not be taken without their consent or knowledge is the most important aspect of the privacy concept.[281] However, this in itself does not completely define our understanding of consumers' interest in such data. The information flow in society at large is another key factor.[282] In a commercial context, the ability of individuals to control their information must be balanced with the businesses' need to understand consumers' demands through the analysis of data and information generated by consumers. This is because businesses usually use their information in creating and presenting a new and better products and services.[283]

Consumers usually reveal private and personal information in exchange for the benefits from transactional relationships. Such benefits enjoyed by consumers must be balanced or given greater consideration than the perceived risk of information disclosure.[284] Consumers' willingness to disclose their information depends on the safety of its storage and the extent to which it can be accessed after the consumers have disclosed it.[285]

Unfortunately, at present, consumers live in a technologically advanced world where information about their purchasing, online browsing and other online activities are easily collected, analyzed, and unfairly used and disclosed, without their consent. For example, in 2006, Apple Inc. released iTunes version 6.0.2, featuring an additional function called the "Ministore" that can offer customized user or consumer recommendations based on the consumers' previous searches and purchases.[286] This function gives consumers better means to acquire more

---

[279] *See* Clarke, *ibid.*

[280] *See ibid.*

[281] *See* Rea and Chen, *supra* note 259, at 168.

[282] *See ibid. See also*, M. J. Culnan and R. J. Bies, *Consumer Privacy: Balancing Economic and Justice Considerations,* 59 Journal of Social Issues 323, 323–24 (2003).

[283] *See* FTC, *Protecting Consumer Privacy in an Era of Rapid Change, A proposed Framework for Businesses and Policymakers, Preliminary FTC Staff Report* (2010).

[284] For a detailed discussion on the issue of consumer information exchange, *see also* Culnan and Bies, *supra* note 282, at 326.

[285] The extent to which consumers will allow access to their personal information also depends on the extent of their access after they have given such information, *see* D. Shubhankar, *Remedying a Technological Challenge: Individual Privacy and Market Efficiency; Issues and Perspectives on the Law Relating to Data Protection*, 15 Albany Law Journal of Science & Technology 337, 358 (2004).

[286] *See* J. Borland, *Apple's iTunes Raise Privacy Concerns,* CNet New, (July 12, 2006), *available at* news.cnet.com/2100-1029_3-6026542.html (visited August 21, 2012).

personalized products and services. However, in addition to facilitating or providing favorite song selections, the personal unique data of each consumer was collected by Apple through the Ministore. Then, the unique data was sent via the Ministore to be analyzed by experts although consumers were not informed of this particular function.[287] Microsoft is another example. It used "Supercookies" to track users and consumers' media player viewing habits, web surfing activities and other data information.[288]

One report shows that privacy concerns are one of the main concerns that undermine people's decision to use the internet.[289] It has been suggested that in online sales, there is an obvious emerging trust gap that renders consumers unwilling to reveal personal information. For instance, a 2001 survey found that a large number of online consumers have declined to give their personal information or refused to buy goods or services from e-merchants because of the uncertainty as to how their personal information was to be used.[290] Moreover, over 40 % of the consumers in the survey avoided visiting certain websites because of their questionable privacy practices.[291] The outcome of this survey suggests that the consumers' concerns about online privacy threaten the use of electronic services.

Therefore, the DPD is one of the mechanisms aimed at protecting the privacy of online consumers by setting up fair privacy practices in the internet market, which give a signal to consumers that the traders in e-sales can be trusted as the collected data will not be used unfairly.[292] The DPD, which mandates the implementation of

[287] *See* K. McElhearn, Kirkville, *iSpy: More on the iTunes MiniStore and Privacy* (2006), *available at* mcelhearn.com/2006/01/12/ispy-still-more-on-the-itunes-ministore-and-privacy/ (visited August 12, 2012).

[288] Microsoft denied having a plan to use this data and provided an explanation of how to turn off this function. However, "the feature is on by default until a user completes a series of steps hidden within a detailed privacy statement. For further discussion on this case, *see* Rea and Chen, *supra* note 259, at 166 and R. Smith, *Microsoft Response to the Window Media Player for Window XP* (February 20, 2002), *available at* computerbytesman.com/privacy/wmp8dvd.htm (visited August 12, 2012).

[289] *See* H. Green, *A Little Privacy, Please,* Business Week, March 16, 1998, at 98–102.

[290] *See* Gurung and Jain, *supra* note 262, at 151–3. The author emphasizes the importance of online privacy concerns, which is closely related to the growth of e-consumer sales, by referring to a long list of online privacy literature supporting his arguments.

[291] *See ibid.* This survey's result is also consistent with the 1997 Privacy and American Business Research, which revealed that approximately only 2 % of consumers are very confident that merchants selling online will handle their personal information fairly. *See* Louis Harris & Associations & A. F. Westin., *Commerce, Communication and Privacy Online: a National Survey of Computer Users* (1997).

[292] This signaling function of fair privacy practice is also necessary to strengthen business and consumer relationships, which is critical in the e-market where the consumer has no direct contact with the seller. Instead, consumers in e-sales have to establish relationships with businesses who are strangers via computer programs that act on consumers' behalf. The provisions of the DPD may help consumers overcome distrust in transactions where there are great distances between the parties by providing assurances to consumers that e-businesses, through their computer programs or employees, will handle the individual data of consumers fairly and the consumers themselves

an appropriate set of fair information processes for all business websites that gather personal information, helps to fill the trust gap and encourages consumers to participate in e-market transactions. When the number of consumers in the e-market increases the number of e-merchants will also increase, leading to more products being offered to consumers and greater competition among merchants. This corresponds to Sects. 4.3 and 4.8 of the Framework on the availability of variety of goods and services at appropriate prices and the consumers' privacy.

In addition, the DPD mainly focuses on individual choices by imposing obligations on merchants to inform consumers that data processing is taking place and making their consent necessary for the data to be acquired. This will serve the same function as product labels and forms of information disclosure that help promote consumers' choices and selections.[293] It will also help facilitate consumers' ability to make more informed choices concerning the disclosure of their information by giving them an alternative of building a relationship with one e-business or its competitor.[294] This corresponds to Sect. 4.4 of the Framework on the freedom of choice and ability to make rational decision.

Although the provisions of the DPD were drafted with the good intention of protecting consumer privacy in the hope of increasing personal information disclosure, which would help facilitate market efficiency in the e-world,[295] the rising tide of consumer privacy concerns in the e-market has continuously and relentlessly increased.[296] It is undeniable that online privacy concerns have not yet been successfully mitigated as a vast number of consumers remain worried and uncertain of the safety of their personal information when entering into e-transactions.[297]

Presently there is increasing criticism being made against the DPD to the effect that, up to now, it has failed to provide adequate and meaningful protection to

---

still preserve the right to control their own information. *See also* Culnan and Bies, *supra* note 282, at 331. Such assurance provided by the DPD is critical and essential in attracting and promoting consumers' relationships, particularly the consumers who make first time online purchases. One survey reported that 71 % of consumers would be willing to give their personal data over the website only if they have an existing relationship with the same business in offline society. *See ibid.* It can be said here that if e-consumers have trust in the businesses' practice, it will facilitate the sharing of information in B2C transactions and the relationship will be built. With respect to privacy concerns in e-sales, the DPD may be a tool to increase growth in the internet market.

[293] *See* Culnan and Bies, *ibid.*, at 331.

[294] In other words, the DPD is also designed to ensure that the appropriate information about privacy is available, accurate and easy to understand for consumers, thereby ensuring that consumers have legitimate choice about how and for what purposes their personal data will be used. *See* Beales, Craswell and Salop, *supra* note 145, at 491–539.

[295] *See* Recitals 4 of the preamble to the DPD.

[296] Despite the creation of various data protection laws in the EU, the widespread violation of data laws and ignorance of good privacy practices continues. This has implications for consumers and the potential growth of online market. *See* Mahony and Flaherty, *supra* note 265, at 339.

[297] The privacy legislation has struggled to keep pace with the rapid growth of technological business models and structures that enable merchants to collect and exploit consumer personal information in ways that often are invisible to consumers. *See* FTC, *supra* note 283, at i.

consumer privacy in e-sales.[298] A discussion about the doubtful effectiveness of various provisions of the DPD follows in the next section.

5.5.2.1 Notice and Consent

Article 6 (1) (b) of the DPD specifies that "Member States shall provide that personal data must be ... collected for specified, explicit and legitimate purposes and not further processed in a way incompatible with those purposes."[299] This requirement makes sure that the data collection must be specifically and explicitly noticed.[300] The underlying rationale is based on the basic information principle for economic analysis of privacy interest, which promotes maximizing the scope of informed self-autonomy.[301]

Consumers should be explicitly notified that their private and personal information will be stored and processed. Consumers can then decide whether they will agree to disclose such information to third parties.[302] The notice regarding the collection of personal data must be "adequate, relevant and not excessive in relation to the purposes for which they are collected and/or further processed".[303] In addition, Article 10 of the DPD requires merchants to provide further information regarding their identity, the purposes of processing the data and so on.[304] All these requirements encourage consumers to enter into e-transactions by ensuring the control of the possible use of their personal information and enabling consumers to make informed choices by freely deciding whether or not to provide the data to the controller or e-merchant.[305] This corresponds to Sects. 4.4 and 4.8 of the Framework on the freedom of choice and ability to make rational decision and the consumers' privacy.

---

[298] Some argue that legislative actions in regulating the internet may be more presumed than real. This is because the internet can never be regulated because of its fast growth and complicate technological involvement. They instead propose an unofficial form of self-regulation on the internet. For the detailed discussion on principal approaches of online data protection, *see* Shubhankar, *supra* note 285, at 337.

[299] *See* Article 6 (1) (b).

[300] *See ibid.*

[301] *See* J. Bagby, E-Commerce Law: Issues for Business 575 (1999). Please note that the main principal objective of the DPD appears in Article 1, which states that it is to "protect the fundamental rights and freedoms of natural persons, and in particular their right to privacy". At the same time, the DPD also balances free trade among Member States by removing any restrictions on "free movement of personal data". Phased differently, if the personal data is appropriately protected in the manner set out in the DPD, the free flow of personal data within the EU zone is allowed. *See* Article 1 (1) (2) of the DPD.

[302] *See* Shubhankar, *supra* note 285, at 356.

[303] *See* Article 6 (1) (b) of the DPD.

[304] *See* Article 10 of the DPD.

[305] *See* Shubhankar, *supra* note 285, at 357.

In this regard, the DPD provides two levels of choice by giving different kinds of consent, namely explicit and unambiguous consent. While Article 8 refers to an affirmative act to indicate explicit consent to allow data to be processed, Article 7 prescribes the definition for "unambiguous" consent. These two Articles attempt to balance the protection of individual interest relating to individual data and the flow of data for market efficiency purposes. "With the possibility of providing personal data but withholding sensitive information, individuals may be more forthcoming in providing consent for the collection for personal data."[306]

For sensitive information,[307] Article 8 may satisfy as an opt-in approach that requires "an affirmative act granting authority to collect and/or use information".[308] For non-sensitive information, Article 7 requires opt-out consent through a clause "provided the related information is easily accessible and comprehensible".[309] The standard of proof for explicit consent is of course higher than the level of unambiguous consent. The affirmative act in electronic communication indicating clear or explicit consent may be clicking the button, ticking an icon or typing a particular word in the space provided on the website. The possible meaning of unambiguous consent in an e-sale transaction may be an "implied consent provided in relation to electronic statements including disclaimers and privacy notices that are not cumbersome to access or confusing to understand", which are specified on the website.

There may be little doubt about classifying these two types of consent in the context of the internet. This is especially true where the communication by e-means may be conducted in numerous forms without rules or limitations. This nature of e-communication brings about unlimited possible acts or required forms that can be designed by e-merchants to use as indicators of consumers' acceptance.[310] For example, the e-merchant may require a consumer to check or unclick a pre-checked icon in front of a privacy notice or the privacy policy may be written or stated in a pop-up window or hyperlinked page.[311] There is a question as to whether or not such means or forms of presentation and acceptance in e-sales can be deemed to constitute explicit or unambiguous consent pursuant to the DPD. This legal uncertainty in determining e-consumers' consent may cause consumers to be reluctant to enter into e-sale transactions.[312] As a result, with a limited number of consumers entering in to e-transactions, e-traders would have no incentive to compete for the

[306] *See ibid.*, at 358.

[307] According to Article 8 of the DPD, sensitive information is personal data relating to racial or ethnic origin, political opinions, religious or philosophical beliefs, trade-union membership, and the processing of data concerning health or sex life.

[308] *See* Shubhankar, *supra* note 285, at 345–6.

[309] *See* D. Rowland and E. MacDonald, Information Technology Law 399 (2000).

[310] For detailed discussion on the unlimited ways of information presentation in the online market, *see* Sect. 5.2.

[311] There is a criticism that the consumer privacy choices in e-sales are often buried by the pre-checked boxes. This mean seems to be ineffective in obtaining meaningful consent or explicit consent. *See* FTC, *supra* note 283, at 60.

[312] *See* Shubhankar, *supra* note 285, at 358.

sales of goods and services in the e-market, resulting in less choice offered in the online market. This contradicts Sect. 4.3 of the Framework on the availability of variety of goods and services at appropriate prices.

As the privacy risks in online sales become increasingly apparent, the disclosure requirements regarding privacy policy under the DPD become longer, more complex, more incomprehensible, and sometimes too difficult for internet consumers to understand. The often encountered problem of information overload on websites leads to situations where the "consumer faces a considerable burden in understanding lengthy privacy policies and effectively exercising any available choices based on those policies".[313] Overly detailed privacy policies may confuse consumers or cause them to ignore the privacy policy altogether.[314] Evidence confirms that consumers are likely to ignore the informed privacy policy and the consents requested by merchants. In one firm' analysis, it was revealed that only 100 out of 20 million consumers who accessed to the company's websites actually visited the merchants' privacy pages.[315] Another piece of research found that about three tenths of Yahoo users accessed the privacy policy the company provided.[316] The results of the focus on notice and consent in the DPD may be ironic because it is widely taken for granted by the public.

Furthermore, although a significant number of e-consumers are vigilant about their privacy and they may be willing to invest effort into protecting it, such effort may take time and may not be practical for most consumers.[317] Some of them may not be able to devote such effort to figure out the related technology on how to protect their online surfing activity, including online purchasing that can easily be collected by merchants even though it takes place against consumers' will.[318] The majority of consumers lack the knowledge and resources necessary to understand how and to what extent their information is used in the cyber world.[319] This lack of understanding, in relation to the terminology that e-merchants employ to manage

[313] This problematic issue of burden in understanding privacy policy has also been the subject of discussion in the US. *See* FTC, *supra* note 283, at 52–3.

[314] *See* F. H. Cate, *The Failure of Fair Information Practice Principles, in* J. K. Winn (ed.), Consumer Protection in the Age of the Information Economy 341, 358–60 (2006).

[315] *See* FTC, *Workshop on the Information Marketplace: Merging and Exchanging Consumer Data* (March 31, 2001).

[316] Although in March 2002 when Yahoo substantially amended its policy allowing marketing messages by telephone and e-mail, causing a high public awareness, the rate of privacy policy visitors in its website increased only to 1 %. *See* S. Hansell, *Compressed Data: The Bog Yahoo Privacy Storm That Wasn't,* New York Times, May 13, 2002, at c4.

[317] *See* FTC, *supra* note 283, at 60.

[318] *See ibid.,* at 29.

[319] Although many studies indicated that many consumers are interested and aware of the danger in providing information through websites, they have no capability or sufficient computer technical expertise to protect their personal data from the possible danger online. For example, they can also not distinguish between safe and unsafe merchants' websites. *See e.g.* G. Milne, A. Rohm and S. Bahl, *Consumers' Protection of Online Privacy and Identity*, 38 Journal of Consumer Affairs 217–33 (2004) and K. Chen and A. Rea, *Protecting Provisional Information Online: A Survey of*

and process consumers' information collection undermines consumers' ability to control their information and to give relevant and appropriate informed consent.[320] The notice and consent provisions under the DPD may not, in practice, be able to help e-consumers make informed choices because the lack of understanding of the complicated terminology of data processing, many tend to refuse to give any explicit permission to merchants to use their personal data or to make non-meaningful choices. Also, these limitations on privacy notice and consent create additional burdens for businesses in informing and requesting consumers provide opt-in consents.

If consumers have concerns about online privacy and are not confident in the online consumer privacy protection provided by the DPD, they may provide false or untrue information or not provide any information at all.[321] In such situations where there is no information in the internet market or the available information is not accurate, the online traders may not be able to offer goods or services that truly meet the demand of the target customers. This type of situation would not be a positive factor in the internet market and traders would not be able to correctly concentrate on focused trading or approaching targeted e-consumers based on their true personal data. Without accurate information, unnecessary solicitation costs of business will be higher.[322] Such costs are likely to be transferred to e-consumers in the form of higher costs of products, services and transactional costs. On the consumer side, if the e-merchants are unable to know the consumers' true interests or demands, causing the marketing or sale strategies of the merchants to not

User Privacy Concerns and Control Techniques, 44 Journal of Computer Information Systems 85–93 (2004).

[320] *See* FTC, *supra* note 283, at 26.

[321] According to the study of Kuanchin Chen and Alan Rea consumers may utilize 3 measures to control their privacy where they are not confident in online privacy protection or there is a possibility that others might collect and use their information, namely (a) falsification, (b) passive reaction and (c) identity modification. *See* Chen and Rea, *supra* note 319, at 85–93 (2004). These situations will negatively affect online market efficiency. This is because in general, consumers' information comprises "individual interest and buying habits", which are necessary for the merchant to develop and procure goods and services to meet the needs and interests of consumers who are the merchant's target. This is in accordance with economic arguments made by the International Chamber of Commerce that "there is a vital need for an unrestricted flow of business information a premise justified by" the four basis reasons, namely the efficient exchange of information and the growth of international trades; the right of free communication; the right of business to access and utilize communication facility and the recognition of modern business communication. *See* Y. Poullet, Privacy Protection and Transborder Data Flow; Recent Legal Issue, in Advanced Topics of Law and Information Technology 29 (1989). Rather than mass offering, all different kinds and qualities of goods and services, personalized information or data enable businesses to narrow their focus on marketing and trading based on previous preferences and control and reduce unnecessary costs. For example, a precise consumer ranking would permit the merchant to correctly approach the rich consumers, who can afford to pay more, with expensive high quality goods or services, meanwhile "consumers of moderate means would pay lower price, closer to what they could afford." *See* Shubhankar, *supra* note 285, at 348.

[322] Weak personal data protection, which allows the free flow of personal information, may help to reduce the cost of doing business. *See also ibid.*

accurately meet the consumers' demands or to approach an incorrect target group. As a result, consumers will need to spend greater time and effort in seeking goods and services that they really need in the market each time they want to make a purchase, without benefiting from the special offers designed by merchants to meet the tastes of a specific target group. This contradicts Sect. 4.10 of the Framework on the reasonable cost of transaction.

5.5.2.2 Control and Security

The DPD contains security and access functions to ensure the consumers' right to monitor and update their personal information after they have allowed someone to collect and process it, alleviating some consumers' concerns on privacy.[323] Article 12 states that consumers shall have the right to be notified of the objective, scope and identity of persons related to the processing of their data. This provides a guarantee to consumers that they have the right to obtain from merchants "as appropriate the rectification, erasure or blocking of data in particular because of the incomplete or inaccurate nature of the data".[324] In addition, Article 6 (1) (d) ensures that personal data must be "accurate and, where necessary, kept up to date; every reasonable step must be taken to ensure that data which are inaccurate incomplete ... are erased or rectified."[325]

These two provisions grant two important rights that prevent potential harm to individual consumers.[326] Firstly, "continuous control"[327] over data is critical for encouraging individuals to share information in the internet market. If consumers do not have control of the information that they have given, they will be hesitant to supply information in the future.[328] Secondly, "security of information processing" is also necessary and "organizations creating, maintaining, using or disseminating personal information must take reasonable precautions to protect it from loss, misuse and unauthorized access, disclosure, alteration and destruction."[329] Without

[323] *See also ibid.*

[324] *See* Article 12 of the DPD.

[325] *See* Article 6 (1) (d) of the DPD.

[326] Please note that the DPD does not grant a general right to object to the processing of personal data, as it is contrary to the objective of maintaining data movement. Article 12 of the DPD states that "rectification, erasure or blocking" will not be done if it is proven that the privacy practice does not involve a disproportionate effort.

[327] *See also* Shubhankar, *supra* note 285, at 359.

[328] *See ibid.* The uncontrolled information may later become a source of unpleasant annoyance for them as the consumers cannot control or update it. The nuisances of junk mail and misplaced telemarketing are examples of unpleasant marketing because they collect the personal data of consumers.

[329] *See* P. B. Maggs, J. T. Soma and J. A. Sprowl, Internet and Computer Law 691 (2001).

technical security or privacy provided by merchants in the internet market, consumers will lose confidence and not be willing to share personal information.[330] Therefore, the DPD puts the duty on merchants to prevent personal information from leaking to unintended recipients and/or to be used unfairly to the detriment of consumers.

The scope of control and security also extends to the trans-border flow of data. Article 25 (i) states that "the transfer of data to third parties outside the EU must take place only in the third countries where such third countries in question ensure an adequate level of protection".[331] This article also indirectly put responsibility on other countries to comply with the guideline of "adequate protection" specified in the DPD.[332]

The control and security functions under the DPD were designed to preserve consumers' benefits derived from the flow of information in the market. However, such overly prescriptive mandatory regulations that place duties on merchants to care for consumers' data, and provide means for consumers to review and amend such data, may impose significantly greater burdens or costs.[333] For example, the e-merchants may have no plan for further use of the consumers' data, but under the DPD they would have to incur substantial expenses in creating computer programs that enable consumers to review and update it.[334] They must also spend significant time and money to safely store consumers' data to prevent it from falling into the hands of unintended recipients who may use such data unfairly. The burden and cost of security duty required by the DPD will ultimately be passed on to consumers in the form of higher prices of products and services while the quality may remain the same. This contradicts Sects. 4.3 and 4.10 of the Framework on the availability of variety of goods and services at appropriate prices and the reasonable cost of transaction.

This is very clear in the case of first party marketing.[335] If the online traders wish to recommend products or services according to consumers' previous purchases on

---

[330] To prevent personal information from leaking to unintended recipients and/or being used unfairly to the detriment of consumers, placing the duty on merchants according to the DPD is one of the measures that helps facilitate and encourage implementation of appropriate protections for consumers' data.

[331] *See* Article 25 (i) of the DPD.

[332] An example of a third country responding to the provisions of the DPD is the US. The US negotiated a safe harbor agreement with the European Commission to satisfy adequate privacy protection prescribed under the DPD. The safe harbor agreement provided clearer and more predictable practices relating to transferring of personal data based on the aim of fostering and promoting international commerce. *See* US Department of Commerce, Export.gov, *Safe Harbour Overview* (April 26, 2012), *available at* http://www.expoert.gov/-safeharbor/shoverview.html (visited August 23, 2012).

[333] Some believe that a detailed series of consent and security requirements may impose significantly more financial burdens on all market players. *See e.g.* FTC, *supra* note 283, at 54.

[334] *See ibid.*, at 55.

[335] First marketing includes only the gathering of information from the consumer "with whom the company interacts directly for the purpose of marketing to that consumer. If the company shares

their websites, according to the DPD they may have to obtain unambiguous consent from consumers.[336] This requirement of the DPD may create an unnecessary and significant burden for e-merchants. Some scholars have argued that first party marketing should be one of a limited set of commonly accepted practices for which the online retailer should not be required to seek consent once the consumer has previously elected to use the product or service in question,[337] constituting consent for the first party marketing. The requirement of consent in this case will become an unnecessary practice in a transaction as it would impose significantly more burden on the online market than any benefit that may be gained.[338]

Some have argued that a flexible approach with less formal regulations on privacy protection as in the approach taken by the US may be more suitable as compared to the provisions of the DPD for today's era of rapid technological change.[339] In contrast to the DPD, the American regulation mechanism favors a "self-regulation" framework for data protection,[340] an approach supported by internet developers and e-merchants.[341] American industry representatives have commented that "overly prescriptive regulations impair the ability of business to develop privacy solutions for consumers at the product level".[342]

From an economic perspective, private regulation may be regarded as profitable because it enables e-merchants to avoid more stringent and different privacy regulations in the borderless internet market.[343]

Although the DPD as a piece of state-created legislation may have the disadvantage of increasing financial burdens on the market as merchants have to comply with mandatory obligations, it may be necessary to provide some protection of privacy as the consumers themselves cannot adequately protect themselves in the circumstances where a sophisticated technology is involved. Some studies have

---

such data with a third party other than the service provider acting on the company's behalf". This would no longer be a first marketing practice. *See* FTC, *supra* note 283, at 55.

[336] This is because the processing of data for the purpose of first direct marketing in internet sales does not fall under the exemption from the requirement to obtain consent from consumers who are the owners of such data pursuant to Article 7 (b)–(f) of the DPD.

[337] *See* FTC, *supra* note 283, at 53–4.

[338] *See ibid*, at 53.

[339] Many have voiced support for self-regulation for controlling privacy in the internet market. *See e.g*. FTC, *supra* note 285, Coteanu, *supra* note 3, at 197, FTC, *FTC Testifies in Support of Federal Legislation Protecting Children's Online Privacy* (September 23, 1998), *available at* ftc.gov/opa/-1998/09/privchil.htm (visited August 17, 2012) and B. Gates, The Road Ahead (1996).

[340] The US promotion of "privacy accepted business practice" through self-regulation with a monitoring agency, such as the FTC, will maintain flexibility in the market that "allows company to innovate in the area of privacy-enhancing technologies." *See* FTC, *supra* note 283, at 35.

[341] *See* Coteanu, *supra* note 3, at 161–3.

[342] *See* FTC, *supra* note 283, at 35. The businesses have named internet users as "Netizens" and proposed "Netiquette", which is "an unofficial form of self-regulation that emphasizes courtesy, respect and self-restraint, as evidence of increasing self-regulation on the internet." *See* Coteanu, *ibid*., at 197.

[343] *See also* Shubhankar, *supra* note 285, at 362.

revealed that consumers do try to protect themselves from online privacy risks, but they do not have an adequate self-protection capability.[344] Therefore, there is a need for governmental interventions such as "new law ... to more effectively monitor business practices".[345]

5.5.2.3 Enforcement

Although the DPD prescribes that e-merchants manage consumers' information responsibly and appropriately, some appear to handle it in an irresponsible or even reckless manner.[346] The Flash Eurobarometer 2003 Survey of business practices indicates that information disclosure under the provisions of the DPD is problematic. From that survey, it is clear that data protection legislation is frequently violated because merchants often do not provide information to consumers, particularly concerning privacy rights. Only 46 % reported that they inform consumers of the objective of data collection and the processes used with respect to it.[347] Only a small number of e-merchants act in accordance with the DPD provision.

This situation can be explained by the low cost of data storage that has brought about an era of limitless data storage, "which creates the incentives and opportunity to find new uses for it".[348] Sometimes, consumers' information may be stored for

---

[344] Individual consumers in the internet market, who often have limited understanding of the technology, are unlikely to overcome the business power of data collecting and processing practices. These practices are very sophisticate and utilize specialized knowledge to run and manage, particularly the e-businesses, which have sufficient incentives to hide its data management activities. Data protection law must be premised on principles that "would enable the market to reach this optimum efficiency but with maximum privacy". This is because the consumers are unable to fight the market power of data collecting, particularly in internet market. *See* Shubhankar, *supra* note 285, at 337, Milne, Rohm and Bahl, *supra* note 319, at 217–33 and Chen and Rea, *supra* note 319, at 85–93. It is interesting to note that although the US privacy protection framework is often regarded as industry's self-regulation, the last few years have seen a rise of legislative mechanisms designed to protect online information privacy for US consumers This may be because the "efficiency of the internet's self-regulation is probably dependent on many more factors that the regulators are willing to accept." *See* Shubhankar, *supra* note 285, at 361. If the recent increasing legislative introductions in the US may be an indication, the effectiveness of the internet self-regulation may not yet be adequate for the real internet market and the legislation may still be necessary.

[345] *See* Milne, Rohm and Bahl, *ibid.*

[346] These include, for example, e-retailers collecting the information directly from their consumers and then selling it to a data broker or a third party that has never had any direct contact with the consumers. It is also possible that online behavioral advertisings, created by online publishers who are usually e-merchants, may allow a third party to collect data of consumers who visited the e-merchant's website. For further discussion of unfair privacy practices in the e-market, *see* FTC, *supra* note 283.

[347] For further discussion on the outcome of this survey, *see* Mahony and Flaherty, *supra* note 265, at 337.

[348] *See* FTC, *supra* note 283, at 25.

future use without prior contemplation and without notice of such to consumers at the initial time the data was collected.[349] A survey on the use of websites revealed that the threat of breach of consumers' privacy is more explicit in frequently used websites to the extent that "when the traffic of all sites surveyed is taken into account, there is a 99 % chance that, during a one month period, a consumer surfing the busiest site on the web will visit a site that collects personal identifying information".[350]

As already discussed, the DPD allow the Member States to prescribe any sanctions in cases of privacy violation under the relevant domestic laws to implement the DPD. This may raise some difficulties, particularly in relation to different enforcement practices in different jurisdictions. Inconsistent sanctions and enforcement practices from one Member State to another may serve to confuse and create legal uncertainty that undermines the effectiveness of the DPD. This argument is confirmed by the European Commission's report which sets out recommendations for the implementation of the DPD.[351] It indicates that the effectiveness and enforceability of the DPD varies among EU Member States.[352] In such cases, merchants who often breach the accepted business practices on consumers' privacy may "cherry pick" the jurisdictions where the sanctions and penalties are relatively light to conduct most of their businesses. This is to avoid potential prosecution and severe sanctions in Member States with stronger enforcement. Such evasive practices take advantage of the different degrees of enforcement and sanctions, meaning that e-consumers in countries with less severe enforcement and sanctions may not enjoy an effective level of privacy protection.[353]

It can be said that the role of the DPD in contributing to consumer confidence on the issue of privacy is not so clear in many areas as has been pointed out.[354] Anna Fielder has mentioned that, despite the introduction of the DPD, a study has shown that there is a "widespread neglect of good privacy practice and lack of compliance

[349] *See ibid.*

[350] *See* Rowland and MacDonald, *supra* note 309, at 341.

[351] For discussion on this report, *see ibid*, at 337.

[352] *See ibid.*

[353] E-traders in such jurisdictions would not be deterred by the relatively light sanctions and continue to unfairly utilize the data of consumers with the aim of maximizing their profits and commercial advantages. In this regards, the UK Information Commissioner has suggested that there is "the need for a strong deterrent and greater attentiveness to the law control by organizations". Such action will send a strong signal to e-businesses that the violator of the DPD will face potentially harsh penalties. This recommendation demonstrates the need for Member States to review and amend their national laws to ensure that appropriate sanction mechanisms for breach of the DPD are in place; and that they are effective and adequate in deterring e-businesses from illegally processing consumers' personal information. *See* Mahony and Flaherty, *supra* note 265, at 339.

[354] Some believe that consumers' confidence in e-sales is very limited because of the failure in online privacy protection, including the ineffectiveness of legislation. *See ibid.*, at 339–50.

with data protection legislation".[355] This leads to serious implications for consumers in e-sales. Some researches have pointed out that many EU consumers still lack confidence in e-sales as they are usually concerned about online privacy and security. For instance, a 2003 survey among UK consumers discovered that six out of ten reported that privacy issues concerning the security of payments is their main concerns whey they are shopping online.[356] Later, in 2005, 10 % of consumers revealed that they have not made any e-purchases because of security concerns.[357] These real experiences confirm that the DPD is ineffective in the e-market setting. It fails to deal with the advanced data collection technology. Due to the nature of the internet, the violation of consumers' privacy is often invisible.[358] The vast majority of consumers are often not aware that their data has been disclosed or even sold without their consent.[359] Even if the consumers learn of such breaches afterwards, they may not be able to bring the offenders to justice as the technology enables e-merchants to very quickly move around and leave the market altogether.

As the DPD cannot satisfy e-consumers who want to protect their personal data, consumers may prefer not make significant online purchases or, if they choose to do so, they may not provide their personal data (passive response) or provide false data (active response) only for the purpose of completing the transactions as previously discussed. In other words, "[w]ithout assurance about Web site security-factoring in privacy and trust considerations-consumers are unwilling to supply the necessary personal information in order to complete an online purchase."[360] As a consequence, the e-merchants would suffer the adverse effects from the "lost or incomplete transactions or partial or incorrect data".[361] This is confirmed by a study that estimates that in 2006, the company Gartner lost more than two billion dollars in profit because consumers do not trust the security of e-commerce.[362] When e-merchants do not possess sufficient and correct data, they will not be able to create or improve their products and services to accurately meet consumers' demands. Without consumers' trust in online privacy, which leads to limits being placed on consumers' participation, the e-market would not be able to grow to its

---

[355] *See* A. Fielder, *Better Compliance: Guidance, Enforcement and Self-Regulation, Paper Present at the Data Protection Conference and Report on the Implementation of the DPD* (2002), *available at* ec.europa.eu/justice_home/fsj/privacy/docs/lawreport/fielder_en.pdf (visited October 12, 2012).

[356] *See* OFT, *Internet Shopping-Some Key Data* (2005), *available at* oft.gov.uk/shared_oft/press_release_attachments/internetshopping.pdf (visited January 12, 2013).

[357] *See ibid.*

[358] *See* FTC, *supra* note 283, at 33.

[359] *See ibid.*

[360] *See* Rea and Chen, *supra* note 259, at 167.

[361] *See ibid.*

[362] *See* E. Schuman, eWeek.com, *Gartner: $2 Billion in E-Commerce Sale Lost Because of Security Fears* (November 27, 2006), *available at* eweek.com/article2/0,1895,2063979,00.asp (visited January 12, 2012).

full potential. This contradicts Sect. 4.3 of the Framework on the availability of variety of goods and services at appropriate prices.

5.6 Interim Conclusion

This chapter illustrates that, unlike the traditional market, the e-market is not only mired with traditional consumer problems such as the asymmetry of information and the lack of bargaining in the formation of standard term contracts, but is also characterized by the technology that gives it its transnational environment where unfair commercial practices can occur more easily because of the manipulation of technology to merchants' advantage. This emergence of the technological interface of the e-market has formed a "technological imbalance" between merchants and consumers.[363] Many legal mechanisms have been attempting to cope with these problems, for instance the governing process of e-contractual formation, the substance of e-terms, the forms of e-communication, proving consumers' cancellation rights, ensuring data management and so on. Consumers usually lack sufficient knowledge in complicated e-communications and encounter new types of online difficulties. Tools designed largely based on old ideas cannot yet efficiently deal with many aspects of such problems that exist online.

For instance, terms and conditions found on web sites can bring potentially drastic outcomes through recognition and validation of e-standard contracts with the unobvious placement because of non-uniform ways of concluding contracts. When considering e-standard form contracts, which are subject to unfair term provisions, e-merchants often incorporate certain provisions to minimize the burden and complexity that may arise from the transnational nature of e-sales. This is especially true when including certain provisions that e-merchants like to put in their e-contracts to avoid costs and hardships associated with the cross border environment such as arbitration clauses, forum selection clauses and applicable law clauses, which may be unfair to consumers.[364] Consumers may also be overwhelmed by the volume of information provided or the number and varieties of means by which that information can be presented, rendering the duties placed on

---

[363] This appears to be inconsistent with the explanation of Cristina Coteanu that emphasizes the unequal power between contractual parties and the technological involvement in e-market. She indicates that "there is a transaction form *contract–as-consent* model to the *contract-as-technological assent* model", including clicking or browsing to express assent and the dominance of technological information which is a result of merchants' control of market behavior which has a detrimental impact on consumers and normal market competitive processes. *See* Coteanu, *supra* note 3, at 63, 129, 206.

[364] Even though the EU law, for example, renders them unenforceable. At the same time, such legal features may be too one-sided, as they do not take into consideration the negative effects on the traders, placing all the burdens, hassles and costs of cross-border dispute resolutions in e-sales solely on e-traders.

merchants ineffective. Furthermore, even though the considerable withdrawal right aims to take away all relevant barriers to distance online contracts, it comes with the unavoidable costs of returning the goods. Consumers are required to bear the cost of returning goods at great distances in e-sales, which may be exceedingly high, ruining the advantages of the withdrawal mechanism. Lastly, e-merchants can easily collect personal data and information about the behavior of consumers without notice or consent and this has been an important concern in the online market which the privacy mechanisms have not yet been able to deal with.

Importantly, the ineffectiveness of the mechanisms reviewed here to cope up with advanced information technology and a quickly developing environment can be evidenced by the current prevalence of unfair practices. The unique and unprecedented characteristics of the internet market itself may well explain the situation. As the costs of entry and exit into the internet market are low, a large number of e-sellers may not be concerned about long lasting potential reputational capital. Some may aim for short term profits and use various aggressive sales techniques, including non-disclosure of information tactics and data gathering conducted without notification, which infringe the provisions of these mechanisms. Perpetrators of such acts can simply escape from the internet market and their legal liability. Together with the trans-border nature of the market, these pose greater challenges to the relevant authorities as their power is often limited within one jurisdiction. Crustina Coteanu may be correct when she asks "[w]ould the consumers have the right to be ignorant in this fast-moving environment? While it is true that the use of information technology requires certain abilities, the goal of consumer protection law should not be confined to the protection of well-informed and reasonably observant consumers".[365]

While this chapter has shown that the substantive mechanisms do not effectively provide access to justice to consumers in B2C e-commerce because of its technological interference, it has yet to explore as to what extent the procedural mechanisms, which relate to the post contractual stage of online relationship, can provide access to justice to consumers. The next chapter will analyze the role of procedural mechanisms, which are essential ingredients to ensure the eventual effects of the substantive mechanisms in achieving the goal for consumer protection.

[365] *See* Coteanu, *supra* note 3, at 183.

Chapter 6
Procedural Mechanisms for Achieving Access to Justice

6.1 Introduction

If consumers in B2C e-commerce are granted substantial rights through a number of substantive mechanisms, as discussed in Chap. 5, while the appropriate procedural mechanisms to ensure effective enforcement are absent or insufficient, the rights provided will be meaningless in reality. To facilitate consumers' access to justice, the credible enforcement of these substantive mechanisms through effective procedural mechanisms is essential. Due to the limitations of traditional private litigation, where an individual consumer dispute is often of a small value, an affected individual consumer will usually not litigate a small claim as his or her individual loss is not economically substantial enough to make initiating a judicial process worthwhile. This is especially true with those *trifle losses* or *scattered damages* cases where the accumulated damages are high and suffered by a widely dispersed group, but the damage to each individual consumer is very low.[1] This situation has led to spirited debate on the question of what are the best tools for consumers' redress. These tools should not be disproportionate to the economic amount at stake in a given case. To deal with this, various attempts have been made in various countries to design one or more sets of enforcement tool such as small claims procedures, collective or group actions, ombudsman and other forms of alternative dispute resolution.[2] The question of whether these enforcement tools

[1] *See* W. van Boom and M. Loos, *Effective Enforcement of Consumer Law in Europe, in* W. van Boom and M. Loos (eds.), Collective Enforcement of Consumer Law 235, 231–54 (2007). This problem is often referred to in German as *scattered damages. See* G. Howells, *Cy-près for Consumers: Ensuring Class Action Reforms deal with "Scattered Damages", in* J. Steele and W. H. van Boom (eds.), Mass Justice Challenges of Representation and Distribution 58, 58–72 (2011).

[2] The increased attention being paid to consumers' enforcement in cross border transactions is confirmed by the various attempts of international authorities. These include the OECD Guidelines for Consumer Protection in Electronic Commerce, the OECD Cross Border Fraud Guidelines, the

S. Yuthayotin, *Access to Justice in Transnational B2C E-Commerce*,
DOI 10.1007/978-3-319-11131-5_6

provide effective means of protecting individual consumer's rights both through providing them with compensation and at the same time modifying corporate behavior to prevent or mitigate legal violations and ensure fair trading practices in B2C e-commerce, requires further careful analysis.[3]

This chapter thus will discuss and assess different procedural mechanisms that have currently been implemented in certain countries. These are examples of more proactive approaches, which appear to be good practices for consumer protection in B2C e-commerce-namely the mechanisms of the EU and some EU Member States.[4] The fact is that the EU consumer laws (including some national laws of Member States) have only recently been developed and thus they have benefited from the accumulated experience and good practices of all of 27 Member States, the majority of which are economically advanced jurisdictions. Therefore, their mechanisms concerning B2C e-commerce present worthy examples for this study.

Similar to the previous chapter, this chapter also applies the multidimensional framework described in Chap. 4 as the benchmark for assessing the effectiveness of each mechanism to identify any difficulties, particularly when dealing with transnational enforcement in the online market. The outcomes of this chapter will bring us to the further discussions in the later chapters, which aim at finding potential solutions to the problems and moving in a direction that will lead to more effective consumer protection mechanisms in B2C e-commerce that constitute the main objectives of this study.

This chapter begins by looking at the procedural mechanisms that are largely based on private litigation processes, namely the small claim and the collective redress mechanisms. This is then followed by a focus on the opposite side of development that reflects the importance of mechanisms in consumer protection such as the use of regulatory agencies. In discussing each mechanism, a brief introduction and description of their functions and structures are provided. The discussion will then explore and evaluate each mechanism by discussing the advantages, disadvantages, and consequences of adopting such mechanisms in the

---

UNCTAD UN Guidelines for Consumer Protection, and the establishment of the International Consumer Protection Enforcement Network, which is an international cooperation with the objective of improving the enforcement of consumer protection legislation.

[3] An effective procedural mechanism is critical to accomplish the ends of both consumer compensation and deterrence against future legal violations. These are the two main objectives of procedural mechanisms. For an explanation of the objectives of consumer redress, *see* H. Kötz, *Public Interest Litigation: A comparative Survey, in* M. Cappelletti (ed.), Access to Justice and the Welfare States 83, 85–9 (1981) and K. J. Cseres, *Enforcement of Collective Consumer Interests: A Competition Law Perspective, in* W. van Boom and M. Loos (eds.), Collective Enforcement of Consumer Law 123, 130, 168 (2007).

[4] Some EU Member States which are economically advanced jurisdictions employ interesting consumer protection features to ensure consumers' access to justice because they have to modify their national laws to comply with the more recently developed EU laws concerning B2C e-commerce. Therefore, their mechanisms present worthy examples for this study. This study selects a number of mechanisms from those countries that have been recently developed and have been the subject of extensive discussions as case studies to reveal the existing difficulties due to the special characteristics of the online market.

online market. To what extent they have been effective in dealing with the main challenges of transnational enforcement in online shopping will be carefully observed.

6.2 The Small Claim Mechanism

Individual private litigation has generally been the traditional means of settling consumer disputes.[5] However, a major issue with such litigation is its inadequacy in providing redress to consumers in cases where the harm inflicted on individuals is dispersed and the compensation each would receive would be greatly outweighed by the cost of enforcement through the courts.[6] A large number of consumers often opt not to exercise their rights when they are violated as litigation in such circumstances does not make economic sense.[7]

As an addition to the traditional civil procedure, the small claim procedure (hereinafter *SCP*), designed to be less expensive and more speedy to complete, has appeared in several legal systems as a response to this particular problem.[8] Academic studies have prevalently conceptualized the SCP as a redress mechanism created in an attempt to improve access to justice[9] and it is often considered "the primary way of increasing access to justice for ordinary people",[10] including those who are individual consumers.

[5] Legally speaking, it has long been accepted that a large proportion of consumer problems and disputes are individual matters. Consequently, they should be settled through pursuing individual private litigation. Also, the fact is that a substantial part of consumer law is private law designed to protect consumer rights. *See* Cseres, *supra* note 3, at 166. *See also* I. Ramsay, Consumer law and Policy, Text and Materials on Regulating Consumer Markets 157 (2007).

[6] These excessive transactional costs, particularly when compared to the low value of most claims, are well known barriers to consumers' access to justice. In this circumstance, traditional private litigation not only fails to compensate for the violation of individual consumer rights, but also fails to deter the unfair behaviors of business institutions.

[7] *See e.g.* OECD, *OECD Conference on Empowering E-Consumers, Strengthening Consumer Protection in the Internet Economy, Background Report' Washington D.C., 8–10 December 2009* (2009), *available at* browse.oecdbookshop.org/oecd/pdfs/free/2498011e.pdf (visited 21 June 2011) and Cseres, *supra* note 3, at 129. *See also* R. van den Bergh, *Should Consumer Protection Law be Publicly Enforced?, in* W. van Boom and M. Loos (eds.), Collective Enforcement of Consumer Law 177, 184 (2007).

[8] *See* P. Cortés, Online Dispute Resolution for consumer in the European Union 17 (2011). For detailed consideration of the common characteristics of the SCP between different legal systems, *see* J. Hill, Cross-Border Consumer Contracts 156–8 (2008). For the qualitative difference of the SCP from the ordinary civil procedure, *see* J. Baldwin, *Is There A Limit to the Expansion of Small Claim?*, 56 Current Legal Problems 313–43 (2003).

[9] *See* Ramsay, *supra* note 5, at 232.

[10] *See* Lord Woolf, *Access to Justice: Final Report to the Lord Chancellor on the Civil Justice System in England and Wales* (1996).

Notwithstanding the variety of domestic laws designed to facilitate a more consumer friendly dispute settlement process by establishing SCP at the national level,[11] the attention of lawmakers at the EU level has largely focused on the development of the SCP at the regional level.[12] This section will explore the EU small claim procedure, which has been recently developed, with an emphasis on cross border small value claims, as a case study to see the consequences that this mechanism has had on the transnational online market.

6.2.1 Overview of Small Claim Procedure

In 2007, Regulation (EC) No. 861/2007 of the European Parliament and of the Council establishing a European Small Claim Procedure (hereinafter *ESCP*) was adopted by the EU aiming to "simplify and speed up litigation concerning small claims, and to reduce cost",[13] as well as to increase consumer confidence to promote the truly integrated EU single market.[14]

One main feature of the ESCP is its application to disputes not exceeding €2,000 in value.[15] In addition, the application of the ESCP is restricted to cross border disputes.[16] This means the ESCP is available only to those cross border cases "in which at least one of the parties is domiciled or habitually resident in a Member State other than the Member State of the court or tribunal seised".[17] However, the implementation of the ESCP does not substitute for the domestic procedure in cross border cases, but is only an optional procedure.[18] The ESCP provides an alternative option for consumers to conduct cross border disputes in addition to the normal civil procedure of their home jurisdiction.

Consumers may initiate their claims by completing an uncomplicated tick-box standard form according to the example provided in Annex 1 (C Claim Form and

---

[11] Detailed considerations of the SCP in a wide variety of national laws of the EU Member States, *see* Hill, *supra* note 8, at 156–7.

[12] The European commission introduced the proposal for the setting up of the European SCP in 2005. *See* Commission of the European Community, *Proposal for a Regulation and the Council Establishing a European Small Claims Procedures* (2005), *available at* eur-lex.europa.eu/LexUriServ/LexUriServ.do?uri=COM:2005:0087:FIN:EN:PDF (visited October 23, 2012).

[13] *See ibid.*

[14] *See ibid.*

[15] There were various perspectives among Member States as to whether small claim procedures should be available in both domestic and cross border disputes. Subsequently, a conclusion was reached to limit its applicability to cross border disputes. For a detailed discussion on this issue, *see* Cortés, *supra* note 8, at 100–1.

[16] *See* Article 3 (1) of the Regulation of the ESCP.

[17] *See ibid.*

[18] *See* Article 1 of the Regulation of the ESCP.

Answer Form) of the Regulation of the ESCP.[19] Traders who are defendants in an ESCP proceeding can defend themselves against the consumers' claims. If the value of a counter claim exceeds the ceiling amount prescribed by the ESCP, the case will fall outside the scope of the ESCP.[20]

A party to a claim being litigated under the ESCP need not be represented by a lawyer but consumers may be assisted by a non-lawyer during the process of litigation.[21] However, in case a lawyer is appointed during the ESCP procedure, the court may grant monetary reimbursements to the successful party, including the cost of legal representation that the court considered necessary and appropriate relative to the disputed amount.[22] If consumers have no legal representation, the judge has the additional duty of assisting them through the procedure according to the ESCP by taking on a proactive role.[23] The court is required "to translate the parties' factual assertions into the legally relevant claims and defence"[24] to ensure the parties' understanding of the claims and its grounds. The court also has to actively seek settlement between the parties whenever it is appropriate during the proceedings.[25]

Written, rather than oral, procedures are required under the ESCP to reduce time and save transactional costs, particularly concerning proceedings conducted abroad.[26] With the reduction in cost and time involved, many consumers may be convinced that initiating a case under the ESCP is worthwhile. Although a wholly written procedure is envisaged, Article 5 (1) of the Regulation of the ESCP specifies that the court shall hold an oral hearing if it considers it necessary.[27] A party may request an oral hearing but the court has the power to refuse such request if "an oral hearing is obviously not necessary for the fair conduct of the proceedings".[28] In practice, a consumer may not apply for an oral hearing because of the additional costs. A video conference or other means of communication can also be used in the hearing as necessary.[29]

Another material element of the ESCP is the relevant costs. The ESCP opts to require the losing party to bear the costs of the proceedings, including lawyer's

---

[19] *See* Article 4 (1) of the Regulation of the ESCP.

[20] *See* Article 4 (6) of the Regulation of the ESCP.

[21] *See* Article 10 of the Regulation of the ESCP. Regrettably, the Regulation of the ESCP does not contain any provision that allows a consumer's associate or consumer organization to act as a plaintiff on behalf of a class of consumers.

[22] *See* Article 14 of the Regulation of the ESCP.

[23] *See* The Preamble para. 2.1.2, Article 9 and Recitals 11, 16 of Regulation of the ESCP.

[24] *See* Article 10–12 of the Regulation of the ESCP.

[25] *See* Article 12 (3) of the Regulation of the ESCP.

[26] This written procedure follows the traditional civil procedure law. Its rationale is based on the practical advantage of reducing the cost and time regarding the process.

[27] *See* Article 5 (1) of the Regulation of the ESCP.

[28] *See* Hill, *supra* note 8, at 161.

[29] *See* Article 8 of the Regulation of the ESCP.

fees.[30] This cost principle is based on the notion that the winning party should not suffer economic disadvantage from pursuing the claim.[31] Nevertheless, to ensure the cost effectiveness of the ESCP, the court is given considerable discretion over the amount of costs awarded to the successful party to "the extent that it is not unnecessarily incurred or disproportionate to the claim".[32]

An important and advantageous element of the ESCP is that it seeks to eradicate the high cost and lengthy delays of traditional cross border enforcement. Judicial judgment conducted in accordance with the Regulation of the ESCP in any Member State is enforceable in other Member State jurisdictions without the need for considering the relevant mutual recognition of judgments.[33] The ESCP removes the intermediate measures as requirements of enforcement in other foreign jurisdictions.[34] However, there is an exception to this enforcement rule for a judgment of an uncontested claim where the defendant has not responded to the claim and participated in its process.[35]

6.2.2 Evaluation of Small Claim Procedure

The main aim of the ESCP is to establish cost-efficient court formalities applicable to small value claims in transnational disputes. Its implementation aims to lower the barriers for consumers to access to justice in transnational e-sales within the EU through such measures as promoting international cooperation, simplifying court procedures and reducing the costs of litigation and enforcement, including those in foreign jurisdictions.[36] With the simplified cross border enforcement process and lower costs, consumers' confidence will increase and the EU market will become truly integrated.[37] In addition, the ESCP is an example of a legislative effort of legal harmonization among the various legal systems of the EU Member States. The use of the ESCP as an optional procedure for small value cross border disputes will also remove the restrictions of the procedures at the national level in countries without small claim procedures of their own.[38] Therefore, it is a step toward the legal

[30] *See* Article 16 of the Regulation of the ESCP.

[31] *See* Cortés, *supra* note 8, at 102.

[32] *See* Article 16 of the Regulation of the ESCP. *See also,* Recital 29 of the Regulation of the ESCP.

[33] *See* Chapter III of the Regulation of the ESCP, which is designed to facilitate cross broader enforcements and eliminates all intermediate processes that are traditionally required for enforcement in foreign jurisdictions.

[34] *See ibid.*

[35] For the detailed consideration on this exception, *see* Cortés, *supra* note 8, at 103.

[36] *See ibid.*

[37] *See ibid.*

[38] This argument is supported by the Commission of the European Community. *See* Commission of the European Communities, *supra* note 12.

harmonization of transnational small value dispute resolution within the EU through cost-efficient procedures. It also encourages consumers to enforce their rights. This corresponds to Sects. 4.10, 4.12 and 4.13 of the Framework regarding the reasonable cost of transaction, the access to effective dispute resolution, and the enforcement of remedies or redress. However, the optimal effectiveness of the ESCP is subject to a number of limitations as discussed below.

6.2.2.1 Limited Scope of the ESCP

The first important concern is the low specified ceiling value of disputes to which the ESCP applies. Due to the diverse economic statuses and different standards of living among various Member States, the ESCP settled on a compromise ceiling amount of €2,000.[39] Many authorities, including the UK Government and the European Economic and Social Committee, have referred to this amount as an "unrealistically low limit" considering the possible outcomes with "disproportionate legal cost" for the dispute settlement that are just under or a little above this monetary limit.[40]

This choice of low ceiling amount has left many disputes with a value exceeding this amount faced with the extreme difficulties of cross border enforcement, especially for consumers who have a higher standard of living in some Member States that always consume higher priced products and services.[41] This criticism is also mentioned in a recent independent report submitted to the European Commission, which claims "the €2,000 limit as too low a limit and one that may not be cost efficient".[42]

In addition, traders who are defendants may easily make a counterclaim in response to consumers' arguments just above the €2,000 threshold, resulting in the case being excluded from the scope of the ESCP.[43] This circumstance is a possible erosion of the effectiveness of the ESCP as bad faith traders can escape from the simplified procedures under the ESCP by doing so. Therefore, the effectiveness of the ESCP may have been frustrating because of its excessively low limit

---

[39] For detailed negotiations about this ceiling amount among Member States, *see* Cortés, *supra* note 8, at 99.

[40] For the UK Government's opinion on this point, *see* the Secretary of State for Constitutional Affairs and Lord Chancellor, *The Courts: Small Claims, Government Response to the Constitutional Affairs Select Committee's Report* (February 2006). For similar argument, *see* The European Economic and Social Committee, *Opinion of the European Economic and Social Committee on the Proposal for a Regulation of European Parliament and of the Council Establishing a European Small Claims Procedure COM (2005) 87 final 2005/0020 (COD).*

[41] *See ibid.*

[42] Leuven Report, *An Analysis and Evaluation of Alternative Means of Consumer Redress other than Redress Through Ordinary Judicial Proceedings* (January 17, 2007), *available at* ec.europa.eu/consumers/redress/reports_studies/comparative_report_en.pdf (visited October 23, 2012).

[43] *See also* Cortés, *supra* note 8, at 101.

that excludes a large number of disputes from its cost-efficient procedure, failing to encourage a certain group of consumers to enforce their rights. This contradicts Sect. 4.12 of the Framework concerning access to effective dispute resolution.

6.2.2.2 Exclusiveness for Transnational Disputes

One other danger is the exclusive application of the ESCP only to cross border disputes. In cases where the consumer and the trader are located in the same jurisdiction, the ESCP does not apply and the enforcement of such cases must proceed in accordance with the ordinary rules of civil procedure. This renders it difficult to resolve many domestic claims, especially those cases where the cross border element surfaced at a later stage of enforcement.[44] One example of this would be in cases where the trader has a branch office in the same country as the consumer, but has no assets in that country on which to enforce judgment. For that to be possible, the mutual recognition of judgments in accordance with the ESCP would have to be obtained. This has left the consumers faced with extreme difficulty in enforcing their rights towards the assets located in a foreign jurisdiction through the ordinary civil process.

Also, with its exclusive application to cross border disputes, the ESCP may ignore small value claims in Member States that do not have their own domestic small claim procedures at the national level.[45] The consumers in those Member States can enforce their rights under the ESCP only if the initial claim includes a cross border element. This means that domestic small claimants are left to continue struggling with the difficulties inherent in conventional litigation.

If access to justice is largely related to the distribution of justice to all "weak consumers" who are unable to protect their rights against traders with more economic power and knowledge, the ESCP appears to fail in accomplishing that task. By overlooking a large numbers of consumers who may fall outside its scope and are unable to enjoy access to justice in commercial activities, the ESCP not only fails to provide effective consumer dispute resolution and redress but also fails to recognize the rights of such group. This contradicts Sect. 4.15 of the Framework concerning the recognition of consumer rights and their roles in the market.

The above claim is especially true in cases where a consumer who cannot settle a dispute and enforce his or her rights in accordance with the ESCP receives a judgment according to their national settlement system and is later unable to enforce it in a foreign jurisdiction. Part of the problem may be that the traditional enforcement process remains so burdensome and the expenses associated with enforcement are often higher than the redress value of consumer claims. Also, traditional cross border enforcement is not automatic and is often associated with very complicated and formal procedures, which require a substantial amount of

[44] *See ibid.*

[45] *See ibid.*, at 100.

time, effort, and money. Due to the exclusive scope of the ESCP, it may not fulfill its own objective as an effective dispute resolution in the transnational transactions of B2C e-sales. This contradicts Sects. 4.12 and 4.13 of the Framework about the access to effective dispute resolution and the enforcement of remedies or redress.

6.2.2.3 Costs of Small Claim Litigation

The ESCP adopts the *loser pays principle*, meaning that the unsuccessful party has to bear all costs of the proceedings including lawyer fees.[46] The basis behind this "no costs" rule for the successful party is that there should not be a monetary disadvantage from seeking legal advice from legal professionals.[47] This rule seeks to avoid discouraging consumers from employing lawyers to represent them in their claims.[48] If they win, the costs can be reimbursed against the losing party. Nevertheless, such rule may put consumers at economic risk in case they are unsuccessful in their claims as they will have to bear the reimbursement of high costs, including the traders' legal fees.[49]

The only qualification to ensure that the loser pays principle would not undermine the cost-effective function of the ESCP is that the court "shall not award cost to the successful party to the extent that they were unnecessarily incurred or are disproportionate to the claim".[50] Jonathan Hill is skeptical of this provision as its specified terms are in practice "hard to assess in the abstract as this provision appears to give courts considerable discretion over the awarding of costs".[51] In addition, despite this limit, from the consumers' general perspective the litigation may still not be worth the risk, especially against foreign traders if compared where the damages they incurred were quite small.

Unquestionably, the litigation cost including loser paid lawyer fees that come with seemingly arbitrary judicial discretion are likely to cause consumers to be reluctant to bring proceedings in accordance with the ESCP, particularly if the value of their claims is less than €2,000 ceiling. Therefore, the ESCP may not in practice eradicate transactional costs, the well-known barrier to consumers redress. This contradicts Sects. 4.10 and 4.12 of the Framework concerning reasonable cost of transaction and the access to effective dispute resolution.

---

[46] *See* Article 16 of the Regulation of the ESCP.

[47] Initially, the EC commission proposal on the ESCP suggested that the unsuccessful party must pay the cost of the proceeding except the lawyers' fees. However, the European Parliament later deleted the exception of lawyers' fees from the draft for the reason that the successful party should not be economically disadvantaged by conducting the litigation, thus encouraging consumers to protect their rights through the ESCP.

[48] *See* Hill, *supra* note 8, at 162.

[49] *See ibid.*

[50] *See* Article 16 of the Regulation of the ESCP.

[51] *See* Hill, *supra* note 8, at 162.

6.2.2.4 Exception of the ESCP

Although the ESCP seeks to facilitate the process of enforcing small claim judgments in foreign jurisdictions through considerably faster and less expensive means, the significant exception of uncontested claims that cannot benefit from the simplified and speedy enforcement process of the ESCP may obstruct it from achieving effectiveness in practice. Defendant traders may be aware of consumers' claims but refuse to participate in the litigation process to avoid possible obligations that may arise from the judgment that will follow by the recognition procedure in other Member State jurisdictions without the need for considering the relevant mutual recognition of judgments under the ESCP.[52] In such situations, the consumers, even if they win the case, will be left frustrated with the classic problems of enforcing their rights in cross border disputes through the ordinary civil procedure rather than the fast track provided by the ESCP.

So far, the above discussion suggests that the ESCP may not be an effective mechanism because it has a number of limitations. For instance, a large number of EU consumers cannot use such tool because of its limited scope of appliance and the risk of transactional cost (because of the *loser pays principle*). As a result, the ESCP may not generate enough motivation for those eligible consumers to employ it. With all these limitations, the optimal effectiveness of the ESCP mechanism in cross border small value disputes of B2C e-commerce may not be as clear as it was originally hoped.

6.3 Collective Redress Mechanism

As pointed out earlier individual consumers who encounter excessive costs and barriers compared to the value of their disputes will often choose to forego seeking redress. This is particularly true "where damage is widespread and individual losses are low, rational apathy prevails among the injured individuals who will not sue".[53] A collective redress mechanism is another procedure designed to solve this problem by merging scattered small value claims and forming a cost-spread method that can encourage hesitant consumers to initiate complaints.[54]

The plaintiff in a collective redress mechanism is a member of a group of consumers in a similar situation. They are faced with and affected by the same unfair business practice of the defendant.[55] The plaintiff brings the case to the court

[52] *See* Cortés, *supra* note 8, at 103.

[53] *See* Cseres, *supra* note 3, at 130, 168.

[54] For a detailed consideration of collective redress, *see e.g.* W. van Boom and M. Loos (eds.), Collective Enforcement of Consumer Law (2007) and W. H. van Boom (eds.), Mass Justice Challenges of Representation and Distribution (2011).

[55] *See* Kötz, *supra* note 3, at 96.

not only on his or her own behalf, but also on behalf of all other class members who are similarly positioned.[56] In other words, the group action is a litigation procedure that "brings together for a single determination the claims of numerous persons against the same defendant that arise from a 'common nucleus of fact'".[57] The judgment in actions brought under such procedures bind all members of the class of consumers who are deemed collective plaintiffs in the case regardless of the outcome.[58] This mechanism is referred to as the collective action, the class action, or the group action depending on the legal system.[59]

The next section will explore the currently debated collective redress mechanisms.[60] To do so, it will look at Swedish law, one of the more recent and the first nation outside the Anglo-American legal tradition to reform its collective redress mechanism, as an example in an attempt to answer the question of whether this mechanism can offer effective protection for consumers in B2C e-commerce.[61]

6.3.1 Overview of Group Action Procedure

The Group Proceedings Act of 2002 (hereinafter *GPA*) containing 50 Sections, came into effect in Sweden in 2003. The GPA provides an avenue for group proceedings when there are many claims against the same defendant that are largely based on a similar ground.[62] In group proceedings, a party engaging in the

[56] *See ibid.*

[57] *See* A. J. Duggan, *Consumer Access to Justice in Common Law Countries: A Survey of the Issues form a Law and Economic Perspective, in* C. E. F. Rickett and T. G. W. Telfer (eds.), International Perspectives on Consumers' Access to Justice 46, 54 (2003).

[58] *See ibid.*

[59] The bundling of claims, or group litigation, can be similarly defined as court litigation initiated by a plaintiff acting on behalf of a specific group and for the benefits of that specified group. The court decision is binding on all the members of that group. *See* K. Viitanen, *Enforcement of Consumers' Collective Interests by Regulatory Agencies in the Nordic Countries, in* W. van Boom and M. Loos (eds.), Collective Enforcement of Consumer Law 81–103 (2007).

[60] The EU is facing difficulties in terms of collective redress. Various Member States have developed and reformed their legislation for collective enforcement over the past few years. *See e.g.* S. Wrbka, S. van Uytsel, M. Siems (eds.), Collective Actions Enhancing Access to Justice and Reconciling Multilayer Interests? (2012), J. Steele and W. H. van Boom (eds.), Mass Justice Challenges of Representation and Distribution (2011) and Boom and Loos, *supra* note 54.

[61] In Sweden, there have been several attempts to improve legal procedures to safeguard group claims. In recent years, Sweden has adopted the reformed traditional group action model. The recent development of collective action in Sweden corresponds to the focus within the EU. *See* A. H. Persson, *Collective Enforcement European Prospects in Light of the Swedish Experience, in* S. Wrbka, S. van Uytsel, M. Siems (eds.), Collective Actions Enhancing Access to Justice and Reconciling Multilayer Interests? 341–63 (2012). *See also* A. Stadler, *Cross-Border Mass Litigation: A Particular Challenge for European Law*, in J. Steele and W. H. van Boom (eds.), Mass Justice Challenges of Representation and Distribution 73–100 (2011).

[62] *See also* Persson, *ibid.*, at 342.

proceedings may plead on behalf of all members of the group without requiring a power of attorney from each member.[63] Under the group proceeding arrangement, many plaintiffs can collectively take action against a single defendant, but it cannot be used by a single plaintiff as a tool to take action against multiple defendants.[64]

According to the GPA, group actions can be initiated by a plaintiff on behalf of a group member, namely, (1) a natural person or a legal entity who is a member of a group (private group action), (2) a consumer association or organization (organizational group action), and (3) the designated public authority (public group action).[65]

However, the public group action will be instituted only when there is a special public interest or the private group action or an organizational group action is not initiated.[66] The public group action is designed to play an active role when the main aim of the collective litigation is "to direct the course of action or to create precedent and promote the development of law".[67]

A group action can be initiated before the competent district courts specified in the GPA. The rationale for this is that these selected courts have the capacity and experience in hearing complex and sophisticated proceedings involving many individuals.[68]

Unless otherwise specified by the GPA, the group action proceedings are conducted under the rules of general civil procedure set out in the Swedish Code of Judicial Procedure.[69] Under the same procedural rules applicable to ordinary civil cases, the court has the power to consider whether a group action falls within its jurisdiction by considering whether such case meets all the special conditions for a group action as prescribed in the GPA.[70] The procedural prerequisites for initiating a group action are "(1) the action is based on the factual circumstances that are common or similar to the group; (2) a group action is not seen as inappropriate because of considerable divergences in the claims; (3) the majority of the claims cannot be equally well-conducted in separate proceedings of the group members; (4) the group is well-defined in terms of the value of the claims, delimitation, etc.; and (5) the plaintiff is well-suited to represent the group.".[71]

---

[63] The detailed provisions of the Swedish Group Proceedings Act of 2002 in English, *see ibid.*, at 346–50.

[64] *See ibid.*

[65] *See ibid.*

[66] *See ibid.*, at 347.

[67] *See ibid.* The competent public authority, namely the Swedish Consumer Ombudsman, will act within that line by promoting community and social interests and "refraining from intervening in the mutual legal relations of individuals, other than in exceptional cases". The Consumer Ombudsman has the sole power to make decisions whether to pursue public group action based on public interests. *See* Swedish Government Bill No., 2001/2002: 107, at 37.

[68] *See* Persson, *supra* note 61, at 348.

[69] *See* Section 2 of the GPA.

[70] *See* Chapter 34, Section 1 of the Swedish Code of Judicial Procedure.

[71] *See* Section 8 of the GPA.

The Swedish group action procedure is an opt-in procedure that requires consumers to actively seek to join or clearly express their intention to take part in the group action.[72] The special requirements and conditions for lodging a group action are prescribed in a very flexible way, thereby allowing judges to exercise their discretion in accepting or dismissing a case filed under a group procedure. If the case filing is accepted, the court must notify the group members as listed in the case filing.[73] The judgment is consequently binding upon all members of the group prescribed in the case filing and in the letters of notification by the court.[74] There is no limitation on civil remedies that are mainly comprised of compensation for damages based on contractual relationship or non-contractual liability that can be granted by the courts according to the GPA.[75] The appeal and enforcement of remedies can be carried out through the normal civil procedure as in ordinary civil cases.[76]

6.3.2 Evaluation of Group Action Procedure Regulation

The GPA is designed to offer dual solutions by both overcoming the individual incentive barriers and providing an optimal deterrent against legal violations. In other words, it is designed to address the shortcomings of traditional private actions, which fail to adequately address all consumer small claim disputes. The group action like the GPA not only "fulfills its historic mission of taking care of the small guy", but also provides "an effective sanction against group injuries".[77]

Bundling the fragmented individual claims carries efficiency advantages to consumers by giving them "a less disruptive and fragmented way of litigation and increasing the merits of claims brought before the courts."[78] The survey conducted by Eurobarometer in 2004 revealed that, in 15 EU Member States included in its study, 67 % of consumers responded that "they would be more willing to defend their rights in court if they are able to join with other consumers who were complaining about the same thing".[79] Therefore, consolidating small value claims

---

[72] *See* Persson, *supra* note 61, at 348.

[73] *See* Section 13 of the GPA.

[74] *See* Section 29 of the GPA.

[75] *See* Persson, *supra* note 61, at 349.

[76] *See ibid.*

[77] *See* M. E. Frankle, *Amended Rule 23 from a Judge's Point of View*, 23 Antitrust Law Journal 295, 299 (1996).

[78] *See* Cseres, *supra* note 3, at 173.

[79] *See* Eurobarometer, *European Union Citizens and Access to Justice* (October, 2004), *available at* ec.europa.eu/consumers/redress/reports_studies/execsum_11-04_en.pdf (visited October 23, 2012).

according to the GPA may be an effective dispute resolution that helps to encourage consumers to protect their rights and increases possibility of litigation in courts.[80]

In addition, another advantage of introducing and implementing a group action procedure under the GPA is its procedural economy.[81] Group actions under the GPA may reduce the burden created by a large number of disputes being initiated by individual plaintiffs, thereby saving the time, effort, and investment of plaintiffs.[82] While the monetary expenses may not be reduced in group action, it certainly provides a "means of vindicating the rights of groups of people who individually would be without effective strength to bring their opponents into court".[83] In other word, group actions clearly remove various forms of transnational costs associated with the handling of claims (non-monetary litigation costs e.g. time, resources, and psychological barriers).[84] This corresponds to Sects. 4.10 and 4.12 of the Framework about the reasonable cost of transaction and the access to effective dispute resolution.

Another rationale supporting the GPA is that it may have a significant impact on business behavior because the risk of facing a large judgment for damages in a group action will force businesses to accept the costs of complying with the law as the least expensive option.[85] This corresponds to Sects. 4.14 and 4.15 of the Framework about the fair trading practices and consumer confidence and the recognition of consumer rights and their roles in the market.

Furthermore, individual consumers are generally considered to be weaker parties who are ill-equipped to assert their diffused rights. They often have to litigate against large business entities with substantial financial means, as well as their legal advisers and information resources.[86] By allowing the claims of multiple consumers to be legally represented by an individual representative, a private organization, or a public authority, the GPA has strengthened the role and significance of individual consumers in the market. Consumers seem to be able to secure better and

[80] *See also* Cseres, *supra* note 3, at 173.

[81] *See* H.-W. Micklit, *Collective Private Enforcement of Consumer Law: The Key Questions, in* W. van Boom and M. Loos (eds.), Collective Enforcement of Consumer Law 12, 17 (2007) and R. A. Nagareda, *Mass Resolution of Mass Tort: Emerging Issues in the United States and the Global Future, in* J. Steele and W. H. van Boom (eds.), Mass Justice Challenges of Representation and Distribution 27, 30 (2011).

[82] *See* Kötz, *supra* note 3, at 96.

[83] *See* B. Kaplan, *A Prefatory Note*, 10 Boston College Industrial and Commercial Law Review 497–500 (1969).

[84] . For example, *Telekon* cases in the Netherlands involving 16,000 plaintiffs led to a long delay of judicial process because of limited capacity and the in availability of competent judges. There is a clear economic benefit of group action in such multiple plaintiff litigation. For detail of the case, *see ibid.*

[85] *See* Cseres, *supra* note 3, at 173.

[86] *See* Boom and Loos, *supra* note 1, at 231.

stronger bargaining positions concerning the settlement with defendant traders.[87] In other words, a consumer class may utilize a group action to challenge a business "on more equal footing".[88] Willem van Boom and Macro Loos have mentioned that "centralization of individual consumers' interests and aggregation of individual consumers' claims may help create bargaining power that isolated individual consumers lack when complaining and claiming for themselves"[89] The GPA can also serve as a tool in ensuring the appropriate market role and bargaining power of consumers. This corresponds to Sect. 4.15 of the Framework concerning the recognition of consumer rights and their roles in the market.

In addition, an action brought by a public authority according to the GPA may help fill the gap in cases where individual consumers and private groups or organizations may not be interested in bringing a group action because of the concern that the private cost of litigation will be greater than the anticipated gain, or where there is a lack of means to finance the litigation.[90] By making consumer cases a state concern and allowing a group action to be initiated by a public authority, the number of group action cases should reach the "critical mass" that makes enforcement function as a deterrent against unscrupulous business practices[91] This corresponds to Sect. 4.14 of the Framework concerning fair trading practices and consumer confidence.

Also, the group action carried on by a public authority on behalf of consumers (e.g. the Consumer Ombudsman, a state agency and so on) may also confirm that such diffused interests of consumers are not being ignored by society, but rather are recognized and actively protected by the state. This corresponds to Sect. 4.15 of the Framework about the recognition of consumer rights and their roles in the market.

However, the above is not to say that the group action procedure under the GPA is perfectly effective without any procedural weaknesses or technical complexities. Over the years after the GPA was first implemented, the number of group action cases has been very small, less than 15 cases in total.[92] Most of the cases were private group actions, with only one group action case initiated by a public authority, and not even a single organizational group action has reached the

[87] *See* Stadler, *supra* note 61, at 75.

[88] *See* Boom and Loos, *supra* note 1, at 231.

[89] *See ibid.*

[90] *See* Bergh, *supra* note 7, at 184. As previously stated, procedural mechanisms aim to protect individual consumer's private interest as well as the social interest at large. Unfortunately, the individual consumer's interest and the interest of society often do not coincide. Group action plaintiffs can be classified into three types, (1) a private plaintiff who is a member of the group and also seek redress for his own damages; (2) a plaintiff who is not a member of the group but a private group which has obtained a legal standing; and (3) a public or state authority who is responsible for initiating a group action for a certain group member. *See* Viitanen, *supra* note 59, at 92. The GPA provisions allow all three types of the plaintiffs to bring a group action to the Swedish courts.

[91] *See also ibid.*, at 184–5.

[92] *See* Persson, *supra* note 61, at 349.

court.[93] This number of cases is far fewer than the Swedish government had initially anticipated. A number of reasons may explain this situation.

6.3.2.1 Cost of Group Litigation

The most asked question when assessing the practical effectiveness of the GPA is how to best finance it.[94] Although the individual private case is too costly and such cost is one of the obstacles for a consumer to bring a case to court, the group procedure case carries a much higher monetary cost than individual cases in normal private litigation.[95] Klaus Viitanen points out that "if group action is wanted to serve as a serious alternative in the settlement of mass consumer disputes, which would also work in practice, the problem of high litigation costs, has to be solved first"[96]

The plaintiff of a group action appears to be exposed to a risk of high litigation cost as the GPA adopted the so called the *loser pays principle*, which would apply to cases under the GPA.[97] This rule applies even when the group action is conducted by a state authority such as the Consumer Ombudsman.[98]

The cost of group litigation under the GPA has apparently become a sensitive issue that bars consumer plaintiffs (either individual consumers or consumer organizations) from forming a group action, thus leading the small number of cases in Sweden.[99] Even though individual consumers may be willing to join as group members or initiate group litigation, an individual consumer tends to encounter a significant financial burden with regard to resources that could support the group litigation because they have no other alternative but to finance their cases from their own savings.[100] Similarly, consumer organizations that are eligible to sue on behalf of consumers also face financial difficulties in bringing group litigation. Evidence shows that some organizations with limited budgets have not been involved in active enforcement as they do not want to take the financial risk of group litigation, particularly in light of the loser pays principle.[101]

---

[93] *See ibid.* and C. Hodges, *Collectivism: Evaluating the Effectiveness of Public and Private Models for Regulating Consumer Protection, in* W. van Boom and M. Loos (eds.), Collective Enforcement of Consumer Law 205, 220 (2007).

[94] *See also* Viitanen, *supra* note 59, at 81.

[95] *See ibid.*

[96] *See ibid.*

[97] *See ibid.*

[98] *See* Persson, *supra* note 61, at 350.

[99] *See ibid.*

[100] Consumer organizations often lack the financial resources and the means to form a class and bring the group action to the court. *See* Cseres, *supra* note 3, at 140, 174.

[101] *See* Hodges, *supra* note 93, at 220.

Alternatively designating a public authority to pursue group actions does not seem to solve this funding problem under the GPA. For example, before initiating a group action under the GPA, the Swedish Consumer Ombudsman, as a competent public authority that can initiate a group action on behalf of consumers, has to carefully assess the financial risk and whether its available budget is sufficient for the necessary costs and expenses if the group litigation case is lost.[102] This is because the consumer ombudsman has to reasonably allocate the funding for its operations and the negative outcome of a group action cannot in turn adversely affect the finances of its other established activities.[103] So far, it can be said that the financial concerns on the costs of group actions has created a barrier for consumers' access to justice, which may be the explanation for why such a small number of group litigation cases have been brought before Swedish courts. This contradicts Sects. 4.10 and 4.12 of the Framework concerning the reasonable cost of transaction and the access to effective dispute resolution.

6.3.2.2 Long Duration and Complexity of Procedure

Time consuming processes may be another problem that has emerged from the GPA. For example, the only group action bought by the public authority under the GPA has taken an extremely long period of time to process through the judicial system. In this case, the Swedish Consumer Ombudsman brought a group action on December 15, 2004 against an energy supplier who failed to provide the required services to 7,000 consumers at agreed prices according to the agreed contractual obligations with the average damage varying from €100 to €1,000 per consumer.[104] As the hearings and proceedings were subject to lengthy delays as the normal rules of civil litigation applied,[105] the District Court rendered a judgment ordering the defendant to pay damages to all consumers concerned in January 2010.[106] After 9 years of litigation, this case is currently under appeal, having no final judgment yet at the time of writing.

The evaluation of the GPA conducted by the Swedish Ministry of Justice also confirms this limitation under the GPA by concluding that the GPA fails to reduce

[102] *See ibid.*

[103] *See ibid.*

[104] For further detail of this case, *see ibid.*, at 349.

[105] "The proceedings were delayed by the respondent asserting among other things that the special procedural conditions under the GPA were not satisfied. The district court overruled the respondent's objection on 20 June 2005. The respondent then took the matter to the Court of Appeals, which dismissed the appeal on 16 December 2006, whereupon the respondent appealed to the Swedish Supreme Court. In a ruling on 25 September 2007 the Supreme Court found no cause for granting a review dispensation. The proceedings were then resumed by the District Court, which, in January 2010, ordered the respondent to pay the damages to the consumers concerned." *See* Persson, *supra* note 61, at 349.

[106] *See ibid.*

the time consuming litigation process.[107] The appeal procedure for a group action case is not separated from the ordinary civil procedure and, as a result, the estimated duration for reaching the final verdict can be as long as 10 years.[108] Also, the same study further points out that the GPA has also not achieved the basic objective of simpler process. The implementation of the GPA seems to be very complicated and difficult in practice.[109] The technical complexities arose because a group action involves a large number of people. For instance, according to the GPA's principle, all members of the group should be notified of the action to give them the opportunity to step into the litigating class and identifying such individual consumers may be an extremely difficult task.[110] The Swedish Consumer Ombudsman confesses that the determination of group members under the GPA is an extremely burdensome undertaking.[111] It can be said that the lengthy adjudicating time and technical complexities of the GPA may be the main obstacles to group actions and a barrier for consumer's access to justice, resulting in the small number of group action cases in Sweden. This contradicts Sect. 4.12 of the Framework about the access to effective dispute resolution.

6.3.2.3 Lack of Consumer Incentive in the Opt-In System

Sweden's proclivity appears to support "a concept that holds the balance between the extension of collective legal enforcement mechanisms and the conservation of conventional European legal traditions"[112] and follows the due process requirement under Article 6 of the European Convention on Human Rights, which specifies that the plaintiff has the right to decide for him or herself whether to take action against the defendant.[113] As a result, the development of a group action under the GPA in Sweden has moved to the *opt-in* system, which requires consumers to actively seek

[107] The Swedish Ministry of Justice appointed a special group to conduct an investigation and evaluation on the GPA. *See* Memorandum from the Swedish Justice Department, *Evaluation of the Law on Class Action Proceedings*, 14 July 2007 (Ju 2007/5800/p) (2007).

[108] *See* Persson, *supra* note 61, at 350.

[109] *See ibid.*

[110] The GPA of Sweden is based on the opt-in system where consumers have to decide whether or not to join the action. Aggrieved consumers should have the opportunity to participate in, or influence the direction of, the case. For a detailed explanation of the principles of the opt-in system, *see* Kötz, *supra* note 3, at 98.

[111] *See* Persson, *supra* note 61, at 350.

[112] *See* Micklit, *supra* note 81, at 20.

[113] This concept of the plaintiff's right reflects the widely accepted view in the EU, which is strongly emphasized in many Member States (like Sweden, Denmark, Finland and Italy). Because of the widespread objections to the American class action system in the EU, the opt-in or opt-out group action has been the subject of debates at the EU level. England has expressed strong support for the development of an opt-in system. In Germany, Article 6 of the European Convention of Human Rights provides that the plaintiff's right to decide whether to take legal action is guaranteed by the national Constitution. *See ibid.*, at 20 and Stadler, *supra* note 61, at 74.

to join or clearly express their intention to take part in the group action procedure as plaintiffs.[114]

Unlike the opt-in system under the GPA, the *opt-out* system assumes that all consumers in a similar situation will automatically be represented in a group action without their consent being required and possibly without them even being notified of such action.[115] The opt-out solution appears to offer an alternative that will more effectively guarantee diffuse interests and the functioning of the market than can be accomplished using an opt-in system.[116] This is because private litigation, including group litigation, will only have a significant deterrent effect on traders' behavior if the number of cases increases significantly. Such an increase is only likely to be accomplished with an opt-out system.[117] The opt-out class action in the US for example has proven to have high deterrent effect in the US market.[118]

While the opt-in solution avoids "a possible clash between the right to be heard under the human right convention",[119] it may not provide sufficient incentive for consumers to participate in a group action. This is because the distribution of compensation to an entire class of consumers usually means that the reimbursement amount for each member will not be substantial. For each individual member of the class, this may not create a sufficient economic incentive to actively seek to join in the group action, which is one of the requirements for consumers under the opt-in system.[120]

However, one should bear in mind that the opt-out approach has also been the subject of criticism as the US style class actions have become subjected to scrutiny.[121] For it to properly work, the opt-out regime requires the leader of the group action to be truly acting in the interests and for the benefits of the entire class and it requires "safeguards to prevent 'fake group actions' instigated with insufficient funding or incompetent and inadequate legal representation with the hidden

[114] Many scholars argue against the opt-in system. *See e.g.* E. Kocher, *Collective Rights and Collective Goods: Enforcement as Collective Interest, in* J. Steele and W. H. van Boom (eds.), Mass Justice Challenges of Representation and Distribution 118, 122 (2011) and Boom and Loos, *supra* note 54.

[115] For a detailed definition and characteristics of the opt-out system and its negative impacts, *see* J. Stuych, *Public and Private Enforcement in Consumer Protection: General Comparison EU-USA, in* F. Cafaggi, H.-W. Micklitz (eds.), New Frontiers of Consumer Protection, The Interplay Between Private and Public Enforcement 63, 81 (2009). Despite the fact that there are criticisms against the opt-out system, in recent years, Denmark and Norway have adopted the opt-out group action procedures, following the American style of class action.

[116] For a detailed discussion of opt-in or opt-out systems, *see* Stadler, *supra* note 61, at 73–100.

[117] *See* Hodges, *supra* note 93, at 220.

[118] It not only offers compensation for individual consumers but also effectively serves as a tool for punitive prosecution to limit unfair business behavior because of the significant number of consumer plaintiffs and cumulative damages. *See* Stuych, *supra* note 115, at 81.

[119] *See* Micklit, *supra* note 81, at 20.

[120] *See ibid.*

[121] *See e.g.* Stuych, *supra* note 115, at 81, Cseres, *supra* note 3, at 173 and Kocher, *supra* note 114, at 130–2.

purpose of failing the claim, thus freeing the tortfeasor from otherwise successful individual claims".[122] Without a safeguard in place, abuses of the opt-out system can easily arise including, for example, excessive litigation, "the creation of a litigation industry that benefits lawyers" or legal blackmail against defendant businesses.[123]

Lessons learned from the US class action may also be another reason why Sweden adopted the opt-in system, which can prevent these types of abuses encountered in the opt-out regime. Nevertheless, one cannot deny that the main criticism of the GPA is the ineffectiveness associated with its opt-in system, which makes it incapable of providing sufficient incentives for group actions. Annina Maria Viola Holmqvist Persson has confirmed that one of the main obstacles to increasing participation in group actions under the GPA is its opt-in system.[124]

6.3.2.4 Difficulties Redress Distribution and Enforcement

If only minimal damage is suffered, consumers will not bother to actively seek redress.[125] This is particularly true in group actions where it is difficult to provide compensation because the damage to each individual consumer is often marginal. From the long experience of US class actions, it has been recognized that a class action might not satisfy all injured consumers if the awards they receive are minimal.[126] Although the GPA is an opt-in system, which is different from the US style class action where group members are identified before the group action commences, the identified consumers may not become active or bother to claim any compensation from the funds raised in the case if the damages they suffered are only marginal.[127]

This problem of redressing such scattered or diffused damages to consumers is even more difficult in cross border cases because of additional burdens (higher costs, more complicated procedures) that exist in transnational processes. Although consumers may have pursued a group action and obtained a judgment against the merchant, the steps to be taken to enforce such judgment against an overseas

---

[122] *See* Boom and Loos, *supra* note 1, at 231, 242.

[123] Details on this issue, *see* Stuych, *supra* note 115, at 81 and Kocher, *supra* note 114, at 131.

[124] *See* Persson, *supra* note 61, at 350.

[125] There are two main reasons explaining the difficulty in enforcing minimal damages in a group action. Firstly, "group members must become active and claim compensation from funds raised or the like; having suffered only minimal damage, they will still not bother to become active". Secondly, "group members often have no evidence to prove that they are entitled to compensation." *See* Stadler, *supra* note 61, at 77.

[126] *See ibid.*

[127] *See ibid.*

defendant may be overwhelming. Such enforcement is certainly more complex and costly than enforcement against a defendant in the same jurisdiction.[128] For example, we may consider a case where a defective product manufactured and distributed by a foreign defendant located in another EU Member State is sold via the internet to Swedish consumers. The injured Swedish consumers in such a case can bring a collective action to a Swedish court under the GPA.[129] The judgment of the Swedish court is likely to be recognized and enforceable in other EU Member States.[130] Nevertheless, one must admit that it may not even be possible to compensate consumers in cross border transactions if they suffered marginal damages.

From a practical perspective, the enforcement of group action judgments against foreign business operators might not be feasible. E-merchants are able to mitigate their possible exposure to enforcement of group action judgments by not maintaining assets or a physical presence in countries that allow group actions, and only conducting business in such jurisdictions via internet or other e-means. This is one way such merchants can avoid having their assets seized to satisfy a judgment made large by the aggregation of individual damages. In this situation where the online environment allows traders to offer products or services in one jurisdiction without a physical presence or any assent required to be located in such territory, it may be impossible to provide consumers with compensation by enforcing a judgment on the defendant's property. This may also frustrate the deterrent effect against both the offending merchant and others because they can avoid sanctions for unfair practices. This contradicts Sects. 4.13 and 4.14 of the Framework concerning the enforcement of remedies or redress and the fair trading practices and consumer confidence.

[128] The argument in favor of the opt-out system points out that it is an effective way to enforce consumers' rights, particularly where the individual damage is very small and individual consumers will not bother to opt-in. However, transnational enforcement under the opt-out mechanism seems to be much more difficult than the opt-in one. The distribution and allocation of very little amounts among group members does not offer a sufficient incentive. This is because the group members in the opt-out system cannot be clearly identified. For the detailed discussion on the difficulties of cross border mass litigation, *see ibid.*, at 73–100.

[129] Under the basic rules of the Brussels Regulation, consumer plaintiffs are eligible to sue the foreign trader defendants in the court of the consumer's domicile. *See* detailed discussion of the Brussels Regulation on this issue, *infra* Chap. 7.

[130] Within the scope of the Brussels Regulation, a class action judgment is likely to be enforced and recognized by other EU Member States under Articles 42–43. However, there is an exception based on public policy under Article 34. An example of the public policy exception is the situation wherein there was a prior group action completed under the opt-out system and later a second group action was initiated in another Member State. The crucial issue to determine by the court is whether the preclusive outcome of the first class action needs to be recognized. For the detailed explanation of recognition and enforcement of cross border group actions, *see* Howells, *supra* note 1, at 82–6.

6.4 Regulatory Agency Mechanism

In the consumer protection arena where there are diffuse and fragmented interests, there is a tendency to establish designated regulatory or governmental agencies that are directly responsible for administering consumers' justice.[131] These may be a separate division of the Attorney General's Office,[132] or an independent governmental agency such as the Fair Trading Office in the UK,[133] the Federal Trade Commission in the US,[134] and the Consumer Ombudsman in Nordic countries.[135] This sub-chapter will explore the well-known governmental advocate modeled on Consumer Ombudsman "who are regarded as being efficient in delivering mass compensation, as well as behavior control"[136] in consumer protection of the four Nordic countries, namely Denmark, Norway, Finland and Sweden. The Nordic Consumer Ombudsmen have been given a wide range of power from supervising the market and regulating unfair contract terms, to taking action for damages and even initiating criminal proceedings with the ultimate goal of enforcing consumer protection laws and policies.[137]

---

[131] So far in Sects. 6.2 and 6.3, we have discussed and considered the procedural mechanisms that encourage and authorize civil litigation by private individuals, private organizations and the representatives of consumer group members, as means of settling consumer disputes. Another possibility is to largely entrust such responsibility to state agencies that have been given the power and duty to directly enforce consumer law by implementing injunctions, sanctions, and sometimes seeking damages on behalf of individual consumers.

[132] The Institutions of Attorney General are usually set up in civil law countries. Their main activities in civil law litigation are usually aimed at helping and protecting individuals who are unable to protect themselves. *See* Kötz, *supra* note 3, at 111.

[133] For details of the functions and duties of OFT, *see* Ramsay, *supra* note 5, at 453–513.

[134] Nordic nations started to establish their national consumer protection systems in the early 1970s. Although there are differences among countries, the core systems are clearly similar. These are usually classified or grouped together as the Nordic model of consumer protection and their best known feature is the Consumer Ombudsman, a regulatory or state agency mechanism. For detailed discussion on this mechanism, *see infra* Sect. 6.4.

[135] They are the main tools of administering and enforcing consumer laws. Their tasks are not limited to private litigation for damages but include granting permission or withdrawing licenses, imposing of fines, initiating criminal cases and so on.

[136] *See* C. Hodges, *Objectives, Mechanisms and Policy Choices in Collective Enforcement and Redress, in* J. Steele and W. H. van Boom (eds.), Mass Justice Challenges of Representation and Distribution 102, 112 (2011).

[137] Enforcement power of Consumer Ombudsman is likely to apply to those foreign traders who are offering their products through the internet and maintain a residence within jurisdiction of the relevant Consumer Ombudsman.

6.4.1 Overview of Consumer Ombudsmen

The enforcement of consumers' interests in Nordic countries largely relies on special regulatory or governmental authorities, namely the Consumer Ombudsmen.[138] The principal activities of Consumer Ombudsmen are "to supervise marketing practices and the use of standard contract terms, but also to promote consumers' interests in general".[139]

In case a wrongdoing is detected, the Consumer Ombudsman must give priority to implementing the soft law method i.e., persuading the targeted offender to voluntarily cease the wrongful practice or the use of unfair contract terms.[140] If the offender agrees, they must sign a written promise to correct their wrongful business practices instead of having the Consumer Ombudsman initiating a legal action.[141]

If the offender is in breach of such written promise, the Consumer Ombudsman will apply the hard law method by instituting a legal action against the offender in a competent court, usually called the Market Court or Market Council. The Consumer Ombudsman also has the power to impose an injunction or place fine on petty offenders.[142] In cases where the merchant is not satisfied with the Consumer Ombudsman's order or decision, the consequences and processes vary among Nordic countries. In Norway, the Consumer Ombudsman's order cannot be easily withdrawn or deferred. The merchant disagreeing with such an order has to appeal to the court for its revision.[143] In other Nordic countries, an injunction made by the Consumer Ombudsman is automatically void if the affected merchant makes an objection within a legally prescribed time period.[144] In response, the Consumer Ombudsman has to take the conflict to the court.[145] However, under urgent circumstances the Consumer Ombudsman in every Nordic country is authorized to impose a temporary injunction that is valid and cannot be repealed until the court begins to hear the case.[146]

The Nordic special court, namely, the Market Court or Market Council, possesses final decision making power to rule whether or not a marketing practice or

---

[138] The laws regulating the four Nordic Consumer Ombudsmen are the Danish Marketing Act, the Norwegian Marketing Act, the Consumer Protection Act of Finland and the Swedish Marketing Act.

[139] *See* Article 5 of the Consumer Agency Act of Finland is an example.

[140] *See also* Viitanen, *supra* note 59, at 87.

[141] *See ibid.*

[142] *See ibid.*

[143] *See ibid.*

[144] *See ibid.*

[145] *See* Article 14 of the Norwegian Marketing Act.

[146] *See* Viitanen, *supra* note 59, at 87.

standardized term in a consumer contract is considered unfair.[147] In Finland and Sweden, the competent courts are called the Market Court, but in Norway, it is called the Market Council.[148] However, they similarly have limited jurisdiction over consumer law cases about marketing and standard terms of contract.[149] In Denmark, a similar court is called the Maritime and Commercial Court of Copenhagen, which has jurisdiction to try all commercial disputes, including marketing and unfair contract term claims.[150] In all Nordic countries, the right of action in consumer matters has been formally granted to the Consumer Ombudsman.[151] However, in case the Consumer Ombudsman does not take action concerning advertising or standard terms, a consumer may file a petition to the court him or herself.[152]

The Nordic Court or Council may impose the following sanctions if an unfair marketing practice is found: (1) an injunction order,[153] (2) corrective advertising,[154] (3) a market disruption fee,[155] or (4) criminal sanctions.[156] It is worth mentioning that, although criminal sanctions are available, the Nordic courts seldom impose criminal sanctions in such cases. The Consumer Ombudsman of Finland once tried to place criminal sanctions against one wrongdoer but the competent court dismissed the charge.[157] In relation to legal expense, the no cost rule will apply to consumer cases initiated in the Market Court or Market

[147] In all countries, these special courts are staffed with well-trained professional judges, consumer experts and representatives of various consumer interest organizations. For example, when the Market Court of Finland hears a case, the panel of judges must consist of three professional judges and at least one, but not more than three, experts. All judges and experts have the same voting rights. *See ibid.*, at 87–8.

[148] These special competent courts were established in the 1970s.

[149] For details on this, *see also* Viitanen, *supra* note 59, at 87.

[150] *See* Article 9.2 of the Finnish Market Court Act.

[151] Consumer cases in Nordic countries can be initiated by the Consumer Ombudsmen. The rights of judicial actions are restricted to the Consumer Ombudsmen in Finland and Sweden. However, if the Consumer Ombudsman decides not to take any legal action, the individual consumer or consumer organization can pursue such action in some circumstances about advertisements and contract terms.

[152] It is more liberal in Denmark. Anyone who has a legal interest over the dispute may take the case to court under Article 27 of the Danish Marketing Act. For the discussion on the right of actions of the Consumer Ombudsman, *see* Viitanen, *supra* note 59, at 88.

[153] This is to stop the trader from committing illegal acts. *See* Article 30.1 of the Danish Marketing Act.

[154] This put the obligation on the trader to correct its illegal behavior by providing totally new advertisements. *See* Article 9 of the Finnish Consumer Act.

[155] This is a special sanction in Sweden. Traders may be ordered to pay a disruption fee if they or their representative's lack of due care results in a legal infringement. *See* Article 22–25 of the Swedish Marketing Act.

[156] In all four Nordic countries, criminal sanctions are available against unscrupulous traders and such actions will usually take place in the court.

[157] This rejection may discourage the Finnish Consumer Ombudsman from bringing a criminal case to the competent court. *See* T. Wilhelmsson, *Administrative Procedures for the Control of*

Council.[158] Under this rule, both parties have to bear their own litigation expenses regardless of the case's outcome.

Unfortunately, the damages awarded for individual cases do not fall within the jurisdiction of the Nordic Market Court or Market Council. An individual consumer wishing to seek compensation for their economic losses caused by a consumer law infringement has to go to the general court.[159] In practice, individual private litigation seems rare because the transactional costs of litigation exceed the expected damage recovery in small value consumer claims.[160] However, in cases where an individual dispute is material in the eye of the general interest of consumers, the Consumer Ombudsman in Finland, for example, may provide financial assistance to that individual to take legal action.[161] Such assistance may include all legal expenses and the amount that the consumer has to pay the other party if the case is not successful[162] Statistics show that the Finnish Consumer Ombudsman provides financial aid to two to six consumer cases per year.[163] One of the main aims of this legal aid is to establish pilot cases to provide precedents and reference of judicial effects in similar circumstances for consumers and merchants.

In the cross border context, in 1987 the Finnish Consumer Ombudsman sued a foreign trader before the Finnish Market Court.[164] In that case, the defendant was a well-known multinational enterprise offering its products to Finnish consumers through TV satellite broadcasts from England to Finland. The court ruled that the Finnish Consumer Ombudsman had the right to sue the multinational company because its marketing and sales techniques were directly designed for and targeted consumers in Finland. Therefore, an injunction order and a fine were granted in favor of the Finnish Consumer Ombudsman.

Marketing Practices-Theoretical Rationale and Perspectives, in T. Junkkari (ed.), Twelve Essays on Consumer Law and Policy 149, 159 (1996).

[158] *See* Viitanen, *supra* note 59, at 91.

[159] *See ibid.*

[160] However, Klaus Viitanen points out that neither the Nordic Market Court nor the Market Council has the jurisdiction to grant compensation to individual consumers. The new group action in Nordic Countries for individual compensation (as discussed in previous Sect. 6.3) may change this pattern in the near future. *See ibid.*, at 88.

[161] The Consumer Ombudsman can determine that the National Agency of Finland should pay on behalf of a consumer to a trader, if the consumer is not successful in the case. *See* Article 9 of the Finnish Consumer Agency Act.

[162] *See ibid.*

[163] *See* Viitanen, *supra* note 59, at 93.

[164] *See* Case no. 1987:13 of the Finnish Market Court.

6.4.2 Evaluation of Consumer Ombudsmen

Based on the overview of the Nordic Consumer Ombudsmen above, they, as public agencies, have been granted wide power to act as both *ex ante* and *ex post* strategy for consumer protection.[165] The resources and mandatory powers of these organizations seem to be more effective weapons than those available in private enforcement. Nordic Consumer Ombudsmen can impose public sanctions (injunctive orders, fines, and so on) that seem to have a greater impact than private enforcement with monetary compensation through litigation.[166] Even though the private enforcement may establish deterrent effects regarding future infringing behaviors and activities of the merchants, the level or degree of deterrence may not be adequate in some circumstances, especially when a large number of consumers lack incentives to pursue consumer cases. Influencing and modifying future behaviors of merchants, the ultimate goals of the procedural mechanisms, may not be effectively achieved by private enforcement alone.

This may be especially true in B2C e-transactions where the burden of transactional enforcement far outweighs the anticipated compensation. Due to the technological interface and transnational nature of the online market, it is very difficult for a private party to identify the location of infringement on consumers' rights. Offenders and consumers seem to lack any incentive to report or provide any information about the infringement because they perceive that any action against overseas merchants in the internet market would be excessively costly and likely to be futile. In this regards, a Consumer Ombudsman may be a more effective tool because it is in a better position to discover infringements on consumers' rights as it has greater investigative tools and power than individuals or private parties.[167]

As a competent state authority the Consumer Ombudsman, possessing resources, knowledge, specialized skill and expertise together with its capacity to impose sanctions, seems to have more influence on behavioral standards in the market. Put it in another way, the Consumer Ombudsman "is able to act both ex ante and ex post and it can impose public sanctions that seem to have higher weight than private enforcement with the compensation sanction.[168] Particularly in e-sales, the

[165] Concerning diffuse and fragmented interests, where the loss value is very minimal, *ex post* mechanisms alone may not be effective. *Ex ante* mechanisms are necessary in this circumstance, given their effectiveness in preventing infringement and reducing the cost of *ex post* mechanisms. Consumers Ombudsmen, with their soft strategies to avoid harm and their power to pursue litigation, can function as both *ex ante* and *ex post* mechanisms.

[166] *See* Hodges, *supra* note 136, at 102.

[167] Without any assistance from the Consumer Ombudsman, some serious infringements in the e-market may continue without discovery and punishment. *See* Bergh, *supra* note 7, at 183.

[168] In diffuse and fragmented interests where the loss value is very minimal, ex post mechanisms alone may not work. Ex ante mechanisms are necessary in this circumstance, giving the effectiveness of prevention of infringement and reducing the cost of ex post mechanisms. Consumers Ombudsman, with its soft strategies to avoid the harm and power to pursue the litigation, can serve as both *ex post* and *ex ante* mechanisms. *See* Hodges, *supra* note 136, at 101–17.

expected compensation through private litigation is considerably less than the likelihood of the transactional cost of enforcement. The Consumer Ombudsman can fill the existing gap, resulting in an improvement of the level of fair trading practices in the market. This corresponds to Sect. 4.14 of the Framework about the fair trading practices and consumer confidence.

Consumers will continue to be the principal actors in defending their own rights via the private litigation mechanism.[169] However, the Consumer Ombudsmen may demonstrate that the interests of consumers are of material interest to the public by actively searching for infringements and bringing offending traders to justice. The role of the Consumer Ombudsman positively shows the recognition of consumers' rights by the state. This corresponds to Sect. 4.15 of the Framework concerning the recognition of consumer rights and their roles in the market.

Another clear benefit of the Consumer Ombudsman is its role in preventing infringement of consumers' rights through soft strategies. The Consumer Ombudsman has the power to use a wide range of flexible measures to prevent possible violations of law. These include issuing advance opinions, providing fair marketing and trading guidelines, and initiating negotiation with merchants regarding standard term contracts.[170] Traders may also have a reason for preferring these soft strategies as they lead to a low chance of unintentional non-compliance and minimal possible sanctions. Other factors favorable to such preventive strategies are the reduction of information, detection, and enforcement costs.[171] The soft approach also tends to be a good measure as supervisions and advanced opinions may secure greater voluntary compliance than repressive or punitive approaches from the state[172] This corresponds to Sect. 4.14 of the Framework about fair trading practices and consumer confidence.

The role of the Consumer Ombudsman in negotiating with merchants and trade organizations concerning standard contract terms in various industries, with the aim of defending consumers' interests and protecting them from unfair practices, can be viewed as performing the duty of representing consumers in negotiations with merchants on such matters, thereby raising consumers' participation and bargaining power in the market. This corresponds to Sect. 4.15 of the Framework concerning the recognition of consumer rights and their roles in the market.

Furthermore, upon discovery of an infringement in case the above persuasive or preventive measures fails, the Consumer Ombudsman will notify the offender and persuade them to cease engaging in such offenses. This is another soft strategy that the Consumer Ombudsman can utilize rather than immediately imposing hard

[169] The consumer disputes tend to be an individual problem as the relevant laws are largely based on private law principles.

[170] *See* Viitanen, *supra* note 59, at 100.

[171] *See also* Ramsay, *supra* note 5. Even though the author discusses the advantages of self-regulation this relies on the voluntary participation of traders in a similar way to soft strategies that focus on the willingness of businesses to cooperate as preventive measures. As a result, they have similar positive effects in the market.

[172] *See ibid.*

penalties on the offender. This soft persuasive measure has apparently become very successful in Nordic countries as it was found that "most traders are in practice more than willing to co-operate".[173] However, it is important to remember the close dependency between persuasive measures and hard law sanctions. Where hard law sanctions are not enforced, the soft method may not be as successful as it has been shown to be so far.[174]

In addition, the Consumer Ombudsman can also provide some assistance to consumers who wish to claim economic losses and damages caused by the violation of consumer law. For instance, the Finnish Consumer Ombudsman has provided financial assistance to a consumer in a cross border dispute against a US trader.[175] In that case, the consumer ordered a product from the internet and the purchase price was charged to his credit card, but he never received the goods. Subsequently the consumer refused to pay the credit card invoice. At the time of writing this thesis, this case is still under consideration of the Supreme Court of Finland. This example seems to illustrate the Consumer Ombudsman's task in relieving consumers of some of the transactional costs of litigation in case disputes arise, particularly involving transnational disputes with substantial costs. This increases the chance for individual consumers to receive compensation for individual economic damages by lowering the litigation barriers.

Nevertheless, all these are not to suggest that the Consumer Ombudsman mechanism is without shortcomings. In fact, its functions appear to be subject to a number of limitations as described below.

6.4.2.1 Lack of Funding

The use of Consumer Ombudsman as the regulatory authority to enforce consumers' rights in place of private litigation does not solve the financing problem. Like any governmental agency, the Consumer Ombudsman has to perform its duties under the constraint of an allocated annual budget. For instance, the annual financial resources of the Finnish National Consumer Agency is approximately €6 million, with which it has to pay the principal expenses such as staff salaries, rent and training.[176] With limited financial resources from the state, the Consumer Ombudsman has to take extreme care in selecting consumer cases to grant financial assistance to.[177] This means many or most consumer cases will not receive any assistance from the Consumer Ombudsman because of lack of funding. Many consumers may be left to replicate the litigation process that often comes with the

[173] This may also be due to the available sanctions under the hard law that can be readily implemented in case the persuasive measures fail. *See* Viitanen, *supra* note 59, at 100.

[174] *See ibid.*

[175] For a detailed discussion of this case, *see ibid.*, at 93.

[176] *See also* Viitanen, *supra* note 59, at 102.

[177] *See ibid.*

well-known transaction costs that are borne by plaintiffs. In this situation, individual consumers may not conduct enforcement activities at socially optimal levels, resulting in the perpetuation of that classic problem of under enforcement of consumer cases.

6.4.2.2 Difficulties of Prioritizing Duties

The Consumer Ombudsman may have difficulties in prioritizing their wide range of tasks and activities, which include not only supervising market practices, regulating unfair contract terms, taking action for damages, imposing sanctions on rogue traders and initiating criminal proceedings, but also promoting consumer's interests in general.[178] Given the number of tasks to be performed, the Consumer Ombudsman might not allocate its resources wisely and its workforce and budget allocation may be dominated by certain activities, while other activities of similar importance may be overlooked. The Finnish Consumer Ombudsman offers a clear example of such risk.[179] The enforcement of competition law appears to dominate the Finnish Consumer Ombudsman's activities. Since 2002, a large number of competition law cases have been filed in the Finnish Market Court. Today, competition law cases are routinely filed and represent over 95 % of all pending cases in the Finnish Market Court.[180] Consequently, the rapidly increasing number of competition law cases has caused delays and longer litigation time for other consumer law cases, particularly cases seeking compensation for damages suffered by individual consumers. This has led to criticism that the Finnish Consumer Ombudsman is failing to fulfill its other roles.[181]

The difficulty in prioritizing its tasks and duties as a special independent supervisory body may result in the Consumer Ombudsman' s failure to fulfill some of its responsibilities, particularly its duty to assist individual consumers to obtain redress for damages, which usually are of minimal value. Geraint Howells confirms that "the danger of relying on regulatory agencies is the obvious one that they may not always prioritize providing compensation to individual consumers. This is understandable given the pressure on their budget...[R]egulators will be even less likely to expend resources when the result will be of only indirect benefit to consumers. They may well feel the deterrence and disgorgement function can be adequately fulfilled by the sanctions they can impose".[182] Consumer Ombudsmen often appear to place excessive emphasis on its role as prosecutor and punisher of

---

[178] The enforcement of consumer protection law is not the sole task of the Consumer Ombudsman. Market supervision, establishing standard contract terms and promoting consumers' interests are its other focuses. See Viitanen, *supra* note 59, at 85.

[179] *See ibid*, at 99–100.

[180] *See ibid*.

[181] *See ibid*.

[182] *See* Howells, *supra* note 1, at 66.

offenders of consumer law rather than helping to obtain compensation for individual consumers. By putting priority on its roles as prosecutor and punisher, the Consumer Ombudsman may not ensure or assist enforcement of individual consumer remedies in practice. Thus, as a mechanism, the Consumer Ombudsman has yet to demonstrate that the diffused and fragmented interests of consumers are not ignored. This is contrary to Sects. 4.13 and 4.15 of the Framework about the enforcement of remedies or redress and the recognition of consumer rights and their roles in the market.

6.4.2.3 Ineffective Sanctions

Once the infringement of consumer law is observed, the Consumer Ombudsman will bring the case to a special court for sanctions available under the law such as an injunction, an order, corrective advertising, a market disruption fee, or criminal sanctions. However, court issued criminal sanctions on consumer cases have turned out to be very rare in practice.[183] The harshest sanctions against unscrupulous traders that have been applied are injunctive orders.[184] This has often been criticized as a toothless sanction, which is unlikely to deter traders from future legal violations.[185]

In the internet market, for example, unscrupulous e-traders who intentionally plan to make quick profits with non-repeating consumers may keep violating the laws. They are not deterred by soft sanctions and may not always worry about their market reputation because they can easily leave and re-enter the e-market with a change of name to avoid consumer complaints and bad publicity.[186] In this regards, Klause Viitanen has called for more attention to be paid to the issue that he identifies as a clear defect in the Consumer Ombudsman mechanism.[187] At present, the prevalence of the infringement of consumer protection laws in B2C e-commerce, could perhaps be explained by the fact that traders do not fear toothless sanctions even though they are imposed by a regulatory agency, like the Nordic Consumer Ombudsman, indicating traders' willingness to ignore consumers' rights and interests in the online market. This contradicts Sects. 4.14 and 4.15 of the Framework concerning fair trading practices and consumer confidence and the recognition of consumer rights and their roles in the market.

[183] This may be because judges and public prosecutors in general do not value the protection of diffuse interests. *See ibid.*, at 100.

[184] *See ibid.*

[185] *See ibid.*

[186] *See ibid.*

[187] He states that "[p]erhaps the biggest problem is that the traditional sanction system does not pay enough attention to the unscrupulous traders who intentionally and repeatedly violate the law in order to increase their sale numbers and profits." *See ibid.*

6.4.2.4 Difficulties of Enforcement

It would be interesting to examine what types of transnational enforcement of consumer law can be carried out by the Nordic Consumer Ombudsmen and whether its enforcement system can be called a success story. Admittedly, the Nordic countries, as EU Member States, are bound under the main EU legal instruments prescribing provisions on power to enforce consumer law in cross border infringements. The most extensive rules regarding the enforcement of consumer law is Regulation (EC) No 2006/2004 of the European Parliament and of the Council of 27 October 2004 on cooperation between national authorities responsible for the enforcement of consumer protection laws (hereinafter Cooperation Regulation) which aims to establish a regional network by requiring Member States to establish national enforcement authorities to establish at least a minimum level of cooperation on common investigation, the gathering of evidence, the sharing of information and coordinating actions against wrongdoers conducting business in multiple jurisdictions. The Cooperation Regulation clearly attempts to eradicate the difficulties of cross border enforcement by improving corporation among the national authorities of Member States. The Cooperation Regulation solely focuses on cross border cases and it clearly states the necessity of "mutual assistance" between various nations through national authorities who are granted power to combat cross border infringements of the 14 EU Directives and 1 Regulation listed in its Annex.[188] The focus of the activity relates to such issues as misleading advertising, unfair terms and distance selling.[189]

Despite the fact that the Nordic Consumer Ombudsmen are competent state authorities who enjoy the benefit of mutual assistance in the international network under the Cooperation Regulation, some defects of this enforcement system remain. First, the technical complexity of the process of transnational enforcement largely exists and remains a significant challenge. Experiences derived from the early EU regulation, namely Directive 98/27/EC of the European Parliament and of the Council of 19 May 1998 on injunctions for the protection of consumers' interests (hereinafter Injunction Directive) that similarly deals with the cooperation among national authorities in cross border situations, may help confirm the unresolved barriers to effective cross-border enforcement.[190]

---

[188] *See* Preamble Recitals 5–8 and Article 4 of the Cooperation Regulation.

[189] Nevertheless, the scope of the Cooperation Regulation will not be extended to those national consumer laws and regulations that falls outside the European Community law. *See* S. Ammerlaan and D. Janssen, The Dutch Consumer Authority: an Introduction, *in* W. van Boom and M. Loos (eds.), Collective Enforcement of Consumer Law 105, 108 (2007).

[190] Transnational enforcement of consumer rules has long been the subject of discussion as many related EU Directives have been left unenforced by Member States and the Cooperation Regulation is not the first law concerning the setting up of an international network for consumer protection. *See* G. Betlem, Public and Private International Enforcement of EU Consumer Law, *in* W. van Boom and M. Loos (eds.), Collective Enforcement of Consumer Law 35, 39–41 (2007).

Also, notwithstanding the availability of the Injunction Directive, it is rarely used or implemented in practice.[191] This may be because the Injunction Directive contains no provisions to simplify the process of cross border enforcement. For example, each authority has to take care of the translation when they communicate and work together among Member States with more than the 20 official languages recognized by the EU and this may cause unpopular implementation of the regulations. Many significant practical complexities such as language barriers, significant formal and official processes and so on appear to remain in existence.[192] The more recently enacted Cooperation Regulation does not appear to offer solutions for the above stated barriers from the past experiences of the Injunction Directive, such as the high cost and complexity of cross border enforcement processes.

It can be said here that even though the transnational enforcement issue has been increasingly stimulating the enactment of regulations in the EU, the classic burdens of cross border enforcement continue to exist and this may be one of the main reasons that the number of cross border consumer cases in the EU is much lower than expected.[193] Like other institutions, the Consumer Ombudsmen, the regulatory agency mechanism, have not yet able to avoid those conventional obstacles to achieving effective cross border enforcement.

Additionally, the legal framework under the Cooperation Regulation explicitly does not cover civil law enforcement and it does not impose any obligation on the national authority to assist individual consumers wishing to litigate against foreign traders to obtain redress for their individual damages.[194] Also, there are no detailed provisions or any practical guidelines for Member States concerning legal actions

[191] There seems to be only a single case brought by the UK OFT against foreign traders based on the provisions of the Injunction Directive. That case was filed against a Belgian trader based on the ground that the defendant circulated unsolicited mail of its catalogues attached with the winning prize coupon to many English consumers. The UK OFT won the case and the defendant had to cease such conduct on the ground that it misled English consumers that if they bought the product, they would be eligible to claim a prize. But in fact there were pre-selected consumers who would receive the prizes. For detailed of this UK action under the Injunctions Directive, *see* Pinsent Masons, OFT Sues Marketer in Belgium, Out-law.com, April 6, 2004, available at out-law.com/page-4439 (visited December 24, 2012).

[192] *See* Betlem, *supra* note 189, at 61.

[193] For example, despite the fact that Nordic countries have amended their legislation to the effect that "in cross border matters, a case may be initiated by petition of a foreign [plaintiff]", at least in Finland, there are no foreign consumers or any other consumer authorities (including the Consumer Ombudsman) from other countries trying to challenge a cross border consumer cases in Finnish jurisdictions.

[194] This appears to be inconsistent with the 2003 OECD Guidelines on transnational enforcement of consumer law. The Guidelines refer to a number of barriers to facilitating and providing effective transnational enforcement of consumer law and suggested the way forward, which includes a recommendation explicitly covering civil law instruments as one of the main concerns. *See* Betlem, *supra* note 189, at 62. The detailed of the OECD guidelines, *see* OECD, OECD Guidelines for Protecting Consumers from Fraudulent and Deceptive Commercial Practices Across Borders (2003), available at oecd.org/sti/consumer/

that national authorities (e.g. Consumer Ombudsmen) can bring against foreign traders on behalf of consumers or how the national authorities may seek to freeze or seize assets of such rogue foreign traders to satisfy judgments in favor of individual consumers.[195] The provisions do not address or touch on the civil law instrument, but rather solely focus on imposing sets of rules and sanctions on business to modify corporate behavior and prevent future legal violations. This means that if the Consumer Ombudsman attempts to recover damages for consumers in a group action,[196] it would similarly have to face the difficulties and burdens of cross border legal enforcement as in the case of cross border litigation conducted by an individual consumer or private consumer organization themselves. Where the individual consumers' damages are not significant, they can be easily overlooked by the Consumer Ombudsmen, especially when it weighs the public cost of obtaining remedies for individual consumers in the transnational environment where the costs are tremendously disproportionate to the economic value at stake.

The EU legislation tends to ignore the remedies for individual economic losses in the cross border environment caused by unfair trading practices and the difficulties of civil litigation processes and private redress enforcement for individual consumers in the same context of cross border matters. Thus, such enforcement systems may not achieve the ultimate dual goals of procedural mechanisms and provide only some level of deterrence against unfair behavior by infringers while failing to deliver individual justice by compensating injured consumers. Consequently, consumers in B2C e-sales may not be able to completely depend on the Consumer Ombudsman as an effective means of accessing justice. This contradicts Sects. 4.10 and 4.13 of the Framework about the reasonable cost of transaction and the enforcement of remedies or redress.

6.5 Interim Conclusion

Effective consumer protection consists of a number of essential ingredients that are interdependent. Legal and regulatory mechanisms include substantive rules that have an impact on the market and related actors will largely depend on the procedural institutional functions that ensure the eventual effects of such substantive rules. The question of how consumer protection law can serve consumer

oecdguidelinesforprotectingconsumersfromfraudulentanddeceptivecommercialpracticesacrossbordershtml.htm (visited March 12, 2013).

[195] *See* Betlem, *ibid.*, at 35–62.

[196] The Nordic Consumer Ombudsmen only provides legal aid to individual consumers who want to pursue a claim for compensation for economic damage. However, the new Nordic group action allows Consumer Ombudsmen to be consumer representatives and act as plaintiffs for a group of consumers. This means that in this new pattern, the duties of the Nordic Consumer Ombudsmen have been extended to taking legal actions on behalf of a group of consumers for their individual compensation. *See* Viitanen, *supra* note 59, at 90.

interests and provide access to justice can be answered by looking at substantive and procedural rules or mechanisms. To create effective mechanisms for online consumers credible substantive tools, rights enforcement methods and appropriate remedies are all essential.

The focus of this study has shifted from the substantive issues discussed in the previous chapter to enforcement and procedural mechanisms in this chapter. Chapter 5 provided some understanding on what kind of behavior in the online market should be regulated or even prohibited to deliver access to justice to consumers in B2C e-transactions. The focus of this chapter thus turned to the question of what would be the optimal enforcement mechanisms to enforce the disciplines or substantive mechanisms by evaluating different procedural tools that have currently been implemented in the online market.

It has long been recognized that a number of consumer problems relate to the fact that traditional private litigation, which is the conventional way of settling consumer disputes, has various limitations that do not provide consumers with economic incentives to individually take legal action. In the last decade, the challenge of seeking more effective and lower cost avenues for consumers that are proportionate to small value disputes has become the main focus in the area of consumer protection policy.

The analysis in this chapter uses some examples that appear to be best suited to reveal the relevant insights on issues concerning online transactions' enforcement. These issues usually relate to distance or the transnational character of e-commerce. The ESCP, which was used as an example here, aims to establish cost-efficient court formalities that apply to small value consumer claims by simplifying procedures and reducing costs. It also seeks to promote international cooperation. Despite its efforts in these areas the ESCP, because of its "loser pays" principle, tends to create considerable financial risks for consumers, particularly where the value of a claim is minimal (not more than the specified ceiling of €2,000) compared to the potential costs and burdens of transnational enforcement that cannot be avoided. In an alternative enforcement framework, Sweden's GPA is similarly designed as a solution to the problems of individual private action. The GPA has also failed to attain the optimal procedural mechanism. The bundling of fragmented individual claims may help reduce the burdensome issues of large number of disputes initiated by many individual plaintiffs, thereby saving the time, effort, and investment of plaintiffs and encouraging consumers to vindicate their rights by joining others in a similar predicament. Nevertheless, many of the GPA's weaknesses (the high cost of group litigation, a lack of consumer incentives in the opt-in system, complexities of process, difficulties of redress distribution and enforcement against foreign traders) have obviously led to the number of cases litigated being far less than initially anticipated.

The analysis of this chapter first reveals that individual consumers, consumer organizations and their representatives face significant impediments if they want to rely on private litigation as a means of settling their consumer claims, including their own limited financial means and a lack of incentives that could promote such litigation. Following from this, the chapter then focused on the use of public mechanisms in the context of consumer protection. The Nordic Consumer Ombudsmen that have been established as a possible solution in response to the fact that private parties, both individual consumers and consumer groups, often refrain from litigation because of its costs outweighing the expected returns. It found that the lack of funding, the difficulties in prioritizing the duties of the Consumer Ombudsmen and the cost and complexity of enforcement, especially in cross border disputes, are among the factors that render public mechanisms for online consumer protection ineffective.

Although the enforcement issue has increasingly stimulated discussion in the online market, the remaining classic burdens of small consumer claims enforcement (because of the excessive time and money required in comparison to the minimal value at stake) plus the additional difficulties of complex processes of enforcement in foreign jurisdictions because of the transnational nature of B2C e-sales, makes it even more difficult to design a mechanism that will efficiently serve the interests of online consumers. In such circumstances, the enforcement activities seem to be limited and incapable of achieving a socially optimal level as there are so many procedural burdens and risks concerning transnational enforcement. These are all contributing reasons for the very limited number of cross border consumer transactions in the online market. This chapter has shown that consumer disputes in online transactions are complicated and expensive and the procedural mechanisms will therefore not be suitable.

Admittedly, a consumer contract, whether concluded online or offline, is a standard term contract. In entering into a consumer contract, consumers seem face the problem of information asymmetry and lack bargaining power regarding pre-drafted contracts. The values of consumer transactions are usually low and the problems about dispute resolution appear to be very much of the same pattern. The discussion in Chap. 5 and this chapter have shown that the issues that the existing mechanisms used in the online market are attempting to resolve are very similar to those in traditional sales. But they do not seem to effectively address the main problems in the e-environment. The advent of the e-market has added technological imbalances and a cross border dimension to the traditional challenges of providing consumer protection. The next chapter will look at the alternative mechanisms of the private ordering, which do not rest on the creation of rules of law, but rely on technological solution and remedies and their significance for achieving access to justice for consumers in B2C e-sales.

Nevertheless, before the private ordering are debated and assessed, the next chapter has to make a detour from the main argument which largely focus on the effectiveness of consumer protection mechanisms and turn to consider the need for legal harmonization in promoting and facilitating the global e-commerce which is one of the important debates concerning B2C e-commerce which cannot be ignored. The question has come into attention whether the legal harmonization can improve consumer access to justice in B2C e-commerce? By exploring the legal harmonization, which largely relied on a governmental regulatory approach and the private ordering, which based on the private affairs in the following chapter, it will help to identify what is the best institutional arrangement that will be deliver the mechanisms which enhancing access to justice in online market, which will shade some light on the way forward to improve consumer confidence in B2C e-commerce.

Chapter 7
Transnational B2C E-Commerce: Legal Harmonization and the Need for a "Second Best Option"

7.1 Introduction

With the variety of consumer law approaches around the world, the harmonization of consumer protection laws has become a heavily debated issue.[1] In scholarly circles, the harmonization of laws is believed to help eradicate uncertainty that may arise from consumer transactions with foreign parties in the borderless online market.[2] Such harmonization is believed to offer consumers greater access to justice and to facilitate the growth of e-transactions by offering a clear perception to consumers and businesses that their expectations will be met at both the domestic and global levels.[3] As a result, the number of confident consumers who like to shop online and make use of the global e-market will increase.[4]

Therefore, legal harmonization has become the subject of recent attention, with the focus being placed on establishing a certain level of uniformity in international consumer protection standards across different countries. However, there are numerous challenges that confront the implementation of this approach, mainly caused by the significant cultural and legal disparities that exist between different

---

[1] From the business perspective, the high burdens and difficulties of e-sale transactions originated from the legal requirement to comply with very fragmented and disparate national consumer protection laws. On the consumer side, it is often said that most consumers who are likely to have very limited knowledge of foreign laws and regulations will not be comfortable and confident enough to enter into transnational e-transactions. This leads to the discussion on the need for harmonization of consumer laws. *See* P. Cortés, Online Dispute Resolution for consumer in the European Union 16–7 (2011).

[2] The regulatory models of consumer protection in e-sales continue to be materially different from one jurisdiction to another and the process of granting remedies appears to be much more difficult for consumers in the e-market. *See ibid.*

[3] *See ibid.*

[4] *See* C Poncibo, *Some Thoughts on the Methodological Approach to EC Consumer Law Reform*, 21 Loyola Consumer Law Review 353, 354 (2009).

S. Yuthayotin, *Access to Justice in Transnational B2C E-Commerce*,
DOI 10.1007/978-3-319-11131-5_7

countries, limiting its effectiveness to deliver access to justice to consumers in transnational B2C e-commerce. A *second best option*[5] in relation to the set of institutional arrangement that can better facilitate the goal of consumers' access to justice in B2C e-transactions may be necessary, which is the main argument that this chapter will try to present.

The structure of this chapter begins with an investigation of legal harmonization approaches in the realms of both private international law and substantive consumer law. This investigation reveals that the experiences with legal harmonization have come with various practical limitations from which suggestions on the second best option for consumer protection in transnational B2C e-commerce can be derived. The chapter then presents the second best option of private ordering, which does not rest on the creation of rules of laws, but rather allows market participants to freely order their own affairs. Various kinds of private ordering mechanisms, including dispute avoidance mechanisms and dispute settlement mechanisms are explored to show that they are able to improve consumers' access to justice and increase consumers' confidence. Nevertheless, some limitations of the private ordering are further explored to determine an appropriate direction that will maximize the potential benefits that may be gained from the second best option of the private ordering, which is one of the main aims of the study and will be addressed in Chap. 8.

7.2 Overcoming the Difficulties from Transnational B2C E-Commerce via Legal Harmonization

7.2.1 Harmonization via Private International Law

With the borderless nature of B2C e-sales, private international law has become the center of discussion as it frames and guides the resolution of consumer disputes.[6] Scholars begin with the premise that consumer litigation is the primary tool used to handle cross border consumer disputes and ensure consumers' access to justice, and

[5] Canadian scholar Richard Lipsey and Australian scholar Kelvin Lancaster explained the theory of the second best in their 1956 literature that if one or more optimality condition cannot be satisfied, it is likely that the following best solution concerns altering other variables away that is presumed to be optimal. *See* R. G. Lipsey and K. Lancaster, *The General Theory of Second Best*, 24 The Review of Economic Studies 11–32 (1956–1957).

[6] *See* J. Hill, Cross-Border Consumer Contracts 9 (2008). *See also* L. E. Gillies, *Adapting International Private Law Rules for Electronic Consumer Contracts, in* C. E. F. Rickett and T. G. W. Telfer (eds.), International Perspectives on Consumers' Access to Justice 359, 380 (2006) and F. Cafaggi, H. W. Micklitz (eds.), New Frontiers of Consumer Protection, The Interplay Between Private and Public Enforcement 32 (2009).

the development of the private international laws is necessary.[7] In considering private international law as an option to improve consumers' protection and access to justice, there are three main issues that need to be addressed, namely: (i) jurisdiction, (ii) applicable law, and (iii) recognition and enforcement of judgments.[8] The following discussion reviews the attempts that have been made to develop private international law. In doing so, the laws of the two largest economies concerning e-transactions, namely the US and the EU, are investigated.[9]

7.2.1.1 Jurisdiction Principles

Jurisdictional matters which relate to "the power of a court to hear and determine a case, and in particular, whether a court has legal authority over a defendant's person"[10] have begun to develop a clear and definite direction for the worldwide e-market where territorial boundaries between states are quite blurred. Although the US and the EU have both been developing jurisdiction principles, the legal concepts and approaches each have adopted are quite different.

The American jurisdiction principle takes into consideration the nature of business activities to determine what constitutes minimum and reasonable contact. A forum selection clause will generally be upheld unless it contains unfair or

[7] For example, J. Hill cited R. Schu's statement that: "The private international law on consumer contracts... has to provide solutions to the question of which is the applicable law to consumer contracts made over the World Wide Web, and it must determine which courts have jurisdiction to hear the case. These questions are not only of academic interest, their answer imply dramatic practical consequences both for the courts and for the people conducting business on Web. If the consumer receives defective goods or if he regrets having made the purchase, he will want to know where to sue the supplier and which law governs his right to damages or to cancel the contract. The supplier, on the other hand, might find himself confronted with foreign consumer protection law which he is not aware of." *See ibid.* and R. Schu, *The Applicable Law to Consumer Contracts Made over the Internet: Consumer Protection through Private International Law*, 5 International Journal of Law and Information Technology 192, 194 (1997). Lorna Gillies makes the same point that consumers have a reasonable expectation of their rights and should be able to imagine where they can enforce their rights regardless of where they are living no matter where the businesses are located. *See* Gillies, *ibid.*, at 380.

[8] There is extensive research with regard to the private international law aspects of B2C e-contracts and the legal harmonization in this area. Nevertheless, the current principles appear to be rather inconsistent and take diverse directions. *See e.g.* Z. S. Tang, Electronic consumer contracts in the conflict of laws (2009), L. E. Gillies, Electronic Commerce and Private International Law, A Study of Electronic Consumer Contract (2008) and D. J. B. Svantesson, Private International law and Internet (2007).

[9] The selection of these two jurisdictions are namely the US and the EU as these two countries always have the highest volumes of B2C e-sales in the global online market. As a result, their private international laws concerning B2C e-sales seem to be the most advanced.

[10] *See* T. Scassa and M. Deturbide, Electronic Commerce and Internet Law in Canada 451 (2004).

unconscionable elements or falls outside the reasonable expectation of consumers.[11] In the absence of a forum selection clause, American courts developed the so-called *minimum contacts* test to apply to internet consumer contracts to determine the reasonable forum.[12] To identify a minimum contact, the *sliding scale test* or the *Zippo* doctrine,[13] which focuses on whether the defendant intends to conduct his or her trading activity with a directly targeted consumer in that forum, is applied.[14] American courts applying this test examine the scale and nature of commercial activities of the website.[15] If the court finds the interactivity of the

[11] For example, in the often cited *Carnival Cruise Lines, Inc. v Shute*, a couple who were domiciled in the US state of Washington bought two cruise tickets from Carnival, a Florida-based cruise service. During the trip, the wife accidently slipped on the ship and was injured. In the ticket sale contract, the jurisdiction clause specified that any dispute must be settled in Florida. The US Supreme Court ruled that the forum selection clause was reasonable and thus valid as such clause was freely bargained for as it was traded off for the low price and it did not cause an undue burden to consumers. The rules set out in *Carnival* were extensively applied to online transactional disputes. *See Carnival Cruise Lines, Inc. v. Shute* 499 U.S. 585 (1991). In following cases, named *Caspi v Microsoft Network, LLC*, the court applied similar reasoning as used in *Carnival*. In *Caspi*, the court ruled that a forum selection clause in Microsoft's online contract was enforceable. *See Caspi v Microsoft Network, LLC* 732 A. 2d 528 (N.J. 1999). *See also* Cortés, *supra* note 1, at 30.

[12] Where there is no forum selection clause, the common law countries will generally determine the jurisdiction based on "their presence of territory of the forum at the time of the service or at the time that the originating process is issued, in the case of a defendant who is present then, but subsequently leaves the territory to avoid service". This traditional approach has become very controversial in internet cases where defendants usually do not have a presence in the territory of the forum, or there are difficulties in identifying the defendants' presence in the territory of the forum. If the nexus between the action and the forum are not clearly constituted, the assertion of jurisdiction may come with many questions. This has also been an issue in the development of jurisdiction principles in the online market. *See ibid.*

[13] The *Zippo* doctrine was developed from the leading case on the issue of jurisdiction. *See Zippo Manufacturing Company v. Zippo Dot Com Inc*, 952 F. Supp. 1119 (W.D. Penn. 1997).

[14] This court precedent involved an internet domain dispute where the lighter manufacturer, Zippo Manufacturing Company, located in the US state of Pennsylvania sued Zippo Dot Com, a California website company. The court had to rule on the question relating to the jurisdictions' assertion as the case was filed in Pennsylvania but Zippo Dot Com objected on the ground of lack of personal jurisdiction as it had neither office nor staff in such jurisdiction. The court rejected Zippo Dot Com's argument citing that Zippo Dot Com is an active website where consumers in Pennsylvania can subscribe to their services and jurisdiction consequently can be asserted. *See ibid.*

[15] The nature of online trading activities can be divided into three levels. First, "an active website" seeking to establish a contractual relationship with persons in other jurisdictions is always subject to the personal jurisdiction of that other jurisdiction. Second, "a passive website" providing online information without any interaction but merely informative nature will not trigger the personal jurisdiction of the viewer's jurisdiction. Third, "a mixed website" where the consumer can receive and exchange information but the site is not particularly soliciting those consumers as contractual parties. The courts will use their discretions to identify whether such interactivities will trigger the personal jurisdiction of consumers.

parties to be at low level, the website operator may not be subject to the personal jurisdiction of the consumer's jurisdiction.[16]

The EU criterion set forth in the Brussels Regulation on the other hand focuses on the location or domicile of the consumer.[17] Article 15 (1) (c) confines a trader to suing in the jurisdiction of the consumer's domicile but grants a consumer an option of bringing an action against a trader in either the consumer's own domicile or that of the trader.[18] Article 17 clearly states that the forum selection clauses shall be deemed ineffective unless they are contractually agreed upon after the dispute arose and are favorable to consumers. This means that the forum selection clause stating that any dispute that arises must be settled in a jurisdiction other than consumer's domicile shall not be enforceable as it is clearly contrary to the Brussels Regulation.[19] If there is no forum selection clause, Article 15 (1) (c) further explains the situation where consumers can bring actions in their home jurisdictions. Based on this rule, when a trader pursues commercial or professional activities in the jurisdiction of the consumer's domicile or by any means, or directs such activities there, such consumer is able to sue in his or her home jurisdiction.[20] The use of consumers' currency or language have become prima facie indicators of a traders' intentions in directing their activities to a particular jurisdiction, giving consumer's the right to bring an action in such forum[21]

---

[16] Bunmi Awoyemi opines that today, large numbers of websites fall within the mixed classification wherein an individual court have to decide whether the website operator may or may not be subject to the personal jurisdiction of the consumer's jurisdiction and the Zippo doctrine, which is out of date, fails to provide predictable outcomes and value.· Instead, it may lead to diverse judicial directions and various incoherent interpretations with the US Supreme Court on the jurisdiction cases. *See* B. Awoyemi, *Zippo Is Dying, Should It be Dead?: The Exercise of Personal Jurisdiction by U.S. Federal Courts Over Non-Domiciliary Defendants in Trademark Infringement Lawsuits Arising Out of Cyberspace*, 9 Marquette Intellectual Property Law Review 37–62 (2005).

[17] The Brussels Regulation forms the forum selection rules in the EU Member States except Denmark. Denmark continues to apply the Brussels Convention, which is an international law ratified by all EU Member States. The Convention subsequently requires all Member States to revise and provide their national laws in accordance with the principles set out in the Convention. In 2000, the Convention was replaced by the Brussels Regulation, another EU regulation directly applicable to all Member States. Any domestic law contrary to the Brussels Regulation will be overruled because the Brussels Regulation as the EU law has the superior status over national laws of Member States. The jurisdictional principles governing international transactions within the EU were generally influenced by "*actor sequitur forum rei*", the famous international law rule with the emphasis that "individual should be sued in the court of the place where they are domiciled". *See* Article 2 of the Brussels Regulation. For detailed discussion on the *actor sequitur forum rei* rule, *see* A. T. von Mehren, Theory and Practice of Adjudicatory Authority in Private International Law: A Comparative Study of the Doctrine, Policies and Practices of Common- and Civil-Law Systems 179 (2002).

[18] *See* Article 15 and 16 of the Brussels Regulation.

[19] In addition, it will be consider an unfair term under the UTD. For detailed discussion on the UTD, *see* Sect. 5.2.

[20] *See* Article 15 of the Brussels Regulation.

[21] However, there are diverging interpretations of what are considered direct activities among the Member States. The UK courts, for example, seem to interpret Article 15 (1) (c) very carefully. In

It can be seen that in the US, contracting parties can agree to specify the choice of forum in their consumer contracts so long as it is not an unreasonable and unfair selection. In contrast, the EU law sets forth a legal standard that clearly favors consumer's interests and disallows forum selection clauses unless the consumer chose the forum after the dispute had already arisen. Due to the abovementioned different approaches, in 2005 the Hague Conference attempted to set up a global agreement on legal harmonization in this area.[22] Unfortunately, the Convention later only adopted the enforcement of judgments in the B2B contractual disputes[23] and appears to have been unsuccessful in addressing the crucial issues in consumer cases, including the above-mentioned divergence of jurisdiction principles.[24] It is often said that such failure was caused by the fundamental disagreement between the US and the EU about the jurisdiction principle in B2C activities.[25]

Crate v Barrel, the English judge held that the website only targeted Irish consumers, rejecting the recognition of consumer jurisdiction despite the fact that the website was available and accessible by the UK consumers. *See Crate v Barrel*, unreported (2000, July 24). *See also* Cortés, *supra* note 1, at 29. This is in contrast to French jurisdiction where the court ruled against Yahoo!, Inc., a US based company, on the ground of French anti-incitement law infringement. In this case, Yahoo!, Inc. sold Nazi memorabilia via its website in English language only and had a filter function barring French IP addresses. It appeared that the English court tends to conservatively rule against a foreign company in the online market while French courts often interpret the Brussels Regulation broadly, extending French jurisdiction to almost all cases sued in French territories. *See French Union of Jewish Students v Yahoo!, Inc.(USA), Yahoo France,* Tribunal de Grande Instance de Paris, Interim Court order, November 20, 2000. Further discussion on this case, *see* R. Ware, *The Use of Jurisdiction Arbitrage to Support the Strategies Interest of the Firm*, 38 University of Toledo Law Review 307 (2006). Another judgment followed the decision in *UFC v AOL*. It ruled the e-contract clauses provided on the website of a US company unfair and unenforceable, certifying French jurisdiction over a foreign company offering transaction online. *See Union Federale des Consommateurs-Que Choisir (UFC) v AOL* R. F. N. 02/03156, Tribunal de grande instance Nanteerre (June 12, 2004).

[22] In the Hague Convention, Article 7 of the Proposed Draft of the Convention on Jurisdiction and Foreign Judgments in Civil and Commercial Matters is subject to most debate. Article 7 specifies that consumers are able to bring an action against traders in the consumers' home country at the time that the contract was concluded or directed to the consumer's country. There are three options to application of Article 7: "(i) The above rule would be used as a default rule when the parties have not entered a contractual clause selecting a forum (ii) The states may enter a reservation that would allow them to respect a jurisdiction agreement only when it has been agreed after the dispute arises. (iii) The second alternative will be implemented in all states, in other words, Article 7 applies unless a jurisdiction agreement was entered into after the dispute arise." *See* Cortés, *supra* note 1, at 33. There was the conflict opinion during the negotiation as the US agrees with option (i) whereas the EU prefers options (ii) and (iii), which are consistent with the Brussels Regulation. *See* P. Nygh and F. Pacar, *Preliminary Draft Convention on Jurisdiction and Foreign Judgments in Civil and Commercial Matters Adopted by the Special Commission* (August 11, 2000), *available at* hcch.net/upload/wop/jdgmpd11.pdf (visited December 26, 2012).

[23] *See* The Convention of the Choice of Court Agreements (July, 2005), *available at* hcch.net/upload/conventions/txt37en.pdf (visited December 1, 2012).

[24] *See* Article 2 of the Convention on Choice of Court Agreements (concluded 30 June 2005) excludes consumer transactions from its application. *See ibid.*

[25] During the conference, the principal conflict arose from American support of the adaptation of the seller's country according to the "original rules" rule, whereas the EU prefers the opposite rule,

7.2.1.2 Applicable Law Principles

Applicable law or conflicts of law principles determine which national law will be referred to and applied in a particular dispute. In general, a court first decides on its competent power, including its jurisdiction to hear a case, and then looks at the applicable legal question.[26] Even though the results of the choice of law clauses in consumer contracts in the US and the EU are similar, differences remain in the recognition and enforcement of such clauses.

This is because the motivations underlying the US and the EU applicable law principles seem to be somewhat different. The US concept seems to be quite flexible to serve business interests, while the EU opts to provide a minimum protection level to consumers as the traditionally presumed weaker parties in consumer sales. On one hand, the EU principles contain a safety net that such clauses shall not deprive a consumer of the mandatory protection provided by domestic legislation, ensuring that they will enjoy the same protection standard as is available to them when they shop domestically.

Article 6 the Rome I Regulation[27] states that a choice of law clause is valid, provided that it does not deprive the consumer protection afforded by the mandatory regulations of the state of the consumer's habitual residence where the trader directly conducts or targets its commercial activities in the consumer's country.[28] This means that if the law selected by a choice of law clause in an e-standard contract limits the rights of a consumer, which are usually recognized and guaranteed according to his or her national law, such clause will be invalid and the mandatory consumer protection rules of the jurisdiction of the consumer's habitual residence will be applied instead.[29] However, such specific protection is designed to only protect passive consumers whom traders target.[30] Passive

called the "country of destination" which is the place of consumer's domicile. *See* Cortés, *supra* note 1, at 33.

[26] *See ibid.*, at 24.

[27] *See* Regulation 593/2008 of the European Parliament and of the Council dated 17 June 2008 on the Law Applicable to Contractual Obligations (The Rome I Regulation). This regulation describes the uniform applicable law principles in contractual transaction for all EU Member States except Denmark. Denmark is still under the Rome Convention 1980.

[28] *See* Article 6 of the Rome I Regulation.

[29] There are number of exceptions such as contracts of carriage and transactional contracts concerning immovable property. *See* Section 6.4 of the Rome I Regulation. *See also* J. Diuckie, Internet and Electronic Commerce Law in the European Union 86 (1999).

[30] This provision divides consumers in B2C e-sales into two types, namely "passive consumers" and "active consumers". On one hand, the passive consumers are those who are approached and invited to enter into B2C e-sales by traders. On the other hand, the active consumers are those who are looking and seeking e-sale transactions themselves. The determination of whether a consumer is passive or active is based on the nature of traders' activities, e.g., when a website pursues advertisement through e-mails or webpages directed to a consumer's country they are usually considered a direct business activity, and the consumers in such jurisdiction are deemed to be passive consumers. *See* Cortés, *supra* note 1, at 28.

consumers can be identified by the nature of a traders' activities, such as whether a website pursues advertisements through e-mail or webpages directed to the consumer's country or uses the language or currency of the consumer's country in its advertisements.[31]

On the other hand, the US tends to allow the parties to freely exercise their autonomy, placing greater value on freedom of contract and providing no such safety net for the choice of applicable law. The three most important laws applicable to transnational B2C e-sales in the US are the Second Restatement of Conflict of Laws (hereinafter *Second Restatement*), The Uniform Commercial Code (hereinafter *UCC*) and the Uniform Computer Information Transactions Act (hereinafter *UCITA*). They similarly give a very broad autonomy to parties in selecting the applicable law while courts are permitted to invalidate applicable law clauses in consumer contracts only if they do not contain any reasonable relationship to the transaction.[32]

In the absence of applicable law clauses specified in a contract, the laws of the US[33] are similar to that of the EU[34]; both specify that the governing law is the law

---

[31] *See ibid.*

[32] The Second Restatement generally guarantees the validity and enforceability of the applicable law chosen by the parties, unless the following are found; (i) the selected applicable law is of a nation that has no substantial connection or relationship to the parties or the transaction; and (ii) the application of such selected law would be contrary to the public policy of a nation "which has a greater interest in the issue, but only when the state would be the chosen one if there was not a contractual clause." *See* Cortés, *supra* note 1, at 27. Similarly, the UCC includes the similar principal governing commercial contracts and transactions, including the consumer cases. The UCITA, which was promulgated with the objective of dealing with e-information transactions, states that the parties to a contract can select the applicable law but, "the choice of law is not enforceable in a consumer contract to the extent it would vary a rule that many not be varied under that law of jurisdiction applicable in the absence of that agreement." This rule seems to depart from the Second Restatement and the UCC where the choice of law clause will be unenforceable if it does not have a reasonable relationship to the transactions. The reason behind the UCITA is to reduce the undue cost of excessive control on the applicable law clause and to increase transactional certainty. With a valid applicable law clause, the parties can obtain clearer legal certainty and understanding regarding the transaction prior to entering into an e-transaction. *See* § 109 (b) of the UCITA. *See also* Cortés, *supra* note 1, at 30.

[33] The Second Restatement specifies that if the parties do not indicate the choice of law, the governing law in an e-contract will be "that of where the consumer is domiciled, that is, the location from where the acceptance was transmitted and to where the goods were delivered." This rule is similar to the EU applicable law approach. For detailed discussion on this issue, *see* A. Zaremba, Civil Justice in Crisis-Comparative Perspectives of Civil Procedure 13 (2005). Similarly, in consumer transactions, the UCC provides that the law governing the transaction will be the law of consumer's location. *See* § 109 (b) of the UCITA.

[34] In case of the absence of a choice of law clause, the Rome I Regulation provides that the applicable law will be the national law where the passive consumer was a resident at the time the contract was concluded. However, if the conditions of the Rome I Regulation prescribed above (e.g. active consumers) are not met, the law of trader's location shall be applied. *See* Art 6 of the Rome I Regulation. In addition, national laws of many Member States will give the presumption in favor of consumers that the consumer contract, unless shown otherwise, was entered into in the

of the consumer's place of domicile. Nevertheless, there is an exception to this under the US law in that the law where the business is located will govern the transaction if the product delivery is accomplished through e-means.[35] This exception appears to concern transactions involving intangible products that can be electronically delivered (such as computer downloads). In these cases, the default governing law is the law of the trader's jurisdiction, making it more favorable to business.

Overall, the US law tends to recognize choice of law clauses even when they seem to be disadvantageous to consumers, providing no safety net and recognizing the law of the trader's place of business in certain circumstances. This approach is driven by economic and commercial reasons in the belief that it will lead to greater choices and lower priced products in transnational consumer sales.[36] However, the American legal regime may create certain difficult situations for consumers as they may fall under the obligations of unfamiliar laws and the legal procedures of foreign jurisdictions where traders are located.

In contrast, the EU applicable law regulations tend to better recognize the interests of consumers. They directly impose greater state interference on applicable law clauses to ensure consumer protection. Traders, especially small and medium sized e-traders, have objected that, because they sell products goods and services across borders, this means that they will have to deal with consumer regulations and complaints under the legal systems of each Member States where they are deemed to engage in business.[37]

7.2.1.3 Transnational Recognition and Enforcement of Judgment

The question of whether a national judgment obtained in one country will be recognized in another has been one of the crucial issues in the global e-market as there are obvious distinctions in consumer laws among various jurisdictions. Today, there is no international agreement to ensure the mutual recognition and enforcement of judgments concerning consumer disputes[38] (except in the EU Member States where there is the ESCP[39]). As a result, even if a consumer has

habitual county of a consumer. The Spanish law, namely the Spanish Ley 34/2002 (Article 29) is for example. *See ibid.*, at 479.

[35] The UCITA provides that the law of the licensor's place of establishment will be applied, if the products are delivered online or by other e-means (i.e. computer software). *See* § 109 (b) of the UCITA.

[36] *See e.g.* Cortés, *supra* note 1, at 28.

[37] *See e.g. ibid.*, at 26.

[38] In cross border consumer cases, the recognition and enforcement of judgments in a foreign state are similar to other civil and commercial cases, depending on the international agreements or bilateral agreements between the two relevant countries (the original country of judgment and the country where the judgment is recognized and enforced).

[39] *See* Sect. 6.2.

obtained a favorable domestic judgment against a foreign trader in a B2C e-sale case, he or she may have no choice but to spend significant time and effort in enforcing such judgment in a foreign jurisdiction. This is because a tool to ensure mutual recognition and enforcement of judgments among different countries does not yet exist.[40] This is likely a major obstacle to consumers seeking justice and compensation in B2C e-sales in practice as it is unlikely to be economical for them to enforce consumer claims against foreign vendors.

7.2.2 Harmonization via Substantive Consumer Law

With the different consumer law approaches worldwide, most consumers who have limited knowledge of foreign laws and regulations may as a result be uncomfortable and lack the confidence necessary to enter into transnational transactions.[41] To solve this problem, the harmonization of consumer protection laws has become a focus of debate.[42] It is claimed that greater access to justice and the growth of

---

[40] This would be relevant in the case where a foreign trader has no branch, representative or asset in the consumer's jurisdiction, and is likely to occur in the online market where small and medium sized traders are able to enter such market without substantial overhead expenses.

[41] From the business perspective, the high burdens and difficulties of e-sale transactions originated from the legal requirement to comply with very fragmented and disparate national consumer protection laws. *See* Chaps. 5 and 6.

[42] The legal harmonization was supported by the United Nations General Assembly. It is recognized that "disparities in national laws governing international trade created obstacles to the flow of trade" and, in 1966, the establishment of the UNCITRAL clearly indicated the UN was taking an active role in removing this barrier. According to the UNCITRAL's general mandatory rule: "is to further the progressive harmonization and unification of the law of international trade and UNCITRAL has come to be the core legal body of the United Nations system in the field of international trade law". Although this model law of the UNCITRAL was not initially intended to apply to consumer contracts, it clearly provides that states may extend the scope of this law beyond the commercial sphere. In other words, the UNCITRAL principles may also apply to e-consumer transactions. *See* United Nations Commission on International Trader Law (UNCITRAL), *Origin, Mandate and Composition of UNCITRAL* (2012), *available at* uncitral.org/uncitral/en/about/origin.html (visited December 12, 2012).

At the national level, for example, the US is increasingly recognizing the need to create a uniform law that is harmonized with international law. "The National Conference of Commissioners on Uniform State Law in recognition of the reliabilities of globalization is working to establish itself in the international arena: With the movement toward globalization, the federal government increasingly participates in the promulgation of private international law conventions that, upon ratification, become preemptive federal law. This disrupts the law in areas such as commercial and family law that historically have been regulated at the state level and that have been the subject to numerous uniform and model laws promulgated by the Conference. The states have a profound interest in, to the extent practicable, having international conventions mesh with their existing laws, influencing the law's development in other countries so that it is compatible with American legal concepts, and harmonizing their own laws with the laws of other countries." *See* A. H. *Boss, The Future of the Uniform Commercial Code Process in An Increasing International World,* 68 Ohio State Law Journal 349, 401–2 (2007) (which cited a work published by

e-transactions can be achieved by offering a clear signal to consumers and businesses that their expectations will be met at both the domestic and global levels.[43] To determine to what extent legal harmonization can effectively address the problem, the EU system of consumer protection provides some insights on the interplay between different domestic national laws and their coordination mechanisms.[44]

In the consumer context, the laws of the EU Member States have been harmonized to, among other things, "create confident consumers who like to shop abroad and make use of the whole internal market".[45] This approach can be seen in the preamble of many EU laws, confirming the existence of a movement towards legal harmonization among the EU Member States (e.g. the CRD[46]). Nevertheless, legal harmonization in the EU stops short of the choice of sanctions and procedural rules that are considered the realm of domestic national laws.[47] This may be because of the influence of the principle of *procedural autonomy* which states that "it is for the domestic legal system of each Member State to designate the courts having jurisdiction and to determine the procedural conditions governing actions at law intended to ensure the protection of the right which the citizens have from the direct effect of Community law".[48]

While leaving some room for the Member States to exercise sovereign authority, the EU laws go "only half way in prescribing national procedural rules for the enforcement of the substantive provisions it sets".[49] Additionally, the experience of

---

Policy Position on International Activities, namely Uniform Activities E-NEWSLETTER (National Conference of Commissioners on Uniform State Laws), May, 2006. *See also* J. A. Puplava, *E-Commerce: Challenges to Privacy, Integrity, and Security in a Borderless World: Use and Enforceability of E-Commerce Contracting: The State of Uniform Legislation Attempting to Regulate E-Commerce Transactions*, 16 Michigan State Journal of International Law 153, 154 (2007). For further discussion on the need for harmonization of consumer law, *see* Cortés, *supra* note 1, at 16.

[43] *See* Cortés, *ibid.*, at 16.

[44] The EU has a single market system and the EU consumer laws as the central laws governing the State Members. The coordination between the State Members and the domestic regulations relating to consumer protection operates within the line drawn by the EU laws, harmonizing their domestic regulations on consumer protection. This is not to say that the EU system is ideal for legal harmonization of consumer law. Nonetheless, it presents a good and clear example of a recent attempt in doing do.

[45] *See* Poncibo, *supra* note 4, at 354.

[46] *See* Chap. 5.

[47] *See ibid.*

[48] This principle was developed by the ECJ decision and it will be applied when there are no relevant rules at the EU level, allowing states to design the procedural rule and sanctions. *See* Case 45/76, *Commet BV v Produktschap voor Siergewassen* [1976] ECR 2043, para. 13. However, there is one procedural rule at the EU level which is the ESCP specifying the procedural rules relating to cross border small claims.

[49] *See* J. Stuych, *Public and Private Enforcement in Consumer Protection: General Comparison EU-USA, in* F. Cafaggi, H. W. Micklitz (eds.), New Frontiers of Consumer Protection, The Interplay Between Private and Public Enforcement 63, 70 (2009). Today, consumer laws of the

negotiation over such arrangements for mutual consensus on legal harmonization in the EU tells that it always difficult.[50] The significant differences in consumer protection laws and procedures currently remain from one Member State to another,[51] France has pursued the consumer protection issue with a focus on strong criminal enforcement while the Nordic countries rely on their consumer ombudsmen and Germany and Belgium prefer consumer disputes to be settled by private enforcement.[52]

Gunther Teubner has made an argument concerning EU legal harmonization that, to be successful, foreign legal transplants must be able to interplay with the structures and relationships among the institutional industries, the government, and the development of the EU's legal norms.[53] The success rate in the EU would be diverse because there are obvious differences in the nature of these institutional bodies in different EU Member States.[54]

At a very general level the divergence in the development of e-consumer protection in the EU and the US is very apparent.[55] In the US, this area of law is largely based on the predominance of a market oriented regime with state intervention permissible only to adjust the market to the extent the economic players need.[56] On the contrary, the EU favors growth that focuses on strong regulatory market control and command, which is the traditional objective of a welfare state.[57] The significant differences among legal systems and traditions that exist in various countries are principal obstacles to achieving legal harmonization.

Member States are still broad and deep divergences. *See e.g.* T. Puurunen, *Choice of Law in European Business-To-Consumer E-Commerce-A Trail Out of a Political Impasse*, Zeitschrift fur Europäisches Privatrecht 789, 790 (2003) and C. Coteanu, Cyber Consumer Law and Unfair Trading Practices 155 (2005).

[50] *See* Cafaggi and Micklitz, *supra* note 6, at 37. For detailed discussion on this difficult situation in EU (regarding the huge debate on the choice between the minimum or the maximum harmonization approach), *see* Poncibo, *supra* note 4, at 353.

[51] *See* Article 11 of the UCPD, for example, requires that "member states shall ensure that adequate and effective means exist to combat unfair commercial practice to enforce compliance with the provisions of this directive in the interest of consumers".

[52] *See ibid.*

[53] *See* G. Teubner, *"Legal Irritants": Good Faith in British Law or How Unifying Law Ends Up in New Divergences*, 61 Modern Law Review 11–32 (1998). On a similar point, a study by K. Freund emphasized the role of interest groups such as politicians, traders and consumers, as well as the relevant institutional structures largely associated with the legal harmonization and foreign legal system transplants. *See* O. K. Freund, *One Uses and Misuses of Comparative Law*, 37 The Modern Law Review 1–27 (1974).

[54] G. Teubner argues that the legal norms underlying the UCTD, for example, will be very divergent because the natures of institutional structures are very different between the two big countries, namely Germany and the UK. *See* Teubner, *ibid.*

[55] *See* Chaps. 5 and 6.

[56] *See* L. Antoniolli, *Consumer Law as an Instance of the Law of Diversity*, 30 Vermont Law Review 855–82 (2006).

[57] The EU is now increasingly developing the relevant e-consumer protection laws and mechanisms. *See* Poncibo, *supra* note 4, at 369.

Due to the deep link between the culture and law of a society, legal transplants from other countries imported through legal harmonization may not be appropriate for the unique culture and society of the importing jurisdictions. For example, the East Asian cultures have always been perceived as less litigious than the Western cultures.[58] The class action or collective action that is closely associated with the US, and subject to wide discussion in the EU at the moment,[59] might not be a suitable mechanism to fulfill what East Asian consumers desire. These differences may indicate that the legal harmonization in the global e-market has become an extremely daunting task.[60] Pushing forward legal harmonization demands a great deal of time, high cost and great effort to adjust all the factors as the EU experience suggests.

7.2.3 The Limits of Legal Harmonization and the Need for a "Second Best Option"

Recent legal harmonization steps that have been taken do not seem to have yet provided satisfactory outcomes due largely to the impenetrable barriers of the cultural and legal diversity. In fact, legal harmonization may not offer a full answer to consumer problems in B2C e-transactions. It may be less relevant in transnational e-sales than many expect. There are a few things worth considering about this.

First, in most situations, the problems arising in e-sales normally turn out to be general contractual or factual issues.[61] "Whatever law is the governing law, a supplier will normally fail to comply with his contractual obligations only if: (i) he misrepresents the nature of the goods or services which are the subject-matter of the contract; or (ii) he fails, within a reasonable time, to perform his side

---

[58] For further discussion on the different legal cultures, *see* N. S. Kim, *Evolving Business and Social Norms and Interpretation Rules: The Need for a Dynamic Approach to Contract Disputes*, 84 Nebraska Law Review 506, 531–40 (2005).

[59] *See e.g.* W. van. Boom and M. Loos (eds.), Collective Enforcement of Consumer Law (2007), Cafaggi and Micklitz, *supra* note 6 and S. Wrbka, S. van Uytsel and M. Siems (eds.), Collective Actions: Enhancing Access to Justice and Reconciling Multilayer Interest? (2012).

[60] One cannot deny that the different development of power, politics and diversity in different cultures may result in diverse approaches to consumer protection. Ideological diversity, different levels of stakeholder power, and different types of organizations all have an influence on the process of designing and implementing laws in each country. This makes legal harmonization relating to consumer protection an extremely difficult or even impossible task.

[61] *See* M. Rutherford, *Documents-only Arbitrations in Consumer Disputes, in* J. Tackaberry and A. Marriott (eds.), Bernstein's Handbook of Arbitration and Dispute Resolution Practice 638, 638–9 (2003). There seems to currently be a common international understanding of what types of trading practices should be regulated, controlled or even prohibited. *See also* K. J. Cseres, *Enforcement of Collective Consumer Interests: A Competition Law Perspective, in* W. van. Boom and M. Loos (eds.), Collective Enforcement of Consumer Law 125, 130, 168 (2007).

of the bargain (for example, by failing to deliver goods which are of satisfactory quality and fit for the purpose or to perform services of an appropriate standard)."[62] These questions are related to the fundamental contractual rules, which are universal in almost all legal systems.[63] In addition, the disputes in consumer transactions tend to turn on factual issues.[64] Examples of these would include cases centered on the question of whether the goods or services were delivered or whether the products correspond to the description contained in the traders' advertisement. Complex questions of law are likely to be quite circumscribed in consumer disputes.[65] In this sense, the applicable consumer law may be of limited importance and legal harmonization may therefore be not so necessary.[66]

Secondly, consumers in e-sales might not be concerned about the issues of conflict of laws and jurisdiction, as they are unlikely to be involved in the formal dispute settlement process because e-sale transactions are usually of low value. It may not be economic sense to expect a consumer to bring an action for a small amount of money against a foreign trader, even if the consumer can bring such an action in his or her own jurisdiction under a familiar domestic law.[67] This is because of the difficulties in enforcing judgments in a transnational environment where a foreign jurisdiction is involved and it is likely to be extremely expensive.[68] An empirical study has revealed that direct negotiation between traders and consumers is the most favorable method when consumers have problems or complaints.[69]

---

[62] *See* Hill, *supra* note 6, at 358.

[63] *See* K. Zweigert and H. Kötz, An Introduction to Comparative Law 546–7 (1992).

[64] *See* Hill, *supra* note 6, at 358–9.

[65] An example of a legal question is the cooling off period issue. If a consumer in the EU purchased a product from a US trader, he or she may expect to return the good within a certain period under the withdrawal right normally granted by the EU legislation, the law of the consumer's domicile. Unfortunately, there is no such law in the US for some kinds of certain products. However, in the online context, it has previously been observed that, even though the US and Canada have no law relating to a withdrawal right, such a right is widely recognized in practice. This means the EU consumers are subject to minimal risk on such issue.

[66] *See* Hill, *supra* note 6, at 358.

[67] Some scholars seem to set the premise on the opinion that, if the law allows a consumer to sue in its own jurisdiction under a familiar national law, the burden of litigation in transactional disputes on consumers will be eradicated. This idea can be found in the EU law, the jurisdictional protection for consumers appears in the Brussels Regulation and the conflict of laws rule based on consumers' interest is included in the Rome I Regulation. *See* Hill, *supra* note 6, at 128. Nevertheless, consumers in practice are not interested in exercising their right in accordance with the law. *See* Commission of the European Communities, *Green Paper form the Commission, Legal Aid in Civil Matters: The Problems Confronting the Cross-Border Litigant* 9.2.2000 COM (2000) 51 final (2000), *available at* eur-lex.europa.eu/LexUriServ/site/en/com/2000/com2000_0051en01.pdf (visited June 12, 2013).

[68] *See* Hill, *ibid.*, at 127–30.

[69] *See* Study Centre of Consumer Law (Katholieke Universiteit Leuven), *An Analysis and Evaluation of Alternative Means of Consumer Redress other than Redress Through Ordinary Judicial Proceedings* (January 17, 2007), *available at* ec.europa.eu/consumers/redress/reports_studies/comparative_report_en.pdf (visited December 12, 2012).

Small value consumer complaints are usually settled within internal after-sale service systems or the traders' internal complaint processes rather than through the intervention of third party dispute resolution.[70] In one recent EU study, 53 % of consumers who had contacted traders when they were unsatisfied with goods they had purchased were either fully or partially satisfied with the trader's response.[71] In 2006, another survey similarly showed that 54 % of consumers who directly negotiated with the traders about the problems were happy with the way traders handled their complaints.[72] These data may signal that private international law may play a limited role in this context because a large proportion of consumer disputes can be satisfactorily resolved through direct bilateral negotiation between traders and consumers rather than through other processes.[73] Jonathan Hill has noted that "it has to be recognized from the outset that the litigation of disputes arising out of cross-border consumer contracts is extremely unusual; all the evidence points to private international law being largely irrelevant in all but a tiny proportion of situations involving cross-border consumer contracts".[74]

Lastly, the prevalent use of direct or bilateral negotiations may result in consumers' rights being framed based on social norms generated by traders in response to market forces and pressures rather than in compliance with legal principles.[75] The role of legal rules may be increasingly limited while the social and market norms play more important parts in the direct negotiation process.[76]

---

[70] *See* International Chamber of Commerce, *Business to Consumer and Consumer to Consumer Alternative Dispute Resolution (ADR) Inventory Project* (2002). However, this is not to say that there will be no chance for the third hand intervention in consumer disputes. If the direct negotiations fail, the third party then comes to assist with the settlement (e.g. online arbitration).

[71] *See* European Commission, *Evaluation of the Pilot Project on Use of European Consumer Complaint form for Consumer Disputes* (2000), *available at* ec.europa.eu/consumers/redress/compl/cons_compl/acce_just13_en.pdf (visited December 12, 2012).

[72] *See* Eurobarometer, *Consumer Protection in the Internal Market* (September, 2006), *available at* ec.europa.eu/public_opinion/archives/ebs/ebs252_en.pdf (visited December 12, 2012).

[73] *See* Hill, *supra* note 6, at Chapter 9.

[74] *See ibid.*

[75] *See* I. Ramsay, *Consumer Redress Mechanisms for Poor-Quality and Defective Products*, 31 University of Toronto Law Journal 117, 129 (1981). *See also* H. L. Ross and N. O. Littlefield, *Complaint as a Problem Solving Mechanism*, 12 Law & Society Review 199–216 (1978).

[76] However, one theoretical concept differently argues that the law still plays a significant role in bilateral negotiations, although it might not directly determine the consequence of the disputes. *See* S. Roberts and M. Palmer, Dispute Processes: ADR and the Primary Forms of Decision Making 114 (2006). "The terms of any settlement are a product of an assortment of the strengths and weaknesses of each party's case; in cross border cases, these strengths and weaknesses include an assessment of the likely outcome of jurisdictional and choice-of-law questions if the case were to go to court." *See* Hill, *supra* note 6, at 362. This picture of the negotiation process was initially referred by R. Mnookin and L. Kornhauser as "bargaining in the shadow of law" in divorce cases, *see* R. Mnookin and L. Kornhauser, *Bargaining in the Shadow of the Law: The Case of Divorce*, 88 Yale Law Journal 950–997 (1979). Nevertheless, it is likely to occur only if the litigation can possibly ensue if the bilateral negotiation fails. *See* H. Jacob, *The Elusive Shadow of the Law*, 26 Law & Society Review 565–90 (1992). *See also* B. G. M. Main and A. Park, *The British and*

Based on the above-assumed factors, the roles of consumer laws and private international law may not be so significant in transnational sale activities and it therefore follows that the conclusion that consumers' lack of confidence in e-sales is because of differences in consumer laws and private international law in various countries may not be so true.[77] Consumers may not be too concerned about the detailed issues of foreign consumer law (as they just want fair treatment and active responses from traders rather than what the law specifies) or conflict of laws and jurisdiction (as they are unlikely to engage in a formal dispute settlement process regarding their usually low value purchases). This is not to say that legal principles are not at all relevant in e-consumer sales as they are clearly necessary in consumer cases involving substantial amounts of money (such as in the case of real property sales or personal injury disputes).[78] Rather, the point is that further development in this area should not be heavily and solely focused on the mandatory traditional law of consumer protection and legal harmonization. Some attention should also be given to other issues such as what effective options exist that can fulfill consumers' needs and positively change their attitude towards transnational sales. To achieve such, an alternative or second best option needs to be considered and developed.

7.3 Towards the "Second Best Option": Access to Justice Through Private Ordering

In general, in designing consumer protection mechanisms in e-sales, the inherent nature of consumers' thinking toward transactions needs to be examined to adopt measures that will be truly effective and satisfactory to consumers. This will also result in an improvement of their confidence in e-sales. In this regards, a large amount of literature on consumers suggests that many consumers are reluctant to

---

American Rules: An Experimental Examination of Pre-Trial Bargaining in the Shadow of the Law, 47 Scottish Journal of Political Economy 37–60 (2000). Unfortunately, litigation in transnational e-sales appears to be very rare, "that any threat of litigation (if there is no negotiation settlement) is almost entirely illusory." Phrased differently, if the negotiation is not successful, there is no credible threat that consumers in e-sales will undertake an action through a more formal method. As a result, bargaining in the shadow of law may actually occur in transnational e-sales. *See* Hill, *supra* note 6, at 366. However, the bargaining in the shadow of law is not supported by any empirical evidence. In contrast, evidence suggests that social norms play a very important role in certain types of negotiation processes rather than the legal rules. *See* e.g. H. Jacob, *The Elusive Shadow of the Law*, 26 Law & Society Review 565–90 (1992).

[77] *See* Hill, *supra* note 6, at 359–9.

[78] Clearly, they provide protection in some degree when consumers purchase online. However, the previous chapters show that the designed protection may only be a novelty as consumers find that unfair business practices are prevalent in the online market because of the fast development of technology that makes it very difficult to vindicate their rights once infringed, especially in transnational e-sales. Thus, the past efforts may be of more symbolic and theoretical significance than of real practical value. *See* Chaps. 5 and 6.

participate in transnational B2C e-sales and their first and foremost concern is about actual transactional issues (such as delivery, refund, replacement, after sale service, apology and so on) rather than legal redress.[79]

Consumers are likely to be very interested in traders' behaviors and how they deal with transactions.[80] Therefore, business behavior needs to be considered. Such understanding can be linked to exhaustive scholarly works on private ordering in online markets which explain various self-regulatory mechanisms that "merchants employ in order to reduce the likelihood of opportunistic behaviors", among their fellow traders.[81]

The following survey of the different private ordering mechanisms will illustrate to what extent private ordering can perform an essential role in fulfilling consumers' interests and becoming the second best solution for better consumer protection in e-sales.[82]

7.3.1 Dispute Avoidance Mechanisms[83]

7.3.1.1 Reputation or Feedback Mechanism

Reputation or feedback mechanisms are designed to help raise consumers' confidence by providing them with detailed information from other consumers and this can be referred to as *an informal third party control*.[84] It brings consumers together

---

[79] *See* e.g. Cseres, *supra* note 61, at 130 and Eurobarometer, *European Union Citizens and Access to Justice* (October, 2004), *available at* ec.europa.eu/consumers/redress/reports_studies/eurobarometer_11-04_en.pdf (visited December 12, 2012).

[80] One scholar suggests that it requires "the change of focus away from the idea of the vindication of rights on an individual basis through the courts and towards dispute avoidance on the collective basis and alternative dispute resolution". *See* Hill, *supra* note 6, at 377.

[81] *See* G. P. Calliess and P. Zumbansen, Rough Consensus and Running Code, A Theory of Transnational Private Law 152 (2010).

[82] The private ordering mechanisms can generally be divided into dispute avoidance and dispute resolution. This classification is similar to the division of *ex ante* and *ex post* mechanisms, which are based on the time of intervention. However, the dispute avoidance mechanisms include the resolution of the disputes at early stages without the full participation of consumers and traders in the settlement processes. *See* Cortés, *supra* note 1, at 59 and Hill, *supra* note 6, at 47.

[83] There are many types of dispute avoidance mechanisms for preventing cross border disputes at earlier stages and the following discussions are on those currently and prevalently utilized in e-sales.

[84] *See* S. Panther, *Non-Legal Sanction, in* B. Bouckaert and G. De Greet (eds.), Encyclopedia of Law and Economics Vol. I 999–1028 (2000). Generally, the gathering and processing of information of the experienced consumers are usually costly because it is unorganized and widespread. *See* Calliess and Zumbansen, *supra* note 81, at 154. Fortunately, the e-communication allows for the first time the emergence of large scale consumer groups and a shared experience network at low cost. The establishment of feedback mechanisms in the information technology sector has brought about a better organized and formalized reputation tool. *See* C. Dellarocas, *The*

to share and exchange experiences and feelings concerning traders and gives consumers the opportunity to learn about the traders before entering into any particular transactions.[85] At the same time, it gives information to traders "with suggestions for improvement in their products or services, and assists them in setting their priorities and in communication toward consumers.[86]

The communication of the feedback mechanism at the early stage enables possible problems and risks to be identified, thereby avoiding further disputes.[87] When the disputes actually arise, the consumer group can through the online reputation system put some pressure on traders and contribute to obtaining better and fairer solutions because they are able to impose reputational sanctions on rogue traders.[88] In this way, there is also an economic incentive for traders to improve their products and services in response to consumers' needs to succeed in the e-market by building up the number of repeated consumers and their online reputation.[89]

Many websites currently enable consumers to review and rate the products and services provided, incorporating the feedback system. For example, the eBay feedback and rating system has created a reputation feature in an online auction forum, which provides potential consumers with the comments of buyers from previous purchases.[90] After each transaction, buyers can assess the specific sellers with a positive, negative or neutral rating.[91] The large volume of assessments creates a rating profile of every seller, the ranking of which is identified by different colored stars attached next to their trading names.[92] The effectiveness of this

Digitization of Word of Mount: Promise and Challenges of Online Feedback Mechanisms, 49 Management Science 1407–24 (2003).

[85] Generally, consumers do not engage in transactions with traders who are likely to be involved in opportunistic behavior or are well-known as bad traders. *See* E. A. Posner, Law and Social Norms (2000).

[86] *See* M. E. Schneider and C. Kuner, *Dispute Resolution in International Electronic Commerce*, 14 Journal of International Arbitration 5, 26 (1997).

[87] *See ibid.*

[88] *See ibid.*

[89] *See also* Hill, *supra* note 6, at 249.

[90] *See* L. Edwards and A. Theuniseen, *Creating Trust and Satisfaction Online: How Important Is ADR?: The UK eBay Experience*, 5 Web Journal of Current Legal Issues (2007), *available at* webjcli.ncl.ac.uk/2007/issue5/edwards5.html (visited June 12, 2013).

[91] Prior to entering into the eBay market forum, sellers and buyers have to register their information online to become members and the databases are available for sellers and buyers to mutually assess each other. *See* Calliess and Zumbansen, *supra* note 81, at 154.

[92] *See ibid.*

mechanism is confirmed by a survey conducted in 2007. It showed that 62 % of consumers in the US usually read reviews available online and 80 % of those who read the reviews written by other consumers admitted that such reviews influenced their purchase decisions in selecting or dealing with a particular trader in case there are similar products or services offered in online market.[93] On the traders' side, some reported that the sale volumes were positively affected by positive reviews from their previous consumers.[94]

7.3.1.2 Trustmarks and Codes of Conduct Mechanism

Trustmarks are usually granted to qualified traders by independent trustmark providers once the set standards prescribed in a code of conduct or practice by the relevant organizations have been fulfilled, thus providing a signal to the market that such traders subscribe to the set standards.[95] Trustmarks can be seals or slogans designed to indicate standards of good business practices in specific areas such as privacy, dispute resolution and online sales. Trustmarks are granted to member traders in exchange for their compliance with the set standards of good practices and, in case the trustmark carriers do not follow the quality standards, the right to use the trustmarks may be withdrawn.[96]

One important function of trustmarks is to raise the standards of traders and to encourage them to comply with a certain standard in terms of business practices and respect for consumers' rights.[97] Once the standards of business practices are raised to a high level, it seems to "boil down to suppliers treating consumers fairly, which can have significant preventive role"[98], avoiding possible disputes. On the consumer side, they are informed of which traders are playing according to the rules (code of conducts) and thus they can avoid rogue traders and disputes.[99]

---

[93] *See* Deloitte and Touche, *Biz Report* (2007) and OECD, *OECD Conference on Empowering E-Consumers, Strengthening Consumer Protection in the Internet Economy, Background Report, Washington D.C., 8–10 December 2009* (2009), *available at* oecd.org/ict/econsumerconference/44047583.pdf (visited January 12, 2013).

[94] *See* OECD, *ibid.*

[95] "Trustmarks offer a functional equivalent to trademarks in that both bundle information on a supplier in an easily accessible form and, thus, replace individual investigations into its reputation." *See* Calliess and Zumbansen, *supra* note 81, at 154.

[96] *See* Cortés, *supra* note 1, at 62.

[97] *See also* Hill, *supra* note 6, at 51, 307.

[98] *See ibid.*

[99] Trustmarks assist consumers in distinguishing traders, who hold trustmark seals, as having high standards in their trading practices and also give the significant benefit to the Small and Medium Enterprises who do not have widely recognized brands and have difficulties in establishing their own trademark in the e-market. *See* Calliess and Zumbansen, *supra* note 81, at 155 and Cortés, *supra* note 1, at 60, 63.

Although many trustmarks have been established following the growth of the e-market, only a few have been successful and reached a critical mass of e-consumers.[100] The case of the Better Business Bureau (hereinafter *BBB*), mutually initiated by the US and Canadian Chambers of Commerce, has for example particularly achieved sufficient penetration.[101] The designed "BBBOnline Reliability Seal" is currently utilized and posted by over 55,000 e-traders on their websites.[102] Traders who are qualified to obtain this seal have to comply with the "BBB Code of Business Practices" which also binds them to the alternative dispute resolution proceedings recommend by the BBB.[103]

Another famous trustmark in e-market is TRUSTe. It was formed by a non-profit organization with the intention "to ensure that its members disclose how personal information obtained by them is handled".[104] It focuses on data and privacy issues by certifying the privacy policies of qualified websites, monitoring traders' privacy practices and resolving disputes concerning privacy matters.[105] If necessary, the TRUSTe provider may revoke the seal from the traders and report any illegal trading practices to the competent national authorities.[106]

Within the EU region, the most well know trustmark regime was established up by a private company called "Trusted Shop".[107] More than 5,000 certified traders have met the prescribed criteria that are fundamentally drawn from the EU regulations relating to distance selling and e-commerce.[108] The functions of the Trusted Shops include the appraisal of safe technological usage, the transparency of prices, consumer service, data issues, refunds and so on.[109] After sales service, which

[100] A trustmarks regime is usually aimed at addressing particular problems and it usually subject to debates within a nation as a means to protect privacy, security of payment, transparent policy (e.g. information, delivery, refund) and so on. *See* T. Wagemans, *An Introduction to the Labeling of Websites*, (2003) *available at* ec.europa.eu/information_society/activities/sip/archived/docs/pdf/reports/qual_lab_bkgd.pdf (visited December 12, 2012) and C. Spletter, *The Significance of Trustmarks in B2C E-Commerce*, LLM Thesis, University of Strathclyde (2003).

[101] *See* Cortés, *supra* note 1, at 62.

[102] *See* Better Business Bureau (BBB), *Better Business Bureau, Start with Trust, available at* bbb.org/online/consumer/default.aspx (visited January 12, 2013).

[103] *See ibid.*

[104] Many big brands are now joining and holding TRUSTe seals such as Microsoft, Yahoo, AOL and Amazon. *See* P. Balboni, Trustmarks in E-Commerce: The Value of Web Seals and the Liability of their Providers 36 (2009).

[105] *See* Cortés, *supra* note 1, at 62.

[106] *See ibid.*, at 63.

[107] *See* Trusted Shops, *Trusted Shops Guarantee*, *available at* trustedshops.co.uk/ (visited January 12, 2013).

[108] *See ibid.*

[109] Trusted Shops also requires the participating traders to settle consumer disputes through an alternative dispute resolution and thus far there have been no court cases between consumers and Trusted Shops traders. Furthermore, the set criterion is regularly updated by the advisory board comprising, among others, traders, consumer protection agencies and scholars. *See* Calliess and Zumbansen, *supra* note 81, at 156.

provide consumers with a multi-language assistance center dealing with any related transactional issues through phone or internet communications, is also assessed under the Trusted Shops regime.[110] However, it has not yet been successful in gaining significant market recognition.[111]

From the above examples, the trustmark mechanism can provide a wide range of private governance, including the development of business norms through codes of conduct, the assurance of good trading practices and the provision of alternative dispute resolution procedures.[112] "The withdrawal function of trustmarks can also work as a powerful sanction mechanism."[113] However, the credibility of trustmarks depends largely on such trustmarks having enough recognition and influence in the market, leading to substantial effects toward the competitive advantage of traders.[114]

7.3.1.3 Electronic Payment Mechanisms

In e-sales, before traders perform their contractual obligations the consumers are required to make advance payment, usually by credit card.[115] In traditional sales, the use of a credit card is associated with the provision of personal identification, the input of a PIN number or security number and the consumer's signature, which all increase confidence in the security of that payment method. Online payments on the other hand only require that the credit card number and period of validity be provided through e-communication.[116] A number of security payment systems have been developed to address consumer's concerns over fraud and thus improve their confidence in e-payments.[117] In such a system, service providers who act as *trusted third parties* play a very important role in ensuring the security of payment.[118] A number of the more important payment regimes are discussed in the following sections.

---

[110] *See ibid.*

[111] *See* I. Ramsay, Consumer law and Policy, Text and Materials on Regulating Consumer Markets 153 (2007).

[112] *See* Calliess and Zumbansen, *supra* note 81, at 157.

[113] Revocation of trustmark seals can be an effective sanction, having substantial effects and putting traders at a competitive disadvantage, only if such trustmarks have enough influence in the market. "Only economically successful trustmarks providers can afford to lost vendors as clients". This means that some trustmarks may not willing to withdrawal the trustmark seal from the traders who fails to comply the set trading standard because the trustmark operation is relied on their membership fee. *See ibid.*

[114] It has been suggested that these can be well achieved not only by a certain period of time (for recognition of branding) but also with financial assistance from public authorities.

[115] This may be because traders have to bear the cost of distance delivery of the products and are under the risk of non-acceptance of the delivered product by consumers as well. However, there is an excepted circumstance (in some countries, namely, Japan and the Nordic countries) where the payment can be made upon the delivery of goods or services.

[116] *See* Coteanu, *supra* note 49, at 31.

[117] *See* Calliess and Zumbansen, *supra* note 81, at 160 and *ibid.*, at 32.

[118] *See* Calliess and Zumbansen, *ibid.*

Chargeback

The chargeback mechanism is based on the policies set by major credit card service providers, namely Visa and Mastercard.[119] It allows consumers to cancel their online credit card payments, in case such payments have been processed without valid authorizations.[120] Upon the receipt of a credit card statement, consumers have a period of 6 weeks to refuse the transaction with the credit card issuer. To reject a charge back request made by a consumer, a trader has to prove that (1) the consumer placed an order for the product, (2) the payment has been processed with the actual consent of the cardholder, and (3) delivery of the product has already taken place.[121] If the trader fails to do so, the charge back request is approved and the amount paid is refunded to the consumer, resulting in the trader being subject to the charge. In this circumstance, issuers of credit cards have shifted the risks and liability online payment fraud to traders.

PayPal

Another payment service is PayPal, an e-payment service provider that transfers money between account holders and "whose services have gained prominence through its use by buyers and sellers on the online auction eBay".[122] PayPal offers a wide range of grounds on which refunds can be requested, including not only the absence of card holder authorization (like the chargeback regime), but also covering other claims involving traders' failure to perform their contractual obligations such as where the goods are not delivered or are significantly different from their description.[123] Money can be easily transferred via email once a user has registered a password protected PayPal account. The amount transferred is credited to the PayPal transferee's account and such credit can be transferred to the bank account of the transferee at any time for withdrawal.

PayPal also expands their services by offering some forms of assistances in dispute resolution[124] and a dispute settlement center has been set up to facilitate

---

[119] *See* Visa, *Rules for Visa Merchants-Card Acceptance and Chargeback, Management Guidelines* (2006), *available at* uiowa.edu/~fustreas/visa_new_acceptance_merchant_responsibility.pdf (visited January 12, 2013) and Mastercard, *Merchant Rules Manual*, (December 12, 2012), *available at* mastercard.com/us/merchant/pdf/BM-Entire_Manual_public.pdf (visited January 12, 2013).

[120] *See* J. Hörnle, Cross-Border Internet Dispute Resolution 39 (2009).

[121] *See* Calliess and Zumbansen, *supra* note 81, at 160.

[122] *See* Hörnle, *supra* note 120, at 42 and Calliess and Zumbansen, *supra* note 81, at 161.

[123] PayPal seems to fill the existing gap of the chargeback system. *See* Calliess and Zumbansen, *ibid.*

[124] The assistance deals with the two types of cases, where (1) the goods have never arrived and (2) where the goods significantly differ from the advertisement or description. PayPal, *Help Center Answers*, *available at* paypal.com/helpcenter/main.jsp;

communication and negotiation between sellers and buyers. This positively resulted in an approximately 50 % reduction in the number of disputes.[125] In case a negotiation is unsuccessful, the consumer can make a formal claim and PayPal will act as an arbitrator who will investigate and examine documents provided by the parties. PayPal settles a dispute by either ordering the trader to make a refund or ordering the consumer to return the goods, providing enforcement to the relevant parties.[126] During the dispute settlement process, PayPal can retain the payment made by the consumer in the trader's account for up to 180 days from the date of payment.[127]

Escrow Service

Another form dispute avoidance relating to online payment is Escrow.com, which is usually recommended by eBay to those consumers engaged in high valued transactions with unknown online traders by eBay.[128] The Escrow service provides an option of online payment similar to a letter of credit. To begin with, a registered buyer or consumer has to deposit the purchased price into an escrow account. Escrow.com then notifies the trader of the receipt of payment. Upon the notification, the trader dispatches the ordered products and provides a proof of delivery to the consumer to receive the deposited purchased price. The purchase price is subsequently released to the trader after the return period has passed without any claim from the consumer. In case of a dispute, Escrow.com will keep the purchase price until the consumer and the trader have reached a mutual agreement.[129] Unlike PayPal, Escrow.com does not provide any dispute settlement services.

---

jsessionid=Q151LhgWG9yLRt1JfbDtTjB2yfvVjY0QG6VLNq2FC0yxFLQn5TzL!397506396?t=solutionTab&ft=homeTab&ps=&solutionId=203832&locale=en_US&_dyncharset=UTF-8&countrycode=RO&cmd=_help-ext&serverInstance=9002 (visited June 1, 2012). In 2002, PayPal was acquired by eBay and their services have expanded. For example, the money back-guarantee service has been promoted. This service enables eBay customers to receive up to US$ 1,000 in reimbursement in case of non-delivery or products not being as advertised or described. *See* Calliess and Zumbansen, *supra* note 81, at 161.

[125] This number is according to the statement of Mr. Colin Rule, the PayPal's Director of Online Dispute Resolution Practice. *See* Practice Ecommerce, Insights for Online Merchants, *'Quick Query: PayPal Exec on Payment Disputes* (April 7, 2008), *available at* practicalecommerce.com/articles/709-Quick-Query-PayPal-Exec-On-Payment-Disputes (visited March 10, 2013).

[126] *See* Cortés, *supra* note 1, at 60.

[127] However, the freezing payment can be done only if the trader has not yet withdrawn the payment and in such circumstances. PayPal will not be responsible for the consumer's loss. *See* Clause 10 of the PayPal's User Agreement, PayPal, *User Agreement* (January 10, 2013), *available at* cms.paypal.com/us/cgi-bin/?cmd=_render-content&content_ID=ua/UserAgreement_full (visited January 28, 2013).

[128] *See* Escrow.com, *Escrow.com Safeguarding Your Online Transactions*, *available at* escrow.com (visited January 28, 2013).

[129] "According to Escrow.com' s terms of trade, after 60 days the matter is passed on to the American Arbitration Association to come to a binding decision. In the meantime, the involved

The above examples demonstrate that the payment mechanisms can generate a realm of private ordering that deal not only with processing input errors, online duplication or authorization, but also with fraud and dispute resolution procedures. These mechanisms essentially improve consumers' confidence in e-payment via credit cards by allowing them to reverse the payment if it was fraudulently processed or the trader failed to perform its contractual obligations. In this scenario, these mechanisms also help to avoid disputes between the consumer and trader because remedies are available to the consumer at a very early stage in the process. Even though the dispute cannot be instantly solved and a complaint is formally formed, some payment mechanisms (such as PayPal) can perform their settlement function as an arbitrator, bringing a fast remedy to consumers in e-sale disputes, especially to those with small valued deals.

7.3.2 Dispute Settlement Mechanisms

Online Dispute Resolution (hereinafter *ODR*) was formed to handle and settle conflicts via technological communication.[130] It encompasses "the whole range of traditional ADR procedures -informal assisted negotiation, mediation and formal arbitration–in so far as the involved parties and neutral third parties communicate via emails or via password-protected web pages, electronically exchange documents and photographs ('written proceeding'), and even negotiation simultaneously in chat-rooms, via phones or in videoconferences ('quasi hearings')."[131] Compared to the traditional forms of dispute resolution, a distinctive difference is that the perceived fundamental interest of ODR is the greater use of communications technology than in the traditional field.[132] In other words, technology takes part

parties are free to turn, for instance, to Square Trade, an online dispute settlement service provider to find an amicable decision." *See* Calliess and Zumbansen, *supra* note 81, at 162–3.

[130] In recent years, the notion that the technological communication employed to conclude e-contracts can be logically used to establish an alternative dispute resolution for settling disputes involving such contracts has received wide attention. In fact, this idea started in the mid 1990s. *See* D. G. Post, *Anarchy, State, and the Internet: An Essay on Law–Marking up Cyberspace* (1995), *available at* temple.edu/lawschool/dpost/Anarchy.html (visited January 12, 2013), M. C. Karanon, *ADR on the Internet*, 11 Ohio State Journal on Dispute Resolution 537–48 (1996) and F. A. Cona, *Application of Online Systems in Alternative Dispute Resolution*, 45 Buffalo Law Review 975–88 (1997).

[131] *See* Calliess and Zumbansen, *supra* note 81, at 157–8 and W. Krause, *Do You Want to Step Outside? An Overview of Online Alternative Dispute Resolution*, 19 John Marshall Journal of Computer & Information Law 457, 460 (2001).

[132] In other words, ODR merely replicates the main traditional forms of alternative dispute resolution and adapts them into the online environment through the transformative arms of technology. *See* Hill, *supra* note 6, at 277.

as a "fourth party" in the ODR process.[133] The following section reviews some worldwide ODR web pages, which are successful providers in the e-marketplace.[134]

7.3.2.1 Automated Resolution System Mechanism

The automated electronic system provides negotiation services without any involvement of a neutral third party.[135] Based on game theory, this system uses a "blind bidding" negotiation function that invites the parties to offer settlement amounts in a number of rounds.[136] Both parties will offer the numbers they have in mind and these numbers will not be disclosed to the opposite side unless they are matched within a certain standard range. Usually, the parties are able to submit three bidding offers and once the bidding amounts between the parties are less than the predetermined range of percentages (e.g., between 5 and 30 %), the automatic settlement will conclude at the middle number of those two bids from the parties.[137]

One of the important automated settlement systems is CyberSettle, which was established in the US in 1998.[138] More than 200,000 disputes with an aggregated value of over US$1.6 billion were settled online through this system. It was initially designed to facilitate the resolution of insurance disputes but later expanded its services to other types of claims, including consumer cases.[139] Under the system,

[133] Generally, the main forms of alternative dispute resolution include; the first and second parties being the disputants, the third party being the neutral party such as the mediator or arbitrator. *See* E. Katsh and J. Rifkin, Online Dispute resolution 93–4 (2001). *See also* Hörnle, *supra* note 120, at 86.

[134] These selected ODR providers discussed in this section seem to be more successful than the others in the online marketplace. An Australian study conducted in 2003 revealed that there were 42 ODR providers established between 1999 and 2000 but 19 of them have closed down. The reasons that some are more successful than others may be that their designed pages can be easily accessed in the online market, their trustmarks are recognized, or their ORD can be used for free or at a very low charge. *See* M. C. Tyler and D. Bretherton, *Seventy Six and Counting: An Analysis of ODR Sites, in* A. R. Lodder, E. Clark, T. F. Gordon, E. Katsh, C. Rule, E. M. Thiessen, B. Verheij, D. N. Walton and J. Zeleznikow (eds.), Essays on Legal en Technical Aspects of Online Dispute Resolution 13–29 (2004).

[135] *See* A. Lodder and E. Thiessen, *The Role of Artificial Intelligence in Online Dispute Resolution, in* E. Katsh and D. Choi (eds.), *Online Dispute Resolution (ODR), Papers and Proceedings of the 2003 United Nations Forum on ODR* (2003).

[136] *See* Calliess and Zumbansen, *supra* note 81, at 158.

[137] The software support system calculates a binding settlement sum "based on the arithmetic means of all offers and given that the final sum remains within a certain range." *See* Calliess and Zumbansen, *ibid.*, at 158. *See also* Hörnle, *supra* note 120, at 81–2.

[138] *See* Cortés, *supra* note 1, at 65.

[139] *See ibid.*

the Rapid Funds regime was set up to rapidly grant settlement funds within 72 h[140] and it also offers telephone communication service as an alternative channel for negotiation.[141] So far, over 200,000 disputes have already been settled by CyberSettle.[142]

7.3.2.2 Assisted Online Mediation Mechanism

Another common type of ODR is online assisted mediation, a process wherein neutral third parties are involved in encouraging the disputing parties to reach a settlement.[143] The assistance from the neutral third parties can be provided in various forms. Beginning with assisted negotiation, it aims to increase the opportunity for communication between disputing parties through the assistance of the third party. For a more complicated process, the use of the management skills of a third party in encouraging the disputing parties to come to an amicable agreement are added in the conciliation and mediation processes. Conciliation is almost identical to mediation, except the conciliator usually proposes certain solutions for consideration by the disputing parties.[144]

Until recently, the leader in providing successful services in this field has been SquareTrade, which was set up by a private company based in the US. It offers services for handling disputes between traders and buyers on eBay with two stages in the dispute resolution process. At the first stage, the disputing parties participate in direct negotiations through an internet web page. If the direct negotiation is unsuccessful, they will then proceed to the second stage of online mediation.

A trader or a consumer can start the process by filing a complaint.[145] The opposite party is notified and asked to voluntarily join the procedure by an e-mail. In practice, the parties are happy to participate in the process because "this was the only manner by which the buyer could get redress and the seller

[140] *See* J. Zissu, *Cybersettle® RapidFund® System to Provide Attorney/Claimant Settlement Funds in Less Than 72 Hours* (October 18, 2004), *available at* prnewswire.com/news-releases/cybersettler-rapidfundstm-system-to-provide-attorneyclaimant-settlement-funds-in-less-than-72-hours-74396727.html (visited January 12, 2013).

[141] CyberSettle also jointly works with the American Arbitration Association (AAA) offering the twin alternatives of the ODR and ADR systems. The parties can initially enter into an automated negotiation made available by CyberSettle. If the negotiation is unsuccessful, they can opt for the ADR services (conciliation, mediation or arbitration) provided by the AAA. *See* Cortés, *supra* note 1, at 65.

[142] The success may be because of the fact that it facilitates and encourages the parties to resolve disputes, and offers an easier, cheaper and faster way of communication. *See ibid.*

[143] Negotiation, conciliation and facilitation are in fact different terms for mediation. *See e.g.* P. Jacobs, *Mediation Now and Then, in* M. P. Barbee, *Newsletter Mediation, International Bar Association Legal Practice Division,* July 2007, at 14.

[144] *See* Cortés, *supra* note 1, at 66.

[145] In doing so, the complaining party has to answer a web-based questionnaire that helps classify the claim type and identify possible solutions.

positive feedback."[146] Once the other party decides to take part in the process, he or she files a response and selects one or more acceptable solutions from the proposed possible solutions. If the offer and selection are matched, the dispute is resolved. If not, the parties are invited to attend a negotiation with the assistance of a mediator. With e-communication, a mediator can easily and quickly assess the nature of the conflict and facilitate the parties in their need for settlements.[147] In addition, the web and software were designed to frame a constructive and friendly environment for negotiation, thus encouraging settlement.[148] According to past experience, online mediations were achieved using technological tools that "limited the free text space, encouraged the proposition of agreements, set deadlines and even shaped the tone of exchange".[149]

Overall, SquareTrade has proven its success as evidenced by the settlement of an impressive 80 % of disputes in the first stage of conjoined resolution with a speedy process of 2 weeks on average. The parties complied with the solutions from the process in 98 % of the disputes.[150] Between 1999 and 2008, SquareTrade handled more than one million cases in over 120 countries in five different languages and employed approximately 2,000 mediators of various nationalities.[151] According to SquareTrade, 80 % of traders and consumers who completed the ODR process said that they were satisfied and will use the services again in the future.[152] In 2008, SquareTrade ceased providing its services at the expiration of the cooperation agreement with eBay.[153]

[146] *See* Cortés, *supra* note 1, at 67 and Calliess and Zumbansen, *supra* note 81, at 159.

[147] *See* Calliess and Zumbansen, *ibid.*, at 158.

[148] *See* Cortés, *supra* note 1, *ibid.*, at 67.

[149] *See ibid.*

[150] *See* Calliess and Zumbansen, *supra* note 81, at 158.

[151] *See* S. Abernethy, *Building Large-Scale Online Dispute Resolution and Trustmark Systems' Proceedings of the UNECE Forum on ODR 2003* (2003), *available at* mediate.com/Integrating/docs/Abernethy.pdf (visited 12 January 2013) and O Rabinovich-Einy, *Technology's Impact: The Quest for A New Paradigm for Accountability in Mediation*, 11 Harvard Negotiation Law Review 253, 258 (2006).

[152] *See* Hill, *supra* note 6, at 285.

[153] The service under the agreement allowed eBay customers to use an assisted negotiation provided at SquareTrade without any charge and an assisted mediation for only US$15. *See* Calliess and Zumbansen, *supra* note 81, at 159. After the expiration of such agreement, eBay established its own system to assist its members in settling claims and problems. eBay, *Resolution Center, available at* resolutioncenter.ebay.com (visited February 12, 2013). During SquareTrade' existence, it has been shown that online mediation can be an effective option for settling consumer claims. According to SquareTrade, it could manage those claims through technology allowing meditators to settle a wide range of disputes from low to medium value consumer claims in an economically efficient way. In other words, small value consumer cases can be practically handled by using a simple, convenient, and inexpensive process where the assisted mediation is conducted via e-mails or web pages. *See* Abernethy, *supra* note 151, at 2.

7.3.2.3 Online Arbitration Mechanism

Online arbitration is identical to traditional arbitration, in the sense that a neutral third party mutually selected by the dispute parties, controls the process and renders a decision based on the arguments and evidence presented to him or her.[154] Online arbitration is generally defined as "the application of dispute resolution skills and resources over a network"[155] and it is entirely conducted via technological communications such as e-mails, web pages and other e-forms of communication.

An example of online arbitration is the model introduced by the UK Chartered Institution of Arbitrators (hereinafter *CIArb*).[156] According to this process, the trader is the only party who is bound by the online arbitration whereas the consumer is free to choose.[157] The process begins with negotiation between the disputing trader and consumer. If a settlement cannot be reached at the first step of the negotiation, the parties will proceed to the second step where a consumer association steps in to assist in resolving the dispute. Again, if such assistance cannot lead to a satisfactory resolution, the consumer can proceed to online arbitration in accordance with the authority of the CIArb. The framework of this model covers claims with a value not more than £ 10,000 and charges only a nominal fee to the disputing parties.[158] In the event that the online arbitration award is considered unfair and unreasonable for the consumer, the consumer is allowed to reject such outcome.[159]

---

[154] As previously discussed in Chaps. 5 and 6, an arbitration clause is usually allowed under the US law, but the situation differs in the EU where it is legally prohibited. Due to this uncertainty on the legally binding effect of an arbitration clause, online arbitration may be considered an unsuitable mechanism for transnational consumer disputes. *See* M. S. Martin, *Keep It Online: The Hague Convention and the Need for Online Dispute Resolution in International Business-to-Consumer E-Commerce*, 20 Boston University International Law Journal 125–53 (2002).

[155] *See* E. Katsh, *The New Frontier Online ADR Becoming a Global Priority* (2006), *available at* umass.edu/cyber/katsh0300.PDF (visited March 5, 2013).

[156] *See* CIArb, *The Professional Home of Dispute Resolution-Worldwide*, *available at* arbitrators.org/WebTrader/index.htm (visited November 13, 2012).

[157] *See ibid.*

[158] *See ibid.*

[159] This is to guarantee that the designed model corresponds to the EU law, which specifies that an arbitration clause that binds consumers is legally void, by ensuring the fairness of arbitration as an alternative dispute settlement. *See ibid.*

7.3.3 The Potentials of Private Ordering in Transnational B2C E-Commerce from the Perspective of Access to Justice

The above discussion of private ordering mechanisms in the e-market has demonstrated that the private tools governing e-contracts, ranging from online reputation to third party intervention by trusted intermediaries to avoid and settle disputes, have been refined to keep pace with the technological and cross border nature of *B2C* e-sales.[160] The impression of these mechanisms is that they clearly come with several advantages.

7.3.3.1 Convenience, Time and Cost Savings: More Effective Mechanisms

The use of the internet, chat, web and video based conferencing and other forms of information technology can overcome the difficulties associated with long distances in B2C e-sales.[161] The parties to e-consumer contracts do not need to travel or have a face to face communication when they want information. It can also speed up the settlement process as the parties have more flexibility in using the mechanisms at any convenient time from anywhere, thereby avoiding the time differences between countries and busy schedules of the parties involved. Additionally, it helps consumers to avoid the potential high cost associated with the choice of forum clauses included in e-consumer contracts where the traders' domicile is designated as the chosen venue in case of litigation, arbitration or other forms of dispute resolutions.[162] This corresponds to Sects. 4.10, 4.11 and 4.12 of the Framework

---

[160] Private ordering mechanisms can work at two levels. They can be employed as a dispute avoidance mechanism, limiting possible disputes arising from B2C e-sales or as a dispute resolution mechanism with the assistance of neutral parties, for resolving consumer disputes.

[161] Private ordering, which allows the use of technological communication, provides meaningful channel to overcome great distances by providing easy and quick communications, reducing costs, time and potential delays, and making dispute settlement processes faster, cheaper and easier to access. *See* G. Kaufmann-Kohler and T. Schultz, Online Dispute Resolution: Challenges for Contemporary Justice 76 (2004), R. Gordon, *The Electronic Personality and Digital Self*, 56 Dispute Resolution Journal 8, 10–1 (2001) and E. Clark, G. Cho and A. Hoyle, *Online Dispute Resolution: Present Realities, Pressing Problems and Future Prospects*, 17 International Review of Law, Computer and Technology 7, 9 (2003).

[162] Consumers are often subjected to clauses indicating a foreign location or venue for any dispute resolution because of the emergence of global e-contracting as previous discussed. It is suggested that a fair arbitration clause should indicate the location of the hearing "at a location which is reasonably convenient to both parties". *See* American Arbitration Association, *Consumer Due Process Protocol* (April 17, 1998), *available at* docs.google.com/viewer?a=v&q=cache:It1QnKtSQV8J:www.adr.org/cs/idcplg%3FIdcService%3DGET_FILE%26dDocName%3DADRSTG_005014%26RevisionSelectionMethod%3DLatestReleased+consumer+due+process+protocol&hl=ja&gl=jp&pid=bl&srcid=ADGEEShaF6NUeTZI_Y9dhn29PxICidhaXZYx4wIFBQ-

regarding the reasonable cost of transaction and the right to conduct dispute resolution in a convenient location and the access to effective dispute resolution.

7.3.3.2 Empowering Consumers Through Communication

The private ordering regime introduces a new line of asynchronous communication that easily persuades consumers and opens them to conducting transactions through an anonymous form of communication that they can cost-effectively use from the comfort of their homes or offices. An informal environment encourages consumers to speak more effectively and place more trust in a trust-building surrounding that can facilitate the settlement of problems arising in transactions and lead to a fair and effective outcome.[163] It also allows parties more time to carefully consider a transaction than is the case in face to face transactions.[164] Additionally, a wide range of private ordering mechanisms allow the parties to start self-fulfilling their demands and preferences and working on the resolution of conflicts at a very early stage. This corresponds to Sect. 4.4 of the Framework concerning the ability to make rational decisions and freedom of choice.

7.3.3.3 Handling Negative Emotion and Psychological Barriers

It has been revealed from the experience of neutral third parties assisting in consumer dispute settlements that "distance leads to a cooling down of acrimonious emotions, and that asynchronous communication gives the party a chance to reflect."[165] Non-face to face communication may give time and opportunity to neutral third parties to rephrase some aggressive messages before delivering them to other parties, avoiding an escalation of the conflict and building a warm environment that fosters settlement.[166]

Private ordering also allows the parties to have more controlling powers over the settlement process and outcomes. Consumers and traders can reach consensus or agreements without the limitations that exist in formal legal procedures. The parties

---

lkMVd62rjC4I80LONhZNxqLx8RNEfONpynKFry7Q17RcLw4zR_NKc7_MZlPLH8ntZ98Ftz-Zl1G_NIOuByuI2B6q84cupFzI-&sig=AHIEtbQCDjAOsJS-3GCGppE_M2okLX6WkQ (visited January 4, 2013).

[163] *See* L. M. Ponte and T. D. Cavenagh, Cyberjustice, Online Dispute Resolution for E-Commerce 24 (2005).

[164] *See* e.g. Kaufmann-Kohler and Schultz, *supra* note 168, at 23, A. Shah, *Using ADR to Resolve Online Disputes* (2004), 10 Richmond Journal of Law & Technology 20, 25 (2004) and B. Baumann, *Electronic Dispute Resolution (EDR) and the Development of Internet Activities*, 52 Syracuse Law Review 1227, 1233 (2002).

[165] *See* Hörnle, *supra* note 120, at 89.

[166] *See* C. Rule, Online Dispute Resolution for Business 66, 72 (2002), R. Gordon, *supra* note 161, at 10–11 and Clark, Cho and Hoyle, *supra* note 161, at 9.

may voluntarily agree upon a solution under a private ordering regime without a third party intervention (except in the case of ODR), resulting in no winner or loser.[167] When parties have voluntarily agreed, there is a better likelihood of voluntary compliance than there is when a court decision has been rendered. This is because the latter often makes one party feel like the loser, resulting in dissatisfaction with the judicial decision. Furthermore, the process of private ordering appears to be informal and flexible, thus removing the need for formal legal representation and increasing the chance of voluntary compliance with the agreement or decision. In such circumstances, the parties need not become involved with traditional legal procedures and enforcement processes that tend to be complicated, time consuming and costly, especially in cross border disputes. As a result, the level of psychological barrier to consumers associated with the complications of traditional dispute resolution will be reduced. This corresponds to Sects. 4.4, 4.12 and 4.13 of the Framework regarding the ability to make rational decisions and freedom of choice, the access to effective dispute resolution, and the enforcement of remedies or redresses.

7.3.3.4 Overcoming Technological Involvement and Transnational Nature

The mechanisms of private ordering are designed and controlled by members of the private sector who normally have superior knowledge and understanding of the technology involved. The systems that they design are thus likely to better handle the potential problems that may arise from the technology than traditional mechanisms, which were designed by policy makers lacking in such knowledge.

With their greater expertise traders can set codes of conduct for their industries that do a good job of following and adapting to the fast developing technology. For example, e-traders appear to know how to design the format of their websites so that material information can be presented to consumers in an appropriate manner, such as through the use of large conspicuous print, by providing actions through which consumers can acknowledge or consent to a contract or by giving an opportunity to review and revise a purchase order before concluding a contract. This corresponds to Sects. 4.2 and 4.14 of the Framework on the accurate and sufficient information and ability to digest information, and the fair trading practices and consumer confidence.

In addition private dispute settlement mechanisms such as automated resolution systems, assisted online mediation and online arbitration, are by their nature extra-

[167] *See* R. L. Wissler, *Mediation and Adjudication in the Small Claims Court: The Effect of Processes and Case Characteristics*, 29 Law and Society Review 323, 324 (1995).

judicial. They can thus avoid any conflicting arguments between parties relating to jurisdiction and applicable law issues,[168] which can be very difficult to resolve and may cause delays and high costs.[169] All these can be circumvented through private ordering mechanisms where disputing parties can reach an agreement without the practical limitations and difficulties of traditional laws and procedures. Moreover, through effective online communication, the parties are able to enforce and take awards immediately once settlements are concluded, thus avoiding the delays that consumers often face in obtaining remedies via traditional face-to-face resolution procedures.[170] The use of technology thus appears to open up new avenues and possibilities for access to justice on a larger scale and it is "an important breakthrough in reducing pre-existing power imbalances ..., by providing access to efficient dispute resolution for disputants with limited resources".[171] This corresponds to Sects. 4.10, 4.11 and 4.12 of the Framework concerning the reasonable cost of transaction, the right to conduct dispute resolution in a convenient location, and the access to effective dispute resolution.

7.3.3.5 Increase Consumers' Access to Justice and Confidence

Although traditional approaches have proclaimed an intention to empower consumers the traditional regulatory mechanism necessary to achieve this goal have not been forthcoming[172] Private ordering is more likely to enhance the role and power of consumers. Consumers can easily share information and their experiences relating to transactions without any geographical limits or costs through private mechanisms such as feedback and rating systems and consumer blogs. This allows consumers to be better organized and empowered by collaboratively setting market

---

[168] Please note that the applicable law can be an issue in online arbitration because its decisions are of a similar nature to judicial judgments, with strict losing and winning parties. For detailed discussion on the applicable law issues in online arbitration, *see* Hörnle, *supra* note 120, at 63–6.

[169] *See* Clark, Cho and Hoyle, *supra* note 161, at 9. The divergent approaches of private international law in different countries, which have been discussed in the previous part, may also add some difficulties.

[170] Some predict that private ordering mechanisms, especially online dispute resolution, "will grow in the coming years due to its ability to transcend borders and escape the constraints of other legal processes less-suited for resolution of e-commerce and international disputes." *See e.g.* International Institute for Conflict Prevention & Resolution, *More More More: CPR Meeting Highlights*, 27 Alternative to High Cost Litigation 125, 128 (2009) and A. J. Schmitz, *"Drive-Thru" Arbitration in the Digital Age: Empowering Consumer through Binding ODR*, 62 Baylor Law Review 178, 182 (2010).

[171] *See* Hörnle, *supra* note 120, at 90.

[172] *See* Chaps. 5 and 6.

standards by signaling their needs through online reputation mechanisms and boycotting those rogue traders who fail to meet such standards.[173] This corresponds to Sect. 4.15 of the Framework about recognition of consumer rights and their roles in the market.

E-traders may actively operate their businesses more carefully along the lines set out in codes of conducts to protect their online reputations, thereby decreasing the likelihood of opportunistic behavior. Empirical evidence obtained by Robert Baldwin seems to support the above assumption. He found that that trading behavior is not totally influenced by regulatory control or fear of legal punishment, but the primary concern is conducting business based on fair trading behavior to build and maintain brand value and reputation as a good enterprise.[174] This is particularly true when a consumer uses a private ordering service (such as chargeback service or ODR), and later he or she can consult with an online reputation mechanism available in a primary market transaction. The effect of an online rating or reputation mechanism is very powerful because it is "given not only to sellers who deliver low-quality goods or to buyers who fail to pay, but also to those who behave uncooperatively in mediation, who do not follow settlements agreed on, or who evade an ongoing ODR procedure of an "e-payment provider via a parallel credit card charge-back and so on."[175] The risk of having sanctions imposed for violating norms through an online reputation mechanism may encourage e-traders to adopt a more flexible approach that takes consumers' concerns significantly. This corresponds to Sect. 4.14 of the Framework concerning fair trading practices.

In this regard, the influences of social and non-legal factors seem to play a part and they might "encourage e-traders to take a more sympathetic approach to the legitimate interests of consumers"[176] by providing trading functions that go beyond what the consumer law required. After sale services and generous return policies, for examples, may constitute effective ways of avoiding possible conflicts as they provide quick responses when complaints arise.[177] Also such approaches ensure

[173] The traditional unaddressed dimensions of consumers' access to justice according to the Framework (Section 4.14 Recognition of consumer rights and their roles in the market) as a result will be positive.

[174] *See* R. Baldwin, *The New Punitive Regulation*, 67 Modern Law Review, 351–83 (2004).

[175] *See* Calliess and Zumbansen, *supra* note 81, at 163. However, it should be noted that there are some concerns relating to consumer rating and reviewing systems as they can be negatively manipulated by some group of market players, leading to a reduction of their value. *See* OECD, *supra* note 93, at 26.

[176] *See* Hill, *supra* note 6, at 361.

[177] *See* C. Schulze and J. Baumgartner, *Don't Panic! Do E-Commerce, A Beginner's Guide to European Law Affecting E-commerce* (2001), *available at* signelec.com/content/download/dont_panic.pdf (visited March 12, 2012). *See also* M. Schellekens and L. van. der Wees, *ADR and ODR in Electronic Commerce in* J. E. J. Prins, P. M. A. Ribbers, H. C. A. van Tilborg, A. F. L. Veth and J. G. L. van der Wees (eds.), Trust in Electronic Commerce 271, 299 (2002).

that traders will not act against the mandatory regulation of even the strongest consumer protection system.[178]

Today, many successful online traders who value their good reputations and repeat consumers, operate "in a way which consumers consider to be reasonable-otherwise they will take their business elsewhere".[179] In such an environment, traders have chosen to satisfy consumers' concerns and interests that go beyond the consumers' legal rights, allowing them to complain on any matters, not limited to those specified by law or those that e-traders are legally entitled to ignore.[180] This consequently create *socio-legal bounds*[181] whereby the participants in e-sales will need to commit to fair and just behavior under social pressure from the collaboration of online social actors, including states, traders and consumers[182], this can be considered a *hybrid order*[183] which helps to reduce the likelihood of opportunistic behavior in the e-market.

In this respect, the necessary interlinkage of different mechanisms occurs in online market. This begins with trustmarks, which rely on the market norms described in codes of conducts combined with the assurance of high standards of business dealings through reputational systems and the assurance of payment security schemes and effective dispute resolution procedures. A study confirms that generous business practices wherein traders positively respond to consumers' needs, such as by allowing consumers to return or exchange goods even in the lack of a legal duty to do so, seem to be driven by efforts to secure repeat consumers.[184] Today, this kind of practice has increasingly become a universal trading practice of many well established traditional stores in many developed countries. Such practices have also been expanded to the online market.

---

[178] *See* Hill, *supra* note 6, at 361.

[179] *See* Hill, *ibid*. The author refers to the study of A Best and A. R Andreasen, *Consumer Response to Unsatisfactory Purchases: A Survey of Perceiving Defects, Voicing Complaints, and Obtaining Redress,* 11 Law and Society Review 701,712–3 (1977).

[180] *See* Hill, *supra* note 6, at 361.

[181] The term *socio-legal bond* is used in a very board scope. It includes not only legal boundaries according to contractual relationships but all kinds of social obligations and responsibilities established by market forces (even though they are not required or described in laws). This includes private ordering regimes. *See* Calliess and Zumbansen, *supra* note 81, at 160.

[182] They are the main stakeholders in the combined approach. The traders (including the third parties who offer private ordering services) will establish their codes of conduct under the supervision of, and monitoring by, the competent state authority to fulfill what consumers' need as indicated by their signals given through feedback and online reputation systems.

[183] Cristina Poncibo proposed a so called *hybrid approach*. This method will help to understand the consumers' problems "as a mix of government regulation, market forces and self-regulation". *See* Poncibo, *supra* note 4, at 362.

[184] *See* Ramsay, *supra* note 75, at 127 and Coteanu, *supra* note 49, at 90.

If traders willingly follow higher standards of conduct, such as by providing contract information, offering fair policies or participating in trustmark schemes and feedback systems, consumer confidence in B2C e-sales can be increased. In addition, as consumers are allowed to share and exchange experiences via feedback and rating systems, traders will gain necessary insights on how to improve business practices and provide services to meet consumers' needs and interests. This will further raise the standards of trader behavior as they compete with each other to provide services that are more responsive to the interests of consumers. Based on this standpoint, private ordering mechanisms will be effective and the likelihood of opportunistic behavior of traders reduced, increasing consumer trust and confidence in the B2C e-sale transactions. As a result, the willingness of consumers to enter into such transactions will increase and consequently the growth of B2C e-sales will be fostered.[185] Thus, the private ordering appears to facilitate consumers' access to justice in almost all multidimensional aspects of the framework, providing better protection for consumers.[186]

It can be safely concluded here that the establishment of private consumer protection mechanisms in B2C e-sales facilitates consumers' access to justice by ensuring fair and just trading practices and providing effective redress that limits opportunistic behavior and fosters the growth of e-commerce by strengthening consumers' confidence in e-sale transactions.

7.3.4 The Limitations of Private Ordering from the Perspective of Access to Justice

Private ordering mechanisms have obvious potential in B2C e-sales, being an alternative to traditional means of improving consumers' access to justice and confidence. However, the introduction of private ordering may face a number of practical challenges.

[185] Today many countries and supranational bodies have shown their enthusiasm in establishing an environment where consumers can be confident of fair trading practices and have an effective mechanism for resolution of their dissatisfactions and obtaining redress relating to e-transactions. However, such efforts have been very slow because in the past several initiatives have produced very little value in practice.

[186] *See* Chap. 4. It is likely to achieve the objectives of various or even all of the dimensions of the framework without creating substantial negative effects on other dimensions.

7.3.4.1 Lack of Face-to-Face Communication

Generally, face-to-face talks, body language, tones of voice, body gestures and facial expressions are important elements for effective communication.[187] Without physical interactions, messages may be misunderstood or misrepresented, causing difficulties for parties trying to consensually and voluntarily come to a solution or an agreement, especially when there is a dispute.[188]

7.3.4.2 Technological Difficulties and Imbalances

Private ordering mechanisms raise important concerns about the ability of consumers to engage in technological processes requiring a wide range of skills. This includes the ability to understand foreign languages, to use e-mail or other online connection or to use related programs and software. An imbalance of technical knowledge and resources still exists throughout the world because computers, internet service, and other digital equipment cost money.[189] This is especially true in remote residential areas where consumers have very limited resources or government regulations prohibit consumers from connecting to high speed internet or other modern forms of communication that consumers need to exchange information, join virtual meetings or video conferences, or do other things that may be required by dispute settlement mechanisms.[190]

---

[187] *See* P. Gilliero, *From Face-to Face to Screen-to Screen: Real Hope or True Fallacy?*, 23 Ohio State Journal on Dispute Resolution 301, 325 (2008).

[188] *See* M. C. Tyler and M. McPherson, *Online Dispute Resolution and Family Disputes*, 12 Journal of Family Studies 1, 11 (2006). Some argue that this challenge may be compensated in some particular ways with the use of technology that replicates face-to-face communication such as video conference or other online technological contacts. *See e.g.* Clark, Cho and Hoyle, *supra* note 161, at 14. But the technological tools may not be able to completely mitigate or substitute for face to face interaction. For instance, body gestures may not be correctly utilized as much as those in a face-to-face meetings when there is a lack of physical contact. Technology is not only an important factor but neutral third parties also have an important role to play in delivering meaningful messages and establishing trust between parties. It is suggested that the training for neutral third parties is necessary. *See* Cortés, *supra* note 1, at 58. Nevertheless, there is an argument that distance communications may be advantageous for dispute resolution by cooling down the angers of the parties as previously mentioned. In addition, the absence of face-to-face interaction may make the parties better off as it avoids possible biases based on sex, physical appearance, religion or nationality. In this regards, the use of asynchronous communication allows parties to truly self-represent without unfair favors or prejudices. *See* L. J. Gibbons, R. J. Kennedy and J. M. Gibbs, *Cyber-Mediation: Computer-Mediated Communications Medium Messaging the Message*, 32 New Mexico Law Review 27, 27, 44 (2002) and Rule, *supra* note 166, at 68.

[189] This imbalance situation is sometimes called the "digital divide". *See* F. Senekal and K. Benyekhlef, *Groundwork for Assessing the Legal Risk of Cyberjustice*, 7 Canadian Journal of Law and Technology 41, 54–6 (2009).

[190] *See also* T. D. Halket, *The Use of Technology in Arbitration: Ensuring the Future is Available to Both Parties*, 81 St. John's Law Review 269, 305 (2007).

7.3.4.3 Fragmentation and Lack of Transparency

Whereas traditional laws and related mechanisms appear to be reliable institutions for consumer protection, private ordering has not fully achieved such an image. There are three important reasons explaining this situation. First, private ordering systems are fragmented as various organizations and private ordering schemes provide relevant guidelines in the form of codes of practice in the e-market.[191] The existence of various schemes within a single global market leads to a lack of coherence, causing confusion among consumers.[192] Secondly, the extent of the participation of traders in voluntary private ordering schemes is not so clear. In a situation where the code owners have no mandatory power to force traders to comply and largely rely on traders' discretion[193], the mechanism may not be successfully implemented in the market as it may not achieve a critical mass. Thirdly, the transparency of private ordering, which is largely based on private implementation without any mandatory state force or clear regulatory control, is often in question, especially when it comes to settling consumer disputes with an obvious disparity in power.[194]

---

[191] A private ordering scheme may be operated by three different types of organization: private bodies, trade cooperatives or associations, and consumer organizations. For example, a Trustmark regime is now operating by the three different types of bodies. These include private entities (such as SafeBuy and WebTraderUK of the UK), commercial associations (such as ABTA) and consumer organizations (such as the Better Business Bureau of the US). *See* Hill, *supra* note 6, at 296. In addition, these three bodies may involve two different systems. The first system may be totally private, where the code owners are a private body formulating the code of practice and running the scheme. In the second system, a governmental or quasi-governmental agency may be involved in the scheme operation by approving or promoting relevant codes of practice designed by a private body. *See e.g.* Hill, *supra* note 6, at 290, 297 and OECD, *Legal Provisions Related to Business-to-Consumer Alternative Dispute Resolution in Relation to Privacy and Consumer Protection* (July 2002), *available at* oecd-ilibrary.org/science-and-technology/legal-provisions-related-to-business-to-consumer-alternative-dispute-resolution-in-relation-to-privacy-and-con sumer-protection_233318385765 (visited January 12, 2013).

[192] For example, a 2002 report indicated that there were over 25 different approval seals and logos for e-transactions across Europe. *See* E. Delgado, *E-Commerce and Trustmarks: Results from SATURN* (2002), *available at* hosteddocs.ittoolbox.com/Delgado022004.pdf (visited January 12, 2013).

[193] *See also* M. Doyle, K. Ritters and S. Brooker, *Seeking Resolution: The Availability and Usage of Consumer-to Business Alternative Dispute Resolution in the United Kingdom* (January 2004), *available at* ncc.org.uk/protectingconsumers/seeking_resolution.pdf (January 3, 2010).

[194] Additionally, the imbalance of power between traders and consumers (e.g. technological ability, information, etc.) seems to discourage consumers from trusting private ordering regimes. Many academic works express concern about the transparency issue in ODR. *See e.g.* Cortés, *supra* note 1, at 78, 79, Coteanu, *supra* note 49, at 94–8. For a detailed discussion on fair and due process in ODR, *see* Hörnle, *supra* note 120.

7.3.4.4 Lack of Funding

The complexity of the technological and cross border issues associated with private ordering mechanisms usually result in high operating cost, especially with ODR services.[195] Many service providers have found it very difficult to offer their services in the B2C e-market unless they are financially supported by membership fees from traders and consumers who use their services.[196] Due to these costs, consumers in the ODR service are for example required to pay service fees that often exceed the small value of their transaction[197] This problem is similar to that with conventional judicial processes, whose high costs provide a disincentive for consumers to seek remedies when their claim are of low value.[198]

---

[195] Many governments are not willing to spend public funds to support the development of private ordering mechanisms. An exception is ECODIR (Electronic Consumer Dispute Resolution) which is funded by the official authorities, namely the European Commission and the Irish government.

[196] *See* Hörnle, *Online Dispute Resolution, in* J. Tackaberry and A. Marriott (eds.), Bernstein's Handbook of Arbitration and Dispute Resolution Practice (2003), at 779–835 and *See* Hill, *supra* note 6, at 282–3.

[197] A number of studies confirm that many ODR services charge service fees exceeding the amounts of typical consumer disputes. The cost charged by the automated settlement system is not always well received by consumers. For instance, SettlementOnline requires 300 US dollars for each claim, whereas CyberSettle costs a minimum of 100 US dollars, depending on the amount of the claim. *See* SettlementOnline, *Settlement Online Pilot Program Proposal, available at* settlementonline.com/Proposal.html (visited March 1, 2013) and Cybersettle, *Cybersettle Online Settlement and Payment Resolution, available at* cybersettle.com/ (visited March 1, 2013). In addition, a 2001 study concluded that thirteen out of twenty nine ODR providers provided dispute settlement services for small value consumer disputes with free or affordable rates. Consumers International Organization, *Disputes in Cyberspace in 2001: Update of ODR for Consumers in Cross-Border Disputes* (November 26, 2001), *available at* consumersinternational.org/media/304196/disputes%20in%20cyberspace%202001.%20update%20of%20online%20dispute%20resolution%20for%20consumers%20in%20cross-border%20disputes.pdf (visited January 2, 2013) and Consumers International Organization, *Disputes in Cyberspace: Online Dispute Resolution for Consumers in Cross-Border Disputes-an International Survey* (December 2000), *available at* consumersinternational.org/media/304925/disputes%20in%20cyberspace-%20online%20dispute%20resolution%20for%20consumers%20in%20cross-border%20disputes%20-%20an%20international%20survey.pdf (visited December 12, 2012) and J. W. Goodman, *The Pros and Cons of Online Dispute Resolution: An Assessment of Cyber-Mediation Websites*, 2 Duke Law and Technology Review 1–16 (2003).

[198] This is especially true in ODR services. *See e.g.* Consumers International Organization, *ibid.*, OECD, *Recommendation on Consumer Dispute Resolution and Redress* 23 (2007) and D. Gawith, *Non Litigation-Based Redress for International Consumer Transaction is Not Cost Effective-A Case for Reform?*, 3 Macquarie Journal of Business and Law 115–50 (2006).

7.3.4.5 Lack of Consumers' Awareness

In order for the private ordering model to work effectively, consumers must be sufficiently well informed and understand how the mechanisms operate. They should also be able to predict how possible problems arising from a transaction can be handled and settled by such mechanisms.[199] This would help keep consumers away from e-traders who are not likely to comply with high standard in their trading practices. In effect, it will result in an increase in the economic incentive for e-traders to join private ordering schemes and keep their trading behavior in line with the relevant codes of conduct to be attractive to consumers. Unfortunately, to date many consumers seem to be unaware of the existence of private ordering mechanisms and where and how to find them.[200] Such economic incentives for trader have not yet been fruitful and seem to be quite minimal, causing private ordering in the e-market to be somewhat ineffective.

On the basis of the above discussion of private ordering as the second best option, the proposal of this thesis is to clarify the shortcomings of private ordering and take them into consideration. Understanding these shortcomings could be helpful in developing a private ordering approach, which appears to have the potentials to deal with the advanced technology and transnational nature of the e-market. Table 7.1 illustrates that, even though various mechanisms serve as inter-linkages in the online market and as an umpire of the private ordering approach in facilitating consumer access to multidimensional justice in B2C e-sales, their apparent shortcomings continue to exist. This leads to considering solutions to these shortcomings to form an effective private ordering system.

---

[199] One of the main difficulties of private ordering regimes is that they have not yet achieved the critical mass of utilization, not because they are not useful or too costly, but rather because the consumers not being aware of their existence. *See also* United Nations, *United Nations Conference on Trade and Development, E-Commerce and Development Report 2003, Chapter 7 Online Dispute Resolution: E-Commerce and Beyond* (2003), *available at* unctad.org/en/Docs/ecdr2003ch7_en.pdf (visited December 1, 2011) and Hill, *supra* note 6, at 295.

[200] A large number of consumers, including those that are well educated, are not likely to be aware of the codes of conduct and the various and fragmented associated private ordering schemes. In addition, it has been claimed that even those who are aware of the available mechanisms, do not trust or have confidence in the private ordering as a tool for reaching a satisfactory solution for problems in B2C e-sale transactions. *See e.g.* Eurobarometer, *European Union Citizens and Access to Justice* (October 2004), *available at* ec.europa.eu/consumers/redress/reports_studies/eurobarometer_11-04_en.pdf (visited November 12, 2012) and Cortés, *supra* note 1, at 78. For example, some evidence indicates a limited success of ODR in the e-market as some pioneering ODR service providers were unable to survive and closed down their operations in recent years. One reason attributable to this unsuccessful experience is the lack of consumers' awareness and understanding over the ODR concept and procedure. *See e. g.* Hill, *supra* note 6, at 298 and Coteanu, *supra* note 49, at 103–5.

Table 7.1 Private ordering, its potentials and limitations from access to justice

Private ordering mechanisms (7.3)		The potentials of private ordering (from the perspective of access to justice) (7.3.3)	The limitations of private ordering (from the perspective of access to justice) (7.3.4)
Dispute avoidance mechanisms (7.3.1)	Reputation or feedback mechanism (7.3.1.1)	Convenience, time and cost savings: more effective mechanism (7.3.3.1)	Lack of face-to face communication (7.3.4.1)
	Trustmarks and codes of conduct mechanism (7.3.1.2)	Empowering consumers through communication (7.3.3.2)	Technological difficulties and imbalance (7.3.4.2)
	Electronic payment mechanism (7.3.1.3)	Handling negative emotion and psychological barriers (7.3.3.3)	Fragmentation and lack of transparency (7.3.4.3)
Dispute settlement mechanisms (7.3.2)	Automated resolution system mechanism (7.3.2.1)	Overcoming technological involvement and transnational nature (7.3.3.4)	Lack of funding (7.3.4.4)
	Assisted online mediation mechanism (7.3.2.2)	Increase consumers' access to justice and confidence (7.3.3.5)	Lack of consumers' awareness (7.3.4.5)
	Online arbitration mechanism (7.3.2.3)		

7.4 Interim Conclusion

This chapter has demonstrated that it may be too much of an exaggeration to simply conclude that consumers lack confidence in transnational B2C e-sales because of differences in the consumer protection laws and the private international law of different countries. Many efforts to improve confidence in B2C e-sales through an improvement of consumer protection by reforming and harmonizing the law do not appear to have had any significant value in practice. The extent of the role of classic types of legal regulation, tends to be limited in transnational e-consumer market. Consumers in B2C e-sales in fact are not so concerned with the laws of traders' countries, or with conflict of laws or jurisdictional issues. A large number of consumers in B2C e-sales often look for actual solutions from traders such as product or service delivery, refunds, replacements, after sale service, apologies and so on. They are very much more interested in the behavior of traders, which gives an indication of the likelihood of their falling victim to opportunistic behavior by those traders. Some attention should also be given to the "second best option" which can truly fulfill consumers' needs and positively change their attitudes in transnational B2C sales.

In this regard, private ordering as a second best option, meaning the various self-regulatory mechanisms that industries have employed with the aim of reducing the likelihood of opportunistic behavior among traders, needs to be considered and developed. In private ordering systems, the usage of technology allows consumers to collaboratively play a role in identifying traders who fail to comply with market standards and share such information among their group on a large scale through online mechanisms. Consumers can exchange their experiences and work together by boycotting those rogue traders who fail to meet market standards. The interests of consumers are thus bundled, becoming more influential in the online market as they are the parties who set market standards by signaling their needs through online reputation mechanism. In this way, socio-legal bounds are created which require business participants to commit to fair and just behavior under market pressure from the social collaboration of online consumers. This, on one hand, facilitates consumers' access to justice as prescribed in Chap. 4 by ensuring fair and just trading practices and limiting the likelihood of opportunistic behavior. On the other hand, it also fosters the growth of e-commerce by strengthening consumers' confidence in e-sale transactions.

However, this chapter's emphasis that one should bear in mind is that such success of private ordering cannot only depend on accessibility, simplicity, speed and low-cost, but is also conditional on the level of social force, consumers' awareness, traders' participation and more importantly the transparency of the system. The intention of the next chapter is thus to discuss how the private ordering as the potential mechanism for achieving access to justice for consumers need to be developed. In other words, Chap. 8 of this study will propose how the private ordering should be implemented to maximize its effectiveness for consumer protection to improve access to justice and consumer confidence in B2C e-commerce.

Chapter 8
Improving Consumers' Access to Justice in B2C E-Commerce: Private Ordering and State as Intermediary

8.1 Introduction

There is no miracle solution that will completely deal with the technological interface of the online market. The emergence of new e-communications has caused issues associated with the advanced technological interface and the borderless nature of online transactions. As there appears to be a lack of consumer confidence in B2C e-commerce, effective mechanisms to protect consumers are needed. Attempts have been made at legal harmonization, a strategy that focuses on the need for an international standard of consumer protection in cross border e-transactions. Due to the divergent regulatory and policy approaches being taken, a high level of harmonization in consumer protection cannot be achieved in the near future and it may not provide a full answer to the issues surrounding B2C online transactions. The previous chapter discussed private ordering which was found to be the "second best solution" because it can play a useful role in widening consumers' multidimensional access to justice in B2C e-sales. The potential of private mechanisms ordering over classic state regulation in a borderless market primarily lie in their speed, lower cost, flexibility and the potential avoidance of regulatory burdens and legal disparities in different jurisdictions. However, private ordering does not come without pitfalls. Difficulties include the lack of accountability and transparency, failures in performance and a lack of awareness. Indeed, there is a clear need to address the deficits that have led to the resurgence of private ordering mechanisms in transnational e-sales.

Therefore, this chapter suggests that the use of an intermediary is a meaningful option in limiting the disadvantages and extracting the benefits of the private ordering mechanisms. It starts by looking briefly at the intermediary concept, what the intermediary does in facilitating private ordering and why they are important in the context of private ordering efficiency and evolution. It then moves on to suggests that the state is the most suitable institution having the capacity and incentive to act as an intermediary in facilitating private ordering in

S. Yuthayotin, *Access to Justice in Transnational B2C E-Commerce*,
DOI 10.1007/978-3-319-11131-5_8

the transnational market. From this point, it then turns to discussing a number of essential aspects that a state, as the most suitable institution to act as an intermediary that facilitates private ordering, should consider in performing its mediating functions. Especially, in the final section, it emphasizes that within inefficient legal systems, the states of emerging markets should actively play the intermediary role in the provision of access to justice for their consumers through the private ordering approach.

8.2 Overcoming Limitations: The Potential of an Intermediary

Some remain skeptical about the future of private ordering but, in fact, more and more scholars are increasingly arguing in favor of private ordering in the online realm.[1] This trend is unlikely to relent. In contrast, as the volume of e-commerce continues to increase along with technological evolution, the utilization of private ordering mechanisms tends to similarly rise. This leads to the question of why, given the fact that it is a meaningful approach with a variety of benefits, have private ordering mechanisms not been used in a way that achieves optimal benefits. This observation gives rise to skepticism in some commentators. The reason is probably that the existence of certain limitations diminishes its advantages.

To gain credibility, the public must give more value and recognition to private ordering. This will increase the willingness of the parties (consumers and traders) to engage in the provision of private ordering mechanisms. Persuasive incentives may be built with the assistance from third parties who act as intermediaries for the success of the private ordering systems by encouraging parties to use and ensure the fairness and efficiency of the private ordering system.

8.2.1 What Is an Intermediary?

The term *intermediary* is defined as a person "who acts between others; an intermediate agent; a go-between, middleman, mediator... Something acting between persons or things, a medium, means..."[2] The essence from the definition appears to be someone or something in the middle who acts as a linkage between some other

[1] *See e.g.* G. P. Calliess and P. Zumbansen, Rough Consensus and Running Code, A Theory of Transnational Private Law 153–80 (2010), I. Ramsay, Consumer law and Policy, Text and Materials on Regulating Consumer Markets 115–6 (2007) and R. van den Bergh, *Should Consumer Protection Law be Publicly Enforce?*, *in* W. van Boom and M. Loos (eds.), Collective Enforcement of Consumer Law 177, 202 (2007).

[2] *See* Oxford English Dictionary 405 (1978). For the general definition and meaning of intermediary, *see e.g.* BusinessDictionary.com, *available at* businessdictionary.com/definition/

things or other parties.[3] Phrased differently, an intermediary mediates, establishes connections, works between, and facilitates relationships between different parties or things.

In determining who is an intermediary, one may have to look at their role in facilitating and defining the relationship between other actors or things as an indication. Phrased differently, in what way and how does a particular thing, actor, or people mediates between two or more different sets of interests. Generally, an intermediary can offer many functional roles that cannot be replaced or constituted via direct interactions. Some essential roles of an intermediary can be identified as follow; *information processing*-covering receiving, aggregating and distributing data; *matching demands and supplies*-including filling or bridging the gap between offers and requirements between two or more parties and/or assisting two parties to come to a mutually beneficial collaboration; *providing trust*-covering ensuring the transparency and accountability within the related inter-organizational or institutional relationship and *providing interoperability*-including arranging infrastructure used by the related organization or institutions.[4]

Each role of intermediary may be of different natures in respect of expertise, knowledge and skills. An intermediary typically specializes in a particular area and works as a conduit for a particular market or a specific field of information.[5] However, the above highlighted roles are general activities and are usually undertaken by all types of intermediary.

Figure 8.1 helps to understand a relationship without an intermediary where information and communication directly reaches the receiver from the content producer with an absence of intervention from an intermediary.

From Fig. 8.2, it can be seen that an intermediary in its "middleman" or "stand-between" role, can help facilitate relationships and enable connections between different persons or things. An intermediary can help straighten the relationship between parties as illustrated by the thick line, showing the stronger connection between two different parties.

---

intermediary.html (visited March 12, 2013) and Thesaurus.com, *available at* thesaurus.com/browse/intermediary (visited March 12, 2013).

[3] *See* R. A. Heverly, *Law as Intermediary*, 2006 Michigan State Law Review 107, 112 (2006).

[4] The four roles were drawn from various literatures, which analyzed different types of intermediary in different files. However, all studies share the same conclusion that these four roles are common activities of intermediaries found in their focused fields. *See* J. P. Bailey and J. Y. Bakos, *An Exploratory Study of the Emerging Role of Electronic Intermediations and Policy*, 1 International Journal of Electronic Commerce 7–20 (1997), Howard Partners, *Department of Industry, Tourism and Resources, Study of the Role of Intermediaries in Support of Innovation April 2007* (2007), *available at* innovation.gov.au/Innovation/ReportsandStudies/Documents/InnovationIntermediariesReport.pdf (visited March 12, 2013) and R. Arendsen and M. J. ter Hedde, On the Origin of Intermediary E-Government Services (2009).

[5] *See* BusinessDictionary.com, *supra* note 2.

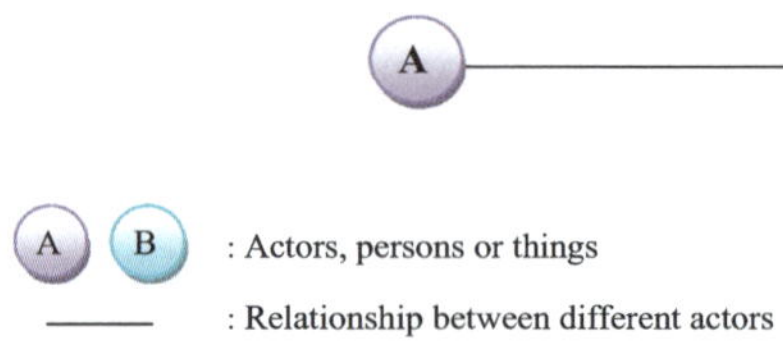

Fig. 8.1 Relationship established directly between two actors without involvement of an intermediary

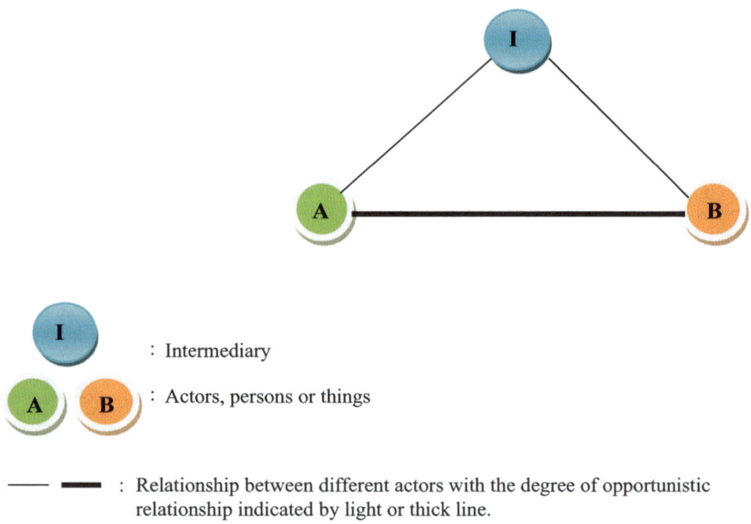

Fig. 8.2 Relationship between two actors with the involvement of an intermediary

8.2.2 What Is an Intermediary in Facilitating Private Ordering?

In the absence of a standard definition of the term intermediary in this field, for the purposes of this study, it will be defined based on the roles and activities usually undertaken by an intermediary in general as explained in Sect. 8.2.1.

Taking into account the above prescribed activities of intermediaries, they "are not simply arbitrators; they create a new interaction scheme where they play a role in ordering and defining a relationship".[6] In the context of private ordering, an intermediary can be considered a neutral third party who plays an integral role in the collaborative tasks of facilitating and supporting various aspects of the private

[6] *See* W. Medd and S. Marvin, Marking Water Work: Intermediating between Regional Strategy and Local practice. Environment and Planning D: Society and Space (2007).

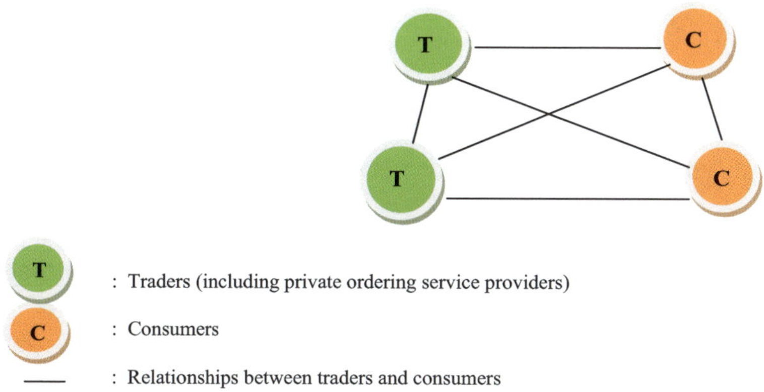

Fig. 8.3 Relationship established directly between traders and consumers in the market without the involvement of an intermediary

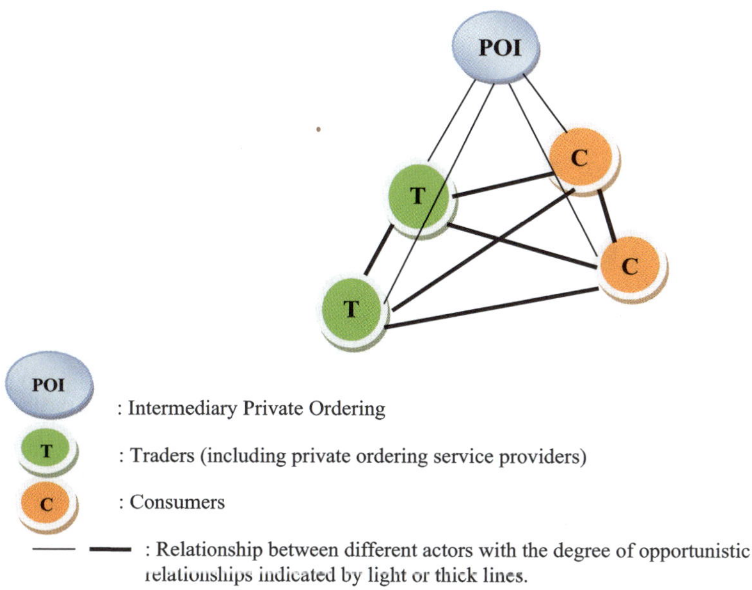

Fig. 8.4 Relationship between various actors in the market with an involvement of an intermediary

ordering approach. The facilitative role can be performed in a variety of ways, from providing information about the available mechanisms, acting as resource providers who ensure access to funding for the operation of private ordering regime and setting standards for mechanisms applicable to systems. These activities of intermediaries attempt to balance different interests and to make a connection between different parties concerning private ordering. In this sense, the parties who are assisted in achieving mutually beneficial collaboration in private ordering are traders (including private ordering service providers) and consumers respectively.

Figures 8.1 and 8.2 may be too simple to illustrate the model of intermediaries in facilitating private ordering in the market. From the increasingly complex social and market nature, there are a vast number of traders and consumers in the market. It shows a model of connections built between only two persons and it should be recognized that some kind of intermediary is necessary in the market where there are countless market players.

Figure 8.3 explains the relationship in consumer markets where traders and consumers directly communicate with each other without the help of an intermediary to facilitate their relationships concerning private ordering.

Figure 8.4 illustrates the case where there are various traders and consumers in the market. With limited financial resources and time on the part of all parties to search for the various choices offered in today's market, an intermediary may help to create faster and more convenient interrelationships between market participants. The role of an intermediary can be to support and strengthen the relationship between traders and consumers, especially with regard to a private ordering system as indicated by thick lines in the figure.

8.2.3 Reasons for an Intermediary in Facilitating Private Ordering

As concluded in the last chapter, market functions and private parties alone may not be able to provide the means of achieving successful private ordering and adequate consumer protection in accordance with the concept of multidimensional access to justice. Part of this stems from a significant trust lacuna, which means that private ordering as a result suffers from a lack of transparency, accountability and public confidence. It may be impossible to bridge the gap between effective mechanisms of private ordering and their actual utilization and recognition by the public without introducing a *third force*, which helps to boost the legitimacy of private ordering by providing appropriate information, awareness and trust.[7] Hence, the third force of intermediaries in facilitating private ordering can be a solution, which may be necessary to create a degree of accountability, transparency, and public trust in private ordering regimes.

[7] As an intermediary is a neutral third party who acts as a conduit for private ordering services offered by traders to consumers, this may help to influence the type of mechanisms available to consumers and create the general standard of private ordering services. Some authors similarly indicate the need for a third force because there is a recognition that the market and existing mechanisms are unable to provide adequate protection for consumers. *See also* Ramsay, *supra* note 1, at 131, 134 and P. Cortés, Online Dispute Resolution for consumer in the European Union 78–9 (2011).

Additionally, the general roles and activities of intermediaries tend to afford the advantages of private ordering to consumers and address a number of gaps and help to fix such system's deficits as discussed in Sect. 7.3.4 (including for example technological difficulties, lack of transparency, lack of funding and lack of consumer awareness). Examples of activities where an intermediary can make contribution are filling informational and knowledge gaps encountered by consumers in recognizing, acquiring and utilizing private ordering mechanisms; providing trust by monitoring, advising and offering guidance on standards for private ordering practices and mechanisms applicable to the system; being a person who secures financial resources for the transparent and accountable outcomes of the system. Therefore, an intermediary can perform a core role in affording the advantages of private ordering whilst limiting its disadvantages and correcting the failures of the market to deliver multidimensional access to justice to consumers, resulting in an increase of consumer confidence in B2C e-commerce.

Furthermore, in recent years, businesses have had greater opportunities because of the fast growth of global e-commerce, which lacks the restrictions of jurisdictional boundaries. When looking at potential business expansion in foreign countries, traders may often feel uncomfortable in unfamiliar environments with different laws and regulations, obligations, cultures, beliefs and tastes.[8] Intermediaries with their local understanding can assist traders to access or transform the local knowledge embedded in different societies that traders can use to develop their business practices aboard (including private ordering services).[9] Especially, the role of the intermediary in providing advice and consultation helps traders to not only identify business opportunities, but also to select appropriate private ordering mechanisms and executing related plans and activities in unfamiliar jurisdictions (Table 8.1).

Table 8.1 Reasons for the use of intermediaries in facilitating private ordering in B2C e-transactions

Justification for Private Ordering Intermediaries (8.2.3)	**To Cure the Private Ordering System's Deficits** (remedying the disadvantages of private ordering listed in Sect. 7.3.4, correcting the failure of the market to deliver multidimensional access to justice and to address the lack of consumer confidence)
	To Foster More Sustainable Transnational B2C E-Commerce

[8] *See also* OECD, *Typologies on the Role of Intermediaries in International Business Transactions, Final Report 9 October 2009* (2009).

[9] *See ibid.*

8.2.4 What Are the Possible Options?

The performance of the intermediary appears to have a direct impact on the efficiency of private ordering systems. When it comes to the issue of who to entrust with the intermediary role, the question is who will be able to most effectively perform the task of facilitating the private ordering system to achieve its optimal effectiveness in adequately protecting and offering multidimensional access to justice to consumers, which will in turn result in an increase of consumer confidence in B2C e-sales. Two important alternative institutional options include private bodies (individuals, industrial leaders, consumer organizations) or public entities (governments, state agencies, quasi-governmental bodies).

The choice between these two institutional options depends on which has more capacity and a greater incentive to carry out the role. It is necessary in choosing between public and private bodies to carefully consider several factors such as the economic resources each possesses, their relative ability to access information, the available tools they have and the quality of their performance.

Private bodies will be more efficient in cases where they are able to stay close to the market and consumers, have better access to information and have a better grasp of the fast developing technology.[10] Private bodies are also less likely to have any disruptive effects in the market and they may be more in tune with consumers' actual demands than public authorities.[11] However, even though private intermediaries may value consumers' interests, they can be ineffective when they encounter difficulties because of a shortage of funding or a lack of economic incentives to do so.[12] With limited material resources (money, tools, workforce and capacity), private bodies may not maximize their efforts in acting as private ordering intermediaries. This is especially true in the cross border environment of the internet where some form of global network or international cooperation is required. Private bodies may not be able to play an important or permanent role in expanding international partnerships geographically. For instance, the Global Network Initiative (hereinafter *GNI*), a non-state organization whose objectives are to address issues of privacy and free expression on the internet,[13] has had very little success since its foundation in 2008.[14] Despite the GNI seeking to ensure global corporate

---

[10] *See also* K. J. Cseres, *Enforcement of Collective Consumer Interests: A Competition Law Perspective, in* W. van Boom and M. Loos (eds.), Collective Enforcement of Consumer Law 125, 130, 173 (2007). The author identifies the advantages of private organization act on behalf of consumers in enforcing their right.

[11] *See ibid.*

[12] *See also ibid*, at 131.

[13] This non-profit organization is a multi-shareholder group, which includes private corporations, academics, and NGOs that would like to participate. *See* Berkman, *Global Network Initiative* (September 15, 2012), *available at* cyber.law.harvard.edu/cyberlaw_winter10/Global_Network_Initiative (visited March 12, 2013).

[14] Many authors discuss the effectiveness of the GNI and they similarly are of the opinion that there are risks and difficulties, which explain why not many companies have decided to uphold the

commitments to fulfill the principles of appropriate privacy and freedom of expression, only three corporations—Google, Microsoft and Yahoo!, American companies with head offices in the US—decided to join and uphold these commitments.[15] The role of GNI seems to be very limited and not so significant in the internet unless it can expand its participation globally.[16] There are reasons why many companies do not find it attractive to join the GNI. Often cited concerns are the requirement of considerable resources to comply with the system (e.g. commitment of time and human resources and budget to finance the system), accountability, and the benefits of participation.[17] In the absence of any pressure and the lack of incentives to join, many companies do not voluntarily do so. This private institution seems to have limited influence on trader behavior and has failed to establish a global network. This unsatisfactory outcome may be because the private bodies lack legitimate power to impose repressive strategies to convince traders to comply and correct the transnational market.[18] There appears to be some danger in entrusting intermediary duty to private bodies. As such, other alternatives that can offer adequate incentives and resources to facilitating private ordering in the market are necessary.

There thus seems to be a good argument for public authorities to act as intermediaries that facilitate private ordering. This is not only because of concerns on the limitation of resources, the lack of motivation and the limited capacity of private groups, but public bodies also seem to be better equipped in terms of their efficiency, resources, accountability, independence and impartiality. Public authorities tend to have more finances and capacity than private bodies have, especially with regard to their expertise, monitoring power and specialization in investigation and other deterrence functions that private parties lack. Also, to effectively impose private ordering standards on the market, in some circumstances the legitimate power of public authorities to place some forms of repressive strategies might be indispensable when traders obviously lack incentives.[19]

Moreover, the state is often considered the most organized and institutionalized body with legitimacy and is a universally accepted institution.[20] Even with the emergence of globalization, the state appears to be well adapted to this new

---

commitments specified under the GNI regime. *See* e.g. *ibid*, at 3, E. Massimino, *Judge the Global Network Initiative by How It Judges Company* (March 3, 2011), *available at* humanrightsfirst.org/2011/03/31/judge-the-global-network-initiative-by-how-it-judges-companies/ (visited May 2, 2013) and L. Downes, *Why No One Will Join the Global Network Initiative*, Forbes, March 30, 2011, *available at* forbes.com/sites/larrydownes/2011/03/30/why-no-one-will-join-the-global-network-initiative/ (visited May 2, 2013).

[15] *See* Downes, *ibid*, at 1.

[16] *See e.g. ibid*, at 5–6, Berkman *supra* note 13, at 3 and J. Jinn, *The Global Network Initiative, Corporate Social Responsibility* (2012), *available at* irps.ucsd.edu/assets/001/503686.pdf (visited May 2, 2013).

[17] *See* Berkman *ibid.*, at 3–4, Downes, *supra* note 14, at 5–7 and Massimino, *supra* note 14, at 3.

[18] *See also* Cseres, *supra* note 10, at 165.

[19] *See also ibid*, at 175.

[20] *See also ibid.*

environment by its ability to listen and respond to outside preferences and to maintain its accountability and independence in the global community.[21] Therefore, the state and its affiliates have the potential capacity to develop their roles in the transnational setting. In other words, the state is likely to be in a better position to support private ordering in the borderless environment than a private body, whose competencies are likely to be limited.

The International Consumer Protection Enforcement Network (hereinafter *ICPEN*), a network of governmental consumer protection authorities from all around the world, is a good example of the success of public bodies in a cross border setting.[22] Members of ICPEN, which has the purposes of protecting consumers' interests, sharing information regarding transnational activities that are likely to harm consumers, and encouraging global cooperation among consumer law enforcement authorities, is comprised of the competent authorities of over 50 nations.[23] By looking at the number of participants alone, the public bodies appear to have a stronger incentive to protect consumers' interests and to look for todays' problem encountered by consumers around the world than private bodies do. This may be because making online markets more transparent and supporting fair and optimal conditions therein corresponds to the conventional duties of the state as guardian of consumer interests.[24]

Furthermore, the traditional role of the state as policy maker and guardian of its citizens bears some resemblance to the activities of an intermediary. State's duties are often seen in various ways, such as through its setting of market standards, enforcing market behavior, empowering consumers by allowing them some protections and guaranteeing their rights, and encouraging traders to conduct business in an appropriate manner. Though they are not usually referred to in the literature on intermediaries, the effects of the state's role support and fit the objectives of an intermediary by positively influencing interactions and helping to create trust between two or more parties in society. Recognition of the fact that the state has been acting in various ways that are closely similar to those of an intermediary is

---

[21] *See also* I. Kaul, *Bye-Bye Westphalian State; Hello Intermediary State—Why Fair Multilateralism Matters*, *available at* ingekaul.net/pdf/upload110908/IS-paper.pdf (visited March 12, 2013). The author explains the changing role of the state today, which departs from the conventional model of sovereignty and the development and adaptation of their roles in the globalized environments.

[22] This global network was formally established in 1992. For details of its aims and functions, *see* ICPEN, *About ICPEN* (2013), *available at* icpen.org/ (visited March 12, 2013). *See also* Ramsay, *supra* note 1, at 118.

[23] For detailed of participants of ICPEN, *see* ICPEN, *Participants* (2013), *available at* icpen.org/for-consumer-experts/who-we-are/participants (visited March 12, 2013).

[24] Based on the traditional principles of consumer law and policy, a consumer is believed to be a weaker party in a transaction who is often incapable of being handed the responsibility for making correct market decisions and avoiding unfair trading exploitation from a trader who is often viewed as a stronger party. Some interventions by public authorities are necessary to provide instruments that make the market more transparent and offer some assistance to consumers. *See* Ramsay, *supra* note 1, chapter 2.

Table 8.2 State is the most suitable institution to serve as the intermediary in facilitating private ordering by affording the advantages of private ordering while correcting market failures in order to deliver multidimensional access to justice to consumers

State as the Most Suitable Institution to Act as an Intermediary in Facilitating Private Ordering (Why?) (8.2.4)			
Have Material Resources (e.g., financial and capacity)	**Have Incentives**	**Accountability and Independence**	**Experience an Specialization**

important in making an argument that the experience and expertise of the state place it in a suitable position to carry out the roles of a private ordering intermediary.

As public authorities tend to have the resources, capacity, motivation, experience, and expertise necessary to perform the tasks of a private ordering intermediary, they should be given preference over private bodies. A further question is how to select a particular form of public body (government, state agency, quasi-governmental body, other government-sponsored entity) to act in the specific role of intermediary. To answer this thoroughly would require more space than this study allows and in fact be an entirely separate topic of study. Therefore, this study only refers to all public chartered bodies as the "state" who should serve as intermediaries in facilitating private ordering or act as a conduit of private ordering services and mechanisms, without trying to determine the specific form of public authority for the specific intermediary task (Table 8.2).

8.3 State as an Intermediary in Facilitating Private Ordering

Next we must consider "the state as intermediary", where the state as a third party offers intermediary services that facilitate a relationship between traders and consumers in connection with private ordering. These important roles include building trust in private ordering interactions necessary to create benefits to the market and making the private ordering approach successful.[25] Under this role, state allows market participants to organize their own affairs without any hard intervention through laws and legislations. In other words, state no longer play its traditional role of market guardian, but rather act as a facilitator of private ordering with the use of soft and nudging strategies such as guidance and advice. In this role, the state may influence the development and implementation of private ordering and the type of mechanisms that is recognized by the market, and the state can

[25] *See also* Bailey and Bakos, *supra* note 4, at 7–20.

become an important actor in any proposed reform of consumers' interest protection under a private ordering regime.[26] This section discusses legitimate reasons that serve as incentives for the state to perform intermediary duties in the provision of private ordering in B2C e-transactions.

8.3.1 Transnational Nature of B2C E-Commerce and Globalization

As international activities and commercial transactions are rapidly increasing with little regard for national boundaries and jurisdictions, the conventional principle of sovereignty based on the notion that the state has exclusive policymaking power within its national territory, and no external forces are allowed to interfere in its domestic affairs, is becoming increasingly questionable.[27] To better enable its citizens to access new global opportunities, the state has to noticeably transform its traditional role of aggregating national preferences into a new role that is more suitable for the transnational environment, including opening its economy and joining the global infrastructure system.[28]

National policies and systems have become more interlinked and interdependent to serve global public goods and international community standards.[29] Many global issues cannot be addressed with an action of one state alone because of their multi-jurisdiction nature, such as the spreading of diseases, e-fraud, international crime and so on. The state has to balance its legitimacy at the national level with the need to for international corporation and partnership, which deepens policy interdependence with foreign preferences.[30] Today, there is a rising recognition of the state's new role, which fits less and less with the conventional sovereignty principle, leading some authors to use the term "intermediary state"[31] in reference to the state's new role.

In the context of consumer protection in the borderless online market, the above idea suggests a change to the role of state. Whereas it has traditionally been conceived as an entity that enforces compliance with its own set policies in the

---

[26] Intermediaries can play a very important role in society and the market. In general, intermediaries might include consultants, government authorities, organizations or private groups. They may influence the relevant type of rules and policies. They may also increase or limit the conflict between the other two parties. *See also* I. Ramsay, *Consumer Redress and Access to Justice, in* C. E. F. Rickett and T. G. W. Telfer (eds.), International Perspectives on Consumers' Access to Justice 17, 34 (2006).

[27] *See* Kaul, *supra* note 21, at 4.

[28] *See ibid*, at 2.

[29] *See ibid*, at 1.

[30] *See ibid*, at 7.

[31] *See e.g. ibid.* and I. Kaul and P. Conceição, The New Public Finance: Responding to Global Challenges (2006).

online market that frequently fails when global challenges are at stake, it should allow private industries to self-regulate and form market standards and norms. This new role of the state in consumer protection, where it facilitates and supports a private ordering approach rather than acting as a conventional regulator in the online market, tends to be necessary in the e-market with its technological and transnational characteristics.

In this new role, the state needs to perform the duties of an intermediary that serves the interests of consumers by preserving the flexible nature of industry self-regulation. Such flexibility will enable the industry quickly adapts to technological changes and the needs of the transnational e-market. This allows the internet environment to be initially regulated by private entities with the state subsequently providing support and monitoring power in its development and evolution as a main facilitator instead of excessively relying on the private sector's self-regulation alone. This serves the two opposite ends of the spectrum—private ordering which allows for the private sector's self-organization (establishing market norms and practices, self-regulation) on one hand and the support of the state authority on the other hand—which would help overcome a number of challenges arising from private ordering and flexibly encompass the collaboration of the industry and the public. This would be consistent with the concept of transnational law regime that "state-backed regulation disappears on the substantive level of primary contract law rules, but should resurface at the meta-level of secondary rules which ensure that the competition of consumer-protection transnational law regime will not lead to a so-called "race to the bottom" in terms of substantive consumer rights".[32] The private ordering regime thus works as mutual compensatory institutional orders between the private regime and the state framework, linking the collaboration of the public, businesses and consumers as social and market actors.[33]

The state acting as an intermediary could make an important contribution to nurturing more stable globalization by allowing and facilitating technological communications to be freely developed by market participants, which supports the growth of opportunities in e-commerce. In addition, transforming the state's role from that of an entity that enforces compliance with its own set of policies to that of an intermediary that supports private ordering may solve the problems concerning the enactment of hard laws in a borderless environment.[34] The benefits include reducing the cost of rule making and enforcement, avoiding state regulatory mistakes as industry experts will determine competent standards, and the fact that regulations set by trade professionals may lead to greater voluntary compliance than state mandatory rules.[35]

Yet, with regard to the intermediary role of the state in facilitate private ordering, transnational partnerships and global networks require further attention, especially

---

[32] *See* Calliess and Zumbansen, *supra* note 1, at 169.

[33] *See ibid.*

[34] *See* Chaps. 5 and 6.

[35] *See* Ramsay, *supra* note 1, at 116.

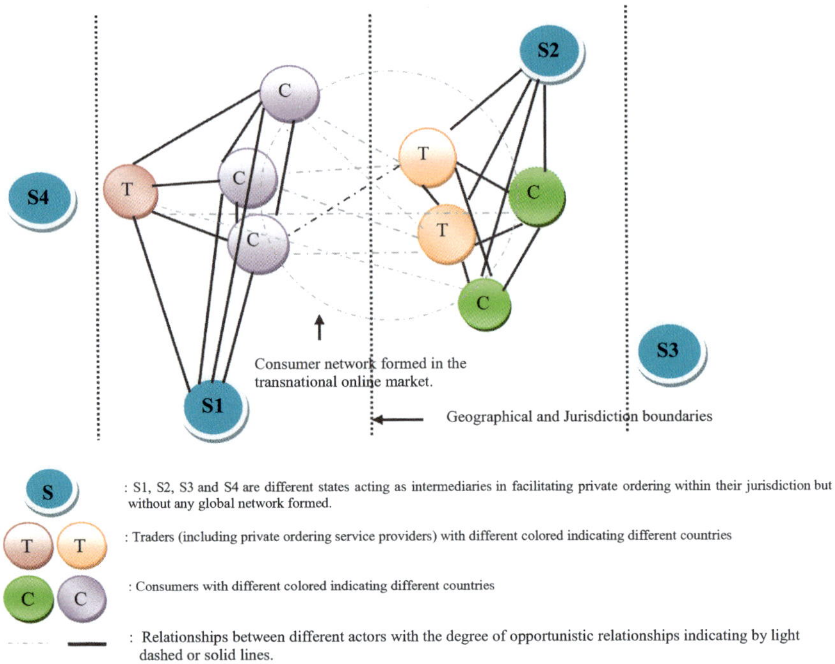

Fig. 8.5 Relationships between various actors in the market with states as intermediaries in facilitating connections and trust in the online environment within a particular jurisdiction without any global network

in terms of collaboration in cross border strategies among various states. It is recognized that many transnational issues in the e-market cannot be addressed through the unilateral action of a single intermediary state, for instance, in the virtual environment where technical difficulties may arise and an unscrupulous trader may disappear before the beginning of any dispute settlement process.[36] It is difficult to address a matter involving multiple jurisdictions by the unilateral action of an intermediary who usually possesses familiarity and expertise relevant to a limited geographical boundary.[37] In the online market, no one state or government (as intermediary) is powerful enough to effectively handle the borderless issues and global challenges and, in dealing with such matters, the use of global networks or international cooperation seems unavoidable.

Figure 8.5 describes the interaction between traders and consumers in the e-market where states, as intermediaries, foster and support possible relationships within their own jurisdiction. If private ordering endorsed by the state as intermediary guarantees and ensures fairness and access to such private ordering services,

[36] *See* Chaps. 5 and 6.

[37] *See ibid.*

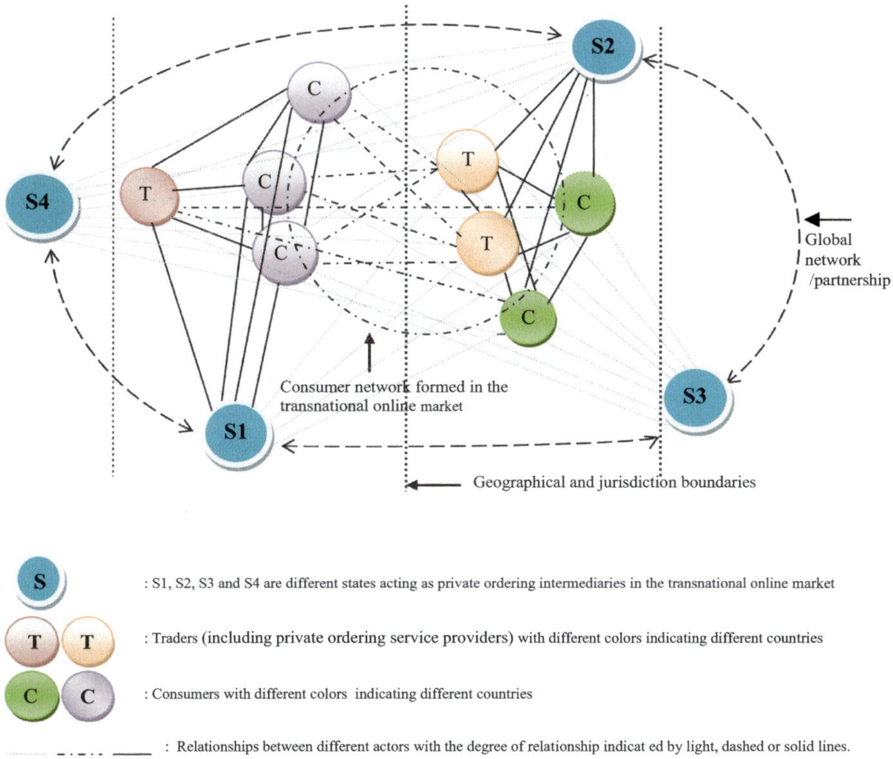

Fig. 8.6 Relationships between various actors in the transnational consumer market with states as intermediaries in facilitating connections and trust concerning private ordering in the distant or transnational online environment through global networks or partnerships

the trust gap between consumers and traders regarding private ordering mechanisms will be bridged and their relationships are likely to be healthier as indicated by the solid lines. However, without a global network, interrelationships between and/or among traders and consumers located in different jurisdictions will be very weak as indicated by the light dashed line.

Figure 8.6 illustrates the important role of global networks or partnerships of different states, acting as intermediaries that facilitate private ordering in the transnational e-market, as seen in the dashed arrow lines. Such global networks tend to better address the borderless online problems, especially with regard to ineffective cross border enforcement. This increases consumer confidence in foreign traders which helps convince consumers to enter into more transactions in the global retail e-market. As a result, the distance transnational relationships between consumers and traders that are usually very weak or do not exist will be built little by little as shown by the dashed lines. Also, with assistance from the intermediary, the private ordering approach can be effective in terms of organizing consumers on a large scale as illustrated in the dashed circle because they can share or exchange information about transactions and collaborate on sanctions against traders who violate norms through private ordering mechanisms (such as online reputation tools) without regard to jurisdictional limits.

8.3.2 Failure of the Market from the Perspective of Access to Justice

Another reason for the state to perform the role of intermediary relates to the fact that the market is unable to self-cure its failure in providing justice to consumers in the online market. As we have witnessed in the previous chapters, private ordering will be optimally effective in providing the multidimensional access to justice to consumers only if an adequate number of consumers participate or are involved in the designed mechanisms, thereby creating sufficient pressure on traders to comply with the code of conduct to avoid being identified as bad traders or to gain a good business reputation. However, consumers are often under the impression that it is not worth the time and effort and they may think there would be no change in practice regardless of whether they make a complaint or share their information and experiences online.[38] As explained by Steven Shavell, the sufficiency of incentives to induce consumers to report or post information about rogue traders depends on the likelihood of reward, the protection from future harm and the desire to punish wrongdoers.[39] Nevertheless, the size of these benefits for individual consumers is usually negligible because of the small value of consumer transactions and as a result many decide not to bother to post damaging online information about bad traders. This of course leads to a low level of consumers' participation in online reputation mechanisms which means that the do not always generate the optimal level of pressure.

To some extent, the market is unable to correct itself through reputation mechanisms and intervention from a third party is needed. This failure of the market may be the central rationale for the state to function as the intermediary in facilitating private ordering as a form of state intervention in the market. In other words, where there is a risk of suboptimal consumer participation in private ordering causing the market to be unable to provide access to justice to consumers, some form of assistance from the state seems to be necessary.

[38] *See also* Cseres, *supra* note 10, at 130.

[39] *See* S. Shavell, *The Optimal Structure of Law Enforcement*, 36 Journal of Law and Economics 255–87 (1993).

Table 8.3 Reasons justifying incentives for the state to act as the intermediary in facilitating private ordering in B2C e-transactions

Incentives Justifying the State to Act as the Intermediary in Facilitating Private Ordering (8.3)		
Transnational Nature of B2C E-Commerce and Globalization (Inefficiencies of traditional regulatory approach in the borderless environment) (8.3.1)	**Failure of the Market from the Perspective of Access to Justice** (Market is not self-correcting but need the state to provide correction) (8.3.2)	**Public Interest Orientation** (8.3.3)

8.3.3 Public Interest Orientation

The recent growth of the private ordering to protect consumers' rights, increase their confidence, and protect the public interest is closely related to the traditional state's duty of providing social justice. For instance, the online reputation mechanism not only protects the individual rights of consumers (by sanctioning wrongdoers via their online reputation), but also prevents future injuries to other consumers by allowing them to share their transactional experiences. Another example is the new dispute settlement type of ODR. It is usually instituted by a consumer with the aim of not only remedying the consumer's own rights but also avoiding future harm to other consumers and punishing traders who act improperly.[40]

In addition, private ordering appears to benefit consumers, the majority of whom are considered a disadvantaged group. This fits with the governmental task of ameliorating social conditions and providing access to justice. Hence, the state may have its own incentive to adjust its role and institutions to the demands brought by private ordering because it not only protects the individual rights of consumers, but also contributes to the public good and public policy (Table 8.3).

8.4 State Role as an "Intermediary" in Facilitating and Extracting the Benefits of Private Ordering

As the intermediary in facilitating private ordering, the state needs to take a number of important areas into consideration to extract and maximize the benefits of the private ordering approach whilst at the same time correcting the system' deficits and the failure of the market to deliver multidimensional access to justice to consumers.

[40] *See ibid.*

8.4.1 Public Funding

One of the main challenges of private ordering is that of cost. A European trustmark provider has for example admitted that the cost of operating and promoting the scheme, especially to obtain a branding, is very high and financing is the main concern.[41] As the estimated annual cost for their operations in all the Member States is around €26 million, the European trustmark scheme found it difficult to be self-sufficient as its self-financing is largely based on the subscription fees made by e-traders.[42] To compare this amount in context, the annual budget of the European Commission for the consumer policy is less than €20 million.[43] This means that the European trustmark provider may not be able to economically afford to exclude clients because in doing so they will lose the membership fees of the traders who fail to comply with their high standards.[44] The criticism of the TRUSTe regime correspondingly emphasizes this point. Even though TRUSTe has managed and settled several thousand disputes, so far it has never repealed a single seal.[45] Dispute settlement services are another example that illustrates the funding problem.[46] The majority of the ODR services require fees that are higher than the amount of typical consumer cases because of the cost of operating such services.[47] In this environment, the effective ODR as a cheaper alternative resolution for the small value consumer disputes has widely been criticized.[48]

In view of the above fact, it is unlikely that private ordering mechanism will be reliable, transparent and effective unless and until an appropriate and viable funding model can be found. The cost of private ordering is born by private industry

---

[41] This is especially true where the trustmark regime relies on the member fees paid by e-traders. The experience of a European trustmark scheme is one example. *See* T. Wagemans, *Got What You Order? in*, ECC (Denmark) *Conference Report: E-Commerce Trustmarks in Europe* (November, 2006), at 16. A number of articles emphasize the financial problems in trustmark schemes and similarly point out the need for financial supports from states. *See e.g.* J. Hill, Cross-Border Consumer Contracts 309 (2008) and Cortés, *supra* note 7, at 63.

[42] *See* Wagemans, *ibid*, at 16.

[43] *See* Hill, *supra* note 41, at 8–9.

[44] *See* Calliess and Zumbansen, *supra* note 1, at 157.

[45] *See* Cortés, *supra* note 7, at 63.

[46] In the EU, most of the ODR services for e-commerce are co-funded by states, businesses, and consumers. There are concerns relating to the effectiveness and fairness of a private funding trustmark system, *see ibid,* at 63, 86.

[47] *See* Consumers International, *Disputes in Cyberspace: Online Dispute Resolution for Consumers in Cross-Border Disputes-an International Survey* (December 2000), *available at* consumersinternational.org/media/304925/disputes%20in%20cyberspace-%20online%20dispute%20resolution%20for%20consumers%20in%20cross-border%20disputes%20-%20an%20international%20survey.pdf (visited December 12, 2012) and J. W. Goodman, *The Pros and Cons of Online Dispute Resolution: An Assessment of Cyber-Mediation Websites*, 2 Duke Law and Technology Review 1–16 (2003), *available at* scholarship.law.duke.edu/cgi/viewcontent.cgi?article=1073&context=dltr (visited December 12, 2012).

[48] *See ibid.*

and it may be more flexible and more innovative as the regulations come from the industries themselves rather than a public authority. However, such an arrangement may lack legitimacy and raise questions about its reliability and transparency. As Jonathan Hill points out concerning funding issues related to the ODR system "[t] here are major problems in finding a business model which enables that the ODR service provider to offer low-cost or free services to consumers while, at the same time, establishing an appropriate degree of independence form business interests (which are, in practice, the major source of funding)."[49] Consequently, private ordering must take place within an institutional framework that extracts benefits from its advantages while limiting its pitfalls. In this regard, the state as intermediary should retain the right to intervene to combat the possible shortfalls of private ordering and, at the same time, allow the private sector to structure its self-regulation to ensure innovative solutions from industry.

Funding from public sources may be necessary to maintain independence and effectiveness and avoid influence from traders while remaining economically attractive to consumers.[50] If not, there is less likelihood for the effective implementation of private ordering mechanisms in the internet market. Currently, there are some positive signs as some ODR services in the EU are now receiving financial support from governments to preserve their independence.[51] The main point to make here is that the private ordering cannot be well operated without cost, and the state should be an active intermediary in this context by spending public money on its evolution.[52]

8.4.2 Information Dissemination

If consumers can think of the possible risks involved in transnational e-sales and know how to limit them by using private ordering mechanisms, they can avoid unreliable traders. This will generate a climate where traders feel that it is advantageous to join trustmark schemes, codes of conduct or other similar schemes to be trusted and selected by consumers. On the contrary, if consumers ignore and do not

---

[49] *See* Hill, *supra* note 41, at 282.

[50] *See* Cortés, *supra* note 7, at 86.

[51] *See ibid.*

[52] There may be another question on policy priorities. How much money should actually be spent by the government on providing access to justice to consumers in e-sales? To spend money on this matter means cutting off or reducing funding for other governmental matters such as defense, health and infrastructure. However, the combined approach, which is based largely on self-regulation, would require less public investment as compared to the traditional state regulatory approach. To support the global economic growth, one important aim is that consumer protection and access to justice need to be achieved to establish an appropriate level of consumer confidence in B2C e-sales.

utilize such accreditation schemes there will be less market pressure put on traders to take part in trustmark schemes, codes of conduct, and other fair trading schemes.

Unfortunately, evidence suggests that today the existing private ordering mechanisms have not full been recognized and exploited by consumers.[53] Trustmarks in B2C e-sales, for example, have not been able to achieve substantial brand recognition in the market.[54] Public awareness of logos or seals of trustmark schemes seems to be minimal.[55] One UK survey confirmed that only 24 % of consumers attempted to find out whether a trader is qualified as a member of any practice code when they shop online, whereas the remaining 75 % do not know the availability of such code or its benefits.[56]

Based on this data, many consumers do not look for or regard any particular seal or logo as an indication that a particular trader complies with a code of conduct or is a member of any trade association before entering into a B2C e-transaction. This means that whether or not a trader has a trustmark seal or logo will not have any influence on consumers' buying decisions. Consequently, the absence of a trustmark seems to have a neutral effect in the e-market as it has no effect or pressure on e-traders to participate in the code of practices of a trustmark scheme.

Therefore, one of the major challenges for the private ordering regime is to gain public recognition. This can best be achieved with the assistance of the state as an intermediary in support of private ordering through public awareness strategies that can help foster overall public recognition of the designed mechanisms.[57] If the state actively takes the information dissemination (e.g. public education) duty into account, consumers with the information provided will be better able to s understand how the system works and how to deal with possible problems before making

---

[53] The ODR service in the EU, for example, is provided by the ECC-Net, which is often referred to as a well operated clearing house, but it has not yet been fully used. *See* Cortés, *supra* note 7, at 86.

[54] *See* R. D. Bruin, E. Keuleers, C. Lazaro, Y. Poullet and M. Viersma, *Analysis and Definition of Common Characteristics of Trustmarks and Web Seals in the European Union: Final Report* (February, 2005), *available at* ec.europa.eu/consumers/cons_int/e-commerce/e-commerce_final_report_annexe_en.pdf (visited November 12, 2012).

[55] *See* OFT, *Internet Shopping: An OFT Market Study* (June 2007), *available at* oft.gov.uk/shared_oft/reports/consumer_protection/oft921.pdf (visited December 12, 2012). *See also* ECC-Net, *Realities of the European Online Marketplace: A Cross-Border E-Commerce Project by the European Consumer Centre's Network* (May, 2003), *available at* ec.europa.eu/consumers/ecc/docs/european_online_marketplace2003_en.pdf (visited November 12, 2012).

[56] *See* OFT, *ibid.*

[57] One of the main issues is the lack of consumer awareness and the need for consumers to be better informed. Governments can provide many strategies to improve public awareness such as providing public education or impose information duties on traders. In other words, the state appears to have the duty to remedy such lack of consumer awareness by providing necessary information sources and offering assistance in raising public trust. The mandatory duty to provide information to consumers is the main form of state intervention concerning this issue. It has been suggested that traders or service providers of the private ordering regime should be subject to mandatory disclosure requirements. An example is the detailed disclosure requirements of the ODR service. But the attempts may be useless if the consumers choose to ignore or not take the available information into account, *see* Cortés, *supra* note 7, at 79.

online purchases.[58] Consumers will be more aware of mechanisms such as trustmarks, ratings or feedback schemes, and the ODR system and as a result they will be able to provide necessary information concerning traders into the market. This will help them conduct *sensible shopping* which can help prevent problems arising from online transactions by engaging with selected traders who engage in fair trading practices that comply with certain codes of conduct and have a good policy on complaint and dispute handling.[59] Once the utilization on of the mechanism has reached an adequate level, it can create a market pressure that serves to incentivize traders to comply with codes of conduct, thereby reducing the likelihood of opportunistic behavior.

The existing function of the FTC is one example. As an independent agency of the American government, one strategy it uses for protecting consumers is to educate consumers on how to shop safely in B2C e-commerce.[60] For EU consumers, a similar function is performed by the European Consumer Centres Network (ECC-Net), a network co-funded by the national governments of Member States.[61] ECC-Net's main objective is to promote consumer confidence in the EU market through, among other things, informing consumers about their rights and remedies in cross-national transactions.[62] Through the functions of state agencies or bodies, plenty needs to be done to promote both consumers' awareness and the recognition of private ordering mechanisms. Nevertheless, the attempts of states alone may not offer a complete solution as the consumers themselves must actually make use of the information disclosed to them.

8.4.3 State Advisory

The success of private ordering also depends on, and needs to take account of, business behavior, including the behavior of private ordering service providers.[63]

---

[58] To increase the awareness of consumers, information is the key element, as consumers should be provided with the necessary information about various consumer protection tools, their benefits and how to use them. With traders' superior knowledge, they should make such information available to consumers. In the context of the combined approach, traders may be motivated according to the self-governing regime and by the state's information requirements making it the traders' duty to provide such information. *See also* C. Coteanu, Cyber Consumer Law and Unfair Trading Practices 150 (2005).

[59] Promoting sensible shopping in the online market is one strategy aimed at helping consumers make better purchasing decisions. *See* OECD, *Report of the Working Party on Information Security and Privacy of the OECD Committee on Consumer Policy (June 2002)* (2002), at 3 and Hill, *supra* note 41, at 48, 380.

[60] *See* G. Spindler and F. Borner (eds.), E-Commerce Law in Europe and the USA (2002).

[61] *See* Cortés, *supra* note 7, at 74.

[62] *See ibid.*

[63] Consumers are not only the purchasers of goods or services of the immediate contract (between seller and buyer), but also consumers of private ordering services supplied in the online market

Unfortunately, evidence shows that the number of traders participating in the established codes of practice is low, even though some well-designed private ordering schemes are available.[64] For example, with regards to trustmark schemes in the EU, e-commerce trustmark and its relevant codes of practice have not be able to produce an environment where significant number of traders agree that "it is sufficiently beneficial to be able to display a seal of approval on their website."[65]

It seems there are only three trustmarks in the EU that have more than 1,000 e-traders participating.[66] The *Euro-Label* scheme has only 500 participants, mostly from Austria and Germany.[67] The rest of the schemes have less than 100 member e-traders.[68] It was estimated that an overwhelmingly large number of e-traders in the EU are now running their business outside any code of practices.[69]

The low growth in traders' participation in private ordering appears to impair its effectiveness and competence as the scheme cannot achieve critical mass.[70] One main reason for this is that there is not enough market pressure on e-traders to join and make their trading behavior comply with the codes being offered. As discussed in Sect. 8.4.2, many consumers are in fact not aware of the advantages of the private ordering schemes and they do not select accredited traders over non-accredited ones.[71] This results in a lack of incentives for traders to join private ordering schemes because they are not likely to be more attractive to consumers and there

---

such as SquareTrade or other ODR service providers. In this context, they are also considered traders, who are one of the market players involved in the development and evolution of the combined approach. Some service providers of private ordering, on one hand, are immediate parties to sales contracts and, on the other hand, are the suppliers of private ordering services as well (e.g. eBay).

[64] For various data supporting the limited level of suppliers' participation in private ordering, *see* Hill, *supra* note 41, at 294–5.

[65] *See ibid.*, at 294.

[66] *See ibid.*

[67] *See* T. Scharmacher, *Is the Business Side Willing to Invest in the Establishment of a Trustmark Scheme?, in ECC (Denmark), Conference Report: E-Commerce Trustmarks in Europe* (November 2006), *available at* ec.europa.eu/consumers/redress/ecc_network/e-commerce_trustmarks2007.pdf (visited March 12, 2013).

[68] *See* J. Trzaskowski, *E-Commerce Trustmarks in Europe-An Overview and Comparison of Trustmarks in the European Union, Iceland and Norway* (2006), *available at* legalriskmanagement.com/PUBLICATIONS/2006_TRUST.pdf (visited January 12, 2013).

[69] *See* Hill, *supra* note 41, at 295.

[70] *See also* C. Rule, ODR for Business 107 (2002).

[71] *See* Hill, *supra* note 41, at 294. Another reason is the lack of traders' awareness. It has been found that more than one-fifth of e-traders are not aware of the availability of the private ordering scheme. *See* OFT, *supra* note 55, at 92.

are no advantages to joining. This is because traders organize and operate themselves based on cost-benefit analysis. They are likely to be involved in an enterprise or activity only if it can be demonstrated to them that the advantages to be gained from implementing it outweigh the costs.[72]

In the environment where there is an absence of incentives, the state authority should take on an advisory role to ensure the participation of traders in accordance with the codes of conduct and other private ordering mechanisms. This appears to be consistent with an often-promoted preventive strategy in consumer protection policies that seeks to discourage traders from engaging in unfair practices and to raise the market standards, thus avoiding possible future economic and other damages caused by unfair trading practices.[73]

Based on this, the state as an intermediary that facilitates private ordering should actively advise and promote the benefits of joining the private ordering scheme among e-traders, especially through the establishment of an online brand reputation. In doing so, the state can point to successful experiences with the private ordering approach. For instance, eBay, established in 1995, is currently the most popular website for internet transactions between small businesses and consumers, with approximately 150 million registered users around the world.[74] To increase the popularity of its websites, eBay attracts public goodwill and spirit among its users, which brings about the establishment of non-state market order.[75] The core of such market order, which regulates the behaviors of members and their relationships, is built around rating systems and trust symbols reflecting consumers' needs and increasing the number of participants.[76] This design of eBay's order relies on the observation of consumers' habits in engaging in transactions. Sanctions for norm violations are also available through the online reputation mechanism called "buyer requirements".[77] This mechanism allows consumers to exclude sellers with negative ratings or poor assessments (e.g. non delivery, no PayPal account, etc.).[78] Also,

[72] This is because businesses are very rational profit-oriented entities. Economic incentives can be used to precisely predict traders' behavior. *See* Cseres, *supra* note 10, at 131.

[73] *See also* K. Viitanen, *Enforcement of Consumers' Collective Interests by Regulatory Agencies in the Nordic Countries, in* W. van Boom and M. Loos (eds.), Collective Enforcement of Consumer Law 81, 84 (2007).

[74] The development of eBay started from advertisements through online auctions, to current mode of e-sales between consumers, especially small size traders. Throughout the world, eBay offers thirty localized websites, with several million sellers and consumers. *See* eBay, *Company Overview, available at* pages.ebay.com/aboutebay/thecompany/companyoverview.html (visited February 12, 2013).

[75] *See* Calliess and Zumbansen, *supra* note 1, at 164.

[76] *See also ibid.*

[77] *See* eBay, *Selecting Buyer Requirement, available at* pages.ebay.co.uk/help/sell/buyer-requirements.html (visited February 12, 2013).

[78] *See ibid.*

other possible sanctions are imposed by eBay itself, ranging from warnings to temporally freezing accounts or the cancellation of a registered membership.[79] It can be seen from the attractiveness of eBay, which fosters the public spirit and caters to consumers' needs, that the intangible business asset of online reputation can help increase sales volume. For example, one empirical study demonstrated that seller's with better eBay reputation received higher prices from auctions.[80] Consumers can easily share information and experiences, especially through feedback or rating systems, and they tend to seek to do business with traders with good online brand reputation.

Although online reputation built by private ordering tools may not be based on law, it can be used to sanction bad traders. Such a tool, which drives consumers away from traders who fail to comply with the market standards established by consumers, is very powerful and cannot be ignored. This type of tool should necessarily be emphasized in public advisory strategies as it can help raise the motivation and economic incentives for traders concerning private ordering through the possible economic pressure of reputation sanctions.[81]

Furthermore, the participation of traders in codes of conduct and high market standards also reflects the concept of *community values* in consumer protection. These community values, which represent fair dealing, honesty, and loss-sharing, often come into a direct conflict with the interests of individual traders.[82] This corresponds with the idea of the *consumerization* of relationships, which is similar to those between patients and doctors or lawyers and clients "with pressure for greater accountability and for more exposure to market forces and challenges to professional dominance".[83] Thus, the state should assume its role in creating public goodwill in the market place by encouraging traders to engage in fair dealing in

[79] The control power of eBay is usually included in the user agreement. Section 4 of eBay user agreement used in Germany is an example. *See* eBay, *The User Agreement (of eBay Germany)*, *available at* pages.ebay.de/help/policies/user-agreement.html?ssPageName=f:f:DE (visited February 12, 2013).

[80] *See* P. Resnick, R. J. Zeckhauser, J. Swanson and K. Lockwood, *The Value of Reputation on eBay: A Controlled Experiment, KSG Working Paper Series No. RWP03-007* (July, 2002), *available at* papers.ssrn.com/sol3/papers.cfm?abstract_id=385206 (visited June 1, 2013).

[81] Such economic incentives for traders also depend upon the awareness of consumers and the utilization of the mechanisms that facilitate the private approach achieving the critical mass. *See* Sect. 7.3.4.5.

[82] Thus, it is not easy for traders to dedicate or contribute to the public goodwill (such as economic efficiency, protection of individual rights) at the expense of their individual interests. For further discussion on the concept of community values in consumer markets, *see* P. R. Stewart and C. R. Sunstein, *Public Programs and Private Rights*, 95 Harvard Law Review 1193, 1238 (1982).

[83] The growing attention on consumerization started two decades ago. Such relationship is reinforced by the functional market forces in mass economy. For a detailed explanation of *consumerization*, *see* Ramsay, *supra* note 1, at 14–5 and R. L. Abel, The legal Profession in England and Wales 306–8 (1988).

accordance with high market standards through the state's advisory and supervision.[84] This will not only result in the development of private ordering but also promote community values and consumerization of relationships that lead to the improvement of market standards as a whole. These advisory roles of the state seems to also offer the advantage of establishing clarity, certainty and market order for businesses at an early stage, thus avoiding incoherence in the system of the private ordering that comes about when dozens of schemes operate simultaneously in a single jurisdiction.[85]

It should be noted that preventive measures of traditional consumer protection law currently used by some states, such as models of standard terms and trading practice guidelines, negotiation and advance state' opinions, can also be adapted and used as advisory strategies of the state acting as an intermediary. The Nordic Consumer Ombudsmen, which have supervision and advisory duties, are good examples of this.[86] It is evident that most traders in Nordic countries are often more willing to corporate with advanced state opinions and advisories given by the ombudsmen than they are with mandatory hard law and sanctions.[87] A similar advisory approach is also found in the UK where the OFT, the best known national government agency acting as consumer regulator, has issued various guidelines for business practices (including Introductory Guidance on Unfair Standard Terms, Guidance on IT Consumer Contracts made at Distance, Guidance on unfair terms in health and fitness club agreements).[88]

8.4.4 State Monitoring

Despite the obvious advantageous features of private ordering over traditional state regulations, including greater flexibility, better economy and quickness, obvious challenges such as the lack of accountability, transparency or performance and potential conflicts with the public interest continue to exist.[89] This may be because

---

[84] The advisory role of the state may not necessarily be based on the law, but it should be created in practice based on the emergence of private ordering during the time.

[85] *See also* W. van Boom and M. Loos, *Effective Enforcement of Consumer Law in Europe, Private, Public, and Collective Mechanisms, in* W. van Boom and M. Loos (eds.), Collective Enforcement of Consumer Law 229–45 (2007).

[86] *See also* Viitanen, *supra* note 73, at 81–104.

[87] For detailed discussion on the successes of the Nordic consumer ombudsmen, *see ibid.*

[88] *See* Cortés, *supra* note 7, at 74.

[89] *See* T. Wagemans, *An Introduction to the Labeling of Websites* (2003), *available at* ec.europa.eu/information_society/activities/sip/archived/docs/pdf/reports/qual_lab_bkgd.pdf (visited December 12, 2012) and J. Hörnle, Cross-Border Internet Dispute Resolution 226 (2009) and Hill, *supra* note 41, at 290–302. *See also* C. Hodges, *Collectivism: Evaluating the Effectiveness of Public and Private Models for Regulating Consumer Protection, in* W. van Boom and M. Loos (eds.), Collective Enforcement of Consumer Law 205, 223 (2007).

the efforts of the private sector alone are not able to effectively ensure that all e-traders will follow fair practice standards set by their leading groups.[90] It is based on the traders' voluntary participation and does not impose any mandatory burdens on them.[91] It is unlikely that such a non-repressive system would be able to achieve the optimal market environment.[92] As a result, some have been calling for public monitoring to ensure the most effective private ordering system.[93]

In general, theoretical and practical experience supports the argument that, when there is an economic, information or technological imbalance of power between parties, it is necessary to ensure that transactional processes are fair. This is a classic rationale for state intervention through consumer protection law and judicial institution in the consumer sales context. "Similarly, in global B2C e-commerce, there exists a demand for a neutral third party that could standardize private ordering service..."[94] There is thus a need for state oversight which will address the accountability deficit in private ordering regimes and assist in the setting of market standards.[95] In other words, the superimposition of state oversight tends to raise the

[90] The existing standards, which are independently developed by numerous providers, lead to confusion and a lack of harmonization, resulting in an unclear direction of consumer protection. Without any specified set of standards or state control and monitoring, the security payment mechanisms of private ordering in e-sales which "provide a remedy to buyers in e-commerce transactions in many instances is not the same as saying that they provide a fair means of dispute resolution." *See* Hörnle *ibid*, at 44.

[91] Economic analysis suggests that traders obey the regulations only if the costs they encounter by acting unlawfully exceed the benefits of acting in accordance with the regulations.

[92] For instance, even the traders and providers of mechanism-related services themselves have always suggested that the issue of unequal technological knowledge and information has to be considered when providing the mechanism-related services by conducting their trade and services in a fair manner and with due process to ensure that the consumers receive a fair transactional business experience and avoid the criticism of creating an imbalance of bargaining power in their private ordering services. In this context, governmental assistance would be necessary to ensure full participation of traders in accordance with the codes of conducts by controlling, monitoring and even providing sanctions for those traders who fail to comply with the minimum standards of fair practice. It has been suggested that the systems should be conceived in a "proactive manner". *See* Coteanu, *supra* note 58, at 96. *See also* A. J. Schmitz, *"Drive-Thru" Arbitration in the Digital Age: Empowering Consumer through Binding ODR*, 62 Baylor Law Review 178, 220 (2010).

[93] It has been widely indicated that a lack of public authorities in charge of assuring compliance of private ordering services may lead to this transparency problem. An example of the move toward state assistance in self-regulation or private ordering is the OFT of the UK, which is the governing power in approving codes of conduct and implementing the Consumer Codes Approval Scheme. *See* OFT, *Consumer Code Approval Scheme: Core Criteria and Guidance* (June 2008), *available at* oft.gov.uk/shared_oft/Approvedcodesofpractice/oft855.pdf (visited January 12, 2013).

[94] *See* Calliess and Zumbansen, *supra* note 1, at 164.

[95] This intermediary role is also consistent with "the responsive regulation", which is emphasized by the autopoiesis theory that focuses on the function of self-regulatory forms in allowing for the integration of the various different institutional systems (political, legal, economic, social, and religious). Such focus has to work in parallel with state regulation set by notified bodies under the Community's New Approach system. *See* G. Teubner, Law as a Autopoietic System (1993) and Hodges, *supra* note 89, at 218–19, 220, 223–24.

level of transparency, thereby addressing some of the disadvantages associated with private ordering mechanisms.[96]

There are several studies supporting a need for state oversight. For instance, in the case of ODR services, if the governmental authority has the power to impose some kind of sanctions on non-complying parties who do not follow the process described in a code of conduct, traders are much more likely to make substantial efforts to find resolutions to consumer complaints, leading to successful voluntary conclusions.[97] Without this kind of incentive, there is a likelihood that traders will not try to settle disputes or try to make their practices comply with the relevant codes of practices.[98] Another study conducted by the OFT found that the voluntary codes prepared by a trade association in the UK will be most effective when there is "the availability of a strong pressure, a plausible threat of statutory regulation..."[99] The study concluded that one requirement for private ordering to work best is "the existence of a governmental supervisory body, with sufficiently strong background power", including the power to impose a code of conduct.[100] The Nordic ombudsmen who can impose injunctive order and conditional fines on traders are an example of state oversight.[101] Another is UK OFT, which has the power to file for injunctive relief concerning unfair terms in consumer contracts for market justice at large.[102] The lack of accountability, transparency, performance and participation in private ordering calls for some degree of state intervention.[103] In other words, private ordering is not privatizing the consumer protection regime but rather serves as a more effective mode of operation for flexible monitoring from the state.[104]

---

[96] *See also* Hodges, *ibid.*, at 223.

[97] *See* Hill, *supra* note 41, at 263.

[98] *See ibid.*

[99] *See* Bergh, *supra* note 1, at 197.

[100] *See also* Hodges, *supra* note 89, at 224.

[101] *See* Viitanen, *supra* note 73, at 87.

[102] *See* Regulation 8 of the UK Unfair Terms in Consumer Contracts Regulation 1994 and Regulation 12 of the UK Unfair Terms in Consumer Contracts Regulations 1999.

[103] *See e.g.* A. I. Ogus, *Rethinking Self-Regulation*, 15 Oxford Journal Legal of Studies 97–108 (1995), J. Black, *Constitutionalizing Self-Regulation*, 59 Modern Law Review 24–55 (1996), I. Bartle and P. Vass, Center for the Study of Regulated Industries, University of Bath School of Management, *Self-Regulation and The Regulatory State -A Survey of Policy and Practice, the Government's Better Regulation Task Force Published a Sequence of Reports Pressing the Advantages of Self-Regulation between 1999 and 2005* (2005).

[104] *See also* Calliess and Zumbansen, *supra* note 1, at 167.

8.4.5 Global Network

Obviously, there are universal standards about international B2B transactions such as the standardized contract terms according to the Incoterms of the International Chamber of Commerce, the model forms of letter of credit, and standard forms referring to the principles of some arbitration institutions. Standardization also occurs regarding transnational B2C activities in cross border transactions. The latter has not yet achieved effectiveness at international level, although some agencies have implemented initiatives with the object of advancing consumer interests and setting a universal standard of consumer protection in the transnational online market.[105]

Today, private ordering appears to be a very incoherent system in the e-market.[106] For example, a single country may have more than one online trustmark scheme. Three e-commerce trustmarks with a substantial degree of prominence are operating in the UK, namely "Internet shopping is safe" or *ISIS*,[107] *SafeBuy*[108] and *WebTraderUK*.[109] On a larger scale, a 2002 report indicated that there were over 25 different approval seals and logos for e-transactions across Europe.[110] That

---

[105] For examples the *econsumer.gov* website, which is maintained by the US Federal Commission is associated with the International Consumer Protection Enforcement Networks (ICPEN), a collaborative venture by the governmental authorities of more than twenty countries. The website was established in 2001 with the main statement that "because the Internet marketplace is a borderless one, sharing your complaint with governmental agencies in different countries will help to keep the Internet safe. It will also prevent other from experiencing the problem you did". It allows online consumers from all over the world to report their complaints against e-traders located anywhere with the main aim that, if fraudulent behavior and other forms of unfair commercial practices come to attention, the relevant governmental authorities can process appropriate action against such rogue traders. Even though this scheme aims to provide international services, access to the service is dominated by the US consumers with a limited number of other countries' complaints. It seems that the *econsumer.gov* website is highly recognized in the US but has yet to achieve effectiveness at the international level. An absence of international cooperation is one of the key causes of this unsatisfactory outcome. For detail of its aims and services of the *econsumer.gov*, *see* Econsumer.gov, *Econsumer.gov-Your Site for Cross-Border Complaints*, *available at* econsumer.gov/english (visited January 12, 2013).

[106] *See e.g.* Hill, *supra* note 41, at 290 and OECD, *Legal Provisions Related to Business-to-Consumer Alternative Dispute Resolution in Relation to Privacy and Consumer Protection* (July 2002), *available at* oecd-ilibrary.org/science-and-technology/legal-provisions-related-to-business-to-consumer-alternative-dispute-resolution-in-relation-to-privacy-and-consumer-protection_233318385765 (visited January 12, 2013).

[107] For the details of *ISIS*' s services offered, *see* ISIS, *Internet Shopping is Safe*, *available at* isisaccreditation.imrg.org/user/pages/homepage.aspx (visited January 12, 2013).

[108] For the details of *SafeBuy*'s services offered, *see* SafeBuy, *Protecting the Consumer*, *available at* http://www.safebuy.org.uk (visited January 12, 2013).

[109] For the details of *WebTraderUK*'s services offered, *see* WebTraderUK, *Details of WebTraderUK's Services*, *available at* webtrader.org.uk (visited January 12, 2013).

[110] *See* E. Delgado, *E-Commerce and Trustmarks: Results from SATURN* (2002), *available at* hosteddocs.ittoolbox.com/Delgado022004.pdf (visited January 12, 2013).

number was increased to 30 different seals and logos in a more recent report.[111] This lack of a coherent framework for transnational accreditation functions leads to a negative perception of the private ordering scheme. As the schemes have been operated by various bodies, they cause confusion among consumers. As Jonathan Hill pointed out in the online market "consumers seem not to know where to turn and do not make as much use as they might of the services on offer."[112]

The use of global networks or international cooperation to deal with this fragmented and complicated transnational environment has been suggested.[113] The OECD's 1999 Guidelines, for instance, suggests that states have to set up international corporation schemes for consumer protection.[114] Such international corporation is also consistent with the idea of new global regulation identified by David Levi-Faur, which includes "the rise of new instruments of regulation that involved increased internal monitoring by corporations; increased international regulation through technical standards; and the diffusion of regulatory ideas worldwide through regulatory networks".[115]

The sharing of information and coordination actions among state agencies or public bodies of different countries will help to ensure the reliability of various implementing systems and the fairness of the online market place. Rogue traders operating in different jurisdictions can no longer use technology to easily escape from one jurisdiction to another if global coordination exists. With global collaboration, once unfair trading practices are brought to attention, the relevant governmental agency is informed and can consequently take action against such trader.

---

[111] *See* Trzaskowski, *supra* note 68, at 25–8. Please note that the same problem exists in B2C e-sale online dispute settlements. A large number of online settlement schemes only deal with specific sectors or industries in the UK. IDRS Ltd., which is a part of the Chartered Institute Arbitrators alone, for example, offers both arbitration and conciliation schemes for several organizations and traders. This may create confusion for users when they search for appropriate services, especially those who are not native English speakers. Also, there are many ADR schemes other than that of IDRS operated by trade associations in the UK. The extensive services of IDRS are said to be poorly organized and the IDRS website is very difficult to navigate to find the relevant information such as the rules or codes of conduct governing a particular type of consumer dispute. For a long list of schemes provided by IDRS, *see* IDRS, *Welcome to IDRS-Your Consumer Redress, Independent Complaints Review and Ombudsman Specialist*, *available at* idrs.ltd.uk/ (visited January 12, 2013) and Hill, *supra* note 41, at 291. It should also be noted that a large number of private ordering schemes have been set up based on the perspective of national transactions. Most schemes have not taken the international aspect into account. For instance, information is generally described in the domestic language are inaccessible to non-domestic residents who are in dispute with traders who are domestic residents.

[112] *See* Hill, *ibid.*, at 237.

[113] The framework of an international collaboration venturing by the government agencies is often suggested. *See e.g.* D. Levi-Faur, *The Global Diffusion of Regulatory Capitalism*, 598 The Annals of the American Academy of Political and Social Science 12–32 (2005).

[114] *See* OECD, *Guidelines for Consumer Protection in the Context of Electronic Commerce* (1999), *available at* oecd.org/internet/consumerpolicy/34023811.pdf (Visited January 13, 2013).

[115] *See* D. Levi-Faur, *supra* note 113, at 12–32.

Today, there is a noticeable growth in global networks and international partnerships among consumer agencies. On a global scale ICPEN, whose members share information and exchange knowledge about best practices, assist others in data exchange, and conduct investigations to mutually combat unfair commercial practices in the online market, has created a global network.[116] For bilateral national cooperation, the Agreement on Mutual Cooperation in Cross-Border E-Commerce Complaints signed by Japan and the US in 2002 is a good example.[117] In case there is a complaint made by a consumer in one country against an online trader located in the other, the relevant competence authorities will work together in all related aspects of dispute settlement, including resolving language barriers.[118] This trend emphasizes the deepening of international cooperation to effectively and efficiently address the transnational issues of the online environment (Table 8.4).

8.4.6 State as Intermediary in Facilitating Private Ordering in the Emerging Market

In general, the state controls the fair and orderly functions of the society by manufacturing numerous rules that affect everyone in the society. Whether poor or rich, people need to access the system of justice because everyone is subject to the law.[119] In today's world, there are many levels of government. They signal that governments are committed, through planning and policies, to ensuring social justice and security and to enhancing the economic and social conditions of its citizens, especially traditionally less privileged groups such as consumers.[120] As a result, the practical commitments of social justice and welfare have conventionally been promoted by public policies of intervention and control of the state.[121]

However, it may be naive to say that the commitments of the state are flawlessly sufficient. This is especially true when looking at the states in the emerging markets, as they have to deal with determining the most suitable laws and policies

---

[116] *See ibid.* at Sect. 8.2.4.

[117] This agreement was signed in 2002 between ECOM ADR, a project operated by the Japanese Ministry of Economy, Trade and Industry together with Next Generation Electronic Commerce Promotion Council of Japan and the US Better Business Bureau (BBB). *See* Calliess and Zumbansen, *supra* note 1, at 174.

[118] *See ibid.*

[119] With tax revenue from citizens, the society requires the state to offer benefits and protections. This puts the state in direct contact with its citizens and imposes a burden on the state in providing justice to all members of society. The long arms of the state are resting on people' shoulders which affects their activities and seem to be necessary to the quest for social justice. *See* L. M. Friedman, *Claims, Disputes, Conflicts and the Modern Welfare State, in* M. Cappelletti (ed.), Access to Justice and the Welfare State 249, 255 (1981).

[120] *See* Chap. 3.

[121] *See also ibid.*

Table 8.4 State as the intermediary in facilitating private ordering whilst correcting the systems' advantages and the failure of markets to deliver multidimensional access to justice to consumers in B2C e-transactions

Aspects to Mediate	State Intervention (Who?)	Suggested Strategy (How?)	Problem Corrected
Public Funding (8.4.1)	Governments (e.g. Some EU governments provide public fund for ODR service providers)	Financial Support for Private Ordering Service Providers (e.g. Trustmarks, ODR)	– Fragmentation and Lack of Transparency (7.3.4.3) – Lack of Funding (7.3.4.4)
Information Dissemination (8.4.2)	State Authorities (e.g. Nordic Consumer Ombudsman) and State Agencies (UK OFT)	Public Awareness Strategies (e.g. public education and training)	– Technological Difficulties and Imbalance (7.3.4.2) – Lack of Consumers' Awareness (7.3.4.5)
State Advisory (8.4.3)	State Authorities (e.g. Nordic Consumer Ombudsman) and State Agencies (UK OFT)	Negotiation with Traders and Advanced State Opinions (e.g. model of standard terms, trading guidelines)	– Technological Difficulties and Imbalance (7.3.4.2) – Fragmentation and Lack of Transparency (7.3.4.3)
State Monitoring (8.4.4)	State Authorities (e.g. Nordic Consumer Ombudsman) and State Agencies (UK OFT)	Warning, Persuading and Some Kind of Sanctions (e.g. injunction order, fines)	– Fragmentation and Lack of Transparency (7.3.4.3)
Global Network (8.4.5)	Governments, State Agencies or Authorities (e.g. ICPEN, Agreement on Mutual Cooperation in Cross-Border E-Commerce Complaints signed by Japan and the US)	International Cooperation Scheme (e.g. sharing information, mutual assistance, coordinating actions against rouge traders in multiple jurisdictions)	– Fragmentation and Lack of Transparency (7.3.4.3)

for each of their respective circumstances.[122] Governments of the emerging markets are attempting to promote economic growth to enhance their economic outlook with the possible adverse result of weakening the demand of a diffuse group of their

[122] People in the emerging economies live in a rapid growing economy. Most of them belong to that lower middle class; some begin to own property-a house, a car, a mobile phone. Their activities are no longer only for social reasons, but also rely on legal relationships. This is because they want to ensure the legal consequences of their activities. When people are acting as consumers in a transaction, if it breaks up, they expect fair consequences, at least in accordance with the law. Consumers in the emerging economies increasingly use the legal system to control society, daily life, and activities. This leads to the introduction of various laws by governments of the emerging market as the part of systematic controls of society through state regulations.

citizens (consumers). These governments have often made clear that their priorities are export growth and having foreign investments play a strong role in their economies to fuel their continuous expansion.[123] To them, it may be of low priority to use public funds to provide for the creation of the appearance of protecting their domestic consumers.

The interests of consumers living in emerging economies may be overlooked due partly to the fact that consumers are very unorganized and voiceless.[124] Consumers have little role in the process of creating relevant laws and policies, while businesses, as well-organized social participants, often have more powerful voices in legal and regulatory improvement.[125] Thailand, one of the emerging economies that continue to heavily rely on exports is an example. The Thai Government may not invest sufficient efforts to promote the interests of Thai consumers. Rather, it places higher priority on external demands to increase the country's economic opportunities.[126] The survey by the National Statistical Office of Thailand confirms this claim by revealing that the Thai public wants the government to make some commitments on consumer matters.[127] Among 106, 620 respondents nationwide, the highest number of 18.3 % of those surveyed want to see the government quickly limit the rising cost of consumer products as the top priority.[128]

Therefore, the question arises as to whether, given the emphasis on economic expansion, governments in emerging countries will establish the necessary bureaucracies to enact and enforce rules that protect consumer interests. This fear is obviously a growing one in the emerging economies, which indeed erodes consumers' confidence in the potential markets the consumers wish to participate in.

In this situation, private ordering mechanisms that can be applied in a state of "lawlessness" may be a solution.[129] Examples of lawless situations include the cross border environment of e-sales, where there are uncertainties arising from applicable laws and institutional litigation, coupled with the relatively non-mature and inefficient legal systems of the emerging market economies.[130] The private

---

[123] *See* C. G. Christopher, Jr. and E. Johnson, *Emerging Consumer Markets: The New Drivers of Global Economic Growth*, 4 CSCMP' Supply Chain Quarterly 2011 (March 18, 2013), *available at* supplychainquarterly.com/columns/201104monetarymatters/ (visited March 23, 2013).

[124] *See* Chap. 3.

[125] This is especially true in export dependent countries where economic development largely relies on their domestic exporters.

[126] *See* Kaul, *supra* note 21, at 5.

[127] *See* MCOT, *Thais Want Government to Curb Consumer Goods' Prices: Survey* (July 5, 2011), *available at* mcot.net/site/content?id=4ff673230b01dabf3c0247ec (March 12, 2013).

[128] *See ibid.*

[129] As Gralf-Peter Calliess and Peer Zumbansen refers to A. K Dixit's book, namely Lawlessness and Economics, Alternative Modes of Governance. *See* Calliess and Zumbansen, *supra* note 1, at 153 (2010) and A. K. Dixit, Lawlessness and Economics, Alternative Modes of Governance (2004).

[130] *See* Calliess and Zumbansen, *ibid*, at 152.

ordering regime tends to be an effective choice for the emerging markets for the three principal reasons. First, as the cost of private ordering is borne by the traders and the industries themselves, the costs of law making and enforcement for the governments of the emerging markets are reduced.[131] Second, the governments of the emerging economies are able to escape from political and other external pressures in making traditional forms of regulations as a result of opening their markets, which indirectly forces them to listen to foreign demands. Third, it allows the state to avoid the responsibility for making unsuitable laws and regulations, especially in a very crucial situation of balancing consumers' interests and the advantages of fast expanding economic growth.

Based on the above reasons, the governments of emerging markets should consider private ordering as a valuable choice and help to actually promote its system by acting as intermediaries in facilitating it. In this regards, it should be noted that the majority of consumers in the emerging economies lack awareness and possess insufficient knowledge to exploit the benefits of private ordering mechanisms, especially when the tools require some degree of technological skills. The social forces created by consumers in emerging markets may not be capable of establishing the optimal market environment, failing to drive adequate participation of traders in accordance with the private ordering. This is why the roles of the state as an intermediary are even more essential in the emerging market economies to limit the potential risks from the lack of technological knowledge and lack of drive to achieve the optimal market environment.

8.5 Interim Conclusion

It is clear that private ordering is a meaningful option for consumer protection in B2C e-commerce, as its mechanisms have the potential to resolve issues associated with the advanced technological interface and borderless characteristic of the e-market. These mechanisms can play valuable roles in widening consumers' multidimensional access to justice and consumer confidence. Its benefits when compared with classical state regulations derive from its speed, lower cost, flexibility, avoidance of regulatory burden and its ability to avoid the problems of legal disparities in different jurisdictions. Nevertheless, there are limitations that diminish the benefits of private ordering which include the lack of accountability and transparency, failure of performance, and lack of awareness. This is not only because of the various limitation on consumers' capacity, awareness and motivation to participate in the regime, but also the limited competence, the failure of market itself to deliver justice to consumers and influence traders' behaviors within the universally accepted fairness that is very essential to the establishment of the consumer protection in the B2C e-commerce.

---

[131] *See* Ramsay, *supra* note 1, at 116.

Indeed, there is a need to address the deficits that lead to the resurgence of private ordering mechanisms to sustain the growing volumes of e-sale transactions. This chapter introduces a proposal for moving forward by considering the "state as the intermediary", a neutral third party playing an integral role in the collaborative task of facilitating various aspects of private ordering as a solution to limit the risks, justifying the optimal market pressure, and the function of the regime. One should not discount the potential of the state as the private ordering facilitator in ensuring that the potentials and effectiveness of private ordering are achieved. Due to its resources, consistency and accountability, the state seems to be in a better position to help shape the private ordering approach to become more effective as compared to a private institutional body which tends to have limited resources and capacity in a single jurisdiction. There are a number of incentives justifying a state to act as private ordering intermediary, including the transnational nature of B2C e-commerce and globalization, the failure of markets to deliver access to justice to consumers and the public interest orientation of the state.

The state, as an intermediary in a private ordering context, needs to carry out the role of ensuring fair trading practices. The private sector should be allowed to establish its market rules and standards and function according to such rules and standards that can quickly adapt to technological developments and consumers' needs. The social and market forces generated by online reputation through the private ordering mechanisms (such as rating or feedback systems) will be driven by the extension of fairness and positive consumer welfare in the market. As a result, the government will not have to be involved in the difficult task of determining the suitability of traditional rules. Rather, private ordering allows an extension of state control through its intermediary role to ensure a fair market environment when direct regulation has proven difficult or inefficient.

It seems clear at the present stage that, to develop efficient private ordering mechanisms that can be implemented, it will be necessary to overcome a number of the difficulties discussed in this study. There are a number of areas that the state, as an intermediary that facilitates private ordering, needs to turn its attention to. First, private ordering services need to obtain public funding to maintain their accountability and independence from private businesses. Greater public financial support would also fill the gap of the existing lack of trust and awareness about private ordering. Second, another key issue is to ensure consumer participation, which can be achieved by utilizing private ordering mechanisms. Such participation can be strengthened by encouraging consumers' involvement via education, fostering public recognition of the efficient private ordering system by putting transparency and accountability in place. Third, the level of traders' participation is also important. If traders' incentives appear limited, the scheme cannot reach the critical mass, thereby impairing the competency of the private ordering system. The persuasiveness of such incentives for traders can be improved through public advising strategies and promoting the benefits of joining the schemes, which resemble the preventive strategy of conventional consumer protection. Fourth, the effective enforcement of private ordering has to be ensured. As it has been demonstrated that private self-enforcement systems based on voluntary participation have been ineffective, public monitoring, oversight and sanctions may be necessary to ensure that traders follow fair standards. Last, transnational issues in B2C e-commerce have to be effectively addressed. With greater economic openness because of e-communication, the unilateral action of a single party alone cannot deal with the transnational challenges of B2C e-commerce and a global network or some similar strategy will need to be formulated and implemented cooperatively in the international community to address various issues concerning the multi-jurisdictional nature of the e-market.

With many existing private ordering services available worldwide, it has the potential to play the main role in transnational B2C activities. The future outlook of the evolution of private ordering seems to be positive. The main reason for this is that private ordering can be effectively applied in a situation of *lawlessness*. In such an environment, the cross border issues and the existence of inadequate or unpredictable legal systems in developing countries create great uncertainties.

So far, the private ordering intermediary role is a meaningful choice for all economies, both mature and emerging, to adapt and change the states' roles to foster more sustainable transnational B2C e-sales. However, to effectively drive these potentials, the way in which the state, as the private ordering intermediary, can complement the private sector's continuous technological development in the online market and how practical elements can be channeled from the public sector to the private realm, have to be clearly drawn and identified. To set a clear line where the government is better placed to serve as the private ordering intermediary and then decide which aspects of private ordering that should be left in private hands in the evolution of private ordering is not an easy task and should be carefully considered.[132] Some tradeoffs and balancing of interests may need to be made between economic efficiency and fairness to consumers in B2C e-commerce. Further detailed studies are certainly needed to continue to provide an answer in this regard which is beyond the limited space allowed in this study.

[132] There is no easy answer to the question on which aspects should be regulated and which aspects should be left in private hands. The debate in the EU concerning how to regulate the ODR process is an example of this difficulty. For the details explanation on this issue, *see* Cortés, *supra* note 7, at 200.

Chapter 9
Conclusion

9.1 Research Summary

Based on the premise that an increase in global economic activities by consumers depends on the expansion of e-commerce, a rational consumer protection strategy should emphasize curing the lack of consumer confidence posed by the problems arising from online contractual relationships. A conclusion that can be derived from the analysis in this study is that the consumer protection mechanisms in B2C e-commerce remain incomplete and that there is an absence of a unified and efficient legal infrastructure, which the consumers can utilize. The issues relating to the distinctive nature of the e-market translated into fragmentation of domestic rules at the national level and efforts at legal harmonization at the international level. However, a lack of consumer confidence in today's e-market demonstrates that comprehensive protective mechanisms have yet to work properly with reference to consumers' needs and preferences. To put it another way, there is a failure in achieving access to justice and providing protection to consumers that directly leads to their lack of confidence. Such confidence cannot be established without taking into account the distinctive features of e-transactions and the nature of consumers' interests that have to be protected in B2C e-commerce.

According to the arguments in this thesis, the particularities of the e-market, which includes its advanced technological interface and transnational nature, require some forms of effective arrangements. From this perspective, one of the main objectives of this study is to seek the adoption of such a meaningful arrangement. A workable consumer protection strategy requires effective mechanisms that allow consumers to achieve effective ways of fulfilling their reasonable expectations and resolving their dissatisfactions that are not disproportionate to the economic value at stake, which is the essence of access to justice. The reliability of the designed mechanisms within the institutional framework must be tested through its ability to deal with the virtual and borderless aspects of the e-market and at the same

S. Yuthayotin, *Access to Justice in Transnational B2C E-Commerce*,
DOI 10.1007/978-3-319-11131-5_9

time to protect and fulfill consumers' concerns by delivering all conditions necessary to satisfy the multidimensional aspects of access to justice.

Although there are no simple solutions for the problems in the e-market and a perfect mechanism may not exist, the private ordering, which relies on technical solutions and remedies, is likely to be a good way forward to improve greater access to justice which help to enhance consumer confidence. When conventional legislation fails to deal with obstacles to the expansion of online trade that arise from cross-border issues and the lack of incentives for litigation, it is better to create and promote effective private methods of increasing standards through codes of conduct, trustmarks, and online reputation mechanisms which help to deliver access to justice and reduce the likelihood of opportunistic behavior in B2C e-commerce. These private ordering methods help foster consumer confidence as traders worry that consumers would not engage in future e-transactions with those traders with a bad online reputation, thereby shifting the commercial practice standards in the e-market. As a result, the present attitude of many consumers that there is a high likelihood of opportunistic behavior in online transactions, which has been undermining the potential growth of B2C e-commerce, will change and render them willing to make online purchases.

Formulating the above argument, which clearly departs from the conventional norms of traditional consumer protection that largely rest on the creation of rules of law, it is no doubt a daunting task. The proposed solution in this study is thus limited in scope by several assumptions, for example the fact that the private institution which is a private ordering mechanism might be a responsive way to achieve access to justice in the e-market in terms of cost, speed and its ability to bypass cross border issues. These key issues seem to be impractical in traditional governmental regulatory regimes.

The use of private ordering seems to be essential in the "lawless" environment of B2C e-commerce, where market actors encounter institutional uncertainties and a diversity of legal and regulatory regimes from one country to the next, resulting in multi-jurisdictional issues.[1] In addition, private ordering also appears to be a valuable alternative to state law in the area of consumer protection where the latter is often influenced by merchants. As such, private ordering contributes a regulatory solution where the protection of consumers, as weaker parties, is the issue.

Private institution with the mechanism of private ordering might be a practical long-term solution for consumers' problems in B2C e-commerce. Nevertheless, it cannot be expected to completely substitute for the conventional framework established by legislation because the need for legal infrastructure to solve consumer problems remains in certain circumstances, such as high value consumer transactions, situations where private ordering mechanisms fail to settle disputes or cases involving criminal wrong doing.

---

[1] *See* G. P. Calliess and P. Zumbansen, Rough Consensus and Running Code, A Theory of Transnational Private Law 152 (2010).

While private ordering's advantages allow consumers to avoid opportunistic behavior by rogue traders and provides a fast and economical solution in, the future such systems need to be able to minimize the difficulties and to deliver the best possible outcomes. A possible way forward is to consider the state, which has the resources and incentives necessary to adjust the market environment, as an "intermediary" that facilitates private ordering. Governments at all levels are likely to create a positive environment for the online market if they as intermediaries make concerted attempts to promote the effectiveness and transparency of private ordering regimes, improve consumer awareness, encourage trader performance and take meaningful steps to establish international consumer protection networks. These movements toward this goal will improve the multidimensional aspects of access to justice that are directly linked to a wide range of preferences and interests of consumers when they shop online and consequently boost consumer's confidence in B2C e-commerce. Without suggesting that we should overlook the possibility that private ordering cannot up hold transparency standards, this study nevertheless emphasizes the value of attempting to achieve consumers' access to justice in the spirit captured by the statement that "imperfect justice for [consumers] is better than no justice for [consumers] at all."[2]

9.2 Research Findings

There are several considerations that should be emphasized within this confined study by way of conclusion. The first part of this research concluded that technological communication has introduced a new global market that allows borderless relationships at low cost. To achieve this potential, effective consumer protection mechanisms for achieving access to justice that are directly linked to consumer trust and confidence are needed to sustain the continuous growth of the global marketplace. The discussion on consumer protection as an effective tool cannot disregard the diverse ingredients of their interests, which are complex, diffuse, and raise new issues in relation to rapid technological changes. Prospective consumer protection mechanisms have to consider the established multidimensional framework, which has the objective of protecting all aspects of justice concerning consumers' activities, blending all social and economic aspects of consumer interests.

The second part of this research recognizes that substantive and procedural tools are interdependent in effecting credible consumer protection strategies. In terms of designing the mechanisms, one main problem with the e-market is that although e-commerce shares many features in common with traditional sales there is the additional problem of inequality in the level of technical knowledge between

[2] *See* A. J. Duggan, *Consumer Access To Justice in Common Law Countries: A Survey of the Issues from a Law and Economics Perspective*, *in* C. E. F Rickett and T. G. W Telfer, International Perspectives on Consumers' Access to Justice 46, 51 (2003).

consumers and traders. This can sometimes cause consumers to encounter technical problems when entering into e-transactions. From a substantive mechanism perspective, it appears that consumers in the online market may be adequately protected than those in physical transactions as many laws have attempted to reconcile the technological inferiority of consumers through such means as information disclosure in relation to online confirmation processes, the introduction of methods that give consumers the opportunity to review their electronic input errors, withdrawal rights and so on. Nevertheless, such substantive protections may be just a novelty because consumers do not find enforcing their rights to be worthwhile, particularly in transactional matters. In this environment, the way wherein unsatisfied issues can be settled depends largely on cost considerations. Procedural mechanisms can only be responsive to these consumer concerns if they also provide effective transnational enforcement. This research has recognized that the development of various procedural mechanisms such as the small claims procedure, collective action and regulatory agency, are only very small parts of the answer to the problems of online transactions because of the lack of economic incentives for small value claimants to use them.

It is worth mentioning that from the view of private international law, which is meant to facilitate civil procedural mechanisms, there is very little that can be done to redress consumers' injuries and improve access to justice with regard to small value disputes in B2C e-commerce. Even in cases where the governing law and forum clauses are favorable to consumers (such as under the terms of European private international law), cross border litigation is not recognized as an effective means for resolving a small value dispute when enforcement has to be carried out in a foreign forum.

One theme of this study is that, from a legal perspective, the law plays much less role in B2C e-commerce than it does in other commercial areas because of its borderless nature. One problem is that many scholars have focused on legal harmonization and private international law while ignoring the fact that the low value of most consumer transactions means that litigation does not offer a realistic solution. In addition, with the aim of achieving integrated global e-market, significant attempts have been made at legal harmonization at the regional and international levels. Such efforts are very challenging and a higher degree of legal uniformity cannot be reached in the short time because of its impracticality given the significant legal disparities still deeply rooted in different countries.

Much of the discussion made in this study emphasizes the fact that there is relatively little other than the idea that the conventional rules of law will serve well in the context of B2C e-commerce. Indeed, the continuous growth in B2C e-commerce depends on the extent of consumer trust and confidence and this can be improved by meeting their expectations when transacting in the e-markets. Such attempts may not be accomplished through the traditional mechanisms as experiences have demonstrated that they are ineffective in nurturing consumer trust and confidence.

The latter part of this study discusses the second best solution of private ordering, which departs from the state's legal order and replaces a public law making entity with a private institution as the principal actor. This proposed approach can become effective when it is designed by a private body whose knowledge is capable of keeping up with the fast expansion of cross border transactions and fast evolving technology. As a result, it can help mitigate the crucial issues of technological complication and costs arising from multi-jurisdictional issues. Private ordering includes various self-regulatory mechanisms of dispute avoidance (codes of practice, trustmarks, systems of rating and feedback) and dispute settlement (automated resolution systems, ODR). These allow consumers to avoid opportunistic behavior by rogue traders by consulting with an online reputation system and, if a dispute arises, afford the cheapest and quickest solution through ODR services. This contributes to consumer satisfaction in the online market as the United Nations Conference on Trader and Development confirmed that "[i]n the online environment, loss of time often causes loss of opportunities and people involved in e-commerce will want to resolve problems in the fastest possible way."[3]

Industries can carry out private ordering with the aim of reducing the likelihood of opportunistic behavior among fellow traders. Within such a system, the usage of electronic communication allows consumers to work together in establishing their borderless network on a larger scale in identifying dishonest traders who fail to comply with market standards through online reputation mechanisms. Consumers are able to share their experiences and collaboratively avoid doing business with rogue traders. Thereby, the interests of consumers will be bundled and they will become influential actors in the market. Under market pressure from such social collaboration of consumers, traders will be pressured to commit to using fair trading practices. As a result, the socio-legal bounds will be established in the market. Clearly, this delivers greater access to justice for consumers by ensuring fair market practices, restricting the likelihood of opportunistic behavior, and fostering the growth of B2C e-commerce by strengthening consumers' confidence.

However, the success of private ordering cannot only depend on the provisions of expertise, flexibility, faster and lower-cost processes, and a potentially lower regulatory burden. It also relies on several other factors, including the social force, consumers' awareness, traders' performance and, importantly, the accountability or transparency of the system.

The conclusion of this study emphasizes the importance of the "intermediary", who plays an integral role in the collaborative task of facilitating various aspects of private ordering. It is a solution that limits the risks and justifies the optimal market pressure and function of private ordering. There are a number of incentives justifying the state to act as intermediary in facilitating private ordering, including the emerging globalization and transnational nature of e-commerce, and the failure of the market to deliver access to justice to consumers and the public interest

[3] The United Nations, *The United Nations Conference on Trader and Development, E-Commerce and Development Report 2003, Chapter 7 Online Dispute Resolution: E-Commerce and Beyond* (2013), *available at* unctad.org/en/Docs/ecdr2003ch7_en.pdf (visited April 18, 3013).

orientation in B2C e-commerce. Within its role as intermediary, the state does not have to face the difficult tasks of creating and evaluating traditional laws and regulations where they have been proven inefficient in dealing with the borderless market.

The state, as an intermediary that facilitates private ordering, needs to pay attention to several areas, including providing public funding to maintain accountability, assuring consumers' participation via education, increasing traders' participation through public advising strategies and ensuring effective enforcement with the use of public monitoring and oversight. Finally, with the borderless nature of e-commerce, a unilateral action of a single actor cannot handle transnational challenges and international collaboration or similar strategies will need to be cooperatively established in the global community to address various issues relating to the multi-jurisdictional characteristics of the e-market.

Private ordering can be effectively applied when there are uncertainties associated with multi-jurisdictional issues and when the legal system cannot adequately or efficiently deal with the online market. It is only a matter of time before the e-commerce stakeholders (consumers, traders, governments and the public) develop the outlook of private ordering. However, it will be a step further to adapt and change the state's role to foster sustainable transnational B2C e-sales. This study attempts to fill a gap in the global debate on how to incorporate private ordering into the transnational e-market. There is significant potential for it to provide multidimensional aspects of consumer access to justice, which is one of the factors that is directly linked to an increase of consumer confidence in B2C e-markets.

9.3 Final Comments and Recommendations for Further Research

Due to the fast technological development that is erasing geographical boundaries, the regulatory system faces crucial choices about whether to rely on conventional mechanisms that have long been serving the consumer market, or to seek a new method that better fits the new multi-jurisdictional global market. Attention has turned to the increasing need for non-state based mechanisms of consumer protection, departing from the hard law approach. There is a continuously growing plethora of literature on private ordering, including this study, as it tends to be a meaningful choice that can foster sustainable transnational B2C e-sales. Private ordering mechanisms have been developed among traders to promote opportunities in commercial online exchanges when there is an absence of legal mechanisms that can effectively convince consumers to enter the market.[4] Traders have to invest in establishing consumer confidence by employing and bundling various mechanisms

[4] *See* Calliess and Zumbansen, supra note 1, at 179.

to respond to consumer concerns concerning the enforcement of e-contracts.[5] Obviously, there is a need for effectiveness and fairness concerning the level of consumer protection where the protection of weaker parties is at stake. Private ordering has developed based on regulatory efforts among traders, consumers, the state and other social market actors that are outside the sphere of traditional governmental law to achieve transnational standards of cross border consumer activities.[6]

To effectively achieve the potential of private ordering, the policy in relation to e-commerce must, at the minimum, allow for the use of private ordering mechanisms. Beyond that, it should also encourage the employment of quality mechanisms by giving incentives to both traders and consumers and ensuring accountability and efficiency. The state which traditional enjoys coercive power to set laws, policies, standards and norms and to enforce compliance with mandatory rules, has to adapt to the new role as past legal applications have not been useful when facing challenges on a global scale. The most important step might be to recognize the suitable role of the state to act as an intermediary that facilitates private ordering in todays' online market as it could offer a potentially important contribution to the development of global B2C e-commerce. In addition, many transnational issues have led to the fact that the unilateral action of a single nation cannot efficiently and effectively address global problems. For the state to effectively play the intermediary role, it must recognize the needs of international cooperation or network establishing a new consumer protection system that will guarantee an effective and prosperous future for the transnational B2C e-commerce.

Today, private ordering mechanisms have not yet achieved their optimal level of usage in the global online market and there is no empirical evidence proving that they are practically correlated with consumers' confidence and their feeling toward online transactions. However, the analysis of this thesis demonstrates conclusively that private ordering is best suited to the true needs of consumers in B2C e-commerce than traditional consumer protection methods in many circumstances. Admittedly, this study may not be able to achieve the conclusion that private ordering is the best choice as it is still in an early stage of evolution and continuously developing. However, the analyses that has already been conducted can provide an essentially sound basis for future positive outlooks on private ordering and can be used to identify the interrelated issues which are worthy of further exploration.

To conclude this study here, some recommendations for further research are essential. The recommendations focus mainly on issues that should be extensively examined in empirical studies such as the extent to which the use of an intermediary can serve as a solution to improve the effectiveness of the private ordering regime. Also, extensive research is needed to examine how the state, as an intermediary, can

[5] *Ibid.*

[6] *Ibid.*, at 180.

successfully complement the private sector's continuous technological development in the online market. It is necessary to set a clear line between the aspects where there is a need for assistance from a state intermediary and where things should be left in private hands. The analysis portrayed in this research could provide a starting point by discussing a number of specific areas of private ordering that obviously need to be filled by the assistance of an intermediary at this early period of its development.

Discussions on the issues of consumer protection in B2C e-commerce are likely to be endless. A plethora of articles, conferences, and surveys has continuously sought many initiatives and strategies in this field. This study highlights a significant challenge, which relates to the question of to what extent the state is willing to spend public money on achieving consumer access to justice in B2C e-commerce through private ordering. If the government spends more on consumer protection in B2C e-commerce, there will be less money left for other areas of state concern. The point made here is that the full function of private ordering cannot be achieved free of cost. Private ordering functions can police the consumer market, take action against rogue traders, and provide a deterrent effect against unfair practices for the benefit of online consumers. As such, it is justifiable for the state to spend public money on providing consumers' access to justice via private ordering. If an important economic objective is to establish a safe and fair global e-market for consumers, private ordering strategies that prevent and help resolve cross border disputes need to be achieved to lift consumer confidence in B2C e-commerce to an appropriate level. It is an indisputable fact that there will always be instances where traders do not comply with contractual agreements and consumers fail to gain redress for their problems. However, if private ordering improves standards in the online market, it will somehow have the effect of limiting the possibility that consumers will suffer from losses.

Bibliography

1. Books and Journal Articles

Abel R. L., The legal Profession in England and Wales (1988)
Akerlof G., *The Market for Lemons: Qualitative Uncertainty and the Market Mechanism*, 84 Quarterly Journal of Economic 488 (1970)
Alboukrek K., *Adapting to a New World of E-Commerce: The Need for Uniform Consumer Protection in the International Electronic Marketplace*, 35 George Washington International Law Review 425 (2003)
Ammerlaan S. and Janssen D., *The Dutch Consumer Authority: An Introduction*, *in* van Boom W. and Loos M. (eds.), Collective Enforcement of Consumer Law 105 (2007)
Antoniolli L., *Consumer Law as an Instance of the Law of Diversity*, 30 Vermont Law Review 855 (2006)
Arendsen R. and ter Hedde M. J., On the Origin of Intermediary E-Government Services (2009)
Arrow K. J., The Limits of Organization (1974)
Atiyah P. S., The Rise and Fall of Freedom of Contract (1979)
Awoyemi B., *Zippo Is Dying, Should It be Dead?: The Exercise of Personal Jurisdiction by U.S. Federal Courts Over Non-Domiciliary Defendants in Trademark Infringement Lawsuits Arising Out of Cyberspace*, 9 Marquette Intellectual Property Law Review 62 (2005)
Bagby J., E-Commerce Law: Issues for Business (1999)
Bailey J. P. and Bakos J. Y., *An Exploratory Study of the Emerging Role of Electronic Intermediations and Policy*, 1 International Journal of Electronic Commerce 7 (1997)
Bainbridge S., *Mandatory Disclosure: A Behavioral Analysis*, 68 University of Cincinnati Law Review 1023 (2000)
Balboni P., Trustmarks in E-Commerce: The Value of Web Seals and the Liability of their Providers (2009)
Baldwin J., *Is There a Limit to the Expansion of Small Claim*, 56 Current Legal Problems 313 (2003)
Baldwin R., *The New Punitive Regulation*, 67 Modern Law Review, 351 (2004)
Baumann B., *Electronic Dispute Resolution (EDR) and the Development of Internet Activities*, 52 Syracuse Law Review 1227 (2002)
Beales H., Craswell R. and Salop S., *The Efficient Regulation of Consumer Information*, 24 Journal of Law and Economics 491 (1981)
Ben-Shahar O., *The Myth of the 'Opportunity to Read' in Contract Law*, 5 European Review of Contract Law 1 (2009)

S. Yuthayotin, *Access to Justice in Transnational B2C E-Commerce*,
DOI 10.1007/978-3-319-11131-5

Best A. and Andreasen A., *Consumer Response to Unsatisfactory Purchases: A Survey of Perceiving Defects, Voicing Complaints, and Obtaining Redress*, 11 Law & Society Review 701 (1977)

Betlem G., *Public and Private International Enforcement of EU Consumer Law*, *in* van Boom W. and Loos M. (eds.), Collective Enforcement of Consumer Law 35 (2007)

Black J., *Constitutionalizing Self-Regulation*, 59 Modern Law Review 24 (1996)

Boss A. H., *The Future of the Uniform Commercial Code Process in an Increasing International World*, 68 Ohio State Law Journal 349 (2007)

Braucher J., *The Repo Code: A Study of Adjustment to Uncertainty in Commercial Law*, 75 - Washington University Law Quarterly 549 (1997)

Braucher J., *Delayed Disclosure in Consumer E-Commerce as an Unfair Deceptive Practice*, 46 Wayne Law Review 1805 (2000)

Braucher J., *New Basics: Twelve Principles for Fair Commerce in Mass-Market Software and Other Digital Products, in* Winn (ed.), Consumer Protection in the Age of the Information Economy (2006)

Budnitz M. E., *Consumers Surfing for Sales in Cyberspace: What Constitutes Acceptance and What Legal Terms and Conditions Bind the Consumers?* 16 Georgia State University Law Review 741 (2000)

Burton S., Principle of Contract Law (1995)

Cafaggi F. and Micklitz H. W. (eds.), New Frontiers of Consumer Protection, The interplay Between Private and Public Enforcement (2009)

Calliess G. P. and Zumbansen P., Rough Consensus and Running Code, A Theory of Transnational Private Law (2010)

Camerer C., Issacharoff S., Loewenstein G., O' Donoghue T. and Rabin M., *Regulation for Conservatives: Behavioral Economics and the Case for "Asymmetric Paternalism"*, 151 University of Pennsylvania Law Review 1211 (2003)

Campbell J. and Carlson M, *Panopticon.com: Online Surveillance and the Commodification of Privacy*, 46 Journal of Broadcasting and Electronic Media 133 (2002)

Cappelletti M. (ed.), Access To Justice and the Welfare State (1981)

Cappelletti M. and Garth B. (eds.), Access To Justice VOL I: A World Survey (1978)

Casamiquela R. J., *Contractual Assent and Enforceability in Cyberspace*, 17 Berkeley Technology Law Journal 475 (2002)

Cate F. H., *The Failure of Fair Information Practice Principles, in* Winn J. K. (ed.), Consumer Protection in the Age of the Information Economy 341 (2006)

Chayes A., *The Role of the Judge in Public Law Litigation*, 89 Harvard Law Review 1041 (1976)

Chen C., *United States and European Union Approaches to Internet Jurisdiction and their Impact on E-Commerce*, 25 The University of Pennsylvania Journal of International Law 423 (2004)

Chen K. and Rea A., *Protecting Provisional Information Online: A Survey of User Privacy Concerns and Control Techniques,* 44 The Journal of Computer Information Systems 85 (2004)

Chirelstein M. A., Concepts and Case Analysis in the Law of Contracts (2001)

Clark E., Cho G. and Hoyle A., *Online Dispute Resolution: Present Realities, Pressing Problems and Future Prospects*, 17 International Review of Law, Computer and Technology 7 (2003)

Clarke R., *Internet Privacy Concerns Confirm the Case for Intervention,* 42 Communications of the Association for Computing Machinery 60 (1999)

Colon-Fung I., *Protecting the New Face of Entrepreneurship: Online Appropriate Dispute Resolution and International Consumer-To-Consumer Online*, 12 Fordham Journal of Corporate and Financial Law 233 (2007)

Cona F. A., *Application of Online Systems in Alternative Dispute Resolution*, 45 Buffalo Law Review 975 (1997)

Cortés P., Online Dispute Resolution for consumer in the European Union (2011)

Coteanu C., Cyber Consumer Law and Unfair Trading Practices (2005)

Cseres K. J., *Enforcement of Collective Consumer Interests: A Competition Law Perspective, in* van Boom W. and Loos M. (eds.), Collective Enforcement of Consumer Law 123 (2007)
Culnan M. J. and Bies R. J., *Consumer Privacy: Balancing Economic and Justice Considerations,* 59 Journal of Social Issues 323 (2003)
de Lima Lopes J.R., *Social Rights and the Courts in* Wilhelmsson T. and Hurri S. (eds.), From Dissonance to Sense: Welfare State Expectations, Privatisation and Private Law 567 (1999)
Dellarocas C., *The Digitization of Word of Mount: Promise and Challenges of Online Feedback Mechanisms*, 49 Management Science 1407 (2003)
Deutch S., *Are Consumer Rights, Human Rights?*, 32 Osgoode Hall Law Journal 537 (1994)
Diuckie J., Internet and Electronic Commerce Law in the European Union (1999)
Dixit A. K., Lawlessness and Economics, Alternative Modes of Governance (2004)
Duggan A. J., *Consumer Access to Justice in Common Law Countries: A Survey of the Issues from a Law and Economics Perspective, in* Rickett C. E. F. and Telfer T. G. W. (eds.), International Perspectives on Consumers' Access to Justice 46 (2003)
Durkin T. and Elliehausen G., *Disclosure as a Consumer Protection, in* Durkin T. and Staten M. (eds.), The Impact of Public Policy on consumer Credit 109 (2002)
Dworkin R., Taking Rights Seriously (1977)
Edwards C., *Freedom of Contract and Fundamental Fairness for Individual Parties: The Tug of War Continues,* 77 University of Missouri at Kansas City Law Review 647 (2009)
Ellison G. and Ellison S. F., *Search, Obfuscation, and Price Elasticities on the Internet*, 77 Econometrica 427 (2009)
Engle K. and McCoy P., *A Tale of Three Markets: The Law and Economics of Predatory Lending,* 80 Texas Law Review 1255 (2002)
Epstein R. A., *Unconscionability: A Critical Reappraisal, Search Term Begin*, 18 Journal of Law and Economics 293(1975)
Epstein R. A., *Contract, Not Regulation: UCITA and High-Tech Consumers Meet Their Consumer Protection Critics, in* van Boom W. and Loos M. (eds.), Collective Enforcement of Consumer Law 205 (2007)
Eskridge W., *One Hundred Years of Ineptitude: The Need for Mortgage Rules Consonant with the Economic Dynamics of the Home Sale and Loan Transaction*, 70 Virginia Law Review 1083 (1984)
Frankle M. E., *Amended Rule 23 from a Judge's Point of View*, 23 Antitrust Law Journal 295 (1996)
Freund O. K., *One Uses and Misuses of Comparative Law*, in Freund O. K. (ed.), Selected Writings (1978)
Friedman L. M., *On Legal Development,* 24 Rutgers Law Review (1969-1970)
Friedman L. M., *Access to Justice: Social and Historical Context, in* Cappelletti M. and Weisner J. (eds.), Access to Justice Vol. II: Promising Institutions 5 (1978)
Friedman L. M., *Claims, Disputes, Conflicts and the Modern Welfare State, in* Cappelletti M. (ed.), Access To Justice and the Welfare State 249 (1981)
Friedman S. E., *Giving Unconscionability More Muscle: Attorney's as a Remedy for Contractual Overreaching*, 44 Georgia Law Review 317 (2010)
Gates B., The Road Ahead (1996)
Gawith D., *Non Litigation-Based Redress for International Consumer Transaction is Not Cost Effective-A Case for Reform?*, 3 Macquarie Journal of Business and Law 115 (2006)
Gibbons L. J., Kennedy R. J and Gibbs J. M., *Cyber-Mediation: Computer-Mediated Communications Medium Messaging the Message*, 32 New Mexico Law Review 27 (2002)
Giddens A., Beyond Left and Right: The Future of Radical Politics (1994)
Gillette C. P., *Rolling Contracts as Agency Problem,* 42 Houston Law Review 679 (2004)
Gilliero P., *From Face-to Face to Screen-to Screen: Real Hope or True Fallacy?*, 23 Ohio State Journal on Dispute Resolution 301 (2008)
Gillies L. E., Electronic Commerce and Private International Law, A Study of Electronic Consumer Contract (2008)

Goodman J. W., *The Pros and Cons of Online Dispute Resolution: An Assessment of Cyber-Mediation Websites*, 2 Duke Law & Technology Review 1 (2003)
Goodwin C., *Privacy: Recognition of a Consumer Right*, 10 Journal of Public Policy and Marketing 149 (1991)
Gordon R., *The Electronic Personality and Digital Self*, 56 Dispute Resolution Journal 8 (2001)
Graubert J. and Coleman J., *The Impact of Technological Change in the Canada/U.S. Context: Consumer Protection and Antitrust Enforcement at the Speed of Light: the FTC Meets the Internet*, 25 Canada-United States Law Journal 275 (1999)
Gumpert G. and Drucker S., *The Demise of Privacy in a Private World: From Front Porches to Chat Room*, 8 Communication Theory 408 (1998)
Gurung A. and Jain A., *Chapter VII Antecedents of Online Privacy Protection Behavior: Towards an Integrative Model, in* Chen K. and Fadlalla A. (eds.), Online Consumer Protection: Theories of Human Relativism 151 (2009)
Hadfield G., Howse R. and Trebilcock M., *Information Based Principles for Rethinking Consumer Protection Policy*, 21 Journal of Consumer Policy 131 (1998)
Halket T. D., *The Use of Technology in Arbitration: Ensuring the Future is Available to Both Parties*, 81 St. John's Law Review 269 (2007)
Halpern C. L., *Public Interest Law: Its Past and Future*, 58 Judicature 119 (1974)
Han P. and Maclaurin A., *Do Consumers Really Care About Online Privacy?*, 11 Marketing Management 35 (2002)
Hanson J. D. and Douglas K. A., *Taking Behavioralism Seriously: Some Evidence of Market Manipulation*, 112 Harvard Law Review 1420 (1999)
Hardy T., *The Proper Legal Regime for "Cyberspace"*, 55 University of Pittsburgh Law Review 993(1994)
Haugtvedt C. P., Herr P. M. and Karders F. R. (eds.), Handbook of Consumer Psychology (2008)
Hemphill T., *Electronic Commerce and Consumer Privacy: Establishing Online Trust in the U.S. Digital Economy*, 107 Business and Society Review 221 (2002)
Heverly R. A., *Law as Intermediary*, 2006 Michigan State Law Review 107 (2006)
Hill J., Cross-Border Consumer Contracts (2008)
Hillman R. A., *Online Consumer Standard Form Contracting Practices: A Survey and Discussion of Legal Implications, in* Winn J. K. (ed.), Consumer Protection in the Age of the Information Economy 283 (2006)
Hillman R. A. and Rachlinski J. J., *Standard-Form Contracting in the Electronic Age*, 77 New York University Law Review 429 (2002)
Hodges C., *Collectivism: Evaluating the Effectiveness of Public and Private Models for Regulating Consumer Protection, in* van Boom W. and Loos M. (eds.), Collective Enforcement of Consumer Law 205 (2007)
Hörnle J., *Online Dispute Resolution, in* Tackaberry J. and Marriott A. (eds.), Bernstein's Handbook of Arbitration and Dispute Resolution Practice 779 (2003)
Hörnle J., Cross–broader Internet Dispute Resolution (2009)
Hörnle J., *The Jurisdictional Challenge of the Internet, in* Edwards L. and Waelde C. (eds.), Law and the Internet (2009)
Horton D., *Flipping the Script: Contra Proferentem and Standard Form Contracts*, 80 University of Colorado Law Review 431 (2009)
Howell G., *The Potential and Limits of Consumer Empowerment by Information*, 32 Journal of Law & Society 349 (2005)
Howells G., *Cy-près for Consumers: Ensuring Class Action Reforms Deal with Scattered Damages, in* Steele J. and van Boom W. H. (eds.), Mass Justice, Challenges of Representation and Distribution 58 (2011)
Huber P., *Flypaper Contracts and the Genesis of Modern Tort*, 10 Cardozo Law Review 2263 (1989)
Ison T.G., Credit Marketing and Consumer Protection (1979)

Issacharoff S., *Can There be a Behavioral Law and Economic?*, 51 Vanderbilt Law Review 1729 (1998)
Jacob H., *The Elusive Shadow of the Law*, 26 Law & Society Review (1992)
Jacobs P., *Mediation Now and Then, in* M. P. Barbee, *Newsletter Mediation, International Bar Association Legal Practice Division,* July 2007
James R., Private Ombudsmen and Public Law (1997)
James R. and Morris P., *The New Financial Ombudsman Service in the United Kingdom: Has the Second Generation Got It Right?, in* Rickett C. E. F. and Thomas G. W. T. (eds.), International Perspectives on Consumers' Access to Justice 167 (2003)
Jarvenpaa S. L. and Todd P. A., *Consumer Reactions to Electronic Shopping on the World Wide Web*, 1 International Journal of Electronic Commerce 59 (1996-1997)
Kahneman D., Knetsch J. L. and Thaler R. H., *Experimental Tests of the Endowment Effect and the Coase Theorem*, 98 Journal of Political Economy 1325 (1990)
Kamp A. R., *Uptown Act: A History of the Uniform Commercial Code: 1940-1949*, 51 SMU Law Review 257 (1998)
Kaplan B., *A Prefatory Note*, 10 Boston College Industrial and Commercial Law Review 497 (1969)
Karanon M. C., *ADR on the Internet*, 11 Ohio State Journal on Dispute Resolution 537 (1996)
Katona G., Psychological Economics (1975)
Katsh E. and Rifkin J., Online Dispute resolution (2001)
Kaufmann-Kohler G. and Schultz T., Online Dispute Resolution: Challenges for Contemporary Justice (2004)
Kaul I. and Conceição P., The New Public Finance: Responding to Global Challenges (2006)
Kennedy D., *Distributive and Paternalist Motives in Contract and Tort Law, with Special Reference to Compulsory Terms and Unequal Bargaining Power*, 41 Maryland Review 563 (1982)
Kessler F., *Contracts of Adhesion-Some Thoughts about Freedom of Contract*, 43 Columbia Law Review 629 (1943)
Kim N. S., *Evolving Business and Social Norms and Interpretation Rules: The Need for a Dynamic Approach to Contract Disputes,* 84 Nebraska Law Review 506 (2005)
Kocher E., *Collective Rights and Collective Goods: Enforcement as Collective Interest, in* Steele J. and van Boom W. H. (eds.) Mass Justice Challenges of Representation and Distribution 118 (2011)
Korobkin R., *Bounded Rationality, Standard Form Contracts, and Unconscionability*, 70 University of Chicago Law Review 1230 (2003)
Kötz H., *Public Interest Litigation: A Comparative Survey, in* Cappelletti M. (ed.), Access To Justice and the Welfare State 82 (1981)
Krause W., *Do You Want to Step Outside? An Overview of Online Alternative Dispute Resolution*, 19 John Marshall Journal of Computer & Information Law 457 (2001)
Landers J. and Rohner R., *A functional Analysis of Truth in Lending*, 26 UCLA Law Review 711 (1979)
Leff A., *Unconscionability and the Code–The Emperor's New Clause*, 115 University of Pennsylvania Law Review 485 (1967)
Leff A., *Unconscionability and the Crowd: Consumer and the Common Law Tradition,* 31 University of Pittsburgh Law Review 349 (1970)
Lemay L., Sams Teach Yourself Web Publishing with HTML and XHTML in 21 days (2001)
Levi-Faur D., *The Global Diffusion of Regulatory Capitalism*, 598 Annals of the American Academy of Political and Social Science 12 (2005)
Lipsey R. G. and Lancaster K., *The General Theory of Second Best*, 24 The Review of Economic Studies 11 (1956)
Llewellyn K., *Book Review on the Standardization of Commercial Contracts in English and Continental Law, by O. Prausnitz*, 52 Harvard Law Review 700 (1939)
Llewellyn K., The Common Law Tradition: Deciding Appeals (1960)

Loos M., *Rights of Withdrawal, in* Howells G. and Schulze R. (eds.), Modernizing and Harmonizing Consumer Contract Law 237 (2009)

Luth H., Behavioural Economics in Consumer Policy, The Economic Analysis of Standard Terms in Consumer Contracts Revisited (2011)

Macaulay S., *Elegant Models, Empirical Pictures, and the Complexities of Contract*, 11 Law & Society Review 507 (1997)

Maggs G. E., *American Law in a Time of Global Interdependence: U.S. National Reports to the XVITH International Congress of Comparative Law: Section VI Regulating Electronic Commerce*, 50 American Journal of Comparative Law 655 (2002)

Maggs P. B., Soma J. T. and Sprowl J. A, Internet and Computer Law (2001)

Main B. G. M. and Park A., *The British and American Rules: An Experimental Examination of Pre-trial Bargaining in the Shadow of the Law*, 47 Scottish Journal of Political Economy 37 (2000)

Mann R. J. and Siebeneicher T., *Just One Click: The Reality of Internet Retail Contracting*, 108 Columbia Law Review 984 (2008)

Martin M. S., *Keep It Online: The Hague Convention and the Need for Online Dispute Resolution in International Business-To-Consumer E-Commerce*, 20 Boston University International Law Journal 125 (2002)

Maxeiner J. R., *Standard-Terms Contracting in the Global Electronic Age: European Alternatives*, 28 Yale Journal of International Law 109 (2003)

McGill S., *Consumer Arbitration Clause Enforcement: A Balanced Legislative Response*, 47 American Business Law Journal 361 (2010)

Medd W. and Marvin S., Marking Water Work: Intermediating between Regional Strategy and Local practice. Environment and Planning D: Society and Space (2007)

Mehren A. T. V., Theory and Practice of Adjudicatory Authority in Private International Law: A Comparative Study of the Doctrine, Policies and Practices of Common- and Civil-Law Systems (2002)

Michael G. A., *Is There a There There? Toward Greater Certainty for Internet Jurisdiction*, 16 Berkeley Technology Law Journal 1345 (2001)

Micklit H.-W., *Collective Private Enforcement of Consumer Law: The Key Questions, in* van Boom W. and Loos M. (eds.), Collective Enforcement of Consumer Law 12 (2007)

Miller G., *The Magical Number Severn, Plus or Minus Two: Some Limits on Our Capacity for Information Procession*, 63 Psychological Review 81 (1956)

Milne G., Rohm A. and Bahl S., *Consumers' Protection of Online Privacy and Identity*, 38 Journal of Consumer Affairs 217 (2004)

Mnookin R. and Kornhauser L., *Bargaining in the Shadow of the Law: The Case of Divorce*, 88 Yale Law Journal 950 (1979)

Mougayar W., Opening Digital Markets: Battle Plans and Business Strategies for Internet Commerce (1998)

Mowbray A., Cases and Materials on the European Convention on Human Rights (2007)

Mukherjee A. and Nath P., *Role of Electronic Trust in Online Retaining: A Re-Examination of the Commitment-Trust Theory*, 41 European Journal of Marketing 1173 (2007)

Nagareda R. A., *Mass Resolution of Mass Tort: Emerging Issues in the United States and the Global Future, in* Steele J. and van Boom W. H. (eds.), Mass Justice Challenges of Representation and Distribution 27 (2011)

Nelson P., *Advertising as Information*, 82 Journal of Political Economy 729 (1974)

Nethin J., *A Comparative Study of Problems in Consumer Protection Laws for Electronic Commerce (E-Commerce) in Thailand and the United States*, 13 Thailand Journal of Law and Policy (2010), *available at* http://www.thailawforum.com/articles/comparative-study-of-problem-5.html (visited January 12, 2013)

Ogus A. I., *Rethinking Self-Regulation*, 15 Oxford Journal Legal of Studies 97 (1995)

O'Hara E. A., *Choice of Law for Internet Transactions: The Uneasy Case for Online Consumer Protection*, 153 University of Pennsylvania Law Review 1833 (2005)

O'Mahony C. and Flaherty P., *Chapter XVII The Legal Framework for Data and Consumer Protection in Europe, in* Chen K. and Fadlalla A. (eds.), Online Consumer Protection: Theories of Human Relativism 326 (2009)

Panther S., *Non-Legal Sanction, in* Bouckaert B. and De Greet G. (eds.), Encyclopedia of Law and Economics Vol. I (2000)

Papazafeiropoulou A. and Pouloudi A., *Social Issues in Electronic Commerce; Implications for Policy Makers*, 14 Information Resources Management Journal 24 (2001)

Perez A. F., *Consumer Protection in the America: A Second Wave of America Revolutions?*, 5 University of St. Thomas Law Journal 698 (2008)

Persson A. H., *Collective Enforcement European Prospects in Light of the Swedish Experience, in* Wrbka S., van Uytsel S. and Siems M. (eds.), Collective Actions Enhancing Access to Justice and Reconciling Multilayer Interests? 341 (2012)

Peterson C., *Truth, Understanding, and High-Cost Consumer Credit: The Historical Context of the Truth in Lending Act*, 55 Florida Law Review 807 (2003)

Poncibo C., *Some Thoughts on the Methodological Approach to EC Consumer Law Reform*, 21 Loyola Consumer Law Review 353 (2009)

Ponte L. M., *Boosting Consumer Confidence in E-Business: Recommendations for Establishing Fair and Effective Dispute Resolution Programs for B2C Online Transactions*, 12 Albany Law Journal of Science and Technology 441 (2002)

Ponte L. M. and Cavenagh T. D., Cyberjustice, Online Dispute Resolution for E-Commerce (2005)

Posner E. A., *Contract Law in the Welfare State: A Defense of the Unconscionability Doctrine, Usury Laws, and Related Limitation on the Freedom to Contract*, 24 Journal Legal Studies 283 (1995)

Posner E. A., Law and Social Norms (2000)

Poullet Y., Privacy Protection and Transborder Data Flow; Recent Legal Issue, in Advanced Topics of Law and Information Technology (1989)

Pridgen D., *Wyoming Division: Speech: How Will Consumers be Protected on the Information Superhighway*?, 32 University of Wyoming Land and Water Law Review 237 (1997)

Puplava J. A., *E-Commerce: Challenges to Privacy, Integrity, and Security in a Borderless World: Use and Enforceability of Electronic Commerce Contracting: The State of Uniform Legislation Attempting to Regulate E-Commerce Transactions*, 16 Michigan State Journal of International Law 153 (2007)

Puurunen T., *Choice of Law in European Business-To-Consumer Electronic Commerce-A Trail Out of a Political Impasse*, 11 Zeitschrift für Europäisches Privatrecht 789 (2003)

Rabinovich-Einy O., *Technology's Impact: The Quest for a New Paradigm for Accountability in Mediation*, 11 Harvard Negotiation Law Review 253 (2006)

Radin M. J., *Human, Computers, and Binding Commitment*, 75 Indiana Law Journal 1112 (1999)

Ramsay I. D. C., *Consumer Redress Mechanisms for Poor-Quality and Defective Products*, 31 University of Toronto Law Journal 117 (1981)

Ramsay I. D. C., Rationales for Intervention in the Consumer Marketplace (1984)

Ramsay I., *Consumer Redress and Access to Justice, in* Rickett C. E. F. and Telfer T. G. W. (eds.), International Perspectives on Consumers' Access to Justice (2006)

Ramsay I., *Globalization, the Third Way and Consumer Law: The Case of the U.K., in* Winn J. K. (ed.), Consumer Protection in the Age of the Information Economy 59 (2006)

Ramsay I., Consumer law and Policy, Text and Materials on Regulating Consumer Markets (2007)

Rawls J., A Theory of Justice (1971)

Rea A. and Chen K., *Chapter VIII Privacy Control and Assurance: Does Gender Influence Online Information Exchange?, in* Chen K. and Fadlalla A. (eds.), Online Consumer Protection: Theories of Human Relativism 165 (2009)

Reith T. T., *Consumer Confidence: the Key to Successful E-Commerce in the Global Marketplace*, 24 Suffolk Transnational Law Review 467 (2001)

Rekaiti P. and van den Bergh R., *Cooling of Periods in the Consumer Laws of the EC Member States: A Comparative Law and Economics Approach*, 23 Journal of Consumer Policy 371 (2000)

Riefa C. and Hörnle J., *The Changing Face of Electronic Consumer Contracts in the Twenty-First Century: Fit for Purpose?, in* Edwards L. and Waelde C. (eds.), Law and the Internet 89 (2009)

Roberts S. and Palmer M., Dispute Processes: ADR and the Primary Forms of Decision Making (2006)

Robertson A., *The Limits of Voluntariness in Contract*, 29 Melbourne University Law Review 179 (2005)

Rosenfeld M., *Contract and Justice: The Relation between Classical Contract Law and Social Contract theory,* 70 Iowa Law Review 796 (1985)

Ross H. L. and Littlefield N. O., *Complaint as a Problem Solving Mechanism*, 12 Law & Society Review 199 (1978)

Rouibah K., Khalil O. E. M. and Hassanien A. E. (eds), Emerging Markets and E-Commerce in Developing Economies (2008)

Rowland D. and MacDonald E., Information Technology Law (2000)

Rubin E., *The Internet, Consumer Protection and Practical Knowledge, in* Winn J. K. (ed.), Consumer Protection in the Age of the Information Economy 35 (2006)

Rule C., Online Dispute Resolution for Business (2002)

Rustad M. L. and Onufrio M. V., *The Exportability of the Principles of Software: Lost in Translations?*, 2 Hastings Science & Technology Law Journal 25 (2010)

Rutherford M., *Documents-only Arbitrations in Consumer Disputes, in* Tackaberry J. and Marriott A. (eds.), Bernstein's Handbook of Arbitration and Dispute Resolution Practice 638 (2003)

Saami Z., *Regulation of E-Commerce by Contract: Is it Fair to Consumers?*, 31 University of West Los Angeles Law Review 163 (2000)

Scassa T. and Deturbide M., Electronic Commerce and Internet Law in Canada (2004)

Schellekens M. and der Wees L. V., *ADR and ODR in Electronic Commerce, in* Prins J. E. J., Ribbers P. M. A., van Tilborg H. C. A., Veth A. F. L. and van der Wees J. G. L. (eds.), Trust in Electronic Commerce 271 (2002)

Schmitz A. J., *Embracing Unconscionability's Safety Net Function*, 58 Alabama Law Review 73 (2006)

Schmitz A. J., *"Drive-Thru" Arbitration in the Digital Age: Empowering Consumer through Binding ODR*, 62 Baylor Law Review 178 (2010)

Schneider M. E. and Kuner C., *Dispute Resolution in International Electronic Commerce,* 14 Journal of International Arbitration 5 (1997)

Scholes A. N., *Information Requirements, in* Howells G. and Schulze R. (eds.), Modernizing and Harmonizing Consumer Contract Law 213 (2009)

Schu R., *The Applicable Law to Consumer Contracts Made Over the Internet: Consumer Protection Through Private International Law*, 5 International Journal of Law and Information Technology 192 (1997)

Schultz T., *Does Online Dispute Resolution Need Governmental Intervention? The Case of Architectures of Control and Trust*, 6 North Carolina Journal of Law and Technology 71 (2004)

Scott C., *Regulatory Innovation and the Online Consumer*, 26 Law and Policy 476 (2004)

Senécal F. and Benyekhlef K., *Groundwork for Assessing the Legal Risk of Cyberjustice,* 7 Canadian Journal of Law & Technology 41 (2009)

Shah A., *Using ADR to Resolve Online Disputes*, 10 Richmond Journal of Law and Technology 20 (2004)

Shanklin W. and King H., *Evaluating the FTC Cooling Off Rule*, 11 Journal of Consumer Affairs 101 (1977)

Shavell S., *The Optimal Structure of Law Enforcement*, 36 Journal of Law and Economics 255 (1993)

Shubhankar D., *Remedying a Technological Challenge: Individual Privacy and Market Efficiency; Issues and Perspectives on the Law relating to Data Protection*, 15 Albany Law Journal of Science and Technology 337 (2004)
Sotrskrubb E. and Ziller J., *Access to Justice in European Comparative Law, in* Francioni F. (ed.), Access to Justice as a Human Right (2007)
Spindler G. and Borner F. (eds), E-Commerce Law in Europe and the USA (2002)
Stadler A., *Cross-Border Mass Litigation: A Particular Challenge for European Law*, in Steele J. and van Boom W. H. (eds.), Mass Justice: Challenges of Representation and Distribution 73 (2011)
Starek R. and Rozell L., *A Cyberspace Perspective: The Federal Trade Commission's Commitment to On-Line Consumer Protection*, 15 John Marshall Journal Computer and Information Law 679 (1997)
Steele J. and van Boom W.H. (eds.) Mass Justice: Challenges of Representation and Distribution (2011)
Stewart R. B. and Sunstein C. R., *Public Programs and Private Rights*, 95 Harvard Law Review 1193 (1982)
Street H., *Access to the Legal System and the Modern Welfare State: A European Report from the Standpoint of an Administrative Lawyer, in* Cappelletti M. (ed.), Access to Justice and the Welfare State 295 (1981)
Stuych J., *Public and Private Enforcement in Consumer Protection: General Comparison EU-USA, in* Cafaggi F., Micklitz H-W. (eds.), New Frontiers of Consumer Protection, The Interplay Between Private and Public Enforcement 63 (2009)
Stuyck J., *Unfair Term, in* Howells G. and Schulze R. (eds.), Modernizing and Harmonizing Consumer Contract Law (2009)
Supanitaya S., Private Organization for Consumer Protection (2001)
Svantesson D. J. B., Private International law and Internet (2007)
Tang Z. S., Electronic consumer contracts in the conflict of laws (2009)
Tasker T. and Pakcyk D., *Cyber- Surfing on the High Seas of Legalese: Law and Technology of Internet Agreement,* 18 Albany Law Journal of Science and Technology 79 (2008)
Teubner G., Law as a Autopoietic System (1993)
Teubner G., *"Legal Irritants": Good Faith in British Law or How Unifying Law Ends up in New Divergences*, 61 Modern Law Review 11(1998)
Thomas M., States, Banks and Crisis: Emerging Finance Capitalism in Mexico and Turkey (2012)
Thomas S., *Does Online Dispute Resolution Need Governmental Intervention? The Case for Architectures of Control and Trust*, 6 North Carolina Journal of Law and Technology 71 (2004)
Thornburg E. G., *Privatisation and Power: Dispute Resolution for the Internet, in* Rickett C. E. F. and Telfer T. G. W. (eds.), International Perspectives on Consumers' Access to Justice 300 (2003)
Trebilcock M. J., *Rethinking Consumer Protection Policy, in* Rickett C. E. F. and Telfer T. G. W. (eds.), International Perspectives on Consumers' Access to Justice 68 (2003)
Tunc A., *The Quest for Justice, in* M. Cappelletti (ed.), Access To Justice and the Welfare State 315 (1981)
Tyler M. C. and Bretherton D., *Seventy-Six and Counting: An Analysis of ODR Sites, in* A. R. Lodder, E. Clark, T. F. Gordon, E. Katsh, C. Rule, E. M. Thiessen, B. Verheij, D. N. Walton and J. Zeleznikow (eds.), Essays on Legal En Technical Aspects of Online Dispute Resolution 13 (2004)
Tyler M. C., and McPherson M., *Online Dispute Resolution and Family Disputes*, 12 Journal of Family Studies 1 (2006)
van Boom W. H. (eds.), Mass Justice Challenges of Representation and Distribution (2011)
van Boom W. and Loos M. (eds.), Collective Enforcement of Consumer Law (2007)
van Boom W. and Loos M., *Effective Enforcement of Consumer Law in Europe, in* van Boom W. and Loos M. (eds.) Collective Enforcement of Consumer Law (2007)

van den Bergh R. J., *Competition Law and Consumer Protection Legislation, in* Hatzis A. N. (ed.), Economic Analysis of Law: A European Perspective 22 (2003)

van den Bergh R., *Should Consumer Protection Law be Publicly Enforce?, in* van Boom W. and Loos M. (eds.), Collective Enforcement of Consumer Law 177 (2007)

Viitanen K., *Enforcement of Consumers' Collective Interests by Regulatory Agencies in the Nordic Countries, in* van Boom W. and Loos M. (eds.), Collective Enforcement of Consumer Law 81 (2007)

von Mehren A. T., Theory and Practice of Adjudicatory Authority in Private International Law: A Comparative Study of the Doctrine, Policies and Practices of Common-and Civil-Law Systems (2002)

Ware R., *The Use of Jurisdiction Arbitrage to Support the Strategies Interest of the Firm*, 38 University of Toledo Law Review 307 (2006)

Weiss R. and Mehrotra A., *Online Dynamic Pricing: Efficiency, Equity and the Future of E-Commerce*, 6 Virginia Journal of Law and Technology (2001), *available at* http://www.vjolt.net/vol6/issue2/v6i2-a11-Weiss.html (visited August 21, 2012)

Wilhelmsson T., *Administrative Procedures for the Control of Marketing Practices - Theoretical Rationale and Perspectives, in* Junkkari T. (ed.), Twelve Essays on Consumer Law and Policy 149 (1996)

Wilhelmsson T., *The Abuse of the "Confident Consumer" as a Justification for EC Consumer Law*, 27 Journal of Consumer Policy 317 (2004)

William F. (ed.), Why The Poor Pay More (1997)

Winn J. K. (ed.), Consumer Protection in the Age of the Information Economy (2006)

Winn J. K. and Bix B. H., *Diverging Perspectives on Electronic Contracting in the US and EU*, 54 Cleveland State Law Review 175 (2006)

Wissler R. L., *Mediation and Adjudication in the Small Claims Court: The Effect of Processes and Case Characteristics*, 29 Law & Society Review 323 (1995)

Wrbka S., *European Consumer Protection Law: Quo Vadis? Thoughts on the Compensatory Collective Redress Debate, in* Wrbka S., van Uytsel S. and Siems M. (eds.), Collective Actions: Enhancing Access to Justice and Reconciling Multilayer Interest? 23 (2012)

Wrbka S., van Uytsel S., Siems M. (eds.), Collective Actions Enhancing Access to Justice and Reconciling Multilayer Interests? (2012)

Wurgler F. M., *Unfair Dispute Resolution Clauses: Much Ado About Nothing?, in* O. B. Shahar (ed.), Boilerplate: Foundations of Market Contracts 45 (2007)

Zain S., *Regulation of E Commerce by Contract: Is It Fair to Consumers?*, 31 The University of West Los Angeles Law Review 163 (2000)

Zaremba A., Civil Justice in Crisis-Comparative Perspectives of Civil Procedure (2005)

Zhang M., *Contractual Choice of Law in Contracts of Adhesion and Party Autonomy*, 41 Akron Law Review 123 (2008)

Zimmermann R., The Law of Obligations Roman Foundations of the Civilian Tradition (1992)

Zweigert K. and Kötz H., An Introduction to Comparative Law (1992)

2. Reports, Working Papers, Thesis, Web Publications and Others

Abernethy S., *Building Large-Scale Online Dispute Resolution and Trustmark Systems' Proceedings of the UNECE Forum on ODR* 2003 (2003), *available at* http://www.mediate.com/Integrating/docs/Abernethy.pdf (visited 12 January 2013)

American Arbitration Association, *Consumer Due Process Protocol* (April 17, 1998), *available at* https://docs.google.com/viewer?a=v&q=cache:It1QnKtSQV8J:www.adr.org/cs/idcplg%3FIdcService%3DGET_FILE%26dDocName%3DADRSTG_005014%26RevisionSelectionMethod%3DLatestReleased+consumer+due+process+protocol&hl=ja&gl=jp&pid=bl&srcid=

ADGEEShaF6NUeTZI_
Y9dhn29PxICidhaXZYx4wIFBQlkMVd62rjC4I80LONhZNxqLx8RNEfONpynKFry7Q17R
cLw4zR_NKc7_MZlPLH8ntZ98Ftz-Zl1G_NIOuByuI2B6q84cupFzI-&sig=AHIEtbQCDjA
OsJS-3GCGppE_M2okLX6WkQ (visited January 4, 2013)

American Bar Association, Jurisdiction in Cyberspace 83 (1999)

Barlow J. P., *Selling Wine without Bottles: The Economy of Mind on the Global Net* (1993), *available at* http://w2.eff.org/Misc/Publications/John_Perry_Barlow/HTML/idea_economy_article.html (visited May 1, 2013)

Bartle I. and Vass P., Center for the Study of Regulated Industries, University of Bath School of Management, *Self-Regulation and the Regulatory State-A Survey of Policy and Practice, The Government's Better Regulation Task Force Published a Sequence of Reports Pressing the Advantages of Self-Regulation Between 1999 and 2005* (2005)

BBC New Asia-Pacific, *China Diary Product Found Tainted with Melamine,* BBC New, July 9, 2010, *available at* http://www.bbc.co.uk/news/10565838 (visited June 12, 2012)

Edwards L. and Theuniseen A., *Creating Trust and Satisfaction Online: How Important Is ADR?: The UK eBay Experience,* 5 Web Journal of Current Legal Issues (2007), *available at* http://webjcli.ncl.ac.uk/2007/issue5/edwards5.html (visited June 12, 2013)

Berkman, *Global Network Initiative* (September 15, 2012), *available at* http://cyber.law.harvard.edu/cyberlaw_winter10/Global_Network_Initiative (visited March 12, 2013)

Better Business Bureau (BBB), *Start with Trust, available at* www.bbb.org/online/consumer/default.aspx (visited January 12, 2013)

Borland J., *Apple's iTunes Raise Privacy Concerns*, CNet New, (July 12, 2006), *available at* http://news.cnet.com/2100-1029_3-6026542.html (visited August 21, 2012)

Brennan T., *Consumer Preference Not to Choose: Methodological and Policy Implications* (2005), *available at* http://rff.org/Documents/RFF-DP-05-51.pdf (visited July 12, 2012)

Brown M., *Evaluating Emerging eCommerce Markets-China and Brazil* (January 31, 2012), *available at* http://www.pfsweb.com/blog/evaluating-emerging-ecommerce-china-and-brazil/ (visited January 12, 2013)

Bruin R. D., Keuleers E., Lazaro C., Poullet Y. and Viersma M., *Analysis and Definition of Common Characteristics of Trustmarks and Web Seals in the European Union: Final Report* (February, 2005), *available at* http://ec.europa.eu/consumers/cons_int/e-commerce/e-commerce_final_report_annexe_en.pdf (visited November 12, 2012)

BusinessDictionary.com, *Intermediary, available at* http://www.businessdictionary.com/definition/intermediary.html (visited March 12, 2013)

CIArb, *The Professional Home of Dispute Resolution-Worldwide, available at* www.arbitrators.org/WebTrader/index.htm (visited November 13, 2012)

Citizen Advise, *Can You Cancel It? CAB/ECC Clients' Experience of Cancellation Rights in Consumer Contracts' CAB Evidence Briefing* (2005)

Child Poverty Action Group, *Paying More and Getting Less: Exclusion from Utilities, available at* http://www.cpag.org.uk/info/Povertyarticles/Poverty120/utilities.htm (visited December 2, 2011)

Chiu L., *Summary of China's Tainted Milk Scandal* (2008), *available at* http://chineseculture.about.com/od/2008milkscandal/a/Milksummary.htm (visited March 12, 2013)

Chowdhury P. R., *Raising Consumer Confidence to Boost E-Commerce Growth* (November 15, 2011), *available at* http://www.bizxchange.in/u47/S-16P-16A-20111115201111151423515756f54b764T-16N-/IT-Zone-Feature-Article.html (visited January 30, 2013)

Christopher C. G., Jr. and Johnson E., *Emerging Consumer Markets: The New Drivers of Global Economic Growth,* 4 CSCMP' Supply Chain Quarterly 2011 (March 18, 2013), *available at* http://www.supplychainquarterly.com/columns/201104monetarymatters/ (visited March 23, 2013)

Commission of the European Communities, *Green Paper form the Commission, Legal Aid in Civil Matters: The Problems Confronting the Cross-Border Litigant 9.2.2000 COM (2000) 51 final*

(2000), *available at* http://eur-lex.europa.eu/LexUriServ/site/en/com/2000/com2000_0051en01.pdf (visited June 12, 2013)

Commission of the European Communities, *Proposal for a Regulation and the Council Establishing a European Small Claims Procedures 15.3.2005 COM (2005) 51 final* (2005), *available at* http://eur-lex.europa.eu/LexUriServ/LexUriServ.do?uri=COM:2005:0087:FIN:EN:PDF (visited October 23, 2012)

Consumers International Organization, *Disputes in Cyberspace: Online Dispute Resolution for Consumers in Cross-Border Disputes-an International Survey* (December 2000*), available at* http://www.consumersinternational.org/media/304925/disputes%20in%20cyberspace-%20online%20dispute%20resolution%20for%20consumers%20in%20cross-border%20disputes%20-%20an%20international%20survey.pdf (visited December 12, 2012)

Consumers International Organization, *Disputes in Cyberspace in 2001: Update of ODR for Consumers in Cross-Border Disputes* (November 26, 2001), *available at* http://www.consumersinternational.org/media/304196/disputes%20in%20cyberspace%202001.%20update%20of%20online%20dispute%20resolution%20for%20consumers%20in%20cross-border%20disputes.pdf (visited January 2, 2013)

Consumers International Organization, *Decision Marketing in the Global Market: Trader, Standards and the Consumer* (2005), *available at* http://www.consumersinternational.org/media/308861/decision%20making%20in%20the%20global%20market-%20trade%20standards%20and%20the%20consumer.pdf (visited January 2, 2013)

CUTS International, *Competition Policy and Consumer Policy* (2005), *available at* http://www.google.com/url?sa=t&rct=j&q=&esrc=s&frm=1&source=web&cd=1&ved=0CDMQFjAA&url=http%3A%2F%2Fwww.cuts-international.org%2Fdocuments%2FCompetition%2520and%2520consumers%2520view.doc&ei=zp9XUaLhCoeCkwXxwoHQDA&usg=AFQjCNG8NJ3Z5rwA6lnWPVdTOtdS6bAurw&sig2=V7e67Z1MhcIsai3DotfRFA (visited March 12, 2013)

Cybersettle, *Cybersettle Online Settlement and Payment Resolution*, *available at* http://www.cybersettle.com/ (visited March 1, 2013)

Delgado E., *E-Commerce and Trustmarks: Results from SATURN* (2002), *available at* http://hosteddocs.ittoolbox.com/Delgado022004.pdf (visited January 12, 2013)

Deloitte and Touche, *Biz Report* (2007)

Downes L., *Why No One Will Join the Global Network Initiative*, Forbes, March 30, 2011, *available at* http://www.forbes.com/sites/larrydownes/2011/03/30/why-no-one-will-join-the-global-network-initiative/ (visited May 2, 2013)

Doyle M., Ritters K. and Brooker S., *Seeking Resolution: The Availability and Usage of Consumer-to-Business Alternative Dispute Resolution in the United Kingdom*, (January 2004) *available at* www.ncc.org.uk/protectingconsumers/seeking_resolution.pdf (January 3, 2010)

eBay, *Company Overview*, *available at* http://pages.ebay.com/aboutebay/thecompany/companyoverview.html (visited February 12, 2013)

eBay, *Selecting Buyer Requirement*, *available at* http://pages.ebay.co.uk/help/sell/buyer-requirements.html (visited February 12, 2013)

eBay, *Resolution Center*, *available at* www.resolutioncenter.ebay.com (visited February 12, 2013)

eBay, *The User Agreement (of eBay Germany)*, *available at* http://pages.ebay.de/help/policies/user-agreement.html?ssPageName=f:f:DE (visited February 12, 2013)

ECC-Net, *Realities of the European Online Marketplace, A Cross-Border E-Commerce Project* 2003 (2003), *available at* http://ec.europa.eu/consumers/ecc/docs/european_online_marketplace2003_en.pdf (visited March 12, 2012)

ECC-Net, *The European Online Marketplace: Consumer Complaints 2004* (2004), *available at* http://ec.europa.eu/consumers/ecc/docs/european_online_marketplace2004_en.pdf (visited March 12, 2013)

Econsumer.gov, *Your Site for Cross-Border Complaints, available at* www.econsumer.gov/english (visited January 12, 2013)

Escrow.com, *Safeguarding Your Online Transactions, available at* www.escrow.com (visited January 28, 2013)

Eurobarometer, *European Opinion Research Group N. 57.2 (April-June 2002)* (2002), *available at* http://issda.ucd.ie/documentation/eb/s3640cod.pdf (visited January 15, 2012)

Eurobarometer, *European Union Citizens and Access to Justice* (October, 2004), *available at* http://ec.europa.eu/consumers/redress/reports_studies/execsum_11-04_en.pdf (visited October 23, 2012)

Eurobarometer, *Consumer Protection in the Internal Market* (September 2006), *available at* http://ec.europa.eu/consumers/topics/eurobarometer_09-2006_en.pdf (visited January 12, 2012)

Eurobarometer, *Consumer Protection in the Internet Market* (October 2008), *available at* http://ec.europa.eu/public_opinion/archives/ebs/ebs_298_en.pdf (visited March 1, 2013)

European Commission, *Evaluation of the Pilot Project on use of European Consumer Complaint form for Consumer Disputes* (2000), *available at* http://ec.europa.eu/consumers/redress/compl/cons_compl/acce_just13_en.pdf (visited December 12, 2012)

European Commission, *Proposal for a Directive of the European Parliament and of Council Concerning Unfair Business-to-Consumer Commercial Practices in the Internal Market and Amending Directives 84/450/EEC, 97/7/EC and 98/27/EC Explanatory Memorandum, 18.6.2003 COM (2003) 356 final 2003/0134 (COD)* (June 18, 2003), *available at* http://eur-lex.europa.eu/LexUriServ/LexUriServ.do?uri=CELEX:52003PC0356:EN:NOT (visited March 1, 2013)

European Commission, *Unfair Contract Terms* (July 4, 2007), *available at* http://ec.europa.eu/consumers/cons_int/safe_shop/unf_cont_terms/index_en.htm (visited June 28, 2012)

European Economic and Social Committee, *Opinion of the European Economic and Social Committee on the Proposal for a Regulation of European Parliament and of the Council establishing a European Small Claims Procedure COM (2005) 87 final 2005/0020 (COD)* (2005)

Fielder A., Better Compliance: Guidance, Enforcement and Self-Regulation, Paper Present at the Data Protection Conference and Report on the Implementation of the DPD (2002), *available at* http://ec.europa.eu/justice_home/fsj/privacy/docs/lawreport/fielder_en.pdf (visited October 12, 2012)

FreeAdvice®, *Cooling-off Rule* (May, 1996), *available at* http://law.freeadvice.com/resources/gov_material/ftc_cooling_off_rule_5_96.htm (visited December 4, 2011)

FTC, *FTC Testifies in Support of Federal Legislation Protecting Children's Online Privacy* (September 23, 1998), *available at* www.ftc.gov/opa/-1998/09/privchil.htm (visited August 17, 2012)

FTC, *Workshop on the Information Marketplace: Merging and Exchanging Consumer Data* (2001)

FTC, *Protecting Consumer Privacy in an Era of Rapid Change, A Proposed Framework for Businesses and Policymakers, Preliminary FTC Staff Report* (2010)

Gillies L. E., *Adapting International Private Law Rules for Electronic Consumer Contracts, in* Rickett C. E. F. and Telfer T. G. W. (eds.), International Perspectives on Consumers' Access to Justice 359 (2006)

Green H., *A Little Privacy Please,* Business Week, March 16, 1998

Griffiths R. T., *History of the Internet, Internet for Historians* (October, 2002), *available at* http://www.let.leidenuniv.nl/history/ivh/chap2.htm#back%20to%20top (visited January 1, 2011)

Hamilton J., *Medical Tourist Creates Thai Doctor Shortage* (November 29, 2007), *available at* http://www.npr.org/templates/story/story.php?storyId=16735157 (March 15, 2012)

Hansell S., *Compressed Data: The Bog Yahoo Privacy Storm That Wasn't*, New York Times, May 13, 2002

Harris J., *Consumer Discretionary* (December 12, 2012), *available at* https://www.fidelity.com/viewpoints/consumer-discretionary-sector-2012 (visited December 12, 2012)

Heitzman J. and Worden R. L. (eds.), *India: A Country Study* (1995), *available at* http://countrystudies.us/india/89.htm (visited November 1, 2011)

Howard Partners, *Department of Industry, Tourism and Resources, Study of the Role of Intermediaries in Support of Innovation April 2007* (2007), *available at* http://www.innovation.gov.au/Innovation/ReportsandStudies/Documents/InnovationIntermediariesReport.pdf (visited March 12, 2013)

ICPEN, *International Consumer Protection and Enforcement Network* (2013), *available at* http://icpen.org/ (visited March 12, 2013)

ICPEN, *Participants* (2013), *available at* http://icpen.org/for-consumer-experts/who-we-are/participants (visited March 12, 2013)

IDRS, *Welcome to IDRS - Your Consumer Redress, Independent Complaints Review and Ombudsman Specialist*, *available at* http://www.idrs.ltd.uk/ (visited January 12, 2013)

International Chamber of Commerce, *Business to Consumer and Consumer to Consumer Alternative Dispute Resolution (ADR) Inventory Project* (2002)

International Institute for Conflict Prevention & Resolution, *More More More: CPR Meeting Highlights*, 27 Alternative to High Cost Litigation 125 (2009)

International Policy Division General Affair Department FUKUI Prefectural Government, *Cooling-off system* (2004), *available at* http://info.pref.fukui.jp/kokusai/tagengo/html_e/konnatoki/9horitu/g_cool/1.html (visited December 4, 2012)

Internet World Stats, *Usage and Population Statistics* (February 17, 2013), *available at* http://www.internetworldstats.com/stats.htm (visited March 1, 2013)

ISIS, *Internet Shopping is Safe*, *available at* http://isisaccreditation.imrg.org/user/pages/homepage.aspx (visited January 12, 2013)

Jain S. and Kapoor B., *Ecommerce in India-Boom and the Real Challenges* (2012), *available at* http://www.vsrdjournals.com/MBA/Issue/2012_02_Feb/Web/3_Sharad_Jain_597_Research_Communication_Feb_ 2012.html (visited January 2012, 30)

Jinn J., *The Global Network Initiative, Corporate Social Responsibility* (2012), *available at* http://irps.ucsd.edu/assets/001/503686.pdf (visited May 2, 2013)

Katsh E., *The New Frontier Online ADR Becoming a Global Priority* (2006), *available at* http://www.umass.edu/cyber/katsh0300.PDF (visited March 5, 2013)

Kaul I., *Bye-Bye Westphalian State; Hello Intermediary State—Why Fair*

Multilateralism Matters, *available at* http://www.ingekaul.net/pdf/upload110908/IS-paper.pdf (visited March 12, 2013)

Kearney's Global Consumer Institute, *E-Commerce is the Next Frontier in the Global Expansion* (2012), *available at* http://www.atkearney.com/documents/10192/348450/2012-E-Commerce-Index.pdf/83c81d46-fa4f-4421-850a-ef501d92afbd (visited December 12, 2012)

Kisyombe M., *Competition and Consumer Protection Policy: A Tanzanian Perspective, Paper for Presentation and UNCTAD Ad-Hoc Expert Group Meeting on the Interface between Competition Policy and Consumer Welfare, Thursday 12 and Friday 13 July 2012* (July 13, 2012), *available at* http://unctad.org/meetings/en/Presentation/ciclp2012_EMCP_S3_Kisyombe_en.pdf (visited March 12, 2013)

Leuven Report, *An Analysis and Evaluation of Alternative Means of Consumer Redress Other Than Redress Through Ordinary Judicial Proceedings* (January 17, 2007), *available at* http://ec.europa.eu/consumers/redress/reports_studies/comparative_report_en.pdf (visited October 23, 2012)

Lodder A. and Thiessen E, *The Role of Artificial Intelligence in Online Dispute Resolution, in* Katsh E. and Choi D. (eds.), *Online Dispute Resolution (ODR), Papers and Proceedings of the 2003 United Nations Forum on ODR* (2003)

Lord Chancellor's Advisory Committee on Legal Aid, *The 26th Legal Aid Annual Reports* (1975-1976)

Lord Woolf, *Access to Justice: Final Report to the Lord Chancellor on the Civil Justice System in England and Wales* (1996)

Louis Harris & Associations and Westin A.F., *Commerce, Communication and Privacy Online: A National Survey of Computer Users* (1997)
Lu S., *On Consumer Confidence in the Online Store* (2009), *available at* http://www.bizxchange.in/u47/S-16P-16A-20111115201111151423515756f54b764T-16N-/IT-Zone-Feature-Article.html (visited January 30, 2013)
L2 Block Digital Digest, *China Leads Emerging Markets for "Retail E-Commerce Potential"* (June 26, 2012), *available at* http://www.l2thinktank.com/china-leads-emerging-markets-for-retail-e-commerce-potential/2012/ (visited December 12, 2012)
Massimino E., *Judge the Global Network Initiative by How It Judges Company* (March 3, 2011), *available at* http://www.humanrightsfirst.org/2011/03/31/judge-the-global-network-initiative-by-how-it-judges-companies/ (visited May 2, 2013)
Mastercard, *Merchant Rules Manual* (December 12, 2012), *available at* http://www.mastercard.com/us/merchant/pdf/BM-Entire_Manual_public.pdf (visited January 12, 2013)
McElhearn K., Kirkville, *iSpy: More on the iTunes MiniStore and Privacy* (2006), *available at* http://www.mcelhearn.com/2006/01/12/ispy-still-more-on-the-itunes-ministore-and-privacy/ (visited August 12, 2012)
MCOT, *Thais Want Government to Curb Consumer Goods' Prices: Survey* (July 5, 2011), *available at* http://www.mcot.net/site/content?id=4ff673230b01dabf3c0247ec (March 12, 2013)
Memorandum from the Swedish Justice Department, *Evaluation of the Law on Class Action Proceedings*, 14 July 2007 (Ju 2007/5800/p) (2007)
Merrill Lynch Wealth Management, *World Wealth Report 2010* (2010)
Nygh P. and Pacar F., *Preliminary Draft Convention on Jurisdiction and Foreign Judgments in Civil and Commercial Matters Adopted by the Special Commission* (August 11, 2000), *available at* http://www.hcch.net/upload/wop/jdgmpd11.pdf (visited December 26, 2012)
OECD, *Electronic Commerce: Opportunities and Challenges for Government* (1997)
OECD, *Gateways to the Global Market Consumers and Electronic Commerce* (1998)
OECD, *Guidelines for Consumer Protection in the Context of Electronic Commerce* (1999), *available at* http://www.oecd.org/internet/consumerpolicy/34023811.pdf (visited January 13, 2013)
OECD, *Report of the Working Party on Information Security and Privacy of the OECD Committee on Consumer Policy* (June 2002)
OECD, *Legal Provisions Related to Business-to-Consumer Alternative Dispute Resolution in Relation to Privacy and Consumer Protection* (July 2002), *available at* http://www.oecd-ilibrary.org/science-and-technology/legal-provisions-related-to-business-to-consumer-alternative-dispute-resolution-in-relation-to-privacy-and-consumer-protection_233318385765 (visited January 12, 2013)
OECD, *OECD Reviews of Regulatory Reform: United Kingdom: Challenges at the Cutting Edge* (2002), *available at* http://www.keepeek.com/Digital-Asset-Management/oecd/governance/oecd-reviews-of-regulatory-reform-united-kingdom-2002_9789264199255-en (visited January 12, 2012)
OECD, *OECD Guidelines for Protecting Consumers from Fraudulent and Deceptive Commercial Practices Across Borders* (2003), *available at* http://www.oecd.org/sti/consumer/oecdguidelinesforprotectingconsumersfromfraudulentanddeceptivecommercialpracticesacrossbordershtml.htm (visited March 12, 2013)
OECD, *OECD Recommendation on Cross Border Cooperation in the Enforcement of Laws against Spam* (2006), *available at* http://www.oecd.org/sti/ieconomy/oecdrecommendationoncross-borderco-operationintheenforcementoflawsagainstspam.htm (visited March 12, 2013)
OECD, *OECD Recommendation on Consumer Dispute Resolution and Redress* (July 12, 2007), *available at* http://www.oecd.org/sti/consumer/38960101.pdf (visited March 12, 2013)

OECD, *OECD Policy Guidance for Address Emerging Consumers Protection and Employment Issues in Mobile commerce* (2008), *available at* http://www.oecd.org/sti/consumer/40879177.pdf (visited March 12, 2012)

OECD, *Typologies on the Role of Intermediaries in International Business Transactions, Final Report 9 October 2009* (2009), *available at* http://www.oecd.org/investment/anti-bribery/anti-briberyconvention/43879503.pdf (visited January 12, 2013)

OECD, *OECD Conference on Empowering E-Consumers, Strengthening Consumer Protection in the Internet Economy, Background Report, Washington D.C., 8-10 December 2009* (2009), *available at* http://browse.oecdbookshop.org/oecd/pdfs/free/2498011e.pdf (visited June 21, 2011)

OFT, *Doorstep Selling, A Report on the Market Study* (2004), *available at* http://www.oft.gov.uk/shared_oft/reports/consumer_protection/oft716.pdf (visited January 12, 2013)

OFT, *Internet Shopping-Some Key Data* (2005), *available at* http://www.oft.gov.uk/shared_oft/press_release_attachments/internetshopping.pdf (visited January 12, 2013)

OFT, *Internet Shopping: An OFT Market Study* (June, 2007), *available at* http://www.oft.gov.uk/shared_oft/reports/consumer_protection/oft921.pdf (visited June 1, 2011)

OFT, *Web Sweep Analysis* (March 2008), *available at* http://www.oft.gov.uk/713560/publications/reports/consumer-protection/oft982 (visited March 12, 2013)

OFT, *Consumer Code Approval Scheme: Core Criteria and Guidance* (June 2008), *available at* http://www.oft.gov.uk/shared_oft/Approvedcodesofpractice/oft855.pdf (visited January 12, 2013)

Oxford English Dictionary (1978)

PayPal, *The User Agreement* (January 10, 2013), *available at* https://cms.paypal.com/us/cgi-bin/?cmd=_render-content&content_ID=ua/UserAgreement_full (visited January 28, 2013)

PayPal, *Help Center Answers*, *available at* https://www.paypal.com/helpcenter/main.jsp;jsessionid=Q151LhgWG9yLRt1JfbDtTjB2yfvVjY0QG6VLNq2FC0yxFLQn5TzL!397506396?t=solutionTab&ft=homeTab&ps=&solutionId=203832&locale=en_US&_dyncharset=UTF-8&countrycode=RO&cmd=_help-ext&serverInstance=9002 (visited June 1, 2012)

Pinsent Masons, *One in Three Airline Sites Break Consumer Laws*, Out-law.com, May 13, 2008, *available at* http://www.out-law.com/page-9113 (visited December 30, 2011)

Pinsent Masons, *OFT Sues Marketer in Belgium*, Out-law.com, April 6, 2004, *available at* http://www.out- law.com/page-4439(visited December 24, 2012)

Practice Ecommerce, Insights for Online Merchants, *'Quick Query: PayPal Exec on Payment Disputes* (April 7, 2008), *available at* http://www.practicalecommerce.com/articles/709-Quick-Query-PayPal-Exec-On-Payment-Disputes (visited March 10, 2013)

Post D. G., *Anarchy, State, and the Internet: An Essay on Law–Marking up Cyberspace* (1995), *available at* http://www.temple.edu/lawschool/dpost/Anarchy.html (visited January 12, 2013)

Robert M., *The Agonies of Too Much Choice*, Financial Time, January 6, 2006

SafeBuy, *Protecting the Consumer*, *available at* http://www.safebuy.org.uk (visited January 12, 2013)

Scharmacher T., *Is the Business Side Willing to Invest in the Establishment of A Trustmark Scheme?, in ECC (Denmark) Conference Report: E-Commerce Trustmarks in Europe* (November 2006), *available at* http://ec.europa.eu/consumers/redress/ecc_network/e-commerce_trustmarks2007.pdf (visited March 12, 2013)

Schulze C. and Baumgartner J., *Don't Panic! Do E-Commerce, A Beginner's Guide to European Law Affecting E-commerce* (2001), *available at* http://www.signelec.com/content/download/dont_panic.pdf 33 (visited March 12, 2012)

Schuman E., *Gartner: $2 Billion in E-Commerce Sale Lost Because of Security Fears*, eWeek.com (November 27, 2006), *available at* http://www.eweek.com/article2/0,1895,2063979,00.asp (visited January 12, 2012)

Secretary of State for Constitutional Affairs and Lord Chancellor, *The Courts: Small Claims, Government Response to the Constitutional Affairs Select Committee's Report* (February 2006)

SettlementOnline, *Settlement Online Pilot Program Proposal, available at* http://settlementonline.com/Proposal.html (visited March 1, 2013)

Smith R., *Microsoft Response to the Window Media Player for Window XP*. (February 20, 2002), *available at* http://www.computerbytesman.com/privacy/wmp8dvd.htm (visited August 12, 2012)

Spletter C., *The Significance of Trustmarks in B2C E-Commerce*, LLM Thesis, University of Strathclyde (2003)

Study Centre of Consumer Law (Katholieke Universitiet Leuven), *An Analysis and Evaluation of Alternative Means of Consumer Redress other than Redress Through Ordinary Judicial Proceedings* (January 17, 2007), *available at* http://ec.europa.eu/consumers/redress/reports_studies/comparative_report_en.pdf (visited December 12, 2012)

Szczepanski K., *The Four-Tiered Class System of Feudal Japan, available at* http://asianhistory.about.com/od/japan/p/ShogJapanClass.htm (visited November 1, 2011)

Tasse R., Faille M. and Henderson G. L., *Online Consumer Protection: A Study on Regulatory Jurisdiction in Canada, the Paper Prepared for the Office of Consumer Affairs, Industry Canada* (July 2001), *available at* http://www.ulcc.ca/en/civil-section/102-civil-section-commercial-law-strategy/electronic-commerce/370-online-consumer-protectionstudy-on-regulatory-jurisdiction-in-canada (visited January 30, 2012)

Thesaurus.com, *available at* http://thesaurus.com/browse/intermediary (visited March 12, 2013)

Trusted Shops, *Trusted Shops Guarantee*, *available at* http://www.trustedshops.co.uk/ (visited January 12, 2013)

Trzaskowski J., *E-Commerce Trustmarks in Europe-An Overview and Comparison of Trustmarks in the European Union, Iceland and Norway* (2006), *available at* http://www.legalriskmanagement.com/PUBLICATIONS/2006_TRUST.pdf (visited January 12, 2013)

UK Broad of Trade, *Final Report of the Committee on Consumer Protection (Monopoly Committee) Cmnd 1781* (1962)

UK National Consumer Council, *Buying Problem: Consumers, Unsatisfactory and the Law* (1984)

UK Office of National Statics, *News Release, Internet Sales Rose by 30% in 2007* (November 21, 2008), *available at* http://www.statistics.gov.uk/pdfdir/ecomnr1108.pdf (visited March 26, 2010)

UNCITRAL, *Origin, Mandate and Composition of UNCITRAL* (2012), *available at* http://www.uncitral.org/uncitral/en/about/origin.html (visited December 12, 2012)

United Nations, *Resolution Adopted by the General Assembly, 39th Session, 16th April 1985 on the Report of the Second Committee (A/39/789/Add2)* (1985)

United Nations, *United Nations Guidelines for Consumer Protection (as expanded in 1999)* (2003), *available at* http://unctad.org/en/docs/poditcclpm21.en.pdf (visited March 12, 2013)

United Nations, *United Nations Conference on Trade and Development, E-Commerce and Development Report 2003, Chapter 7 Online Dispute Resolution: E-Commerce and Beyond* (2003), *available at* http://unctad.org/en/Docs/ecdr2003ch7_en.pdf (visited December 1, 2011)

US Council for Public Interest Law, *Balancing the Scales of Justice: Financing Public Interests Law in America* (1976)

US Department of Commerce, Export.gov, *Safe Harbor Overview* (April 26, 2012), *available at* www.expoert.gov/-safeharbor/sh overview.html (visited August 23, 2012)

Visa, *Rules for Visa Merchants - Card Acceptance and Chargeback, Management Guidelines* (2006), *available at* http://www.uiowa.edu/~fustreas/visa_new_acceptance_merchant_responsibility.pdf (visited January 12, 2013)

Wagemans T., *An Introduction to the Labeling of Websites*, (2003), *available at* http://ec.europa.eu/information_society/activities/sip/archived/docs/pdf/reports/qual_lab_bkgd.pdf (visited December 12, 2012)

Wagemans T., *Got What You Order?, in* ECC (Denmark), *Conference Report: E-Commerce Trustmarks in Europe Report* (2006)

WebTraderUK, *Details of WebTraderUK's Services*, *available at* http://www.webtrader.org.uk (visited January 12, 2013)

Wigder Z. D., Bahl M., Willis K. and Varon L., *Trends in India's eCommerce Market* (August 23, 2012), *available at* http://www.assocham.org/arb/general/Forrester_Trends_In_Indias_eCommerc.pdf (visited January 12, 2013)

Working Group on Electronic Commerce and Consumers, *Principles of Consumer Protection for Electronic Commerce, a Canadian Framework* (1999)

Zissu J., *Cybersettle® RapidFund® System to Provide Attorney/Claimant Settlement Funds in less than 72 Hours* (October 18, 2004), *available at* http://www.prnewswire.com/news-releases/cybersettler-rapidfundstm-system-to-provide-attorneyclaimant-settlement-funds-in-less-than-72-hours-74396727.html (visited January 12, 2013)

Printed by Printforce, the Netherlands